THE JACOB LAWRENCE SERIES ON AMERICAN ARTISTS

THE JACOB LAWRENCE SERIES
ON AMERICAN ARTISTS

Storm Watch: The Art of Barbara Earl Thomas by Vicki Halper

Elizabeth Catlett: An American Artist in Mexico by Melanie Anne Herzog

Dox Thrash: An African American Master Printmaker Rediscovered by John Ittman

Alfredo Arreguín: Patterns of Dreams and Nature / Diseños, Sueños y Naturaleza by Lauro Flores

Yun Gee: Poetry, Writings, Art, Memories edited by Anthony W. Lee

Portraits of a People: Picturing African Americans in the Nineteenth Century by Gwendolyn DuBois Shaw

The Prints of Roger Shimomura: A Catalogue Raisonné, 1968–2005 by Emily Stamey

Joe Feddersen: Vital Signs by Rebecca J. Dobkins, Barbara Earl Thomas, and Gail Tremblay

Ruben Trejo: Beyond Boundaries / Aztlán y más allá edited by Ben Mitchell

William H. Johnson: An American Modern by Richard J. Powell et al.

Queering Contemporary Asian American Art edited by Laura Kina and Jan Christian Bernabe

QUEERING CONTEMPORARY ASIAN AMERICAN ART

EDITED BY

LAURA KINA AND

JAN CHRISTIAN BERNABE

University of Washington Press

SEATTLE AND LONDON

Queering Contemporary Asian American Art was supported by a grant from the Jacob Lawrence Endowment, established through the generosity of Jacob Lawrence, Gwendolyn Knight, and other donors.

This book was also made possible in part by funding from the DePaul University Research Council, the Asian/Pacific/American Institute at New York University, and the Center for Art + Thought.

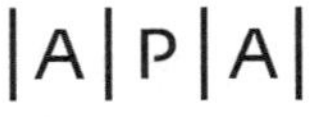

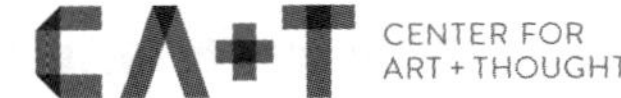

Printed and bound in the United States of America
Design by Katherine Wong
Composed in Minion Pro, typeface designed by Robert Slimbach
21 20 19 18 17 5 4 3 2 1

University of Washington Press
www.washington.edu/uwpress

Library of Congress Cataloging-in-Publication Data
Names: Kina, Laura, 1973– editor. | Bernabe, Jan Christian, editor.
Title: Queering contemporary Asian American art / edited by Laura Kina and Jan Christian Bernabe.
Description: Seattle : University of Washington Press, 2017. | Includes bibliographical references and index.
Identifiers: LCCN 2016027925 | ISBN 9780295741376 (pbk. : alk. paper)
Subjects: LCSH: Asian American art—21st century. | Group identity in art. | Art and society—United States—History—21st century.
Classification: LCC N6538.A83 Q44 2017 | DDC 701/.03—dc23
LC record available at https://lccn.loc.gov/2016027925

Cover image: *Niagara* by Kim Anno, 2013. Oil on inkjet on aluminum. 36 x 42 in. Collection of Berkeley Art Museum. Courtesy of the Berkeley Art Museum

The paper used in this publication is acid-free and meets the minimum requirements of American National Standard for Information Sciences—Permanence of Paper for Printed Library Materials, ANSI Z39.48–1984. ∞

In memory of

KARIN HIGA

(June 19, 1956 – October 29, 2013)

CONTENTS

CHAPTER 4 **QUEERING METHODOLOGY**

CHAPTER 5 **QUEERING SUBJECTIVITY**

CHAPTER 6 **QUEERING MIXED RACE**

CHAPTER 7 **QUEERING ASIAN AMERICA**

FOREWORD

In a catalog essay on Ruth Asawa's retrospective exhibition, *The Sculpture of Ruth Asawa: Contours in the Air*, Karin Higa expounds on the wonders of Ruth Asawa's ability to manipulate the sensuous and kinetic elements of a piece of wire in the form of a line into a volumetric gray-silver mesh. Contingent on its interaction with light and shadow, Asawa's dynamic looped-wire sculptures simultaneously appear iridescently opaque and transparent. Linking this transformative state of her sculptures with Asawa's own ability to navigate and negotiate different kinds of spaces and identities, Higa highlights how the artist's early life and Japanese American identity were formative in her art making and sensibility as an artist before she attended Black Mountain College. There, Josef Albers's *matière* courses and pedagogical approach informed her work and validated "her cultural heritage," but in turn her art, as Higa points out, exemplified the concept which entailed taking materials and objects out of their conventional contexts in order to create new visual, sensual, and haptic experiences.

Karin would never claim Asawa or her art as queer. But her interdisciplinary approach, which foregrounds the vicissitudes of the artist's life circumstances and expands rather than shuts down discussion of Asawa's art, serves as a befitting prototype for many of the readings in *Queering Contemporary Asian American Art*. In her reading of Asawa in "Inside and Outside at the Same Time," Karin performs her own kind of *matière*, simultaneously unraveling the inside and outside of Asawa's works by juxtaposing her early history at her parents' farm, attendance in progressive schools, and internment experience at the Santa Anita detention facility during World War II with her time at Black Mountain College in order to complicate the trajectory and culmination of her art practice and, in direct relation to this anthology, to underline the ways that bodies matter.

Nonnormative Asian Americans bodies and queer theory matter in Laura Kina's and Jan Christian Bernabe's exciting anthology in ways that revitalize the critical capacity and relevance of Asian American art as a means to mediate, negate, and open new fields of meaning. Extending David Eng's and Alice Hom's pioneering *Q&A: Queer in Asian America*—which foregrounded gender and sexuality as integral categories of analysis and the productive importance of queer studies in the understanding of Asian American history and law, the editors' mobilization of recent queer scholarship on temporality and space that unbind time and history from disciplinary and marketplace timelines enable scholarship on Asian American art to be in excess of current conceptual categorical paradigms. Neither methodical nor arbitrary, the anthology is conceived here as a sideways inquiry; a mash-up of queer theory in combination with interdisciplinary concepts—including Kandice Chuh's subjectless critique, Victor Bascara's critique of model minority imperialism, Amelia Jones's intersubjective contingency, Sarah Ahmed's discussion of will, and Jose Muñoz's conceptualization of hope as a form of hermeneutics—that insightfully rearticulates the past-potential future of Asian American art.

On another level, the anthology is in part a tribute to Karin Higa, her commitment to Asian American art, and her innovative thoughts of it as a field of study. Her influence on the field was especially felt in a landmark gathering of scholars at a National Endowment for the Humanities seminar that took place at New York University in the summer of 2012, organized by Margo Machida and Alexander Chang. There, at one of the morning sessions, in her understated no-nonsense way, Karin metaphorically analogized Asian American art scholars as ants, citing the imperative of ants to create and burrow new paths of inquiry, to open up Asian American art as a relevant field in the twenty-first century.

The eclectic array of essays, interviews, and art is an invaluable follow-up to this seminar and a constellation of conversations in response to Higa's imperative. Serving as a symbolic counterpoint to the figure of the "model minority" as an ant who assimilates in order to secure stability and success, but also accepts isolation and division from other Asian Americans, racialized minorities and queer bodies, the editors figure the scholars and artists gathered here as rogue ants, creatures who are already generally perceived as a necessity and a nuisance. Following the spirit of critique deployed by a number of queer scholars who interpreted the 2015 Supreme Court decision's formal recognition and legal right of same-sex couples to marry under the Fourteenth Amendment as reinforcing heteronormative forms of kinship and reproduction and foreclosing other kinds of queer romance and relations, the anthology refuses the recognition that offers Asian American art as a safe but contained haven of an established disciplinary future.

In distinction to the culture of scarcity in which Asawa lived and worked, the artists and writers featured here are making and writing about art during a time of precarity. Neoliberalism, in combination with the globalization of art, has reduced the role of art to a kind of spectacle or a financial investment. Art schools such as Rhode Island School of Design (RISD) have recently been getting a new form of attention from Wall Street, as a productive site for the breeding of unicorns—a term coined by Asian American venture capitalist Aileen Lee to describe start-ups whose value exceeds one billion and which are dependent on high risk and a horizon of future returns. Against this background in which venture capitalists have become a contemporary version of art patrons and the rest of us are figured as entrepreneurs, forced not only to take risks but to be at risk—demanding constant assessment and recalibration of individual over collective priorities—the anthology takes risks in re-engaging the protracted pursuits of racial and social justice and identity politics, symbolized in their renewed belief in the search for a mythical unicorn.

Embracing queer theory's resignification of failure as an oppositional refusal of received terms, discourses, and timelines that reductively place Asian American art as the outcome of a failed identity politics, the talented and committed writers and artists here look for alternative ways of folding subjects and objects into alternative categories of analysis and structures of belonging and being-with. Their belief in the unicorn is not about the existence of this mythological animal, but about what it represents: unrealized possibilities and futures to come, which revolve around not projected profits but rather ways to challenge dichotomies of looking at Asian American art, and past and present arrangements of the world vis-à-vis queer theory's challenge to normalized structures of time and space. Their intentions correspond similarly to José Muñoz's conception of queerness as an ideality—"to see and feel beyond the present"— in a manner that meets Karin's challenge in creating multiple modalities and portals to see Asian American art anew.

Susette Min
University of California, Davis
January 16, 2016

ACKNOWLEDGMENTS

"We are the termites of art history," the late Asian American scholar and curator Karin Higa bluntly posited of our interdisciplinary practice as artist-scholars-activists invested in the project of Asian American art and the dismantling, or nibbling away, at the white hegemonic pillars of art practice, history, and criticism. *Queering Contemporary Asian American Art* is an outgrowth of the lectures and conversations that emerged from our participation, along with Karin and many of the authors and artists in this book, in the National Endowment for the Humanities Summer Institute at the Asian/Pacific/American Institute at New York University, July 9–28, 2012, "Re-envisioning American Art History: Asian American Art, Research, and Teaching," which was organized by art historian Margo Machida and curator Alexandra Chang. In this groundbreaking setting, the group "Que(e)rying Asian American Art," for which the title of this anthology is named, was formed. This anthology owes a lot to the collaboration and discussion of all its members. We continued this dialogue and "termite" activity in subsequent years through our continued and often informal communion over good food and drinks as well as our participation at various annual meetings and conferences, including Association for Asian American Studies, American Studies Association, College Art Association, Critical Mixed Race Studies, and Critical Ethnic Studies. Jan Christian Bernabe's curatorial work through the Center for Art + Thought provided the opportunity to curate the multiplatform virtual exhibition *Queer Sites and Sounds* and its offline show and symposium at UCR ARTSblock. The volume also builds upon Laura Kina's 2013 University of Washington Press anthology and exhibition *War Baby / Love Child: Mixed Race Asian American Art,* which she co-authored and co-curated with Wei Ming Dariotis, for the DePaul University Art Museum and the Wing Luke Museum of the Asian Pacific American Experience.

We would both like to thank the Asian/Pacific/American Institute at New York University and the Center for Art + Thought for sponsoring this project. Kina would like to thank DePaul University for their financial and in-kind support for the research and production of this book with her 2014 and 2016 University Research Council grants, 2014 College of Liberal Arts and Social Sciences Summer Research and Development grant, visiting speaker and travel support from the Department of Art, Media, & Design, and major funding from the Society of Vincent de Paul Professors. Bernabe would like to thank Kristina Elstner for her transcription services. Bernabe would also like to thank Sarita Echavez See and David Lloyd, as well as George Bernabe and family for their financial sponsorship of this book.

At the University of Washington Press, we would both like to thank senior acquisitions editors Regan Huff and Ranjit Arab for encouraging this book into existence and for editor in chief Larin McLaughlin's continued to commitment to diverse voices and visions. This project owes much to lives and artwork of twentieth-century modern and contemporary Asian American and diasporic artists of an earlier generation who were or are LGBTQ identified—Bernice Bing, Tseng Kwong Chi, Shu Lea Cheang, Lenore Chinn, Richard Fung, Pipo Nguyen-duy, Alfonso Ossorio, Hanh Thi Pham, Martin Wong, and the many others who have shaped Asian American art—and to critical currents in contemporary scholarship whose flow we hope to join. In particular, we find an affinity with queer theorist Judith "Jack" Halberstam; queer of color scholars Sarah Ahmed, David L. Eng, and the late José Esteban Muñoz; and Asian American art scholars Margo Machida and Sarita Echavez See. Special thanks to *Amerasia Journal* for allowing us to reprint Valerie Soe's article in this book. Finally, we would like to thank all of our contributing authors and featured artists and offer a note of thanks to Harrod J Suarez for reading our essays and offering critical feedback over the course of the project.

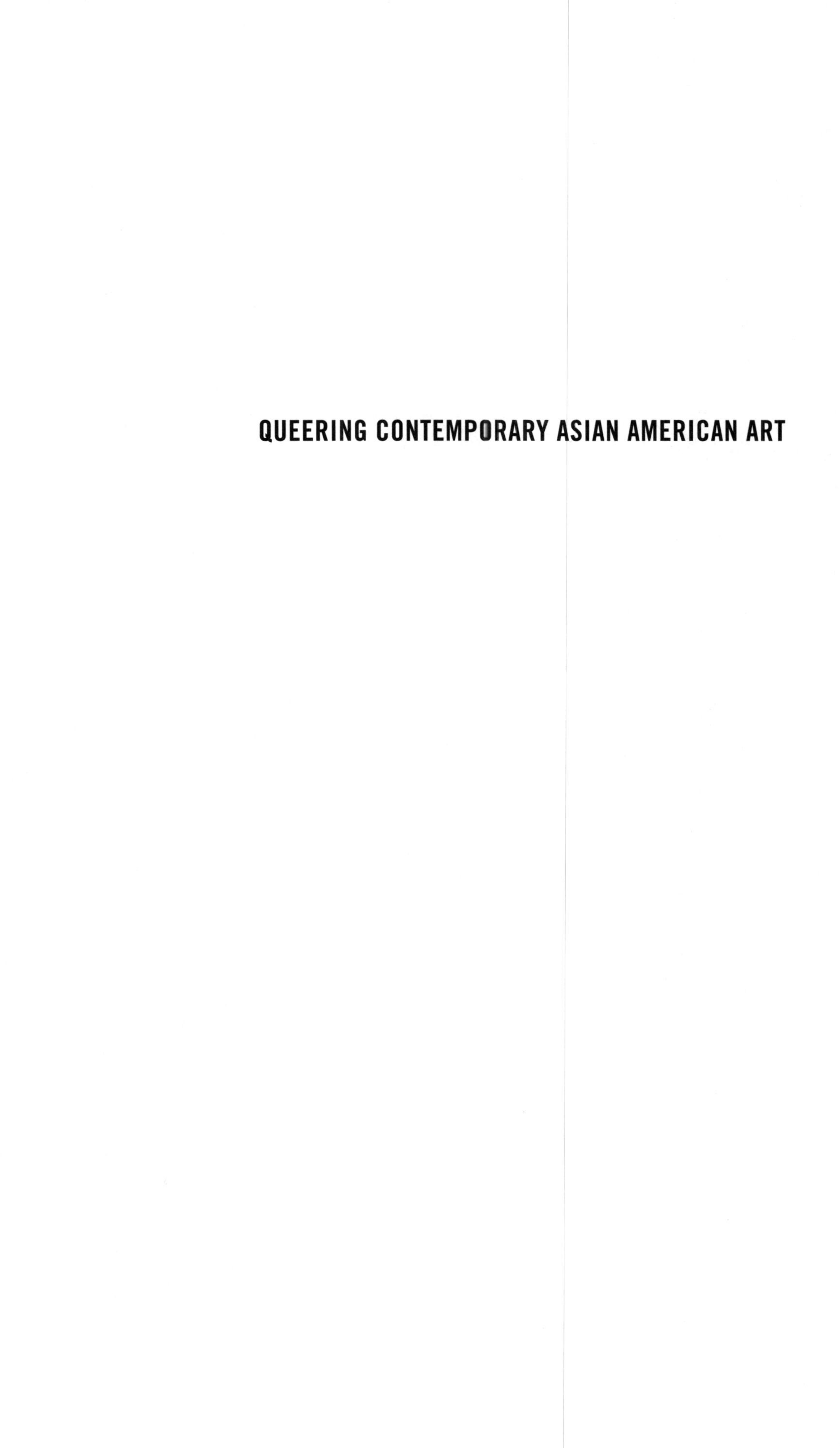

QUEERING CONTEMPORARY ASIAN AMERICAN ART

Introduction

For the Love of Unicorns: Queering Contemporary Asian American Art

JAN CHRISTIAN BERNABE AND LAURA KINA

Queer used to mean "strange," evacuated of any whimsy or novelty. The term was spoken in the most derogatory manner. The mere mention of the word still evokes sadness and perhaps even fear in those who were its targets. In this way, the deployment of *queer* was meant to banish or estrange individuals from the heteronormative domestic and, in a broader sense, the national sphere. Said with malice or disdain, *queer* was a slur, notes Heather Love.[1] Indeed, for a generation that lived through the 1950s and 1960s, the term can still sound grating and cringe-worthy. For a generation growing up today, words like *fag* and *dyke* are akin to *queer* in their negative affect. Unlike the former words, *queer* was reappropriated in the 1980s by the very communities targeted by the term. As part of the larger political and epistemic strategy of the LGBTQ (lesbian, gay, bisexual, transgender, and queer) movement, *queer* was reclaimed to create the spaces for open dialogue and inclusion of nonnormative genders and sexualities.

By the 1990s, the cultural and political currency of *queer*, as the editors of "What's Queer about Queer Studies Now?" note, lay in its "commitment to interrogating the social processes that not only produced and recognized but also sustained and normalized identity."[2] Following this vein, we use *queer* as a verb, precisely for what the editors have called "its broad critique of social antagonisms, including race, gender, class, nationality, and religion, including sexuality."[3] We use *queer* as a verb not to evacuate the term of the body and the body politic. Quite the contrary, in its transitive form, *queer* ineluctably produces queer bodies through its very embrace of the nonnormative.[4]

Queering Contemporary Asian American Art is a product of *undisciplinarity*, a resistance to normative models of being—indeed, a form of misbehaving that produces both intentional and unintentional Asian American queer networks and communities. Much like the self-described "disabled pin@y-amerikan transgender queer" and New Jersey–based artist Kay (or K.) Ulanday Barrett's poem "Brown Out Shouts!," *Queering* is a shout-out to LGBTQ and feminist artists of color, brown artists like Barrett, whose creativity and survival thrive at the interstices of an already racially marginalized Asian American body politic. Barrett, who uses the third person plural, declares in their poem:

> *because without explanation, we exist*
> *and you, you like all of our ancestors before,*
> *you live it so fiercely that even when injustice sets in,*
> *this rumbling sky houses your breath and*
> *that is better than any survival story,*
> *that, that is joy being born.*[5]

If to misbehave is to witness "joy being born," then to *queer* is to participate in a type of unruly and yet alimentary cultural and knowledge production that perhaps, as Barrett suggests, "is better than any survival story." *Queering* enacts a form of disciplinary resistance driven by queer bodies and practices. It is at once emancipatory in its production of queer jouissance and politically charged by its very emergence in the contemporary moment.

Indeed, with its focus on contemporary Asian American art, *Queering Contemporary Asian American Art* arrives at a pivotal and often contradictory moment in the wake of over a decade of colorblind "postracial" rhetoric concomitant with the simultaneous rise in post-9/11 Islamophobia. We write at a moment of heightened racialized and sectarian religious violence in the United States and throughout the world. On the international front, our focus has been on the victims of terrorism and the rise of ISIS (Islamic State of Iraq and Syria). Our domestic attention has been focused on the deaths of far too many unarmed young black men. And yet, violence against queer and transgender people of color remains virtually unnoticed by society at large. This disparity of empathy was evident during the neoliberal celebratory moment that followed the US Supreme Court legalization of same-sex marriage on June 26, 2015, and the simultaneous media frenzy over Caitlyn Jenner's very public transition only a few weeks later with her *Vanity Fair* cover.[6]

Queering arrives during the second decade of the twenty-first century, a time in which Asians in the United States continue to be framed as well-behaved "model minorities" or still perceived as FOB (fresh off the boat) foreigners, perpetually clueless, cunning, and conniving.[7] Understanding the very real material and political stakes of representation and misrepresentation, this anthology is not so much a multiculturalist corrective as it is an embrace of what queer theorist Jack Halberstam, in *The Queer Art of Failure,* calls the productive value of "failure."[8] Associating failure with Asian America might seem counterintuitive or even anticapitalist in a world networked by transnational economies. In the context of racial politics in the United States, failure stands counter to political and cultural recuperative projects by communities of color that seek historical redress for the consequences of exclusionary laws based on race. Nonetheless, failure should not be dismissed too hastily, for it is the lens of failure that illuminates the forces and imperatives of success, producing benchmarks of normativity

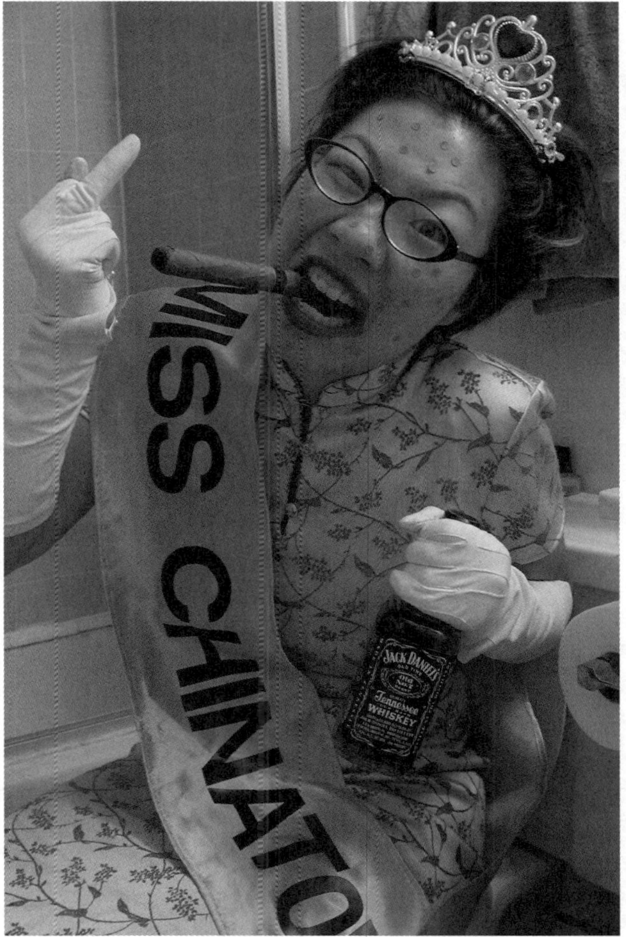

FIGURE I.1

Kristina Wong (American, b. 1978)
Fannie Wong, Former Miss Chinatown Second Runner Up, 2001

Performance publicity still
Digital image
Courtesy of the artist
Photo: C. Pete Lee

within Asian American communities and the intentional or unintentional exclusion of queer bodies and practices.

San Francisco–based Chinese American performance artist Kristina Wong's culture-jamming character *Fannie Wong, Former Miss Chinatown Second Runner Up* (figure Intro.1) is one example of how Asian American artists are pushing back against Asian American heteronormative expectations of success. Take, for example, Amy Chua, author of *Battle Hill of the Tiger Mom*, who epitomizes the disciplined and disciplining Asian American "Tiger Mom." Her book reinforces images of Asian American "Tiger Moms" who teach their children not to make waves; encourage them to play the violin or piano; accept nothing but straight *A*s; push their children to go to an Ivy League school; and nag them to get married, become a doctor or engineer, and ultimately to produce grandchildren. Chua and those who have ingrained her parenting method reinforce a telos of racial success that has sealed off any opportunity for transgression. Moreover, the very notion of Asian American racial success perpetuates the very dangerous "model minority" myth that has been used as a racial wedge against other people of color.[9] For to transgress normative structures is to fail—and failure, of course, cannot be an option.

Rather than concerning herself with "breaking the bamboo ceiling," Wong began crashing Asian American parades and other "respectable" community events in 2001, as a character she describes as "a pimple-faced, cigar-smoking, whisky-drinking" lady "whose claim to fame is that she was a former Miss Chinatown 2nd Runner Up (of what year, she cannot say, for she is a *lady* after all)."[10] Wong's character is too crude to be anything like the sexy cultural icon of Miss Chinatown. Her performance thus calls into question precisely the politics of respectability as a cultural construct based on assimilative imperatives in Asian American communities—imperatives governed by normative modes of femininity. The failure of Wong's character to heed such gender imperatives from the Chinese American community becomes a critique of the larger forces that have normalized both the mother's role in rearing her daughter as well as her daughter's want of an idealized femininity that surrounds her and that the pageant reinforces. Wong's performance of a type of failed Asian American femininity captures how Asian American racialization in the United States is always already tied to normative ideas of gender and sexuality within a racially marginalized community, and more broadly inside the United States writ large.

These normative ideas of gender and sexuality are not specific to the Chinese American community. Other Asian communities in the United States contain ethno-specific variations of normative gender and sexual expectations. Take, for example, the *Unsuitable Girls* (2007) series (plate 1) produced by South Asian American artist Swati Khurana, in collaboration with photographer Anjali Bhargava. Khurana, as described in the project's statement, "created a series of trophies with engraved text that celebrate our reluctant, disheveled, un-proper selves."[11] If trophies are objects given to celebrate successes, Khurana disrupts the "trophy-success" paradigm through her focus on South Asian females who have failed to live up to "socially accepted norms" within the South Asian community.[12] Bhargava pictures South Asian women posing with their trophies. These trophies signify the women's failure to live up to South Asian heteronormativity, with engravings on the trophies that point to why these women are "unsuitable girls," including "Least Suitable Girl," "Most Apprehensive Fiancée," and "Least Dutiful Wife." For Khurana, these trophies are markers of transgression that come at a social cost. Failing to submit to heteronormative imperatives always induces displacement within the social order of the domestic household or the larger community. While the women pictured in the portraits are marked with a negative attribution by their respective trophies, these women take ownership of their "Unsuitable Girl" awards, transforming the very spaces in which they are located and the people with whom they share their locations and whom they encounter. Describing these "unsuitable girls," Khurana remarks on the transformation that failure inspires: "We love our families while challenging them to accept us and the communities and families *we create*."[13] What the series pictures, then, are alternative South Asian queer spaces—spaces that interrogate heteronormativity and its cultural consequences—wherein liberatory expression by South Asian women is possible on their own terms.

As has been shown by Wong's and Khurana's work, racial transgression comes at a cost to the social order of the family unit and of the larger Asian American community. Indeed, it is this order that at once coheres individuals to others within their racially marginalized communities and, in a broader sense, constitutes Asians as part of the nation's body politic. According to the 2010 US Census, Asians represented the fastest-growing racial group in the country, with 60 percent of the growth coming from migration from abroad.[14] Five years later, in 2015, the *Economist* boldly proclaimed, "The Future's Asian," in reference to the influx of Chinese students and H1B highly skilled Indian migrants who have overtaken Mexicans as the largest group of new migrants to the United States.[15] With the increase in the Asian population, culture becomes a site in which the stakes of succeeding or failing for Asians at the social, cultural, *and* political spheres are at their highest. Lisa Lowe reminds us, "It is through the terrain of national culture that the individual subject is politically formed as the American citizen."[16] It comes as no surprise, then, that embedded within cultural production by Asian Americans are material and bodily stakes tied to communal and national belonging. That is, cultural production produces the terms in which Asians can and do self-represent, participate, *and* reap the benefits of the nation as citizen-subjects—squarely conveying allegiance to the biopolitical governance of citizens by the nation. For the nation to succeed, its citizens must reproduce, not only on the corporeal level but in replicating national culture on the abstract level in order to be a part of the imagined heteronormative community at large. Asian American citizenship in relation to national culture, which itself is underscored by heteronormativity, eschews and attempts to foreclose on opportunities for any type of transgression by Asians in the United States, be it racial, gendered, or sexually oriented. *Queering*, however, recognizes the limits and slippages in the management of Asian American cultural production—specifically, artistic practices—and shines a light on the bodies, spaces, and practices that thrive on the periphery, all of which are in constant interrogation of the heteronormative. If success constitutes the emergence of the Asian body within the larger national landscape, failure marks this Asian body as queer and as a critical analytic with which heteronormative bodies and practices must reckon.

How, then, do we confront Asian bodies whose figurations or presences are absent from artistic and photographic production, if indeed cultural production facilitates the means to self-represent or articulate the terms by which Asian groups delineate their social and cultural positionality in the United States? Clearly, projects that visualize the successes of Asian bodies within cultural production advance a collective, if not heteronormative, sense of belonging for a racially marginalized community—feelings of belonging that are in constant negotiation for citizen-subjects in the United States precisely because of their racial status. Asians who misbehave or practice transgressive cultural politics through their expressive practices pose a direct challenge to racial, gender, and sexual normative boundaries. While self or community representation in cultural production works to cohere notions of belonging to a racialized minority, Asian American artists who identity as LGBTQ may choose to disidentify with representational practices that are devoted solely to representing Asian American bodies and spaces. And while it might be facile to speculate on whether such Asian American artists have internalized the "model-minority" myth, we might consider how their art could be performing other types of critical cultural and political work, which nonetheless still has stakes in maintaining heteronormative privileges espoused by the Asian American racial minority group. As Eun Jung Park observes regarding Korean adoptee artists in chapter 5, "Their works show engagements with normative pressures; pressures that are constitutive of a neoliberal subject such as family, nation-state, religion, and sexual orientation."

The work of Los Angeles–based Chinese American photographer Jeff Sheng, for example, is invested in identificatory practices and politics that foreground mainstream LGBT (with the *Q* for *queer* notably missing) rights—a subject matter that cuts across race and gender—over directly confronting Asian American racial marginality at large through his photography. He is a frequently invited campus speaker, and his work has garnered mainstream press, including *ABC World News, BBC Radio, CNN*, and the *New York Times*,[17] and was featured at the 2012 London Olympics by the Federation of Gay Games at the Pride House for LGBT athletes and their families. Sheng's *Don't Ask, Don't Tell* photography series (2010–present), particularly the first two completed parts, situates his political concerns within the fight for LGBT inclusion and visibility in the US military prior to repeal of the Don't Ask Don't Tell (DADT) policy in 2011.[13] The series features closeted LGBT military servicemen; each portrait hides the identity of the individual because LGBT servicemen were not allowed to serve openly. If the faces of servicemen are not pictured in *Don't Ask, Don't Tell*, the students in Sheng's earlier *Fearless* series (2003–present) are given full visibility. In *Fearless*, Sheng photographs out LGBT-identified high school and college student athletes. While the politics of visibility underscores both photographic projects, Sheng is not particularly interested in highlighting race as an organizing principle for who gets photographed and who is left out. As a gay-identified artist, Sheng, through the subject matter of his work, reveals that he is a stakeholder in LGBT culture and politics. And while his sexual orientation potentially locates him on the margins of a heteronormative Asian American racial minority group, the subject matter of his photographs may unwittingly or deliberately, as queer theory scholar Jasbir Puar writes, "support forms of heteronormativity and the class, racial, and citizenship privileges they require."[19] That is to say, Sheng's investment in the mainstream LGBT political movement, as depicted in particular through the documentation of military servicemen during DADT, may indeed be participating in the production of *homonormativity*. This cultural and political work of bringing forth homosexual citizen-subjects into the juridical and representational realm in the United States does not necessarily undermine heteronormative privileges but rather sustains, as Puar points out, "the national and transnational political agendas of U.S. imperialism."[20] We might consider how Sheng's work participates in a politics of LGBT respectability and inclusion—a type of anti-utopian and antirelational political organizing that José Muñoz connects to "gay pragmatism"—and at what cost to other queers of color and gender queer bodies that are disenfranchised, ironically, by the mainstream LGBT rights movement.[21] Conversely, we might consider how Asian America, as a racial and political project, has systematically excluded LGBTQ representations. Our book is thus situated within women of color feminism and a queer of color critique, which as Grace Kyungwon Hong and Roderick A. Ferguson write in *Strange Affinities: The Gender and Sexual Politics of Comparative Racialization*, are comparative methods that "profoundly question nationalist and identitarian modes of political organization and craft alternative understandings of subjectivity, collectivity, and power. . . . Women of color feminism and queer of color critique reveal the ways in which racialized communities [and for our project, we might add LGBTQ communities] are not homogeneous but instead have always policed and preserved the difference between those who are able to conform to the categories of normativity, respectability, and value, and those who are forcibly excluded from such categories."[22]

In *Cruising Utopia: The Then and There of Queer Futurity*, Muñoz counters the "antirelational thesis" in queer studies advanced prominently by Lee Edelman in *No Future: Queer Theory and the Death Drive*. Edelman argues for a future in which "the Child" stands at the core of the heteronormative logic of the political that structures the social order; it is as if to say the fight for the Child is a fight for our heteronormative future. Thus queerness, as Edelman states, "names the side *not* 'fighting for the children,' the side outside the consensus by which all politics confirms the absolute value of reproductive futurism."[23] That is to say, the future horizon is always already structured by the Child, and for Edelman, a radical queer politics would resist participating in a reproductive futurism by embracing the "death drive."[24] Muñoz, however, envisions more hope for queerness than the rhetoric of queer negativity that Edelman's polemics posit. Indeed, for Muñoz queerness "*is* always in the horizon," and he argues "the essential need for an understanding of queerness as collectivity."[25] Unlike Edelman and other proponents of the antirelational thesis, Muñoz welcomes identificatory markers of difference that constitute queerness as a collectivity and thus shape the queer horizon that he envisions. Pointedly, Muñoz states, "Antirelational approaches to queer theory are romances of the negative, wishful thinking, and investments in deferring dreams of difference."[26]

Rather than deferring dreams of difference and isolating the Child as the sole social catalyst for all things that have yet to come, *Queering* takes on a relational positioning by welcoming identificatory markers of difference within Asia America, which constitute for us the queer horizon. The queer Asian American horizon that we propose is invigorated by cultural imaginations of the artistic and visual cultural workers found in this book and others which, because of publishing constraints beyond our control, we could not include. Our intent was never to write a comprehensive compendium of contemporary Asian American art. Rather, we *cruised* the corpus of contemporary Asian American art and art criticism to find a selection of artists and scholars whose work, we think, captures how queerness might inform a type of critical cultural, social, and political engagement and practice that broadens the terms we use to discuss race, gender, sexuality, citizenship, and so forth, within the Asian American body and cultural politic.[27] The anthology thus turns to art and visual cultural production to, as Muñoz writes, "glimpse the worlds proposed and promised by queerness in the realm of the aesthethic."[28] It is within the spaces of art and visual culture that we see the makings of an Asian American queer futurity—a forward time and space that does not shun the past but rather renders it a source of inspiration for Asian American artists working in the present. Muñoz writes, "The past is a field of possibility in which subjects can act in the present in the service of a new futurity."[29]

An Asian American queer horizon constitutes a type of utopian thinking that critics might call out as isolated inside a postracial bubble. But that type of criticism warrants pause as it evacuates our arguments for an Asian American queer futurity of the very people working collectively to achieve social justice in the United States. It also dismisses the creative aspirations and imaginations of the cultural producers working today who are always already confronted by normative notions of identity and culture found within Asian America, and more broadly the United States. We recognize that an Asian American queer horizon cannot be disassociated from the historical fundament that is tied to the emergence of Asian Americans as a racial group, as race itself is a social construction enshrouded by historical contingencies. Asian American queer futurity is about thinking about Asian American sociality with renewed vigor for the potentialities that are in store.

In *For the Love of Unicorns* (2014) (plate 2), a digital short film by Los Angeles–based artist Genevieve Erin O'Brien, the filmmaker centers a narrative of imagining utopia through the eyes of the unicorn-loving child Kylan. Kylan, a mixed-race child, is excited to go to the Celestial Carnival, which purports to have a real unicorn, only to find that she's been duped. "That's not a real unicorn," she exclaims. "That's a goat with a party hat!"[30] The ringleader responds to Kylan, "If you want a real unicorn, you gotta use your imagination, kid." At this point, the child leads the call for social action and starts to chant, "No Unicorn, No Peace," while the carnival's disenfranchised queer and racial minority laborers—"We are not clowns. We are queens!"—begin to chant for the formation of a union. "No Union, No Peace!" As all are chanting, Kylan closes her eyes and imagines until a unicorn appears. A woman is heard singing "Unicorn Song" in the background: "That dream can come true, it all starts with you." One by one, the kids in the audience follow Kylan's lead, closing their eyes and imagining unicorns until they appear floating above them.

By centering on the child as the film's protagonist, we might easily conclude that the future is indeed governed by the Child, as Edelman posits in *No Future*. But what if we shift our attention from the Child—on which, as Edelman argues, the future is contingent—to the unicorn or, more specifically, the act of believing in its existence. The collective (or coalitional) practice of imagination animates everyone (the social) in the carnival and, more symbolically, everyone in the beyond. Kylan's chanting inspires the collective practice of imagination not only for the other children and parents in the audience but also for the queer and racial minority laborers of the carnival. The fight for the future is, thus, not for the Child alone, but rather for the collective actions of a broader social field that energizes a call for social justice by imagining the unicorn, fictional or not. Indeed, the unicorn represents what Muñoz calls "the promise and potentiality of the ornament," which inspires a "radically democratic potentiality."[31] Muñoz writes, "Queerness is that thing that lets us feel that this world is not enough, that indeed, something is missing."[32] In *For the Love of Unicorns*, queerness indexes the fantasy of the unicorns, and their imaginary status offers viewers (us) a renewed sense of the collective and coalitional practice of hope, aspiration, and imagination on which an Asian American queer futurity must rely. As the film comes to a close, the woman singing the unicorn song sings the following lines: "Believe in moonbeams and rainbows. A world where anything goes." With her fist in the air, Kylan finally declares, "I believe! My heart eyes are working."

Like Kylan, we too believe. We believe in the transformative potential of cultural production as well as the creative imaginations of the artists found in this anthology and their crucial roles in securing a queer future that is inclusive of differences within Asian America. It is through queering that we seek to advance critical visions and new modalities that perhaps stand amiss in current discussions and scholarship of contemporary Asian American art. With a bit of pixie dust and collective imagination, we hope that this book can be part of the journey towards an Asian American queer horizon.

ASIAN AMERICAN HISTORY AND STUDIES

The artists and authors in this book are indicative of the scope of Asian American history and communities. This project is part of the larger field of Asian American studies, a political identity, movement, and discipline that emerged in the 1960s from the civil rights movement and the third world movement protests of the Vietnam War. The history of Asians in the Americas, of course, begins much earlier, in the mid-fifteenth century with Chinese explorers in the Americas and, in the sixteenth century, Filipino sailors arriving through the Spanish galleon trade along with Indian and Chinese so-called coolie laborers on cotton and sugar plantations. Just to name a few well-known historical markers: Chinese began arriving by the thousands to "Gold Mountain" during the California gold rush of the 1850s, and later in the 1860s to build the transcontinental railroad. The 1882 Chinese Exclusion Act cut off all Chinese immigration and severely restricted subsequent Asian immigration. It was not until the 1965 Immigration and Nationality Act (the Hart-Celler Act) was passed that the United States again saw a flow of migrants from Asia. While a good number of our contributors date to these first waves of immigration, many more came as part of the post-1965 wave of political refugees following the Vietnam War, such as artists Lan Thao Lam and Việt Lê or artist Anida Yoeu Ali, whose family fled the Khmer Rouge in Cambodia. Others, like artist Wafaa Bilal, are part of more recent refugee communities who came to the United States during the Iraq War. The military and war are major points of connection for many of the participants in this book. Kiam Marcelo Junio, for example, became a naturalized citizen through service in the US military. Still other artists, such as Deann Borshay Liem and Mihee-Nathalie Lemoine, covered in the chapter by Eun Jung Kim, came as Korean adoptees—a recent child migration that cannot be disconnected from the legacy of the Korean War.

According to the Center for American Progress, this past decade has seen more immigrants "come to the United States from Asia than from any other region in the world, making Asians the fastest growing immigrant population in the United States. These immigrants bring their diverse cultures, language skills, and different economic and demographic traits from various Asian countries and the Indian subcontinent." Recent Asian immigrants have come to the United States primarily through family-sponsored visas, temporary work permits and student visas, including highly skilled H-1B visa workers from India, and "Asian immigrants comprise a significant portion of undocumented populations."[33]

Asian America as a moniker encompasses multiple countries of origin and is generally understood in racial and ethnic terms. While East Asians and Southeast Asians are typically the default for this category, South Asians and sometimes West Asians and Pacific Islanders have had more tenuous ties. The borders and boundaries remain porous and often contested—dare we say *queer*—with competing colonial histories and varying degrees of geographic, cultural, and religious affiliation. The very names for each Asian American community and identity change over time and context. Are Filipinos Asian or Pacific Islander? Does West Asia exist, and if so, when does it become the Middle East? Are South Asians *really* part of Asian America at all?

Just to use our own biographies as examples, artist and coeditor Laura Kina hails from a multiracial Anglo (Spanish/Basque, French, English, Irish, Scottish, Dutch)–Japanese American family. Her paternal ancestors immigrated from Okinawa to the US territory of Hawai'i in the early part of the twentieth century as sugar plantation workers. Her great-grandparents became naturalized citizens following the 1952 Immigration and Nationality Act (McCarran-Walter Act). Growing up on the Big Island, her father remembers identifying as Oriental and Japanese, although he knew he was Okinawan. Today, *Oriental* is typically considered racially offensive, and these Asian working-class migrant laborers are now considered by some academics and Native Hawaiian activists to be part of a "settler-colonizer" history. Kina identifies as Asian American, but we found in our interviews with millennials (those born between 1980 and 2000) that they no longer relate to this political term, instead identifying as people of color. Kina's Okinawan community has reclaimed, to use the Okinawan term, an *Uchinanchu* indigenous identity and builds transnational ties through peace activism, family and Okinawan association networks, and cultural festivals, such as the World Wide Uchinanchu Festival held every five years. Kina, like artists Kim Anno, Sita Kuratomi Bhaumik, Maya Mackrandilal, Zavé Gayatri Martohardjono, and Saya Woolfalk featured in this book, is also part of the increasingly mixed-race Asian American population in the United States.

Coeditor Jan Christian Bernabe's parents are immigrants from the Philippines, arriving after the 1965 Immigration and Nationality Act. Like many other Filipinos, Jan's father enlisted in the US Navy, and this paved the way for his parents to become naturalized citizens. After the defeat of Spain during the Spanish-American War, the United States acquired the Philippines and transformed it into a colony, which it remained until Philippine independence was won in 1946 through the Treaty of Manila. American colonialism in the Philippines facilitated the recruitment of Filipinos into the US military, often in low-ranking positions. Bernabe's father was not the first in his family to enlist in the navy; his grandfather on his mother's side enlisted almost twenty years prior to his father's enlistment after World War II and Philippine independence. Bernabe and his brother are first-generation Americans who grew up on military bases in Japan, Guam, the Philippines, and California. Debunking the presumption of migration being unidirectional, in their retirement Bernabe's parents live half the year in the Philippines and the other half in the United States.

ASIAN AMERICAN ART HISTORY

Queering Contemporary Asian American Art is a critical engagement with the emergent field of Asian American art—artists, artistic praxis, and criticism. This anthology owes its foundation to art historical projects that have recuperated a once forgotten historical archive of artistic and photographic production by artists of Asian descent from the mid-nineteenth century through the 1970s, which resulted in the publication of the such seminal texts as *Picturing Chinatown: Art and Orientalism in San Francisco* (2001), *Asian/American/Modern Art: Shifting Currents, 1900–1970* (2008), and *Asian American Art: A History, 1850–1970* (2008).[34] These books and others have sought to frame and locate artwork and photography produced by Asians in the United States against or within a Western art historical canon; in doing so, these scholarly works serve as critical interventions through their focus on the way race delegitimizes and thus excludes artistic production by Asians in the United States in relation to the Western canon of art. We are under no illusion that these types of scholarly projects are no longer necessary. Indeed, given Asian American art history's relative youth, it would stand to reason that more art historical work would help ground the field of study institutionally. With institutionalization, however, comes the potential to be disciplined by art historical methods—in other words, to ossify ways to *query* the subject that disallow queerer scholarly interventions.

The authors and artists featured in this anthology have come to contemporary Asian American art through diverse and often organic routes, with only two authors, Alpesh Kantilal Patel and Eun Jung Park, having come through "traditional" PhD art history training. Our contributors have been schooled in or work in scholarly, community, or activist realms in American studies, art criticism, Asian American studies, critical mixed-race studies, curatorial studies, ethnic studies, film, LGBT studies, literary studies, performance, philosophy, studio art, visual cultural studies, women's and gender studies, and queer theory. As such, the methodologies and critical frameworks we bring to this project are interdisciplinary and intersectional but with a common focus of queering the archives, criticism, and production of what has been a Eurocentric art world. Even as we participate in our "termite activities," to quote the late Asian American scholar and curator Karin Higa, of nibbling away at these hegemonic foundations, we are cognizant of what Swati P. Shah points out, in her analysis of Brooklyn-based artist Chitra Ganesh's work, as the Western art world's tendency to assimilate interventions such as feminist, queer, or Asian art "within a framework that requires aesthetic, political, and national boundaries in order to reproduce itself. . . . [T]he story of the art historical record is that of categorizing the canon into the knowable forms and places of the 'universal' Western canon."[35]

In Chitra Ganesh's 2014 *Eyes of Time* (plate 3), a site-specific installation commissioned for the Brooklyn Museum, Elizabeth A. Sackler Center for Feminist Art (December 14, 2015–July 12, 2015), a large-scale wall painting of Kali, the Hindu goddess of destruction and rebirth, picks up themes of "female power and plurality" from the center's adjacent permanent installation of Judy Chicago's *The Dinner Party*. Indicative of her larger practice, the mural includes drawing, painting, collage, and assemblage and draws from "a broad range of material, including the iconography of Hindu, Greek, and Buddhist mythology, 19th century European portraiture and fairytales, archival photography, and song lyrics, as well as contemporary visual culture such as Bollywood posters, anime, and comic books" to explore "ideas of femininity, empowerment, and multiplicity."[36] Ganesh has long been interested in hidden, excluded, and queer narratives in her often doubled and dismembered figures. Her aesthetics are that of excess—of exceeding and thus transforming limits. Shah argues that Ganesh's work—which has been categorized as "queer," "feminist," and "South Asian American"—"provokes these categories by exceeding them, urging the viewer to consider the histories of myth within the figures that populate her images, as well as the history of mythmaking that structures the narrative of the canon itself. . . . Chitra Ganesh's work abstracts this narrative, pulls it apart, and looks intently for what remains."[37] So, too, do we hope to provoke the emergent category of Asian American art history through our embrace of undisciplinarity and excess.

In Nirmal Puwar's *Space Invaders: Race, Gender and Bodies out of Place,* she notes, "Some bodies are deemed as having the right to belong, while others are marked out as trespassers, who are, in accordance with how both spaces and bodies are imagined (politically, historically and conceptually), circumscribed as being 'out of place.'"[38] Asian American art scholarship and analysis and Asian American bodies are still largely "trespassers" in Euro-American Western art worlds, but they have also benefited from the West's spike of interest in contemporary *Asian* art (as distinguished from *Asian American*), which followed the past decade's rise of China and India as a global economic forces. Following these economic shifts, contemporary artists, galleries, and museums across Asia, including emerging Southeast Asian markets, are readily promoting artwork with overt Asian content to the Western art world. As Mellissa Chui, the former curator of Asia Society, invokes in *Contemporary Art in Asia: A Critical Reader*, one only has to recall the storming of the "citadel of the New York artworld" when in 2008 "two major museums presented retrospectives of Asian contemporary artists: Cai Guo-Qiang at the

Guggenheim and Takashi Murakami at the Brooklyn Museum."[39] The state of mainstream American contemporary arts, however, continues to promote anti-identitarian and deracialized art—form taking precedence over content. The contemporary Asian American artist stands somewhere in between, betwixt the larger forces and pressures of the contemporary global art market, the recuperative and community-oriented goals of Asian American studies, and the experiences of being an artist of color. But despite the dominance of the "postracial" discourse of the 2000s and possibly because of the increase in Asian contemporary art, this past decade also saw a marked increase in publication on Asian American art.

This anthology builds upon and is in conversation with key publications on Asian American art. For example, *Asian America* is defined in a diasporic framework rather than solely by US national identity, immigration narratives, and one-directional hemispheric perspectives. We have adopted Alexandra Chang's use of *diaspora* as a verb, in which Asian American art is created by the "formation of communities of affinity through the practice of active linkage and connection including performative interaction and cultural production."[40] We have taken up the archivist challenge from scholars such as Gordon Chang and Mark Johnson to document our present moment and record biographies of Asian American artists who may not yet be known in the canon of art history.[41] As with Elaine Kim's *Fresh Talk/Daring Gazes* (2003), we bring artists and scholars together in conversation. We have inherited an "unsettled vision" of Asian American art and methodology from our antidisciplinary godmother, Margo Machida. By this we mean seeing the borders of Asian America as heterogeneous and dynamic with an attention to generational differences, waves of immigration, and points of contact, confluence, and departure. Through our use of collaboratively edited artist interviews, we continue Machida's formulation of oral hermeneutics as "an exploratory form of dialogic engagement that seeks to share interpretive authority with artists by linking the use of oral history methods with a hermeneutical orientation towards textual interpretation."[42] Although this book is not overtly a recuperative project, we do share an impulse to "trouble borders" and conceptions of Asian America, diverging from an exclusive East Asian focus.[43] In much the same way that Sarita Echavez See's *The Decolonized Eye: Filipino American Art and Performance* (2009) used theory to focus beyond the artwork and artist, the thematic essays in this book use theoretical and sociological analysis to explore postcolonial identity and the reaches of US empire. The metadiscourse in which this book participates—of examining legacies of Orientalism, moving beyond binaries to hybrid and Third Spaces—stems from foundational work by postcolonial theorists (e.g., Homi K. Bhabha and Edward Said), but it is in queer of color theory and queer methodology that this book finds its second home.

ON QUEERING

Insofar as queer bodies immediately gesture to the corporeal, so too do they point more broadly to other bodies that reside outside of (hetero)normative centers: bodies of knowledge, repertoires of performance, and intellectual and artistic production, among others. The continued usage of *queer* today as a form of identification for individuals and communities, its discursive usage and interventions within the intellectual and political spheres, and its salience to cultural production and critique reflect the word's transformative potency. For this anthology, we deploy *queer* as an axis of critique—whether via queer acts, readings, and practices or through the very queer bodies of artists that navigate across heteronormative domestic and diasporic landscapes. Taken together and in all its formations, *queer* brings to light the cultural, economic, racial, and political processes that continue to constitute Asian American identities and art practices as fixed or stable loci of cultural production. That is to say, *queer* recognizes the myriad ways in which contemporary cultural production and producers are influenced by global flows of bodies and information, whether through transnational migrations or digital media flows or through transnational creative economies of labor and representation. Put simply, (to) *queer* contemporary Asian American art signifies the dynamism of the contemporary moment—a welcoming of sorts—while also acting as a means to broaden our understanding of the ways *(hetero)normativity* acts as a generative constraint in society writ large, even within the very Asian American communities in which many of the artists featured in this anthology locate themselves and their artistic practice *or* are positioned and claimed by others.

CHAPTERS IN BRIEF

This book is meant to trouble the archives of American art history and to reimagine and queer a past in which the very absence of the "nonnormative" Asian American body describes the contours of its presence. A post-9/11 understanding of the presumed threat of the corporeal brown, Asian, and Arab body is examined, as is the virtual but still racialized and gendered body in the context of our present digital age. Generational differences and parallels are drawn between earlier waves of socially engaged Asian American activist art and current practices and politics of identity by artists of Asian American heritage. The eight chapters and interviews have been organized by keywords and should be read in a relational manner.

In "Queering Surveillance," we look at how artists use sousveillance (self-surveillance) to counter the presumed objective view of state surveillance of suspect bodies, namely that of Muslim and brown and black males.

Literary scholar Harrod J Suarez's "'You Blushed': Queering Surveillance after 9/11 in the Work of Jill Magid and Hasan Elahi" argues, in the vein of Asian American studies scholar Kandice Chuh, for a "subjectlessness of queer Asian Americanist critique." He examines images in which the Asian American queer body at first seems to be absent but is in fact present in the very framework of the gaze. He looks specifically at Bangladeshi American artist Hasan Elahi's ongoing *Tracking Transience* project —a response to his FBI racial profiling case. Elahi live-streams a barrage of data about his daily life, including all the hotel beds he sleeps in, tacos he eats, and toilets he uses, but never includes his actual body. "By putting everything about me out there, I am simultaneously telling everything and nothing about my life." This is contrasted with Jill Magid's project *Evidence Locker,* in which the artist in 2004 donned a conspicuous red coat and had herself surveilled by the Liverpool police over the course of thirty-one days, all the while relating to the camera/anonymous viewer as if it were her lover. It should be noted that neither Elahi nor Magid is queer identified, and Magid is also not of Asian heritage. It is Suarez who performs a queer Asian American reading of their artwork to chart "forms of biopolitical intimacy that effectively seduce the surveiller such that his (the pronoun is used instructively) authority is compromised."

In our joint interview, "Performance, Surveillance, and Sousveillance," Elahi is then given agency in a conversation with Iraqi American artist Wafaa Bilal about their shared experiences as brown "suspects" and their artistic strategies for incorporating performance, surveillance, and sousveillance. Billal discusses his 2010 *3rdi* project, in which "he surgically implanted a camera into the back of his head to live-stream pictures every minute for a year to literally and metaphorically, in reference to his life as an Iraqi Gulf War refugee, record the places he has left behind," and his 2007 *Domestic Tension*, a month-long live installation project where he locked himself in Chicago's Flatfile Gallery and provoked people to "shoot an Iraqi," allowing anonymous users to log on to a website to shoot him with a remotely controlled but very real paintball gun.

"Queering Time" pairs "Pacific Standard Time" by Mariam B. Lam with an interview with Southeast Asian diaspora artists Việt Lê and the artist collaborative Lin + Lam (H. Lan Thao Lam and Lana Lin) to, as B. Lam states, "rehistoricize and transnationalize or geopoliticize" queer temporality. Mariam B. Lam's essay highlights works by Lin + Lam, Nguyen Tan Hoang, Eliza Barrios, and Việt Lê to examine the ways in which contemporary artists "negotiate aesthetics and politics in today's rapidly developing Southeast Asian region against deeply layered and contested geopolitical terrains, architectural markers, and spatial histories." She critically "queers" the emergent field of Southeast Asian American / diasporic art across three themes: field formation / pedagogy, (il)legibility, and exhibition politics.

In Laura Kina's conversation with Việt Lê and Lin + Lam, "Promiscuous Time Traveling (On Leaving and Returns)," they explore "queering time and their proximity and distance to Vietnamese history and memory." The dialogue centers on *thanotourism* (death tourism) in Vietnam and how, in Lê's 2012 "Love Bang!"—a "time traveling, trans, love triangle"—and Lin + Lam's 2010 installation "Tomorrow I Leave," each artist was compelled to sample songs by the Vietnamese antiwar singer Khánh Ly. Of Ly's iconic song "Biển Nhớ," H. Lan Thao Lam recalls, "This song played regularly over the [Pulau Bidong] refugee camp intercoms as people left and arrived. . . . It's such a heart-wrenching emblem of Vietnamese 1970s pop music, and was banned after the war ended." Ly's voice has thus become a marker of time and a vehicle to travel back in memory, but the narrative is disjunctured. Mariam B. Lam points out that Ly's "song resonates very differently for various demographics—for those who came of age during the war with vexed romantic departures . . . the refugees who heard the song played in camps each day as someone left, or the diasporic youth . . . who grew up with it as household reminders of parental nostalgia. . . . Past, present, and future verb tenses are not required in Vietnamese grammatical forms, with communication rendered from context clues of the past imperfect or subjunctive future." For Việt Lê, who samples a Nancy Sinatra song covered in French by Ly, his video becomes both a temporal and musical mash-up sung/rapped in three languages—Vietnamese, English, and Khmer. *Love Bang!* "talks about this transnational movement of culture, memory, cultural production—how it gets absorbed and then reconfigured."

In "Queering Affect," Jan Christian Bernabe's essay, "Filipino Diasporic Queer Killjoy: Recuperating Failure in Jeffrey Augustine Songco's *Guilty Party* and *BOMH* Series" resists the recuperative efforts at representation so often associated with Asian American studies. His analysis of an interview with Songco argues instead that Songco is a Filipino "queer killjoy, a troublemaker, a queer artist who is drawn to and images bad subjects. His work facilitates the production of affective oscillations, feelings of negativity, ambivalence, anxiousness coupled by humor." "I always have some kind of worry or nervousness, like some kind of weird feeling, strange, queer feeling, if you will, that I need to resolve," says Songco. Bernabe homes in on this sense of nervousness, which he believes is "caused by the burden of representation and the weight of racial belonging" and by the very "strange, if not queer, relationship between Filipinos and US empire."

Kenneth Tam explores subjects of masculinity, awkwardness, intimacy, and desire in his work. In his interview, Tam, who is a self-described "Chinese-American straight" male, discusses how he negotiates masculinity and explores homosocial desire in his videotaped encounters with strangers he solicits via Craigslist in *The Compression Is Not Subservient to the Explosion; It Gives It Increased Force* (2011).

In "Queering Methodology," we begin with "Queer Zen" by art historian Alpesh Kantilal Patel, who argues that because the queer Asian American subject is largely missing from pre-1980s art history, the only way to explore queer sexuality and transnationality, which is so important to this volume during this period, is to unmoor Asian American art history from its anchor in Asian genealogy and consider it as discursive knowledge. By doing so, he finds that the artworks of American artist Cy Twombly, Roland Barthes's reliance on Zen to characterize them, and more recent conceptual overlaps between queer and Zen to explore sexuality in mid-twentieth-century abstraction all suggest that a queer relation to sexuality and transnationality has always been part of the hegemonic archive of art history.

Where Patel questions if one need be of Asian heritage to be claimed as part of Asian American art history, media/installation/performance artist Eliza Barrios wonders, in her interview with coeditor Jan Christian Bernabe, if one need be queer identified for work to qualify as queer. Barrios reflects on her methodological approach and how art and activism in her individual and culture-jamming collaborative practice with Mail Order Brides/M.O.B. (along with Reanne Estrada and Jenifer Wofford) have shifted since the 1990s in terms of queer and Asian American identity, curatorial frameworks, and the philosophical implications of the ephemeral nature and planned obsolescence of digital technology. Her poetic digital projections, such as *Solace* (1995), disrupt urban environments of commerce, promote self-reflection, and ask questions about our geospatial relationships.

Kim Anno's interview, "Queer Traveler," flips the script of Orientalism as she, as a multiracial Asian American queer-identified person, appropriates Western iconography of nineteenth-century landscape painting and notions of the sublime in her *Grand Tour* series. She examines her competing desires to covet, possess, touch, and queer the places and spaces where she travels against her environmental concerns and the terms of her visibility in art history.

In "Queering Subjectivity," we continue looking at how voids and absences in effect describe the very presence of their formation. While identity is explored across all of the chapters of this book, here we focus on the related and intertwined concept of subjectivity—that is, the effect of external factors on subject formation, such as the socially constituted nature of mutual recognition between self and other. Art historian Eun Jung Park centers on "Risky Subjectivity" in looking at the artistic practice of three Korean adoptee artists, Kate Wall, Deann Borshay Liem, and Mihee-Nathalie Lemoine, who "deliberately denaturalize origin narratives and reconceptualize the social contingency of subjectivity." Her chapter raises the visual metaphor of mise en abyme in the case of Korean adoptees, whose "self-portraits are a synecdoche of the mise en abyme, that is, the self positioned among multiple mirrors in which the reflections of the self are multiplied into infinity towards oblivion." Park notes that Korean adoptee artists may look for a sense of self and empowerment and "justification of subjecthood" that "often rests in the past, the histories, the familial alignments—the things that are often located in an archive." Her essay asks us to consider, "But what if your past has been eradicated? Eradicated by what, by whom? Who or what has the power to eradicate a past?"

In "Dazzle," our joint conversation with Greyson Hong and Kiam Marcelo Junio, we talk about subjectivity in relation Hong's 2013 new media project *Funereal Archive* and Junio's Jerry Blossom personae and 2012–14 multimedia series *Camouflage as a Metaphor for Passing* and their identities as queer, transgender Asian Americans. Junio's performance, textile, costume, and sculptural installation works are about an absent presence and camouflaging oneself: "I'm seeking to ask to what extent we make ourselves visible and invisible in order to survive." Junio was born in the Philippines, served seven years in the US Navy, and became a naturalized U.S. citizen. "I was coming from the perspective of passing in the military as straight, heteronormative . . . then pulling outside of that and delving into queer theory and passing in society and gender presentation." Kiam sees camouflage as particularly charged in the Filipino experience, "as we have often been called 'the invisible minority.'" While both artists share their biographies in depth in this interview in terms of nationality, race, gender, sexuality, and kinship, Greyson, whose mother emigrated from South Korea, has moved "away from the storytelling confessional structure." Rather, he is interested in how our individual histories overlap. *Funereal Archive* explores genealogy and kinship in response to his grandfather's passing. Presented as a PDF file of personal, familial, and sampled text and images, it lives disembodied on the Internet and is virtually devoid of affect. The work addresses how the structures of colonialism, postcolonialism, and "the notions of race, class, and gender have affected" his relationship with his grandfather.

In chapter 6, "Queering Mixed Race," artist and coeditor Laura Kina draws on interviews with artists Maya Mackrandilal and Zavé Gayatri Martohardjono to investigate how their work questions the boundaries of contemporary Asian American representation and how they recognize their intersectional mixed-race and queer positionalities in their studio practice. The essay focuses on Mackrandilal's 2013 *Seated Woman*, a seven-hour performance where she channeled her grandmother and explored the "invisible authority of the museum and the power dynamics of the gaze upon the Other that it engenders," and Zavé Gayatri Martohardjono's 2013 performance *Brother Honeyqueen's Dance of Darkness*, a Butoh study of the half-human/half–sun deity warrior king Karna from the Hindu epic poem *Mahābhārata*.

Kina's conversation with Sita Kuratomi Bhaumik and Saya Woolfalk continues the discussion on how being mixed-race might decenter or broaden the way we understand *Asian American*. Bhaumik and Woolfalk express how their "double minority" identities and hybrid cultural backgrounds as an Indian/Japanese-Colombian and Japanese/African American have influenced their interdisciplinary studio methodology to queer archives and discuss their "mutual penchant for forming faux institutes—Bhaumik's *Curry Institute* (2011) and Woolfalk's *Institute of Empathy* (2008)."

Finally, in chapter 7, "Queering Asian America," we begin with "Open-Source Identities" by Asian American filmmaker and scholar Valerie

Soe. Identity politics take center stage as she surveys the ways in which Asian American artist/activists Scott Tsuchitani, Gaye Chan, and Hasan Elahi "use online platforms, public interventions, and socially engaged art practice to subvert and resist oppressive economic, political, and social systems" that build on the overtly political "creative strategies of previous Asian American artists." She additionally argues that the Free Art Movement—including Tsuchitani, Chan, and Elahi's work—which embraces open-source principles that "seek to bypass or circumvent capital-based systems of exchange in the distribution of creative work," is part of a much older native gift economy. Our digital moment and "open-source" technology is thus characterized more in terms of social behavior than advances in the mechanics of technology.

In the final two interviews in this anthology, we selected artists to represent pre- and post-1965 immigration reform Asian American communities—a historical paradigm that has come to represent Asian American history.

Tina Takemoto's queer experimental music videos *Looking for Jiro* (2009) and *Warning Shot* (2016) queer heteronormative, hypermasculine Japanese American history and memory of World War II. Takemoto employs queer speculation to create a gay imaginary for the lives of two Japanese American bachelors, Jiro Onuma and James Wakasa, who, as a result of President Franklin D. Roosevelt's 1941 Executive Order 9066, were among the over 127,000 West Coast individuals of Japanese descent who were mass-evacuated and incarcerated—many of them US citizens or legal permanent resident aliens. Her drag king performance as Jiro Onuma was a way "to think about the experience of an adult gay man in camp" and how "a lot of the time would probably be filled with boredom and longing and how to create a kind of internal life for that character to have a space for fantasy and desire." In *Warning Shot*, Takemoto questions the circumstances of the death of James Wakasa on April 11, 1943, in Topaz concentration camp at the hands of US military police. Using the "Rashomon effect," the video flashes back to recount Wakasa's death from different perspectives. "One death. Three versions of the crime," the video asks. "Was it justifiable homicide, an accidental fatality, or second-degree murder?" Her work mines historical archives to create an Asian American queer futurity, as it also draws connections to present-day activist and protest movements, such as Black Lives Matter, in resisting police brutality and the historical erasure of facts from the public and official memory.

Anida Yoeu Ali's interview by Laura Kina represents the generations of immigrants who came to the United States post-1965. Ali's work is rooted in performance but "spans mediums, themes, and borders." Ali discusses her *Buddhist Bug* series (2011–present), "which combines Muslim and Buddhist iconography to explore her diasporic identity as a Muslim Khmer woman and war refugee returning to Cambodia after three decades in the United States." The *Bug* is a gender-queer saffron-colored soft sculpture that Ali inhabits with her own body in live performances, with iterations as photos and videos. Her use of textiles that “can pack up very easily and then unpack to become something expansive . . . speaks so much to my refugee experience—that idea of carrying just the clothes on your back.” Ali, who began her career as a graphic designer and spoken word artist, talks about the failure of written or spoken language and has since, similar to Zavé Gayatri Martohardjono, come to rely on Butoh dance traditions and movements to communicate across cultures.

Across seven thematically framed essays paired with nine original artist interviews and an afterword by Kyoo Lee, we explore contemporary currents and experiences in Asian American art, including the multiple axes of race and identity, queer bodies and forms, kinship and affect, and digital identities and performances. As a critical modality, queering troubles, for example, binary and reductionist critiques of Asian American art that simply employ the lens of “East meets West”; challenges the East Asian American–centrism of art objects and artists of study and decenters geographical biases of Asian American art production (New York and California foci, for example); and embraces interdisciplinary and theoretically informed methodologies that engage readers to understand global and historical processes through contemporary Asian American artistic production. This interdisciplinary anthology at the intersection of queer theory and Asian American studies hopes to harness Asian American difference as a crucial point of departure for the study of contemporary Asian American art.

Chapter 1

Queering Surveillance

"You Blushed": Queering Surveillance after 9/11 in the work of Jill Magid and Hasan Elahi

HARROD J SUAREZ

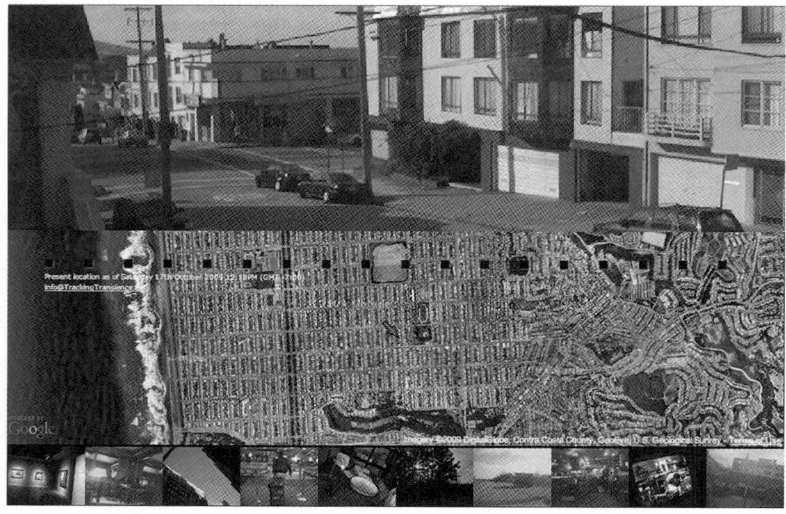

FIGURE 1.1

Hasan Elahi (American, b. 1972)
Tracking Transience
Screenshot from trackingtransience.net
Live website, launched 2003, ongoing
Courtesy of the artist

Hasan Elahi's *Tracking Transience* (plate 4, figure 1.1) is an ongoing project that appears online (trackingtransience.net). The site collects images of where Elahi is at any given moment, while also providing GPS coordinates for his recent whereabouts. The origins of the project shed light on what it might mean to surveil oneself. In a *New York Times* op-ed piece, he explains that he was unable to enter the United States through the

Detroit Metropolitan Airport on June 19, 2002. A naturalized citizen born in Bangladesh who grew up in New York, he was interrogated about his whereabouts on the day after 9/11. Elahi writes, "Fortunately, I'm neurotic about record keeping. I had my Palm P.D.A. with me; I looked up Wednesday, Sept. 12, 2001 on my calendar. I read the contents [to the official]: 'pay storage rent at 10; meeting with Judith at 10:30; intro class from 12 to 3; advanced class from 3 to 6.' We read about six months of my calendar appointments. I don't think he was expecting me to have such detailed records."[1] After a series of inquiries into Elahi's background that continued for half a year, including polygraph tests, he was cleared of suspicion.

But in preparing to travel abroad after the background check, Elahi decided to contact the FBI, willingly offering the details of his trip. "I wanted to make sure that the bureau knew that I wasn't making any sudden moves and that I wasn't running off somewhere. I wanted them to know where I was and what I was doing at any given time," he writes. It is a counterintuitive move: shouldn't one seek to challenge surveillance or, in the least, shield oneself from it? After 9/11, while some of those subjected to racial profiling sought to demonstrate their patriotism, others rejected such a mandate and challenged its racist assumptions. But it is here that the alternative offered by *Tracking Transience* begins. He continues:

> Soon I began to e-mail the F.B.I. I started to send longer e-mails, with pictures, and then with links to Web sites I made. I wrote some clunky code for my phone back in 2003 and turned it into a tracking device.
>
> My thinking was something like, "You want to watch me? Fine. But I can watch myself better than you can, and I can get a level of detail that you will never have."
>
> In the process of compiling data about myself and supplying it to the F.B.I., I started thinking about what intelligence agents might not know about me. I created a list of every flight I've ever been on, since birth. For the more recent flights, I noted the exact flight numbers, recorded in my frequent flier accounts, and also photographs of the meals that I ate on each flight, as well as photos of each knife provided by each airline on each flight.[2]

Grid upon grid, image after image—it appears as if very little of Elahi's life in the last decade has not been subject to documentation, and he indicates that the server logs show visitors to the site include the Department of Homeland Security, the CIA, the National Reconnaissance Office, and the Executive Office of the President.[3]

It is important to recognize what Elahi accomplishes in using a tactic of exposure and revelation through self-surveillance. On one hand, the

Transience website is a polyglot assortment of images that are hard to organize and seem to lack coherence. It is, as Elahi puts it, "deliberately user-unfriendly. A lot of work is required to thread together the thousands of available points of information. By putting everything about me out there, I am simultaneously telling everything and nothing about my life. Despite the barrage of information about me that is publicly available, I live a surprisingly private and anonymous life."[4] In doing so, he actually thwarts the objective of surveillance: to organize a profile of a subject/suspect. But he thwarts it not by running away, by seeking privacy from those who would surveil him, but by running toward the camera, arms wide open, offering himself and his whereabouts to whomever cares to inquire or log on. He shows the most intimate details of his life—the toilets he uses, the meals he eats, the beds he sleeps in—such that we get lost in his life. We don't obtain knowledge about him; instead, we very nearly come to live with him.

By staging what is in many ways an inappropriate survey of his life, Elahi's art sets up an alternative critical response to the conventional wisdom that privacy is the best way to resist surveillance. It is an alternative whose significance arrives through a queer reading, if we understand *queer* to refer to what Mel Chen calls "the social and cultural formations of 'improper affiliation,' so that queerness might well describe an array of subjectivities, intimacies, beings, and spaces located outside of the heteronormative."[5] The discomfiting intimacy of Elahi's work precisely constitutes an "improper affiliation" between the surveiller and the surveilled. In this essay, I argue that a queer reading of both Elahi's and Jill Magid's art charts forms of biopolitical intimacy that effectively seduce the surveiller such that his (the pronoun is used instructively) authority is compromised. By constructing an improper affiliation grounded in intimacy and desire rather than empirical data, these artists point to the limits of the purportedly objective comprehension of the surveilled subject/suspect.

Further raising the stakes of this argument, I suggest that Magid and Elahi enable a queer Asian Americanist critique of surveillance. Kandice Chuh argues for Asian American studies as a "subjectless discourse" insofar as it does not have a normative or essential subject, given the heterogeneity inherent to the category.[6] Indeed, what is perhaps most striking about *Tracking Transience* is that Elahi's body never appears in the surfeit of images. The images are literally subjectless and yet together compose something like a corpus, or body, of details orienting us toward Elahi's whereabouts and doings.

To draw attention to intimacy is already to disrupt the category of the subject/suspect. While surveillance may assume the subject to be a suspect, I contend that insofar as it is a category organized according to the protocols of a heteronormative biopolitics, the subject itself is suspect. Rather than reproduce the logic of subjectification that locates meaning in individuated subjects/suspects, the focus on intimacy calls for an intersubjective analysis. Thus, it hardly matters whether Elahi, Magid, I, or you identify as queer or Asian

American. It is the intersubjective desire—the desire that exceeds the subject of heteronormative biopolitics, the desire that draws me to Elahi and Magid just as they are drawn to systems of surveillance—that enacts the subjectlessness of queer Asian Americanist critique. It is the intimate and affective relations across bodies and texts that deliver a robust critique of surveillance.

While Steve Mann's "sousveillance" project—which attempts to surveil the surveiller, often literally using another camera to record the surveillance and closed circuit cameras in order "to empower individuals in . . . their encounters with organizations"[7]—has served as the "prevailing artistic response to surveillance,"[8] Magid and Elahi do not seek to take on such roles. Kirsty Robertson suggests that many of those working with sousveillance as a tactic have a "relative privilege" that potentially adheres to "an invisibly gendered virtualization of the omniscient male gaze."[9] Mann himself has admitted that "universal surveillance/sousveillance may, in the end, only serve the ends of the existing dominant power structure"—and this is especially true if the response results in the construction of a resistant *subject*.[10] To construct resistance along the terms of the subject—again, constituted through what I will claim has its foundations in heteronormative biopolitical surveillance—is to remain within the logic of these dominant structures.

Rather than aspire to become surveillers of their own vis-à-vis Mann, Magid and Elahi inhabit the role of the surveilled, drawing attention to themselves as subjects of surveillance after 9/11. But in doing so, it is not as if they simply succumb to the demonstrably inescapable force of biopolitical surveillance. As Magid writes to a surveiller with whom she cultivates a romantic intimacy, "I did not critique your system; I made love to it. You blushed."[11] If sousveillance functions as a critique that unwittingly reinforces the very terms of surveillance, its very power, then intimacy arrives as a queer relation to power. To be clear: the power is not so much in the surveillance itself, but in the form that enables the surveilling relationship—that is, the form of the subject who offers herself to be surveilled. If that subject is put under erasure through the intimacy and affect that Elahi and Magid explore in their respective art, then surveillance loses sight of its objective.

CONSENSUAL SEX

Paul Virilio describes contemporary society as operating according to "the banalization or popularization of global surveillance, or to put it another way the DEMOCRATIZATION OF VOYEURISM on a planetary scale."[12] Cameras and wiretapping are only concrete forms of the *general social field of surveillance*. What Virilio establishes as the universalizing and democratizing distribution of voyeurism and surveillance ought to be understood as an effect of the consensus politics that serves as the foundation for global capitalism at both geopolitical and biopolitical levels. Consensus politics works according to the narrative of the end of history, such that liberal-capitalist democracy emerges as the final horizon to which each nation, in uneven relation to each other, aspires. The confluence of capital and democracy marks this consensus, confirming for Jacques Rancière that the "absolute identification of politics with the management of capital is no longer the shameful hidden secret behind the 'forms' of democracy; it is the openly declared truth by which our governments acquire legitimacy."[13] In order to preserve and encourage the capital flows constituting liberal democratic practice, a consensus forms around, among other things, the need for surveillance to manage and repress the threat of difference, especially after 9/11. To participate in a society governed by the logic of consensus, one has little choice but to submit to a culture of surveillance.

While surveillance operates at a geopolitical level to manage terrorism and other threats to the consensus, it must also be understood as working at the biopolitical level of the subject; these two levels are part of the selfsame system. In its biopolitical form, we become subjects through our consent to behave as such; it is as individuated subjects that we are granted social and legal status—citizenship, family, and so on. Biopolitics takes on what Foucault refers to as a "capillary" form, an instructive analogy given that biopolitics works by regulating and disciplining bodies even and especially at minor, dispersed levels.[14] The site of power is a dispersed and extensive process, nebulous and more insidious than explicit coercion. Such a mobile, decentralized network enables power to shift and adjust to different conditions and contingencies. Jodi Melamed, for instance, writes that in the United States, "this means a new flexibility in racial procedures, so that racism constantly appears to be disappearing according to conventional race categories, even as neoliberal racialization continues to justify inequality using codes that can signify as nonracial or even antiracist."[15] Writing about overseas Filipina workers, Neferti Tadiar contends that "it is possible to conceive of domestic enslavement as part of an ongoing process of production of a new 'race,' which has as yet no discernible collective identity, but exists only as a changing pool of workers fulfilling class, gender and nationality specifications. We are apprehending a process of racialization that has not congealed into a fully-developed discourse of 'race.'"[16] The biopolitical and the geopolitical are thus mutually constitutive, working to manage populations on an ad hoc basis and primarily motivated by the need to reinforce the consensus.

Consensus politics informs gender and sexual constructs as much as it manages racial formations. Lee Edelman, for instance, critiques the "reproductive futurism" that subtends contemporary politics, arguing that the various angles and positions of any issue—taxes, gay marriage, war, immigration, and so on—consensually organize around the figure of the Child, the symbol of hetero-reproductive progress, guaranteeing "heterosexuality [as] the assurance of meaning itself."[17] The surveilled subject is constituted through the heteronormative. But we not only submit and subject ourselves to surveillance; we also become conduits and transmitters of surveillance, as if pace Virilio by way of Foucault there were a will to surveillance. Anthony Downey argues that the "rhetoric and aesthetic of surveillance is not only about a will to truth, the production of truth/knowledge, it also imbricates the observer within a system of knowledge that includes the production of criminological, juridical, and sociological models for the study of normative and, crucially, aberrant forms of behavior. . . . [W]e need to address how the use of surveillance produces, through a process of internalisation, the very behaviour we witness."[18] A more insidious biopolitical web of surveillance stretches across social, economic, and political relations—stretches, that is, from the micro levels of lived experience (the communities to which we belong, the pleasures and struggles of daily life) to the macro levels of geopolitics.

The question we are left with is in what ways we may propose to challenge the regime of heteronormative surveillance that structures geopolitical and biopolitical relations. Within queer theoretical debates, Edelman proposes, in a rather polemical fashion, to reject society outright. Building on Leo Bersani's earlier work on queer negativity, Edelman suggests that given the heteronormativity which stabilizes social being and belonging, there is not only no space for queer sexual relations, there is a mandate to eradicate queer difference. Queerness is not to be incorporated into the expansive reach of liberal multiculturalism; it "can never define an identity; it can only ever disturb one."[19] Rather than reconstitute a politics around a queer subject, like Asian American for Kandice Chuh, for Edelman queer is precisely subjectless. Insofar as political and social meaning itself is thoroughly constituted within heteronormative parameters, queer marks the absence of meaning, presence, and identity. It is an improper affiliation and appellation.

But in Edelman's polemical introduction that I have been citing, instability emerges in the category queer. For most of the chapter, Edelman uses Lacanian psychoanalysis to produce a concept of the queer in its negativity and subjectlessness. But when he writes that "those of us inhabiting the place of the queer may be able to cast off that queerness and enter the properly political sphere," it is unclear what it means to "inhabit the place of the queer."[20] What is a negative place? The problem is not academic: what it leads to, in the rest of the chapter, is the reconstitution of the queer as a subject position: "Queers must respond to the violent force."[21] Even as he continues to refer to the provocative notion of queer as part of the psychoanalytic breakdown of the subject, Edelman conjures up a resistant queer *subject*. In doing so, he loses the intersubjective and affective possibilities afforded by the subjectless turn. Indeed, when one pores over the incisive and stringent critiques of Edelman, especially from Jack Halberstam and José Esteban Muñoz, each of whom espies other archives that offer a glimpse of alternative futures, it is precisely the intersubjective and affective dimension that they draw on. For Halberstam, Edelman misses out on "dyke anger, anticolonial despair, racial rage."[22] For Muñoz, there is also racial hope: "All babies are not the privileged white babies to whom contemporary society caters," he writes.[23] In other words, the "future is only the stuff of some kids. Racialized kids, queer kids, are not the sovereign princes of futurity."[24] There are all sorts of improper affiliations that Edelman, in reconstituting the queer subject, misses out on.

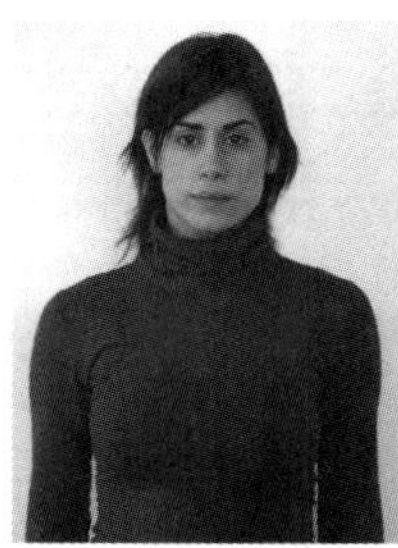

Dear Observer,

Make me a diary and keep it safe. Take care that it is mine.
Hold this photograph of my face. Keep all our entrieds in order.
Put the letters in your desk file and images in your evidence locker.
You can edit out everyone else.

I will fill in the gaps, the parts of my diary you are missing.
Since you can't follow me inside, I will record the inside for you.
I will note the time carefully so you will never lose me.

Don't worry about finding me. I will help you. I will tell you
where I am, what I am wearing, the time of day... If there is anything
distinctive about my look that day, I will make sure you know.

Hold on to my diary for at least seven years.

I am enclosing a check. Use it for whatever expenses you have.

Sincerely,

Jill S. Magid

FIGURE 1.2

Jill Magid (American, b. 1973)
One Cycle of Memory, 2004 from the Evidence Locker project

Printed book (page)
8.25 in x 5.75 in (21 x 15 cm)
Courtesy of the artist from One Cycle of Memory in the City of L.

QUEER INTIMACY IN *EVIDENCE LOCKER*

In *Evidence Locker* (2004–present) (figure 1.2, plate 5), Jill Magid spent thirty-one days between January and February 2004 in Liverpool, England, being surveilled by police using cameras located throughout the city. The maximum time that footage is maintained before it is erased is thirty-one days. To obtain access to any footage, an individual must submit a nine-page access form within that time frame.[25] Magid submitted one form for every day she was surveilled. These forms comprise *One Cycle of Memory in the City of L*, a text that complements *Evidence Locker*. The project is ongoing because it now takes a digital form: evidencelocker.net provides a starting point, but interested viewers can only obtain access to the forms by registering their e-mail addresses. The registration page comes with important messages. For instance, "To access my evidence locker, you must agree to be my witness."[26] There is also a disclaimer: "The emails and the locker they open are confidential and intended solely for you, the witness to whom they are addressed." The forms are separated into thirty-one separate e-mails, and registrants have the option of receiving them hourly or daily.

Magid actually instructed the police to surveil her; she wore a bright red coat—a nod to Jean-Luc Godard's film *Le mépris* (*Contempt*, 1963), which informs her project—to make her easy to identify in the footage, and she told the police where she would be each day. The forms do not consist of the typical bureaucratic discourse. Even as they identify where she was, the time, and other empirical details, they take an epistolary form. As the description on her website says, "Magid chose to complete these forms as though they were letters to a lover, expressing how she was feeling and what she was thinking . . . an intimate portrait of the relationship between herself, the police and the city."[27]

I registered in early May 2014. The first e-mail I received had the subject line "prologue"; it was a brief message addressed to the "Observer"—the surveiller, which originally was a male-gendered police officer, but now is the registrant, who could be anybody. It tells this Observer that Magid "will fill in the gaps, the parts of my diary you are missing. Since you can't follow me inside, I will record the inside for you."[28] Each of the thirty-one letters that follow includes links to a page on her website that resembles a rack for what appear to be thirty-one cartridges or cases, perhaps the size of DVDs. Clicking on one reveals the surveillance footage for that day. In the third letter, she writes, "I stood in the center of the street, in the red coat under my umbrella, and looked at you. I paused and looked right at you," but the footage is unstable and brief, making it hard to spot her.[29] It isn't until the fourth day that she appears in the frame, wearing her bright red coat. Part of the fifth letter takes the form of a dialogue between the Observer and Magid:

> *Should I follow you?*
> *You can. I just wanted to let you know I was going out.*

How long should I follow you?
Just as far as you want to.
I would follow you to the end of the world.
Motorcycle and all?
Would you like that?
Yes.
Then I will. Don't talk to any strange men.
Ok.[30]

The intimacy increases with each letter. In the eighth letter, she writes about taking a pregnancy test, revealing that the "porcelain soft-boiled egg holder with flower decal that is located on the wooden shelf of the kitchen above the bread bin has been used as a receptacle for a small portion of my urine."[31] In the tenth letter, she conjures up a scene wherein the Observer meets her at the Swan, a bar. He wears "black leather," while she wears "high red boots."[32] At the next bar they go to, "I got to know you. You told me more about what you do. You were taught the ways of the street. On the street you can scan a crowd. You can approach people and ask questions. From behind your windows, all this changes. Your approach can be intrusive. You can still scan the crowd, find that same person and follow him, but you don't like to, and it's not really fair. And you will be accountable."[33] Throughout the work, Magid constructs the Observer as a man, and their relationship extends beyond surveillance.

Critics have been quick to identify *Evidence Locker*'s gender politics. Elise Morrison argues that Magid achieves a "savvy feminist critique of surveillant epistemology overlaying the 'disciplinary gaze' of surveillance with the 'male gaze' of mainstream cinema," which she then interrogates, "challenging [its] gender-neutrality . . . to construct a space for feminist subjects of surveillance."[34] Deriving insights from Judith Butler's work on gender and performativity, Morrison's argument "suggests that the invitation for 'anyone' to become a panoptic watcher constitutes a radical potential within the carefully controlled disciplinary institution. If anyone can occupy the central guard tower . . . then there is potential for a different kind of looking, a different kind of repeating and deployment of the disciplinary gaze of surveillance."[35] The fluid and mobile circulation of biopolitics does not render us entirely beholden to its hegemonic and normative force. Morrison suggests that "by investing in the personal, affective experiences of watching and being watched, Magid constructed an embodied and lasting critique of the limitations of visual surveillance and its ability to capture an intricate record of a person."[36]

Maintaining a hetero structure in order to critique it remains in place for other parts of Magid's oeuvre, such as in *The Barragán Archives* (2013), where Magid looked into the politics of managing the archives of the late architect Luis Barragán. While she was able to study his personal archives in Mexico, she was not able to obtain access to his professional archives, which are managed by a Swiss furniture company that acquired them in 1995 for a new foundation in Barragán's honor. While much of the project raises questions about what it means to have one's archives split up in such a manner, in an interview Magid describes the project along intimate lines, referring to Federica Zanco, who runs the foundation: "I start thinking of the archive as her lover, which also makes her seductive to me as a person, but then I also think, Okay, if the archive is her lover, then who am I? . . . I'm the other woman in this post-mortem love triangle. . . . While she's immersed in his professional life, I'm immersed in his personal life. So we're kind of two halves of the whole."[37]

Queer intimacy appears to take multiple forms in this project. On one hand, Magid describes the relations among her, Zanco, and Barragán (or his archive) as a love triangle. The archive standing in place of Barragán's body marks an ambivalent construction: either it represents the extension of heteromasculinity such that a collection of files and documents can take on its privilege, or its proxy status marks a substantive transformation that alters heteromasculinity into something other than itself. Nevertheless, Magid narrates it as if she and Zanco are vying for the archive's attention. At the same time, it is striking that the archive is split into personal and professional collections. Its body is divided. Furthermore, Magid reports transferring her desire from Barragán to Zanco. It might be understood as a reimagining of Eve Kosofsky Sedgwick's discussion of male homosociality, wherein the figure of the woman only emerges to deflect the sexual desire, permitting a distinction between homosociality and homosexuality. But Magid stages the narrative in order to reveal the desire that Barragán's archive actually fosters between her and Zanco. Queer female desire is negotiated through Barragán's absent male body and through the archive that stands in its place.

We may also obtain a queer critique in *Evidence Locker*. While the disjointed movement of images in surveillance footage reveals a very manipulated surface, the intimacy she generates in her letters—which, remember, are actually access forms—is smooth and continuous. Reading the letters gradually reveals a romance narrative that she controls through her subjection to the camera, through choreographing her own surveillance at the hands (or eyes) of the Observer as both police and e-mail correspondent. It may be understood as a question of sexual agency. Morrison continues:

> The close personal relationship that Magid forms with her detective-Observer gives body to the systemic love affair that Magid has with the entire surveillance network of Liverpool. In fact, Magid describes her commitment to building a deep and meaningful human connection with her Observer through the techno-human interface of Liverpool's surveillance system as "making love" to the surveillance system. This phrase, like the famous fashion model dictum "make love to the camera," bespeaks an

intimate, one-on-one relationship between the viewer and the viewed. The scenes and conversations Magid records between herself and her "Observer" pointedly re-frame the relationship between surveiller and surveilled. Rather than a disciplinary association, theirs becomes a libidinal, intimate, and even loving contract, an affair played out in the surveilled cross walks and cafés of Liverpool.[38]

In making the "entire surveillance network" blush through her insistence on being surveilled, Magid cultivates a rapport that exceeds its normative protocols. Her letters reveal an intimacy and affect that go beyond what the system is supposed to accomplish, and in going beyond, she tracks an alternative and improper path within the regime of surveillance.

TRACKING INTIMACY

Building on this analysis, there are three formal ways in which we may trace a queer Asian Americanist critique in *Evidence Locker* and *Tracking Transience*. First, there is the technical processing of (moving) images, which distorts any constructions of reality on which surveillance relies. Magid emphasizes a distinction between the filming of the footage and what is relayed in the footage provided after submitting an access form: the footage is filmed in real time, whereas the relayed footage is provided at three frames per second, which is evident on viewing it. All of the movements are stilted; there is a clear gap between each frame. The disparity produces in visual form what Magid implies is true about the surveillance footage in general. In letter 15, she writes that "I am your subject; I relate myself to the city by the way you frame me in it. I know when you see me and when you don't. You can't hear me or smell me or touch me. You know what I wear and where I go. When I pick up the phone, you don't know who is speaking to me, unless I am speaking to you. I like that."[39] Having been subjected to the camera's gaze, she nevertheless alleges to know more than it does about her life. With a return rate of three frames per second, the camera produces meaning through the excising of images, manufacturing a stilted and distorted visual diegesis.

Elahi achieves something similar in *Tracking Transience*. Note, first of all, the time lag and time freezing that occur in his online self-surveillance. Like the transformation of surveillance footage from continuous real-time video to the stuttering aesthetic of three frames per second, the images that Elahi uploads wrench the continuous time of consensual heteronormative biopolitics out of its naturalized status. Against the proposition that we have reached the end of history through the advancement of capital and its facilitation through heteronormative narratives of progress and the future, Elahi freezes time with his still imagery. Even more intriguing is that much of the website actually creates a sense of motion, and thus of temporality. The first image that appears is revealed through continuous panning; even though the image itself is static, we see it emerge gradually—the screen moves. There is no ability to control the flow of images, either—the screen automatically shifts after a few seconds. The site thus functions according to a very manipulated motion and temporality that is staged, revealing not just the image but also the artifice of any naturalized temporal structures.

Second, both Magid and Elahi exercise a degree of control over their self-surveillance. Magid orchestrates much of what appears to the camera. She tells the Observer where she will be, where he can find her. She tells him of Godard's *Le mépris* to encourage him to be more assertive in directing her where to go. In letter 23, she tells him, "Yes, study me. It does not have to be invasive. It would be better if you could talk to me, while I do this, you say. If you can speak to me you can tell me what to do, where to be, and if I am in danger. If you can speak to me, you can protect me when my eyes are closed. We decide to get me an earpiece," and in the penultimate video, the Observer finally does direct her. She appears in a busy city square, eyes visibly closed. She appears to move according to what we can only presume are the Observer's directions. She nearly walks into an oncoming tractor but is able to avoid it. A stranger stops her and asks if she needs assistance. In the final video, she is seen riding away as a passenger on the back of a motorcycle.

By purposefully obfuscating the navigation of his website, Elahi also maintains a degree of what some might call agency. As he has suggested, part of what the project does is flood the visual and epistemological field with information about his whereabouts. The images are not contained in a manner of organization discernible to the viewer; if we accept this as a form of agency similar to Magid's in orchestrating her movements and surveillance, and finally leaving Liverpool, it is a different kind of agency, one that does not rest its hopes on the binary structures of surveiller and suspect/subject. Agency emerges beyond the subject, in the evacuating of the subject through the deluge of images that flood Elahi's website. Magid and Elahi thus destabilize the categorical distinction of surveiller and surveilled by politicizing intimacy and affect. Rather than propose an escape, they inhabit the position of being surveilled, and of the racialized, gendered, and sexualized implications of being gazed at, without understanding such a position as purely disempowering. They exploit the power of being surveilled, seducing those who may look upon them, thereby enabling themselves to make the system blush.

The third form in which queer Asian Americanist critique emerges has to do with the transference, in both projects, of the surveiller from the official to the random online voyeur, although the projects diverge in terms of what such transference achieves. For Magid, the shift of the Observer from a police officer manning a surveillance camera to viewers of the project's website generates another kind of queer intimacy, improper affiliations, especially given the diverse possibilities offered by the viewer's own identity. The letters are e-mailed to us with a sense of privacy; we are made privy to her thoughts, perceptions, and feelings. The transference from an institutionalized authority figure of the state to a random individual curious about the project is significant. If the conventional narrative of surveillance is dramatized in Althusser's narrative of interpellation, wherein the officer produces a subject who responds to his hail, Magid's transference is striking. At first, one is tempted to read it as marking the arrival of biopolitics—who needs an officer's interpellative surveillance when anonymous citizens can transmit the same power? A slight corrective is in order, though: Magid—the subject of surveillance—is the one who hails us to surveil her. At its worst, it is not that we surveil others, but that we seek to be surveilled, that in being observed we find validation—not unlike the phenomenon of seeking attention through "likes" and "favorites" on Facebook and Twitter. Magid e-mails us her letters addressing us as the Observer. In doing so, she does not just make us recognize our complicity in surveillance; we are also forced to recognize her complicity as a subject, which she constructs only to dismantle it via the improper affective relation. Kinship, affinity, and intimacy are generated in doing so.

Elahi's *Tracking Transience* also trades on complicity in terms of marking us as voyeurs who can surveil him. But two aspects in particular structure how complicity works differently from *Evidence Locker*. First, due to the surfeit of images with dramatically little context that populate his website, intimacy takes on a different, subjectless character. The images are impersonal, almost clinical and sterile, but nevertheless offer a different kind of intimacy that structures our complicity, our vicarious participation in Elahi's life. Here is an image of a toilet taken in his hotel room in Pittsburgh. A plate of *ma po tofu* in Los Angeles, a hamburger in Tokyo. Second, in sharp contrast to Magid's figure, which is the central focus of *Evidence Locker*, its raison d'être especially in working with and against the gendered gaze, Elahi's figure never appears in the frame. His body is never produced—except that in some ways, it is, insofar as the corpus of images tracking where he goes and what he does effectively functions to reconstitute the body in its lived, racialized experience. *Tracking Transience* plays on the context of racial profiling after 9/11 that served as the origins of the project, but it substitutes a series of images for his body. The images, in this sense, become racialized insofar as they are associated with his suspect whereabouts that we track online.

CODA

While I have contextualized *Evidence Locker* and *Tracking Transience* as providing alternatives to sousveillance, they also call to mind other artistic efforts taking on surveillance. For instance, one thinks of Sophie Calle's *The Detective* (1981), in which Calle hired a private detective to follow her. Knowing she was being watched, Calle went to sites that held personal significance for her, a form of knowledge that the detective would not be able to access. The piece emphasizes the stark difference between institutionalized knowledge and intimate, affective knowledge, a distinction that is also at work in *Evidence Locker* and *Tracking Transience.* Kirsty Robertson draws a connection between Calle's and Magid's pieces, suggesting that both mine "the fissures of the surveillance system to reconfigure earlier feminist debates, avoiding essentialist definitions of the body, but looking for fluid subjectivities, alternative gazes, and embodied resistance within the anxious urban spaces of contemporary capitalism."[40] While *The Detective* and *Tracking Transience* maintain the separation, *Evidence Locker* more explicitly entangles the surveilled and the surveiller into a romance narrative. Intimacy intervenes in the biopolitical, whereas Calle and Elahi keep the two separate.

Part of a larger project, Walid Ra'ad's *The Operator #17 File: I Think It Would Be Better If I Could Weep* (2000) consists of surveillance footage taken at the Corniche, a path that follows the coastline in Beirut. Ra'ad and the Atlas Group allegedly obtained the footage from officials. The footage shows a Lebanese security officer who "secretly diverts state surveillance cameras in order to shoot footage of the sunset."[41] The sentimental footage is purposeful: Ra'ad and the Atlas Group claim that the operator of camera 17 was relieved of his duties for moving the camera, though the operator claims "he only filmed the sun when it was about to set and subsequently went back to his operations, and added that in doing so he was fulfilling a childhood dream: when growing up in East Beirut he had always yearned to watch the sun set from the Corniche in West Beirut."[42] Ra'ad's video uses intimacy to disrupt the scene of surveillance. Ra'ad's operator is a surveiller who inserts a human longing—and one that is contextualized by the Lebanese Civil War (1975–1990)—into the tedious and mechanical work of surveillance.

One of the auxiliary yet insightful texts appended to *Evidence Locker* is an e-mail correspondence between Magid and the City Watch Operations Manager in charge of the Liverpool CCTV that takes a nod from Ra'ad's work. Near the end of the transcript provided on the *Evidence Locker* website, she wonders aloud, "Imagine if the CCTV cameras could be used to record beautiful moments and interactions in the city instead of watching for problems? Just a nice thought!"[43] The official responds, "We often see and record such events but sadly in the cold world of crime and disorder this is not evidence. But as you say we can use our imagination and have nice thoughts. I believe some people though use their imagination and have naughty thoughts." In the wake of 9/11, both *Evidence Locker* and *Tracking Transience* demonstrate the continuation and enhancing of surveillance regimes to manage populations, and they play within the texture of its field, developing critical forms of intimacy that challenge the heteronormative and biopolitical consensus of surveillance from within its very terms.

Performance, Surveillance, and Sousveillance: A Conversation with Wafaa Bilal and Hasan Elahi

JAN CHRISTIAN BERNABE AND LAURA KINA

On July 7, 2014, Jan Christian Bernabe and Laura Kina caught up with Wafaa Bilal (New York) and Hasan Elahi (Maryland) via conference call to talk about their use of surveillance and sousveillance. After a mistaken post-9/11 racial profiling incident by the FBI in 2002, Elahi began his open-ended Tracking Transience *project, in which he broadcasts his location and posts photos of his "hotel rooms, train stations, airports, meals, beds, receipts, even toilets."*[1] *In Bilal's* 3rdi *project (2010), he surgically implanted a camera into the back of his head to live-stream pictures every minute for a year to literally and metaphorically, in reference to his life as an Iraqi Gulf War refugee, record the places he has left behind.*

HASAN ELAHI: I was born in Rangpur, Bangladesh, in 1972, a few months after the independence of Bangladesh in the transition from East Pakistan to Bangladesh. My mom and I came to the United States in 1979, and my father came a couple of years before. We moved to New York City, which in a lot of ways was just like Bangladesh—everything was chaotic. "It's just like home," my parents would say. I grew up in New York and went through the public school system and way too many colleges to keep track of. I finished grad school at Cranbrook Academy of Art in 1996. Eventually I got into the academic business, and I now teach at the University of Maryland and live in Baltimore.

WAFAA BILAL: I was born in Kufa near Najaf, Iraq, in 1966. I stayed in that city until I moved to Baghdad in the mid-eighties—during the Iraq-Iran War. By the end of that decade, we were forced to leave Iraq. We traveled and ended up in Kuwait and Saudi Arabia in refugee camps. In 1992, I made it to the United States. I landed in New Mexico. That's where I got my BFA in studio art at the University of New Mexico. Then I moved to Chicago and got my MFA in art and technology from the School of the Art Institute of Chicago in 2003. I spent about eight years in Chicago and then moved to New York City, where I now live and teach at New York University.

JAN CHRISTIAN BERNABE: How do you as artists and people identify in the public sphere?

HE: Wafaa, I think both you and I get pigeonholed, identified, and plugged into a lot of different things—whether it be a Middle Eastern show, a subversive show, or a military show. We've had this experience where we are "that person." If we start at that point of identifying practice, I don't really affiliate myself with a particular type of practice or particular type of material or medium. I'm a photographer. I make video work. I make sculptural work. I think a lot of it is talking about looking at ways of negotiating and navigating ideas. Wafaa, I love your photographic works, and you're incredibly skilled in photography. You teach photography. You're a professional photographer, but I don't think that's your only identification.

WB: I totally agree with you. I don't think you can hold us down to one medium, and I always believe that the project determines the medium, not the other way around. Especially with our work—it's very responsive to a situation. It reflects our political environment. We need to balance how we want to target our audience. Is it a gallery? Is it in a physical platform? Is it a virtual platform? We start thinking about how you reach your audience using that specific medium.

HE: A term that works very well for our type of practice is "methodologies of working." I think given the type of work, there's a lot of insertion from the audience.

WB: Hasan, I like that idea of insertion because if you think about how we go about our own work, it's not like we are inserting ourselves into that situation. It has to do with how we go about executing a specific project. This has a lot to do with the status of art—at least in current times it has changed a lot. We are no longer broadcasting; rather we are triggering something and seeking response to that trigger.

HE: If anything, we are stepping outside and holding a mirror up; a lot of this has to do with dualities of us growing up in multiple cultures and code-switching back and forth. It was really amazing watching you in Dubai [the two were at Art Dubai in March 2014], where you switched back and forth from English to Arabic. Going back and forth between these multiple worlds—we do that. It's one of those things that's inherent in us as multicultural, multilingual immigrants. With all this hybrid background, it's inevitable that we are going to be bouncing back and forth between these worlds.

WB: We do exist in these two worlds. Hasan, I know you grew up here, but I think your cultural inheritance is not just in New York but exists in both places. In my situation, I do have family back in Iraq, and I am here but I'm mentally split between these two places even though I physically exist in one and not the other but still on a daily basis I think about the two places, and what makes the situation even more dire is that these two places are at war. Hasan, you have been put in the same category because of where you come from.

HE: I was born thirty-six days after the war of independence ended. I'm sure that has something to do with my upbringing. Of course, my father and my uncles were involved in it. I want to go back to this thing of immigration and this idea of immigrants. One of the things that happen is that we've assimilated very well into our adopted culture. I think of that and our assimilation into various types of practice in respect to making art—whether we need to do a performance, or a type of sculptural piece, or an immersive installation work.

WB: That's really important because we, as people who exist in both places, are trying to reach an audience that has a comfort zone, and we have assimilated to that zone and become part of it. How do you connect this audience to a place that is far away physically and emotionally removed from them? It becomes a matter of filtering the conflict through a local language people can understand. By language, I don't mean language itself but rather the society; how you create that trigger becomes very important. That isn't easy unless you are within that culture.

JBC: Wafaa, I was introduced to your work at a conference where Ronak Kapadia was doing a critique of your work using a queer framework. How comfortable are you with this kind of reading?[2]

WB: As an artist conceiving a project, I really don't have control over how that project can stand up, because an art practice is an assigned value to an act, and if we think what we created is very open ended and dynamic, then what other people assign to it might be completely different than what I intended. But it makes the work have multiple existences, multiple lives, multiple meanings. To start with, I didn't assign "that value" or "this value" to the art or the object, but rather I am opening a platform. And the platform has to have multiple players in order to become a very dynamic thing.

HE: Wafaa, I think you hit it right on the head when you talked about assigning value. It's not that your work can only be read in one way. Your work can be read in so many different contexts, and each of those reads has many interpretations that springboard from it. I think that's the sign of a really strong body of work. When people are able to have these really heavy reads and intellectual conversations that are completely different and exist in different worlds, there is some magic happening there.

JCB: Hasan, your work also speaks to that richness. In *Security & Comfort v. 3.0* from the *Tracking Transience* project (2007), you photographed all of those toilets (plate 4). I was drawn to how private that space is and how you were teasing out this intimacy. It's very Duchampian and very queer! Wafaa, your *3rdi* project (plate 6) is also very powerful in how it functions as a mirror to society.

HE: You should see my Instagram feed and what I put on every single day, and that's [toilets] the *only* thing I put on Instagram by the way.

WB: I get the feed all day!

HE: Yes, there is a smartass side to that, of course. Yes, there is the Duchampian read that's obviously there but there are also a lot of other things that are happening underneath. One of the things to keep in mind, and Wafaa, I know you have been in much more traumatic situations, but when you are face-to-face with authority—Saddam Hussein in your case[3] or the FBI in my case[4]—when you are face-to-face with someone on that side of the table with that much power of life and death over you, you are basically reduced to your animal functions and you become the ultimate Other. You become the animal and you do whatever you have to do to get out of that situation. It's a very primal instinct.

On the other end of the spectrum of the formalist art side, you look at the photographs of Bernd and Hilla Bechers[5]—every single blast furnace, every single chimney, every single water tower. You look at this cataloging, this continuous chronicle where everything is presented purely as evidence. This is evidence of what has happened there, but you don't know what the conversation was. You don't know who else was there. Look at some of those beds [in his *Tracking Transience* database of all the beds Hasan has slept in while traveling], which is such a private space. Yes, there are obvious references to Felix Gonzales-Torres with the images of the beds, but that image functions differently here, and with that many different beds, they can't possibly be my own bed.

WB: It's interesting that you point to the Bechers. The Düsseldorf School was very reactive to the gooey sentimental postwar images. I hear you talking about the emotion removed from these pictures, but they indicate something completely different. They almost open up the subject.

HE: They open it in a different direction. It goes back to that mirror, holding up that mirror—if it looks sad, desolate, and depressing, maybe that's the state of living we are in right now in our own political world.

WB: To me it goes back to the idea of a local language that people cannot understand but rather assign something to.

HE: It's assimilation. It really is. It's assimilating into various modes and contexts.

LAURA KINA: How did the two of you meet?

HE: We've been following each other's work forever. The place we first met was, of all places, in Istanbul. Joseph DeLappe put us together on a panel at International Symposium on Electronic Art (ISEA) in September 2011, "If You See Something Say Something: Art, War, Surveillance and the Sustainability of Urgency in the Post 9/11 Era." That was the first time we met in person, but we had so many overlaps with mutual friends over the years.

LK: In both *3rdi* and *Security & Comfort*, you're dealing with surveillance, as you mentioned, but also sousveillance—surveying yourself. Can the two of you talk about how you engage the topic of surveillance as users, makers, and subjects, and what this means to you as racialized subjects?

WB: The *3rdi* project is surveillance but also *sousveillance*—we are monitoring ourselves with our work. With the *3rdi*, there is a trying as a photographer and artist to lose subjectivity over the picture. I'm trying to remove what Roland Barthes called the most powerful thing a photographer has—his index finger.[6] Trying to remove that power, trying to remove the power of what the eye sees and what you assign to that photograph by pointing the camera, by cropping the pictures; all of this is removed and what's left is . . . There's no such thing as the fusion of body and machine, but when it becomes mundane, a never-ending thing that is automated, that shoots without the knowledge of me, what's left is the context of where I existed for any time in a year.

HE: *Security & Comfort* is one of the databases with *Tracking Transience*, a larger body of work that has generated some seventy thousand images by now: all the rest-stop pictures off of the interstates, all of the tacos that I've eaten in various street stalls in Mexico City, all of the beds that I've slept in, and dozens of other categories. *Security & Comfort* is the database of all the toilets I've used. It's one of the nodes of the larger network. There's even an entire hidden database from the very early days when I wore a little cell phone camera around my neck. The pictures were taken automatically. I hated the images, and I was so disappointed in the way they looked. Even though I'm not trained in photography, maybe this is where this deep-down, ingrained Düsseldorf idea of photography comes into my head. It drove me crazy to the point that I had to stop the automated capture. But now with the iPhone being my main camera, I'll pull it out and take the picture without realizing it.

WB: Hasan, when I had the camera in my head, one thing I promised myself is to never turn myself into the camera—to never turn around and take a picture, which was one of the hardest aspects. In the beginning it was fine because the body is not assimilated yet to the apparatus, but then the body starts tensing when the camera is about to take the picture, and then the hardest aspect of it is not to turn around if there is something interesting and take a picture. It goes off every minute, and I could tell the shutter was going to go off because the camera—I put it to sleep to save the battery and then I wake it up—it makes this tiny motor sound in the camera lens, and then I would have to say, "Okay, you made a promise, don't break the promise."

HE: I'm wondering if these parameters that you've set up changed across the year?

WB: I tried to really stick to what I had set up. You know its history with the rejection of the camera on the head, and I started wearing it on my collar.[7] . . . I don't think it changed very much but what changed is looking back at these images and examining them and seeing how much as artists we are obsessed with the idea of making. Most of the time I was either in the studio or on my office chair making something but not really being in the physical situation. I think that changed me as a person. There is a sort of obsession and maybe not a healthy obsession, and the obsession comes from this responsibility that's placed on us because we are from these two different places. The revelation here is that you have to live where you are and enjoy that life.

JCB: There is something very subversive in your work with your obsession to track and archive, especially mundane and vernacular things. Can you speak to the ways in which photography no longer becomes this rarified thing?

WB: There is an article written by Nicholas Mirzhoeff on photography, and while so many people predicted that photography was about to die, Mirzhoeff said, "Wait a minute; that prediction was wrong," and then he announced the *death* of the death of photography and told these former critics they're wrong.[8] The reason for that is the technological shifts. If one has almost exclusive access to the medium by being a photographer, because you know what you should do, that's one aspect; the second is that photography became so ubiquitous in changing our lives and influencing us in a way we cannot perceive; the third and most important is how the new generation and the people who adopt these technologies subvert the power structures and change it. Power is about limited access. Now the apparatus is inverting the power structure. What was once private is now within all our power to make public. This confessional stage is empowering us and is becoming the signature of this generation. I no longer have anything to hide.

HE: The other thing, Wafaa, is a real critical moment where there are more cameras than there are photographers in culture; and many of those cameras are fully automated. These machines are continuously photographing, continuously archiving, and continuously broadcasting. The autonomous camera has caused a radical shift in photography, releasing that power to the machine to take that photograph. Best of all, that camera does not care for the photographer! Whether it be the traffic camera, the surveillance camera, or that satellite up in space, none of them care whether there is a photographer or not.

LK: I'm wondering if you could link this up to the post-9/11 "War on Terror" and a lot of the civil liberties that we've given up and the subsequent rise in Islamophobia in the United States?

HE: There is an inextricable link between art and warfare and the different art movements and art practices that have resulted from our experiences with warfare. The birth of Dadaism is a perfect example, where the culture was trying to make sense of the world after the wreckage and tragedy of World War I. There is a similar pattern when you look at the "War on Terror." Even though we've invaded other countries over three hundred times since independence, the United States has only declared war eleven times in history.[9] We are currently at war with "terror," but how does terror—an undetermined enemy—give up? How does terror say, "The war is over. You guys win"? We've put ourselves in a perpetual war, and this has significant cultural implications. When we live in a culture of perpetual war, it's only natural to react with corresponding perpetual documentation. The perpetual "selfie"—that holding up of the camera—is the cultural reaction to the "War on Terror."

JCB: You raise the point of the ubiquitous selfie, but I wonder how much the user is thinking that what he or she is doing is motivated by these technologies of surveillance?

WB: I think it's important to make a distinction between surveillance and sousveillance. Surveillance is looking without the knowledge of the person you are looking at. Sousveillance is a very meditative way of presenting and broadcasting yourself. There is a shift in the distribution channels, and the shift helps bring these platforms that cater to us, that cater to our ego and reach a massive audience. That act itself of sousveillance has been adopted by groups and individuals who like to reach as many as they can for whatever reason—broadcasting yourself or a message.

HE: I think the technology of the selfie is so far removed from the act of taking a selfie that we don't make a direct connection. There are so many different levels of mediation along the way. When you are driving down the street using your GPS, you're not thinking, "Oh, this is what guided missiles use," or when we use the Internet and send each other e-mails, we're not saying, "This was a project created for the military to be able to communicate securely in case the Russians blew up some big telephone exchange system back in the Cold

War." A lot of the pieces of technology that have become common every day have a military origin.

WB: It's back and forth. One example is the National Security Agency, which has to capture so many private conversations with just a machine doing it, not individuals doing it.

HE: This automation is interesting. We already talked about how the camera doesn't care for the photographer. The images taken with these automated cameras are not meant for human consumption. The images are purely meant for machine reading, because it is physically impossible for humans to read fifty exabytes of image data—you just can't. That's the latest way of monitoring everybody and recording everything that's taking place on the Internet. That's what the NSA is doing at the Utah Data Center.[10]

JCB: Part of my question is this taken-for-grantedness of the technology and photography, and the ways in which you two really bring it back to the importance of the mundane, the banal, and tell your audience, "Wait a minute, it's not just the selfie or the toilet."

WB: Sometimes you are so in it you don't recognize this is part of our daily practice. Unless we see it reflected on a different surface, then we acknowledge that person who holds the mirror.

HE: We are fully embedded in this, and it's not something we can extract out of. I don't think that's an option given our current technology. I can only imagine how embedded this will become in the future.

LK: Wafaa, earlier you talked about being in two places at once and that your mind is also in Iraq. With the current events happening right now with the takeover by ISIS,[11] can both of you talk about your relationship to Iraq and Bangladesh and where you are currently?

WB: It's really hard to see what is happening on the ground in Iraq and to see how it's so confusing to everybody what has taken place. I cannot separate myself from that situation. I'm in an obsessive mood these days. What has surprised me is that I no longer want to get my news from the networks because every one of them has an agenda. What I resort to now is checking on Twitter and what people are loading on Facebook posts. To me it is uncensored, in a way. I'm seeing these mass executions, and they are loaded by the people who are doing them! No network will broadcast that to me. Then I make up my own mind; the crowd decides to bring these matters into the forefront to be public. For the first time, I'm not listening to networks but going to the crowd itself to tell me what is happening.

HE: There is a technological shift where now there is an immediacy. Not only are the networks giving you the stadium-seating kind of image, but now you have individuals—the people taking the selfies—who are live-tweeting events as they occur.

WB: Hasan, you mentioned "unmediated." I think they do have bias but no spin.

HE: There is a spin but it's direct one-to-one rather than one-to-millions or going through traditional media filters. In the past, it may have taken days or weeks to get images of these types of events, but now we are seeing it happen in real time. As that explosion is going off, we are seeing a YouTube clip of it. That's really changed photography as we know it.

WB: It's so true that it is changing everything we know. Yesterday I was looking at what is unfolding on Facebook. Here is the crowd saying there is this attack against the country, and we can expose who is doing it but we aren't going to wait for anyone to tell us what to do. We, as a group of people, are going to do it.

HE: Laura, in regards to Bangladesh, our two cases are quite different in that I came over as a child whereas Wafaa came over as an adult to the United States. Those are huge differences, but also think about the time. When the war took place in Bangladesh, in 1971, it was a very different era technologically. I'm thinking back to how Wafaa is getting his news and his Twitter feeds right now as it's happening, and it makes me think about my parents' generation and how information got out. In 1971, this was a very localized event, whereas now there is a much broader reach.

JCB: Wafaa, can you speak about how you use your body and how you conceptualize the Arab male body and recuperate it?

WB: What is happening here is that the body functions as a trigger. If we think of the body as having its own language, what I'm soliciting from my audience is a corporeal reaction as well as a cerebral reaction. The mind analyzes and blocks ideas it may not like. By triggering a visceral reaction, the viewer's body essentially overrides what the brain is trying to tell them. By using the participant's body directly, [I am bypassing] what their mind is telling them they know. This way, on one level, you have an intellectual engagement; on the other, it is a very corporal, very body-to-body connection. That's why when you look at my works in *Shoot an Iraqi*[12] (plate 7), when you look at . . . *and Counting* (2010), what you are really looking at is your body placing itself automatically in that situation, and this happens because of the immediacy of performances—how the body is used in performance, how it is unequal to any other medium since it is immediate and the reaction is immediate.[13]

JCB: You place yourself in these very vulnerable positionalities.

WB: That's a big part of it, because vulnerability triggers a response—a visceral response from the audience.

JCB: Hasan, in your photos the body is absent but we can feel it—there is an affective lingering of the body in your picturing and surveillance. How do you locate the Arab male body, or do you even identify as Arab?

HE: No, I'm only Arab if we go by what Homeland Security thinks: "All those people are the same." I'm Bengali, and we're far from Arabs. Unfortunately, in the United States, we often interchange *Muslim* with *Arab*. That's very problematic. People assume I'm Arab because my name is Elahi, but that's not correct either, since the name has its historic roots in Iran, but my family isn't Iranian or Persian. There are a lot of incorrect assumptions, and to add to the complications, we don't seem to understand secularism in Islam. We know that not every Jew is Orthodox. We know that not every Christian is Amish. We understand how secularism works among Jews and Christians, but why do we think that every Muslim is a radical Wahhabi Saudi? Unfortunately it's not just a *Fox News* sort of attitude, but quite prevalent across an educated population in the United States. Here's where it gets really interesting. If you call an Irish person English, it can be quite offensive, yet we have difficulty understanding that not all Muslims share the same national origin. We are dealing with a great degree of variance in cultures that span globally from Morocco to Indonesia. Add in Muslims in the United States, and then secular Muslims—it gets really complicated and that identification of "Arab" just does not make sense.

JCB: I wonder if that's symptomatic of this ubiquity of technology that we've been talking about.

HE: No, I don't think it has to do with technology at all. It's symptomatic of our society—if you are not one of us, then you are one of them.

WB: We can't blame it on technology, but rather we blame it on a society that doesn't want to be engaged even though their own government is waging these wars and aggressions. Ultimately it is the responsibility of the citizen to check on the government to see what it is doing, in a very simple way. We can't have one-size-fits-all.

HE: That's really ironic, because we talk about our American culture as being very inclusive. We think of ourselves as a very diverse country and culture—and we are, but it's problematic when cultural differences between Northern and Southern Europe are celebrated, and many parts of the rest of the world are conflated as monolithic.

WB: It's the brown color, man!

HE: We can laugh about this, we can make jokes about this, but at the same time this is exactly how my investigation was triggered. The authorities received a report that "an Arab man had fled on September 12th and was hoarding explosives." Never mind that I'm not Arab, never mind it wasn't the 12th, never mind I didn't have explosives—none of that matters because whoever reported me created an idea of a person they wanted to see.

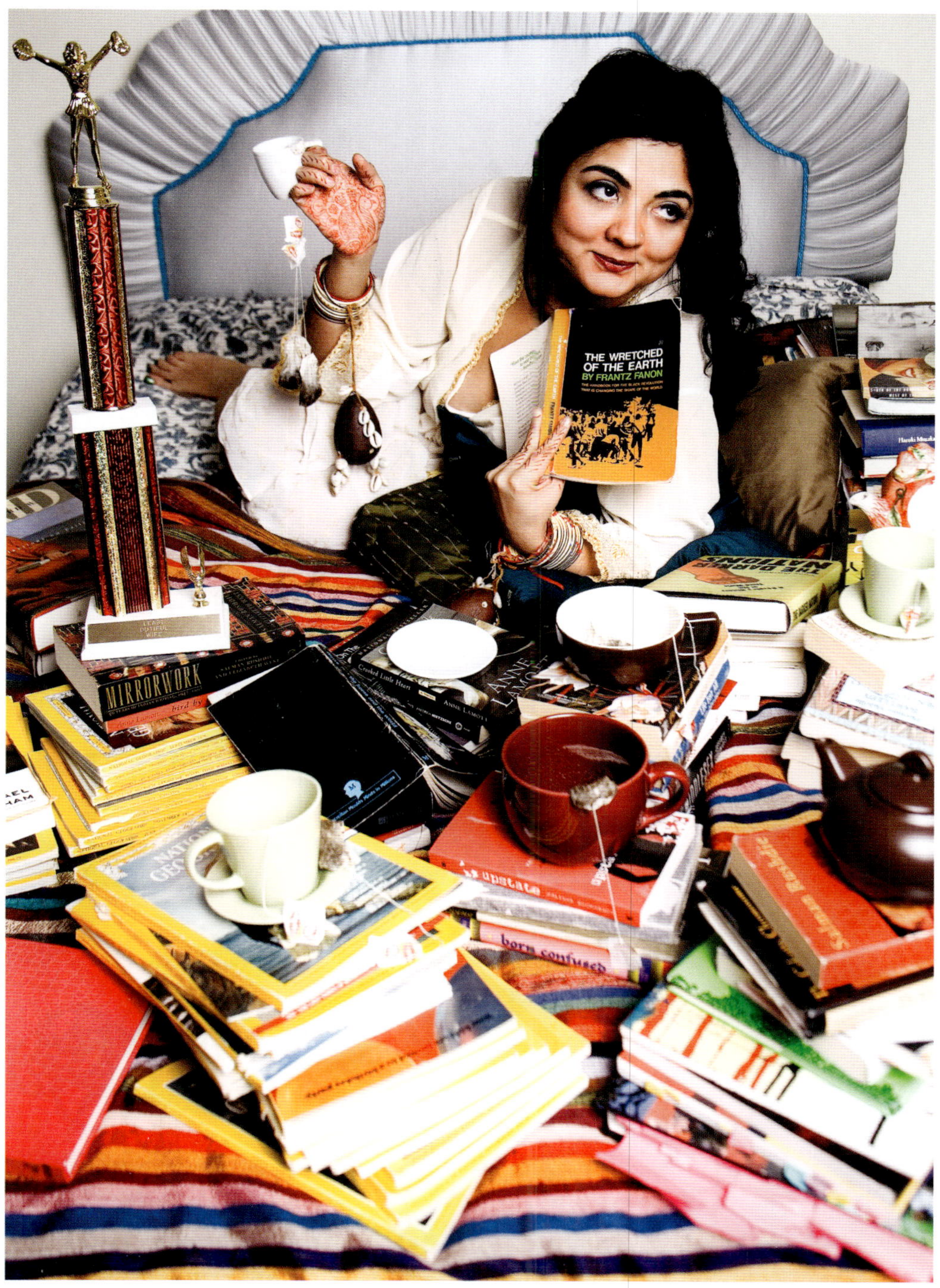

PLATE 1

Swati Khurana (Indian/American, b. 1975) and Anjali Bhargava (Canadian/American, b. 1977)
Unsuitable Girls: Least Dutiful Wife, 2009

Digital C–Print
30 x 20 in. (76 x 51 cm)
From the *Unsuitable Girls* series by Swati Khurana and Anjali Bhargava

Photo: Anjali Bhargava. Courtesy of the artists.

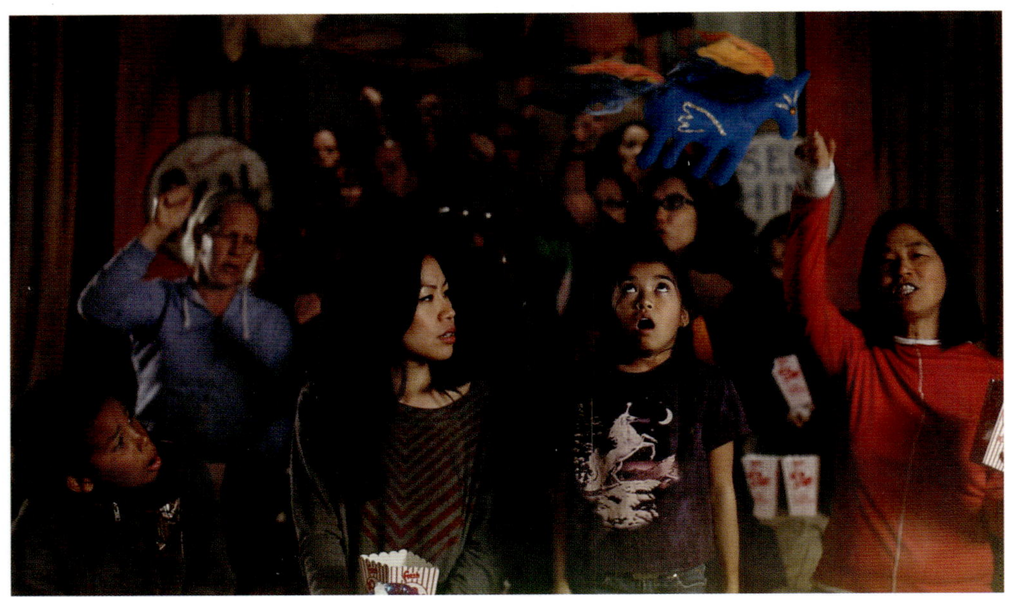

PLATE 2

Genevieve Erin O'Brien (American, b. 1974)
Film still of Kaylan and her mom in *For the Love of Unicorns*

5 min, digital color narrative, 2015
Courtesy of the artist.

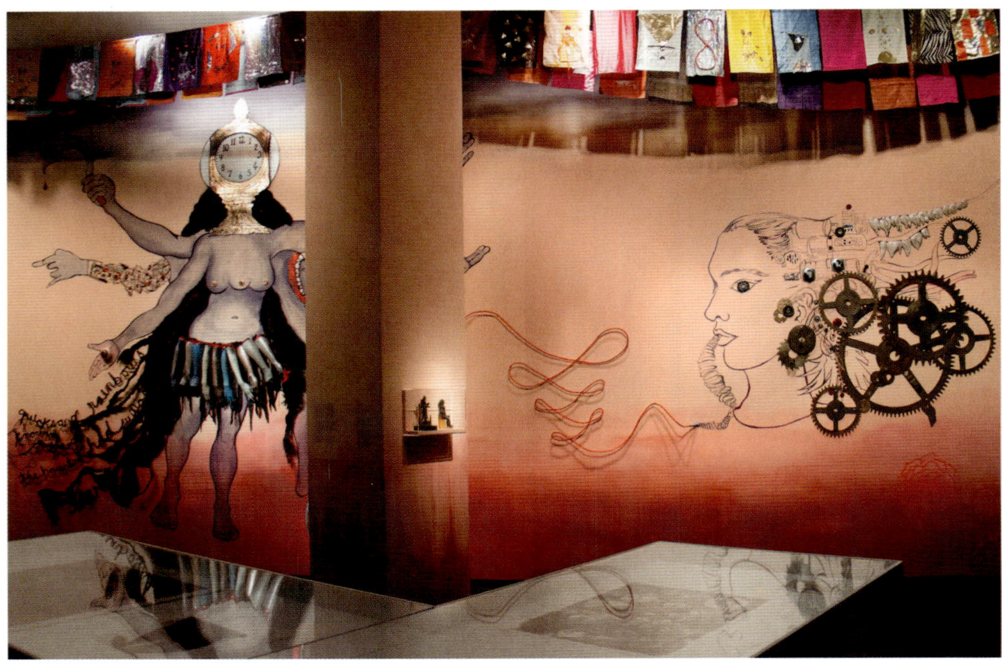

PLATE 3

Chitra Ganesh (American, b. 1975)
Chitra Ganesh: Eyes of Time, Brooklyn Museum, December 12, 2014–July 12, 2015 (installation view)

Mixed media on wall
186 x 564 in. / 15.5 ft. height, approximately
47 ft. width (472.5 x 1,432.5 cm)
Courtesy of the artist and the Brooklyn Museum, Elizabeth A. Sackler Center for Feminist Art
Photo: Jonathan Dorado

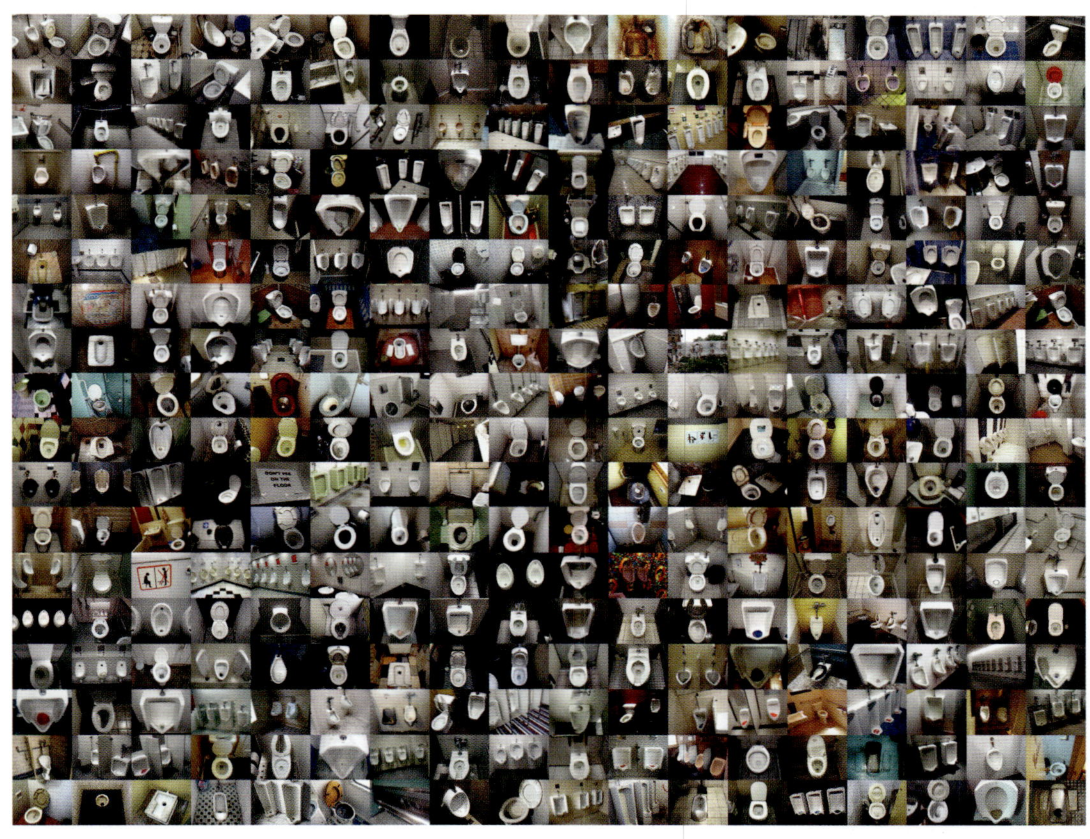

PLATE 4

Hasan Elahi (American, b. 1972)
Security & Comfort, 2007, from the ongoing *Tracking Transience* project

C-print
59 x 118 in. (150 x 300 cm)
Courtesy of the artist

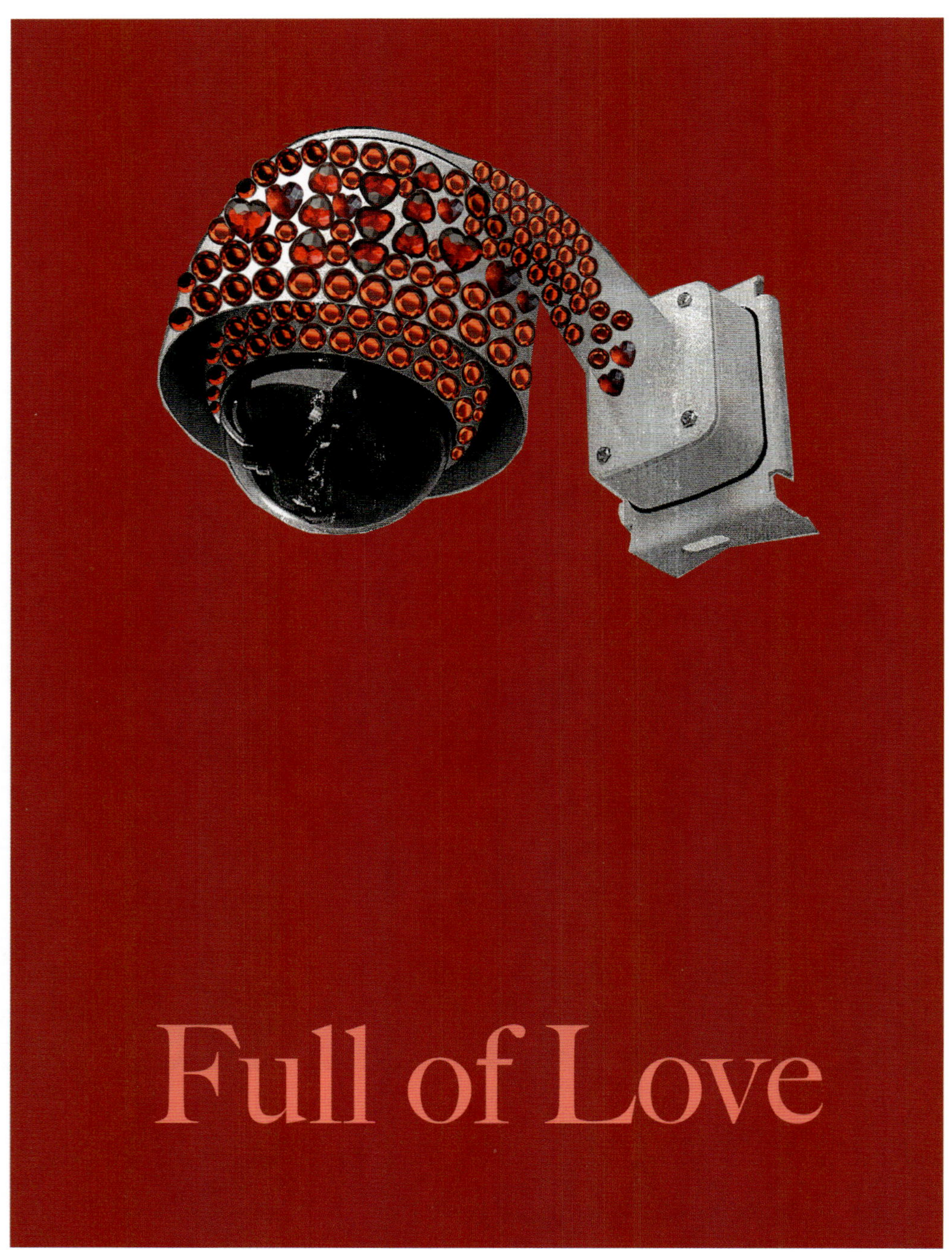

PLATE 5

Jill Magid (American, b. 1973)
Full of Love, 2001, from the *Evidence Locker* project

Silkscreen
Dimensions variable
Courtesy of the artist

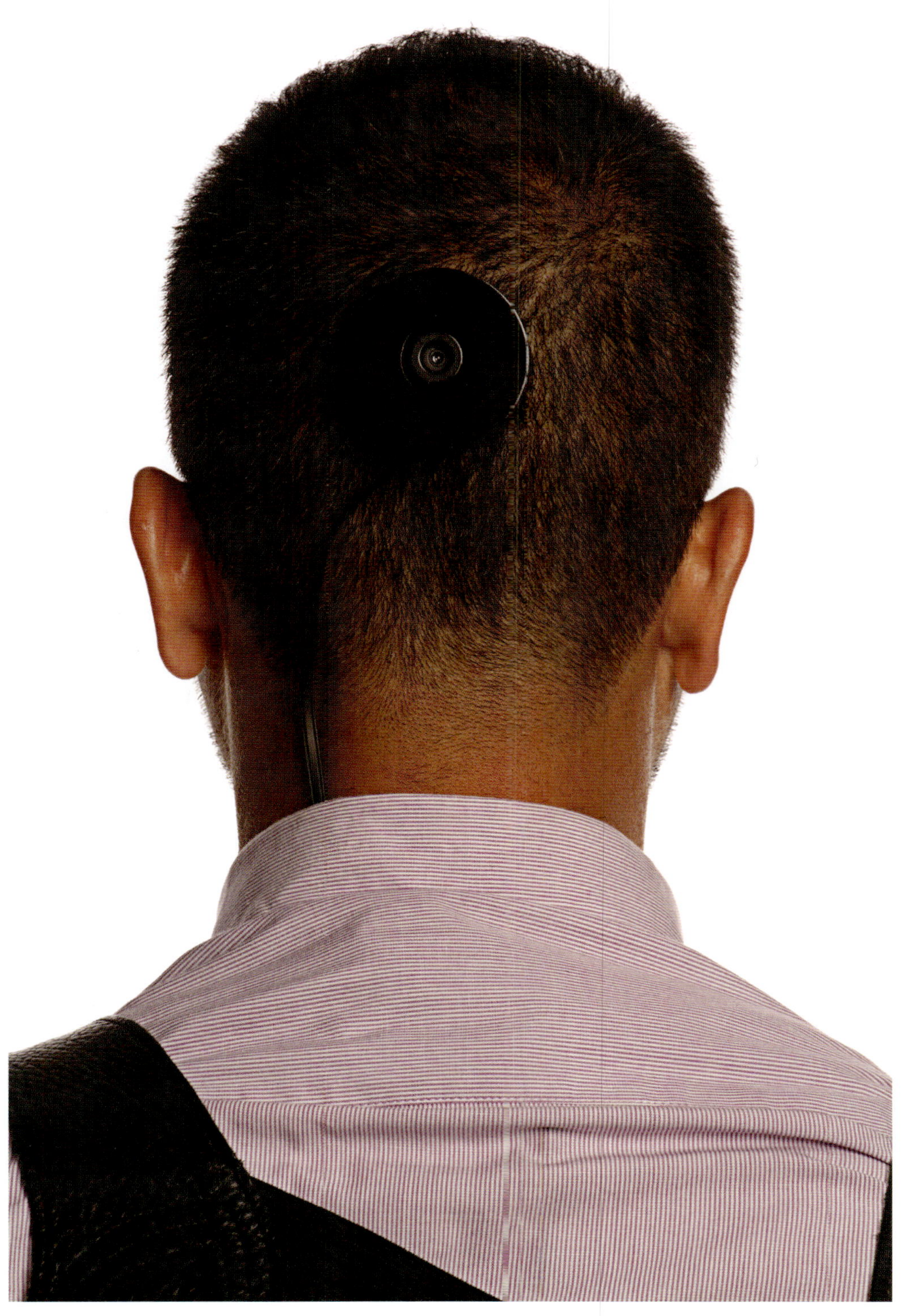

PLATE 6

Wafaa Bilal (Iraqi, b. 1966)
3rdi, 2010–2011

Year-long performance
Courtesy of Driscoll Babcock Galleries

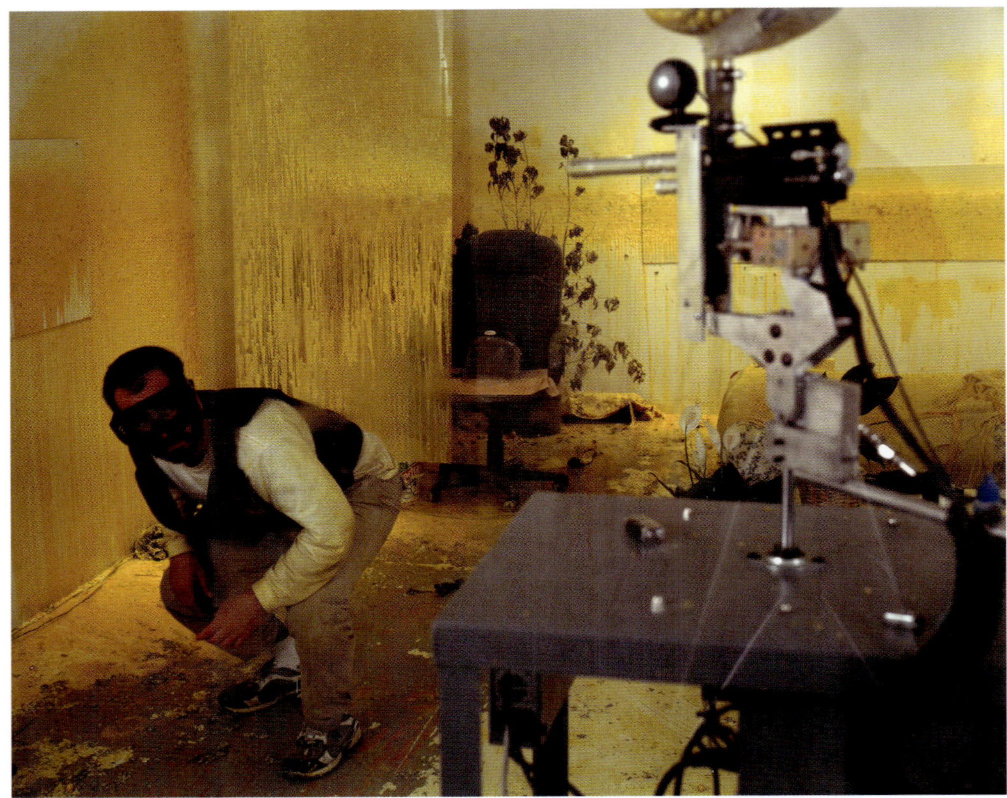

PLATE 7

Wafaa Bilal (Iraqi, b. 1966)
Domestic Tension, 2007

Performance

This image was reproduced in Wafaa Bilal and Kari Lydersen, *Shoot an Iraqi: Art, Life and Resistance under the Gun* (San Francisco: City Lights, 2008).

PLATE 8

Lin + Lam (Lana Lin, American, b. 1966; H. Lan Thao Lam, Canadian, b. 1968)
"Caution US Government" (a component of *Unidentified Vietnam*), 2006

Digital C-prints, 16 x 20 in. (40.64 x 50.8 cm) each photo
Mixed-media installation with photographs, sculptures, 16mm projector and 16mm film loop, video, and parabolic speakers
Courtesy of the artists

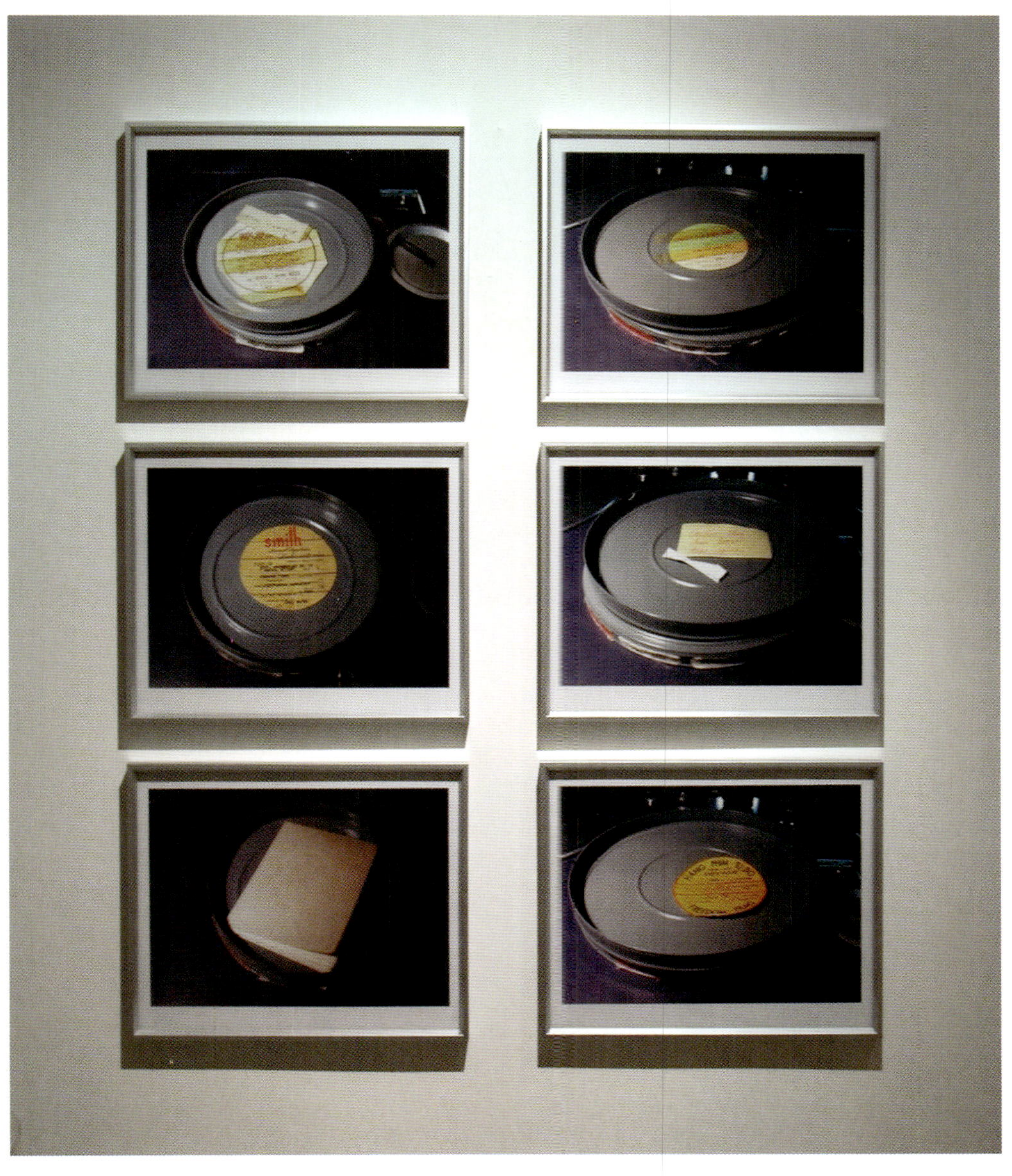

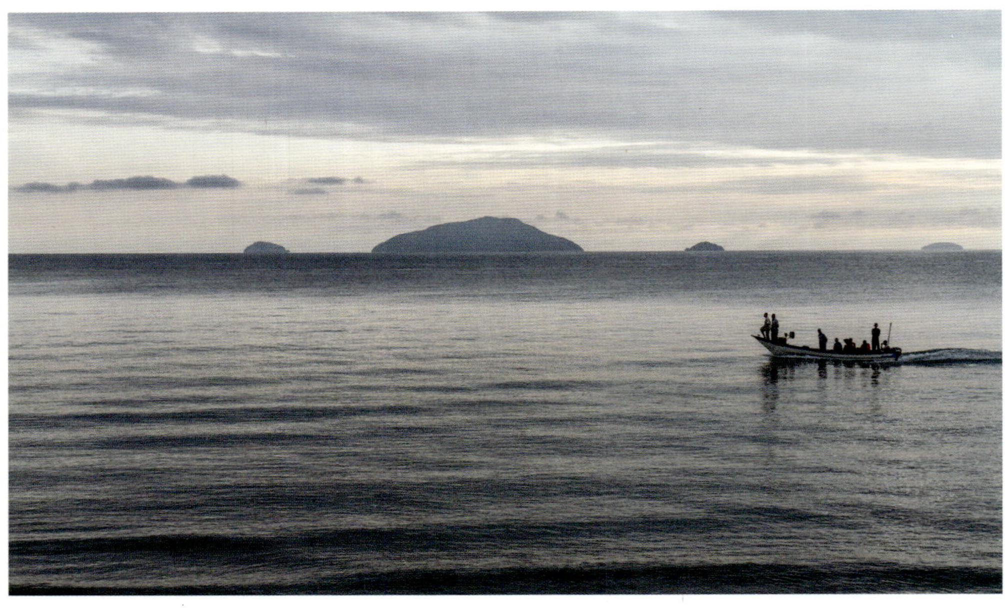

PLATE 9

Lin + Lam (Lana Lin, American, b. 1966; H. Lan Thao Lam, Canadian, b. 1968)
Tomorrow I Leave, 2010

Digital C-print
35 x 60 in. (89 x 152 cm)
Courtesy of the artists

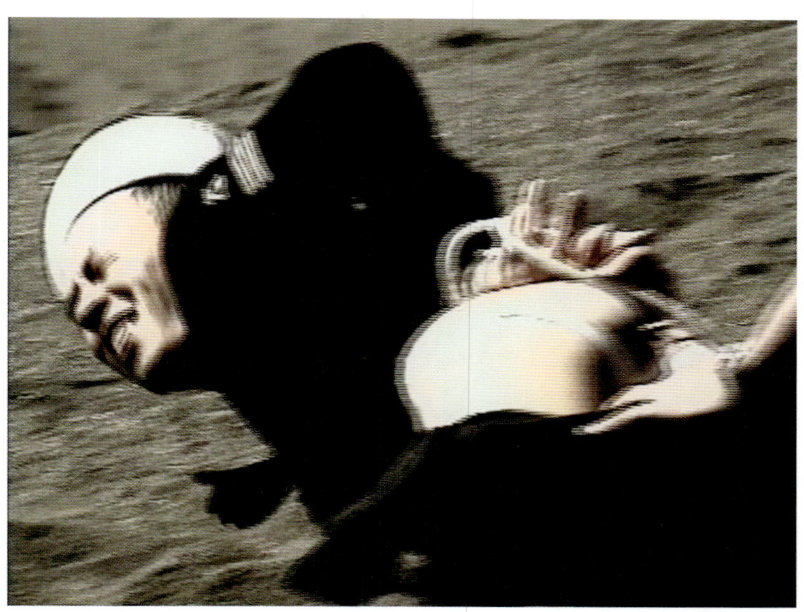

PLATE 10

Nguyen Tan Hoang
(Vietnamese/American, b. 1971)
PIRATED!, 2000

Beta-SP Video, 11 min.
Courtesy of the artist

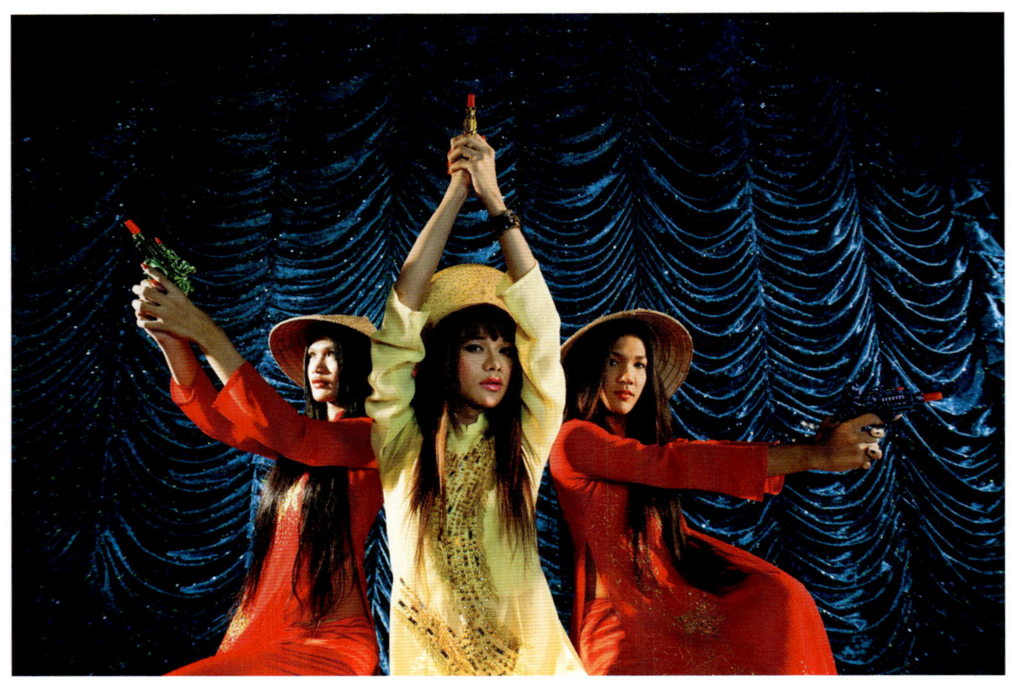

PLATE 11

Việt Lê (Vietnamese/American, b. 1976)
Charlie's Angels (of History), 2013, from the *Love Bang!* series

Digital C-print (vinyl banner)
60 x 100 in. (152 x 254 cm)
Courtesy of the artist

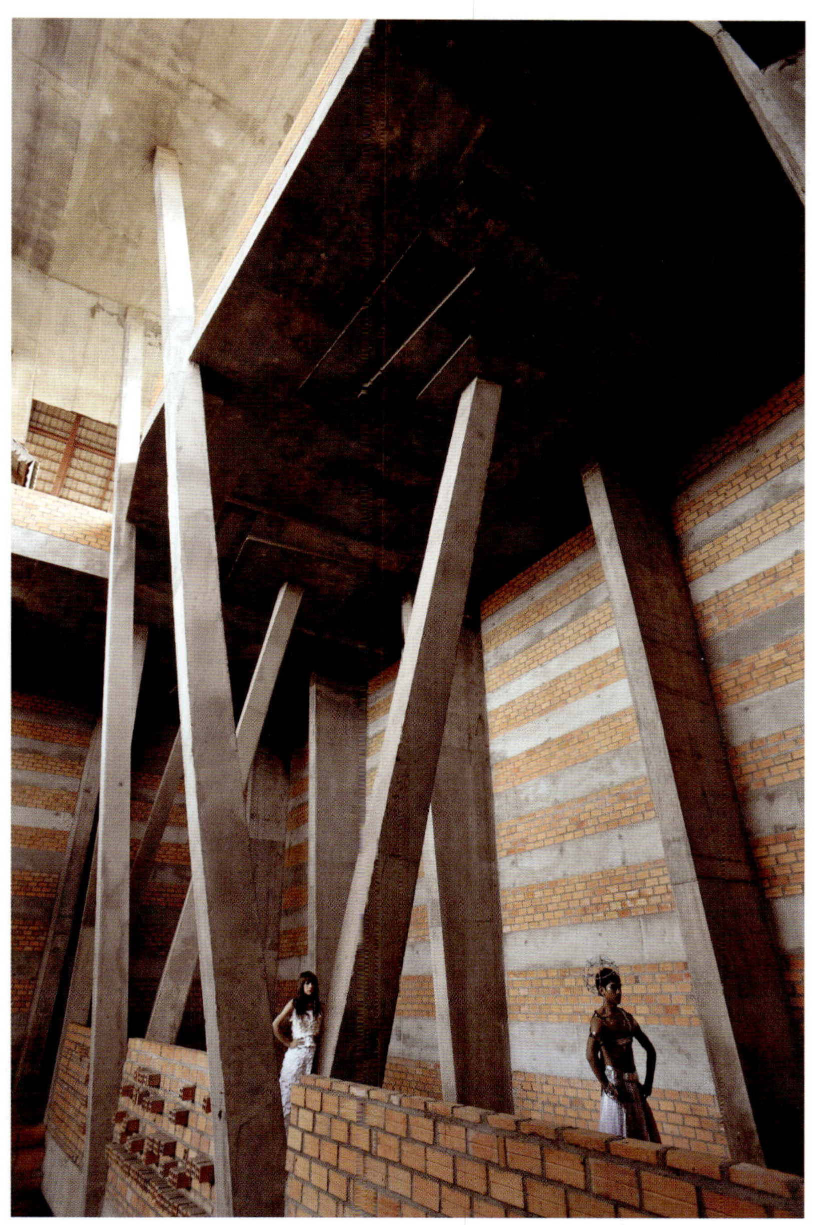

PLATE 12

Việt Lê (Vietnamese/American, b. 1976)
Untitled (Shaft), 2013, from the *Love Bang!* series

Mixed media: C-print on banner, video
5:31 TRT video
300 x 100 in. (762 x 254 cm); banner, dimensions variable
Courtesy of the artist

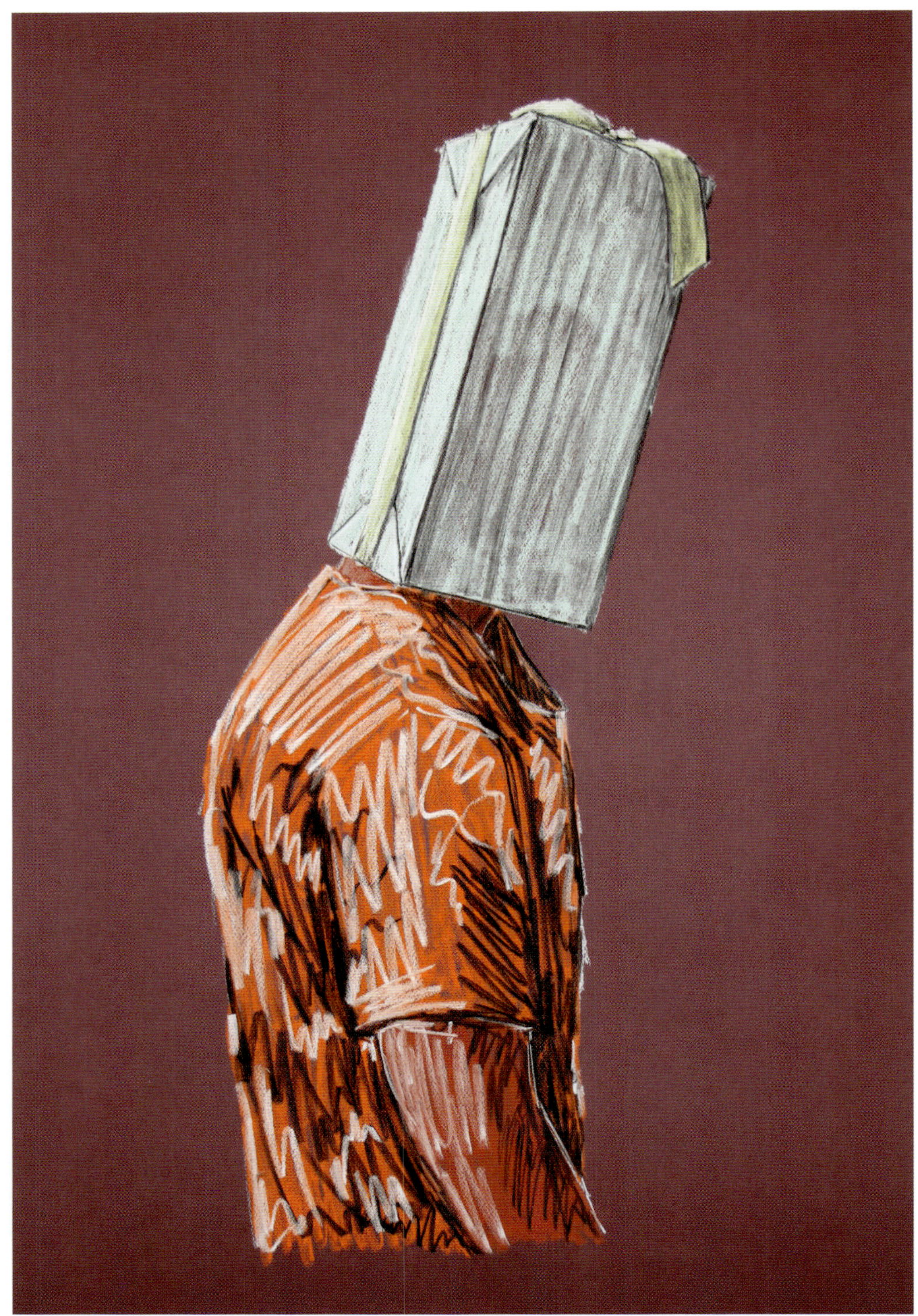

PLATE 13

Jeffrey Augustine Songco (American, b. 1983)
Guilty Party #3, 2014

Chalk pastel on paper
40 x 28 in. (100 x 70 cm)
Courtesy of the artist

PLATE 14

Jeffrey Augustine Songco (American, b. 1983)
BOMH #1, 2009

Digital inkjet print
30 x 20 in. (76 x 51 cm)
Courtesy of the artist

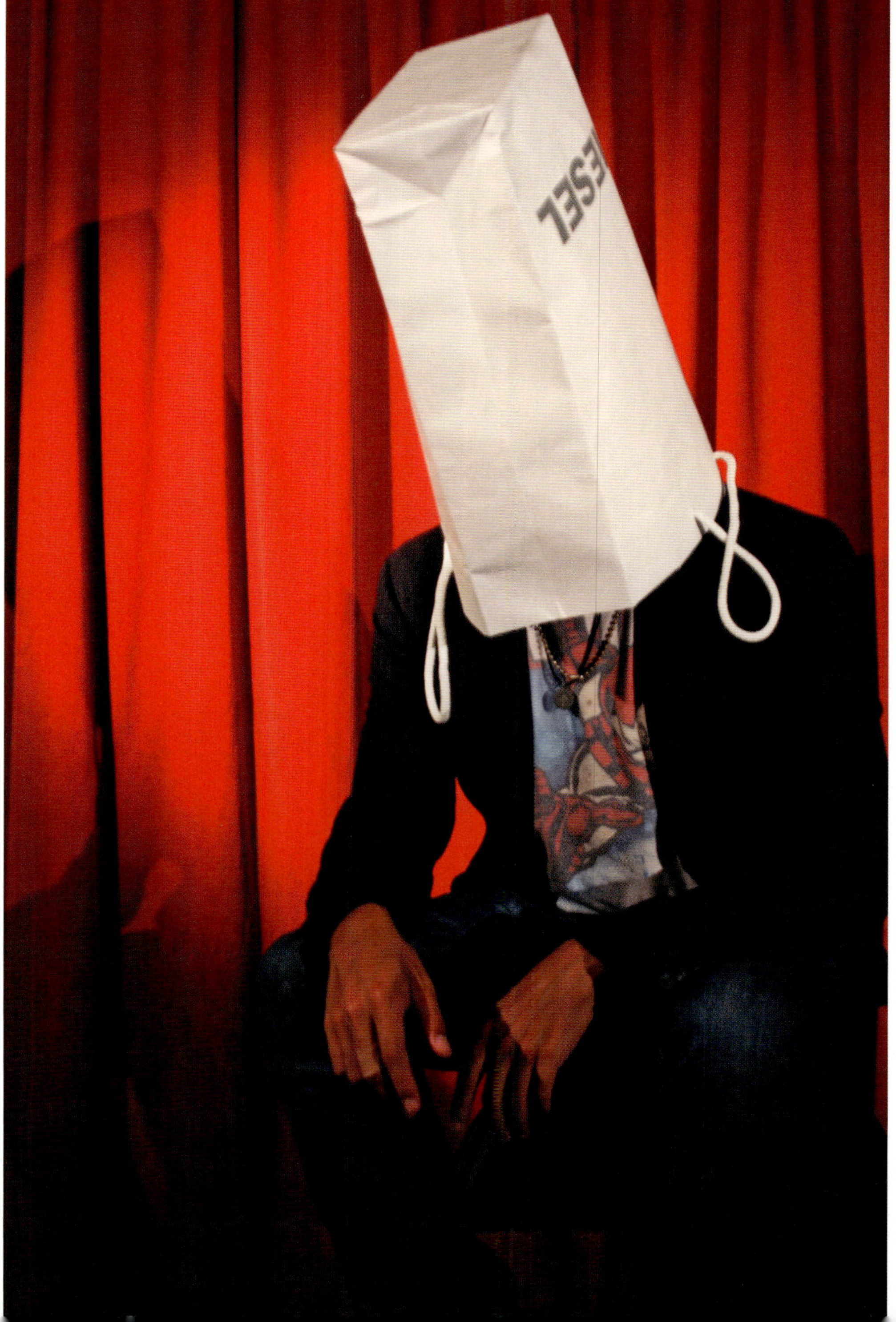

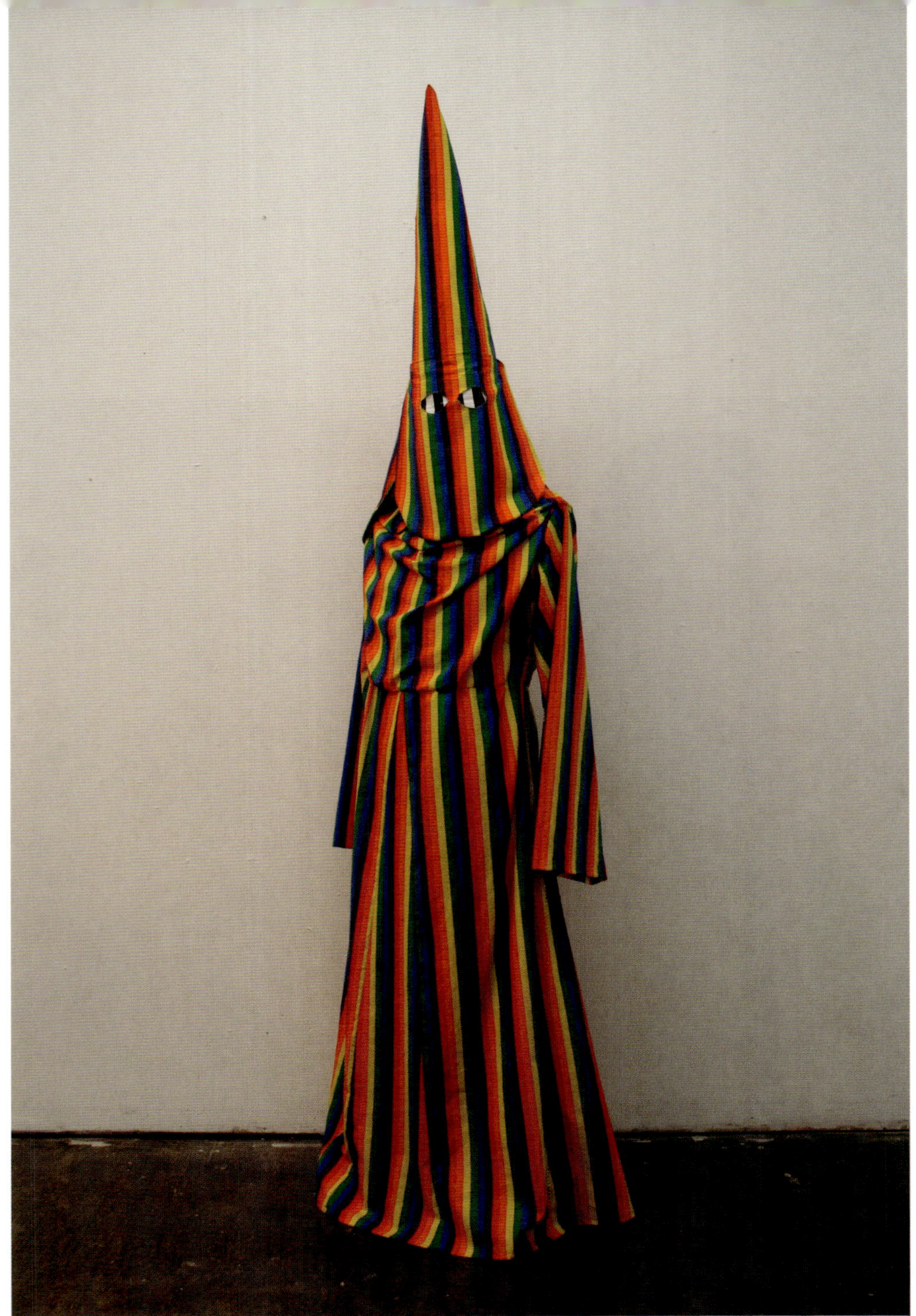

PLATE 15

Jeffrey Augustine Songco (American, b. 1983)
GayGayGay Robe, 2011

Cotton and paper on dress form
20 x 30 x 80 in. (51 x 76 x 203 cm)
Courtesy of the artist

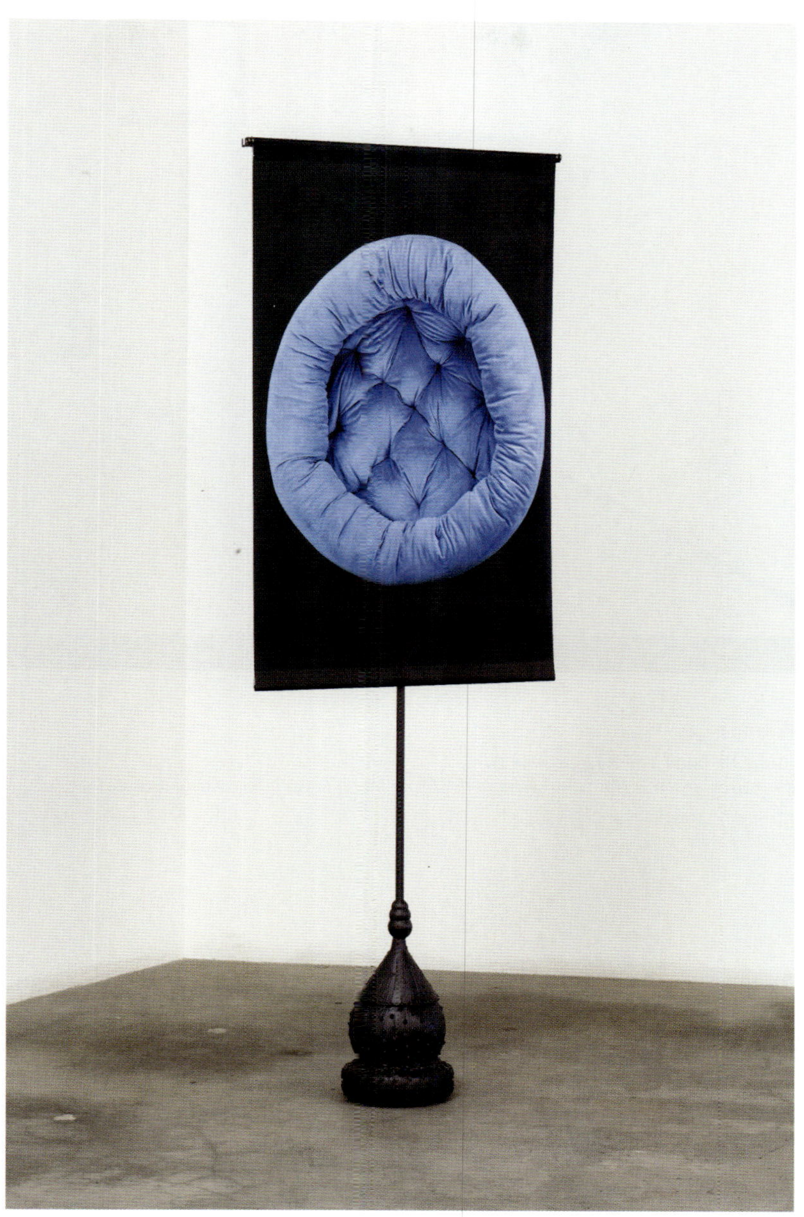

PLATE 16

Kenneth Tam (American, b. 1982)
Blue Pillow with Stand, 2013

UV ink on polyvinyl, steel, urethane, resin, paint
10 x 30 x 87 in. (24 x 76 x 221 cm)
Courtesy of the artist

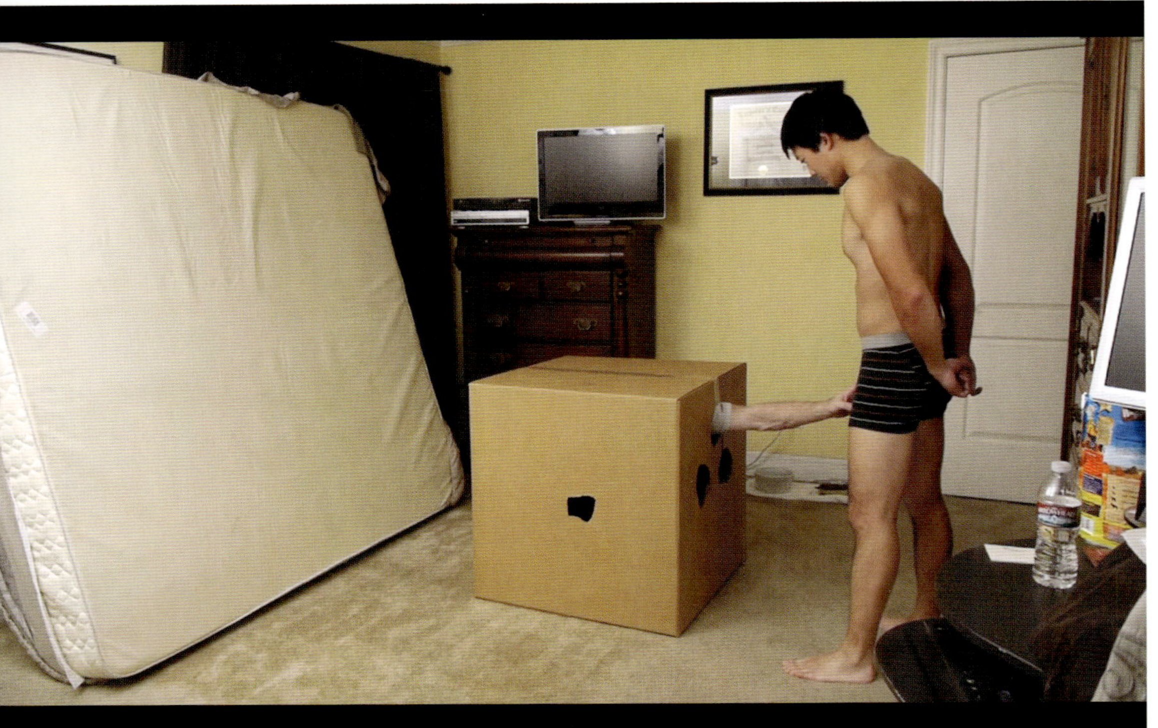

PLATE 17

Kenneth Tam (American, b. 1982)
The Compression Is Not Subservient to the Explosion; It Gives It Increased Force, 2011

HD video, 11 min. 25 sec.
Courtesy of the artist

ACROSS TOP

PLATE 18

Cy Twombly (American, b. 1928)
Ferragosto IV, 1961

Oil paint, wax crayon, and lead pencil on canvas
65¼ x 78⅞ in. (166 x 200 cm)
© Cy Twombly Foundation
Image courtesy Gagosian Gallery

ACROSS BOTTOM

PLATE 19

Cy Twombly (American, b. 1928)
Ferragosto II, 1961

Oil, oil crayon, and pencil on canvas
64¾ x 78⅞ in. (164 x 201 cm)
Hirshhorn Museum and Sculpture Garden,
Smithsonian Institution
Gift of Joseph H. Hirshhorn, 1966
Photography by Lee Stalsworth

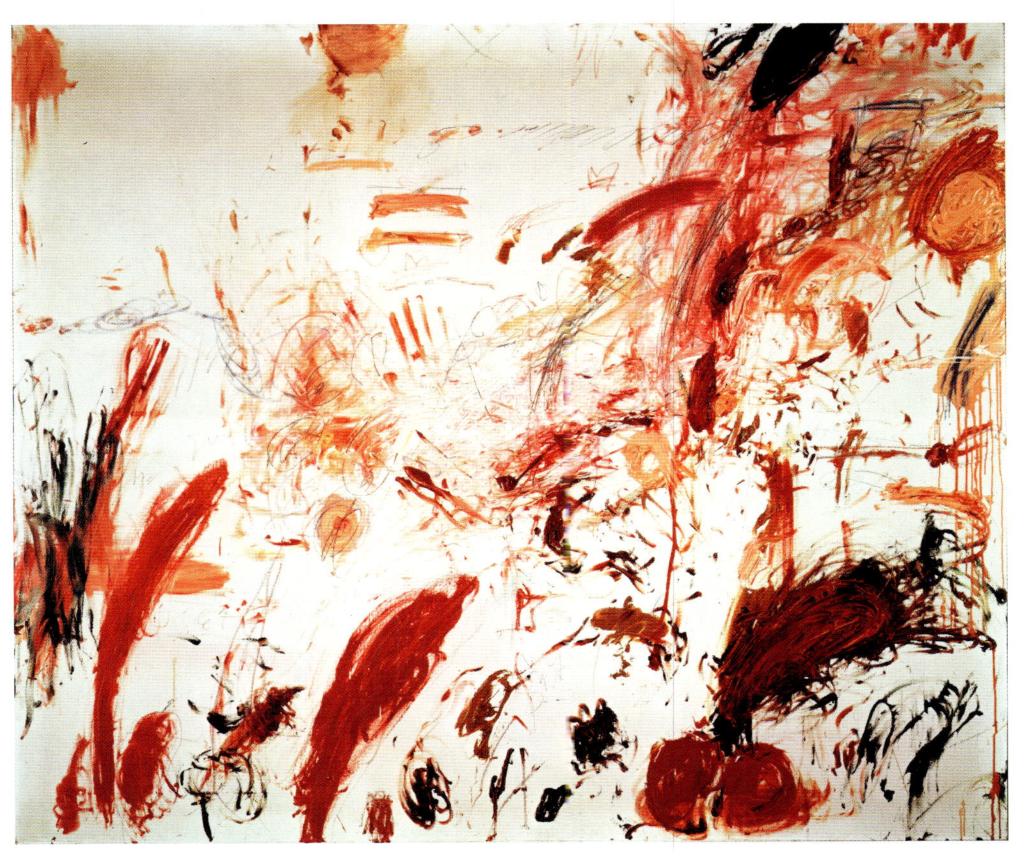

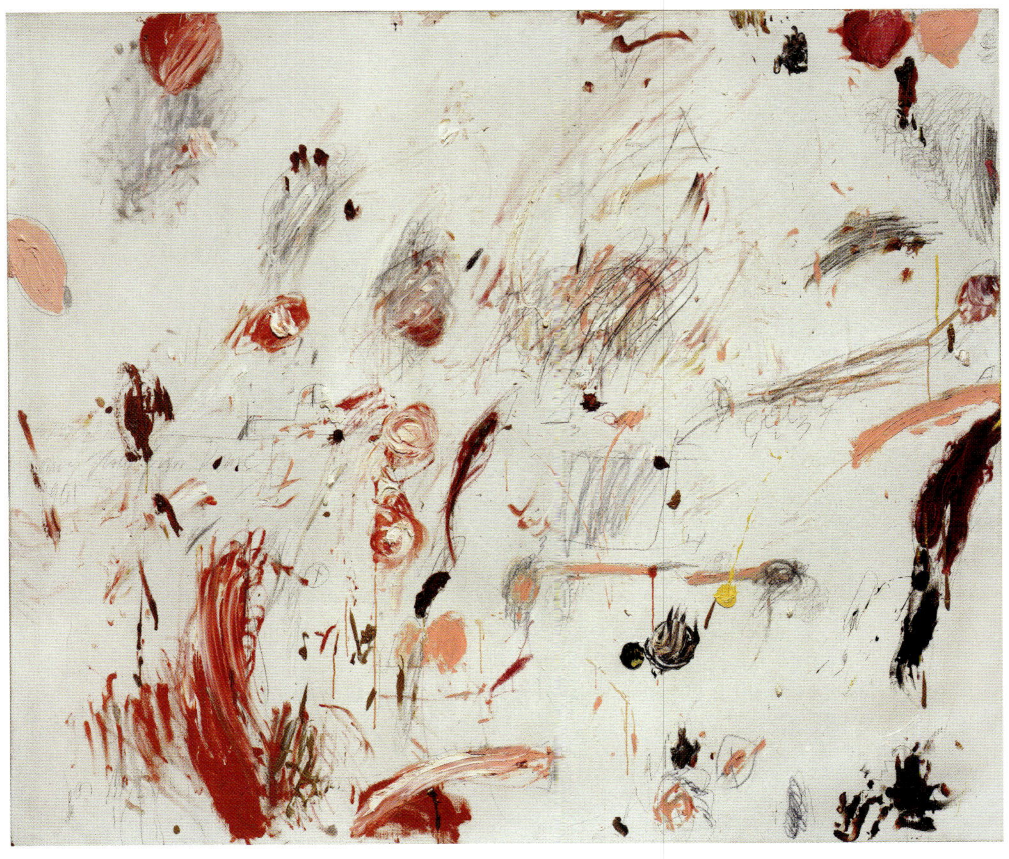

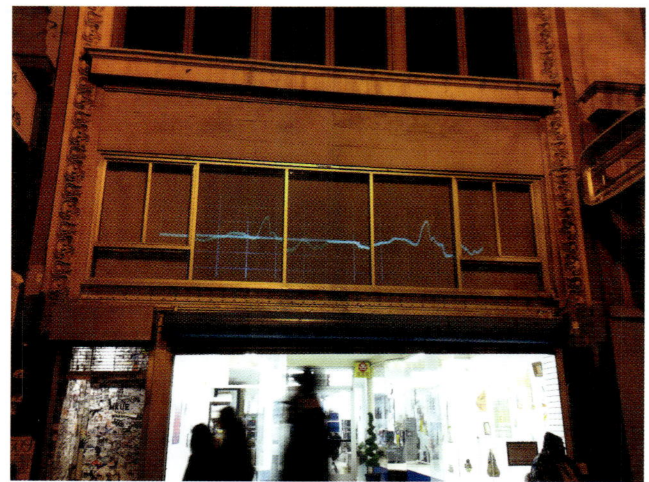

PLATE 20

Eliza Barrios (American, b. 1968)
Solace, 1995–present

Video projection, Luggage Store Gallery, San Francisco, CA
Courtesy of the artist

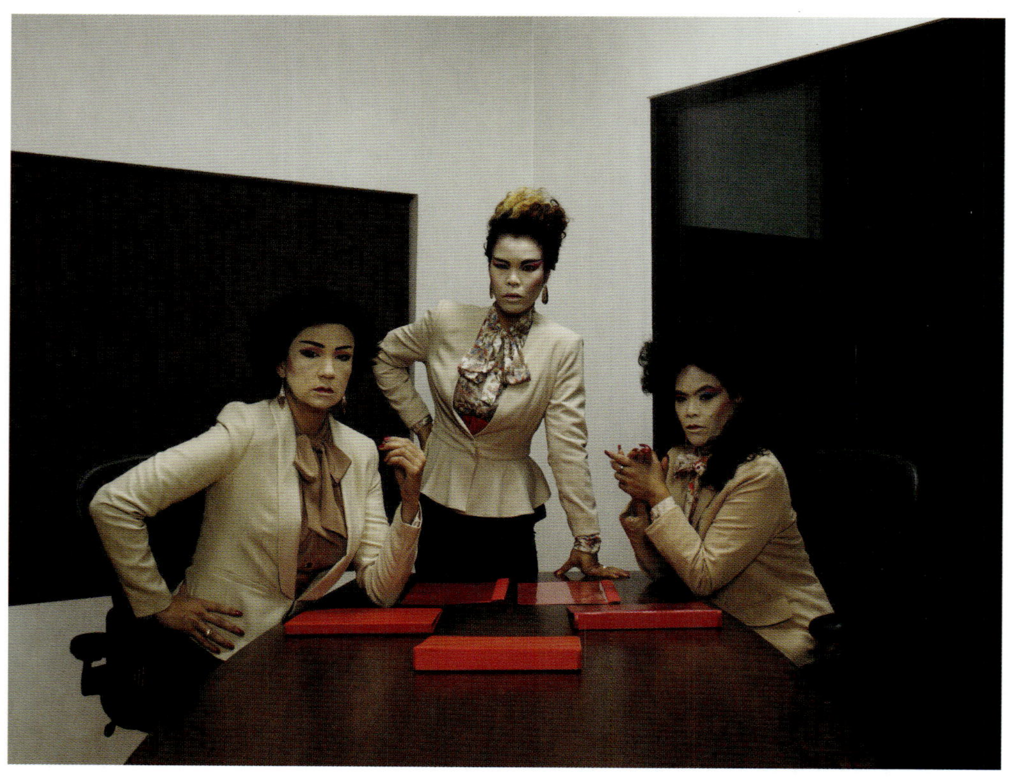

PLATE 21

Mail Order Brides/ M.O.B. (Eliza O. Barrios, Reanne A. Estrada, Jenifer K. Wofford)
Manananggoogle: Conference, 2013

Archival pigment print
32 x 43 in. (81 x 109 cm)
Courtesy of the artists

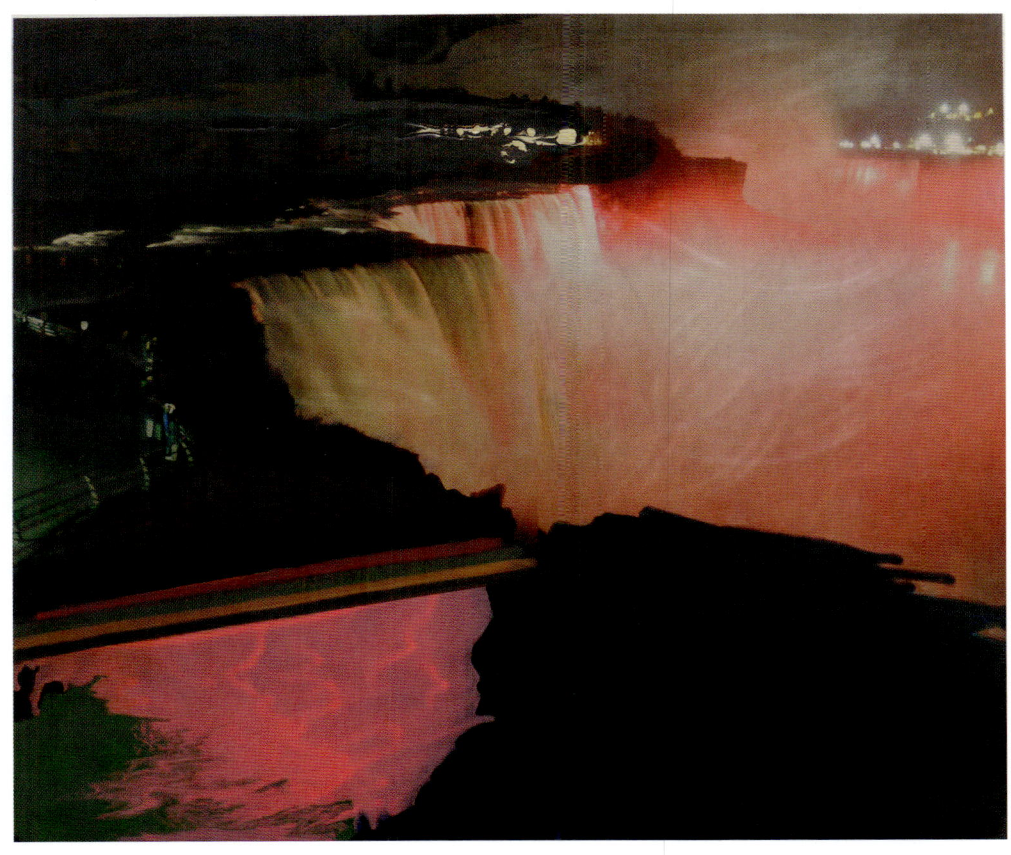

PLATE 22

Kim Anno (American, b. 1958)
Niagara, 2013

Oil on inkjet on aluminum
36 x 42 in. (91 x 107 cm)
Collection of Berkeley Art Museum
Courtesy of the Berkeley Art Museum

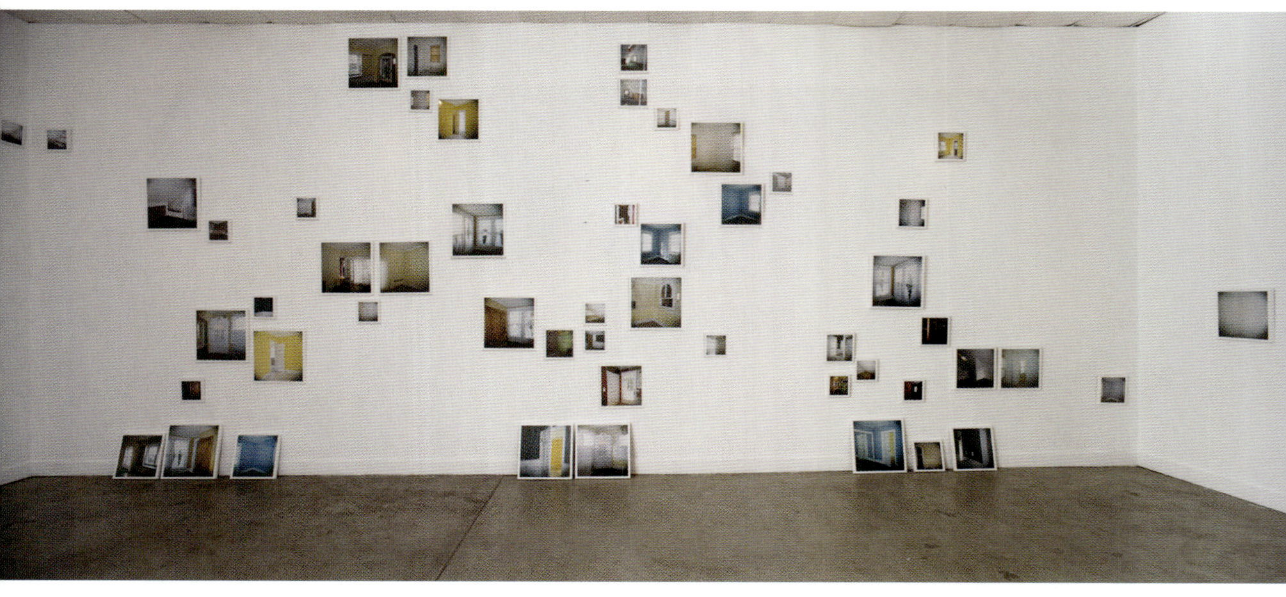

PLATE 23

Kate Wall (American, b. 1978)
When the peaks of our sky come together, my house will have a roof, 2008

Dimensions: varying by installation
Courtesy of the artist
Photo: Pablo Mason

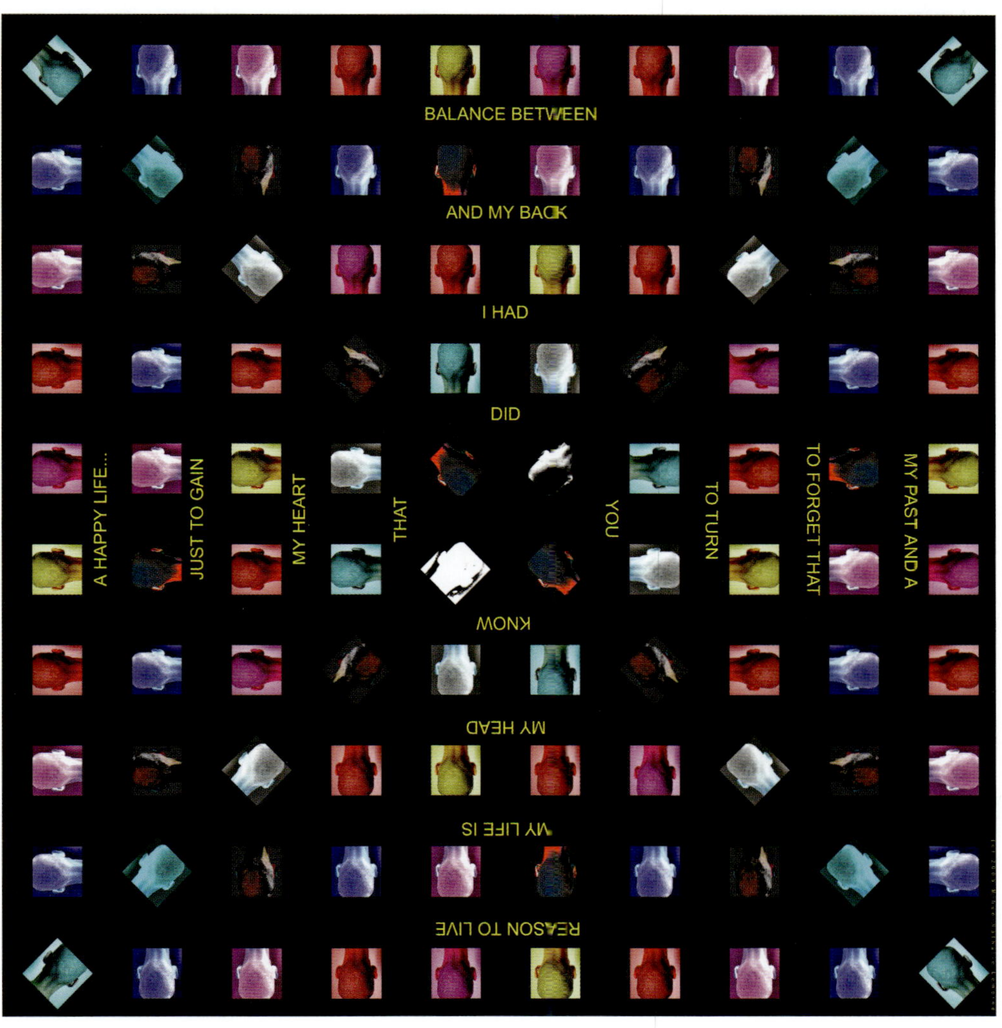

PLATE 24

Mihee-Nathalie Lemoine (Belgian, b. 1968)
100 Me (Baek Me), 2003

Digital print
Variable: 39 x 39 in. (100 x 100 cm)
© 2003 mihee-nathalie lemoine, S/Korea

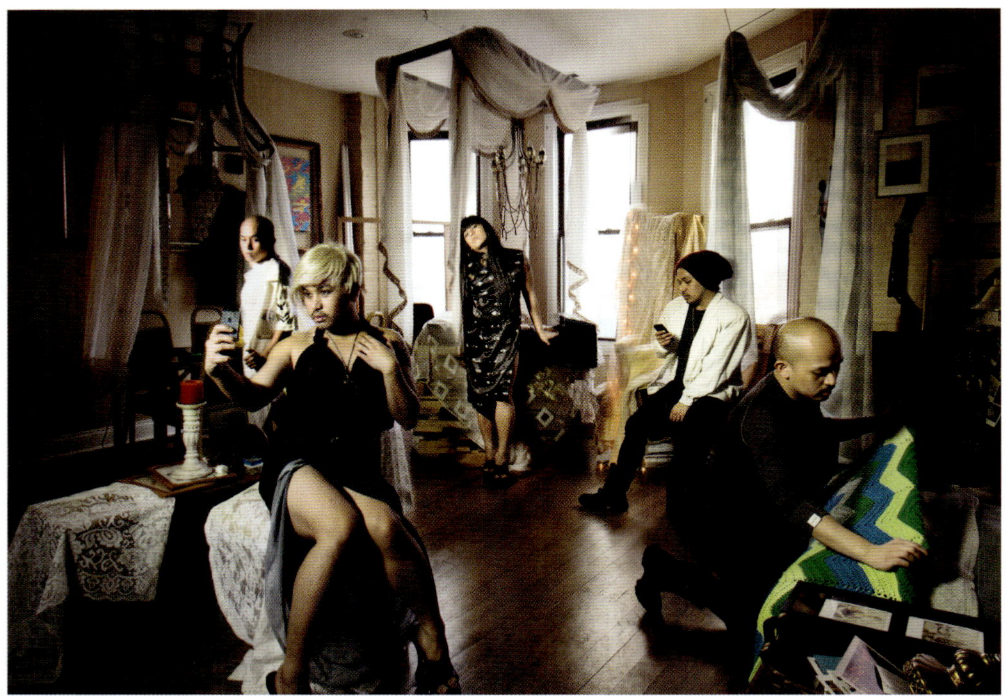

PLATE 25

Kiam Marcelo Junio (Filipino/American, b. 1984)
Model Minority Composite, 2013

Archival inkjet print
17 x 23 in. (43 x 58 cm)
Courtesy of the artist
Photo: Jacqueline Friedberg

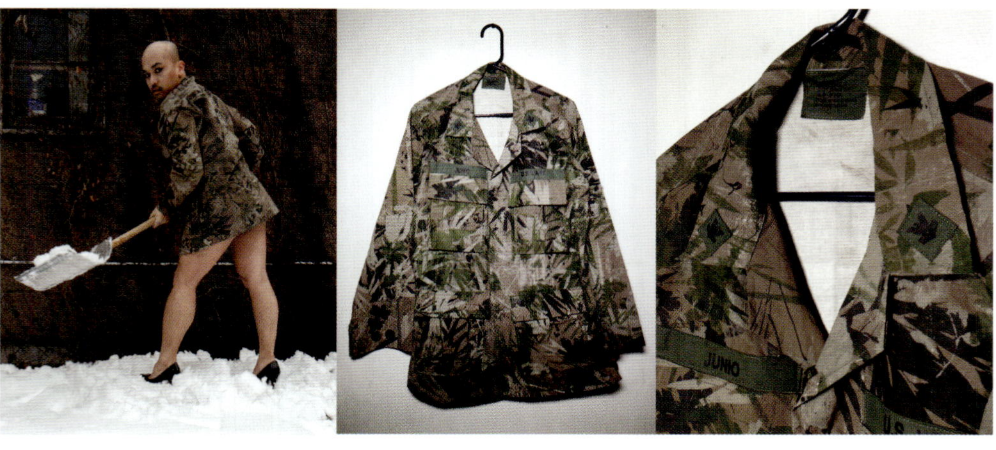

PLATE 26

Kiam Marcelo Junio (Filipino/American, b. 1984)
Camouflage as a Metaphor for Passing: Crypsis I, 2013

Replica of artist's military-issued camouflage jacket, size XS, silkscreen on cotton, poly thread,plastic buttons.
Courtesy of the artist
Photo: Jacqueline Friedberg for Anatomy/Gift/Association

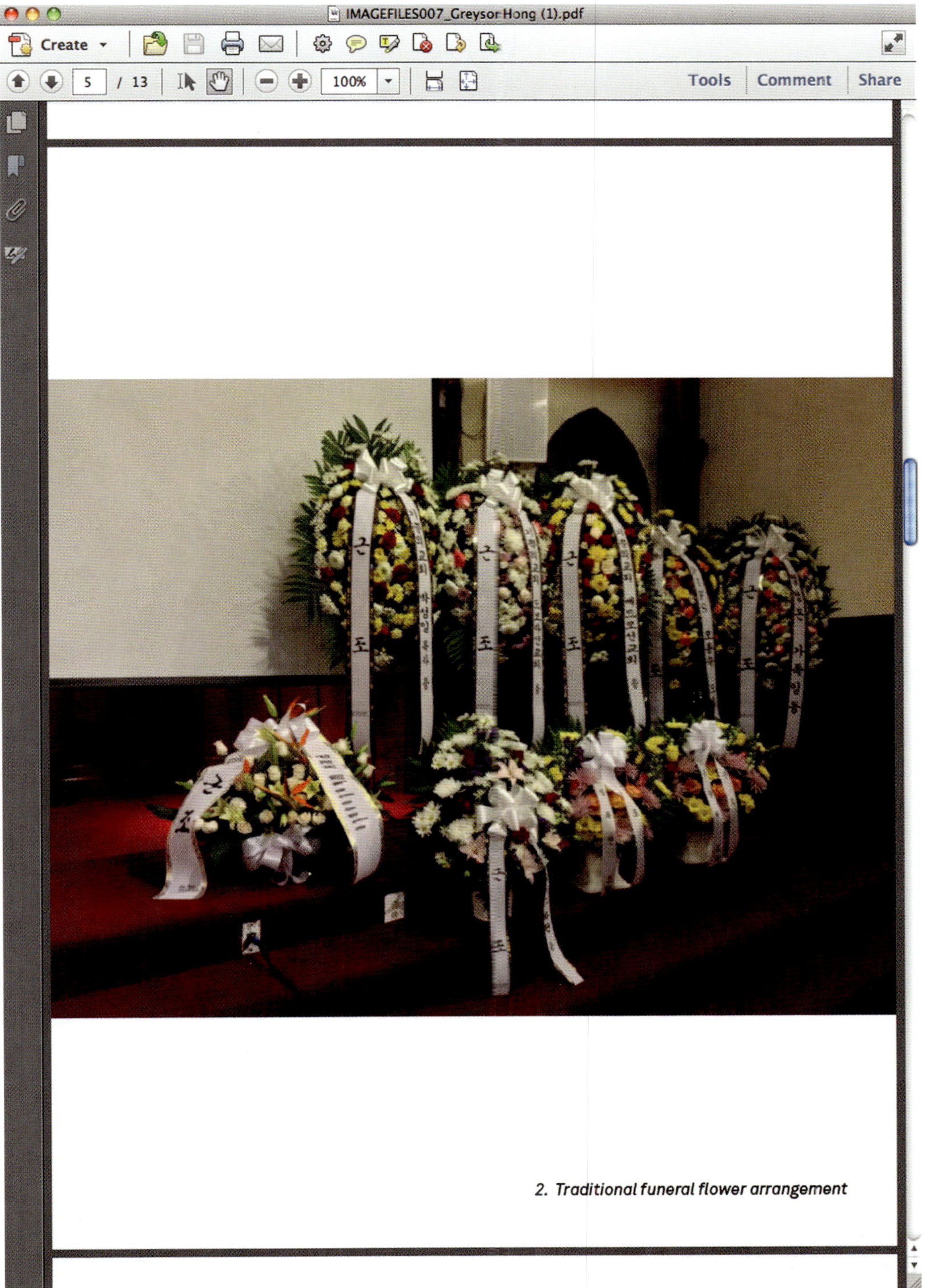

PLATE 27

Greyson C. Hong (American, b. 1982)
Funereal Archive, 2013

PDF
Detail of an 11-page, 1MB PDF document
Courtesy of the artist

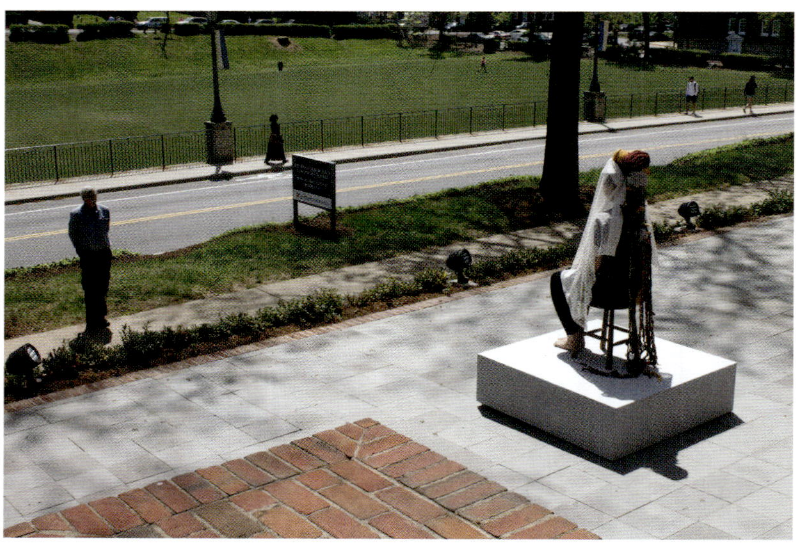

PLATE 28

Maya Mackrandilal (American, b. 1985)
Seated Woman, 2013

7.5-hour durational performance, April 23, 2013, Fralin Museum of Art at the University of Virginia
Courtesy of the artist

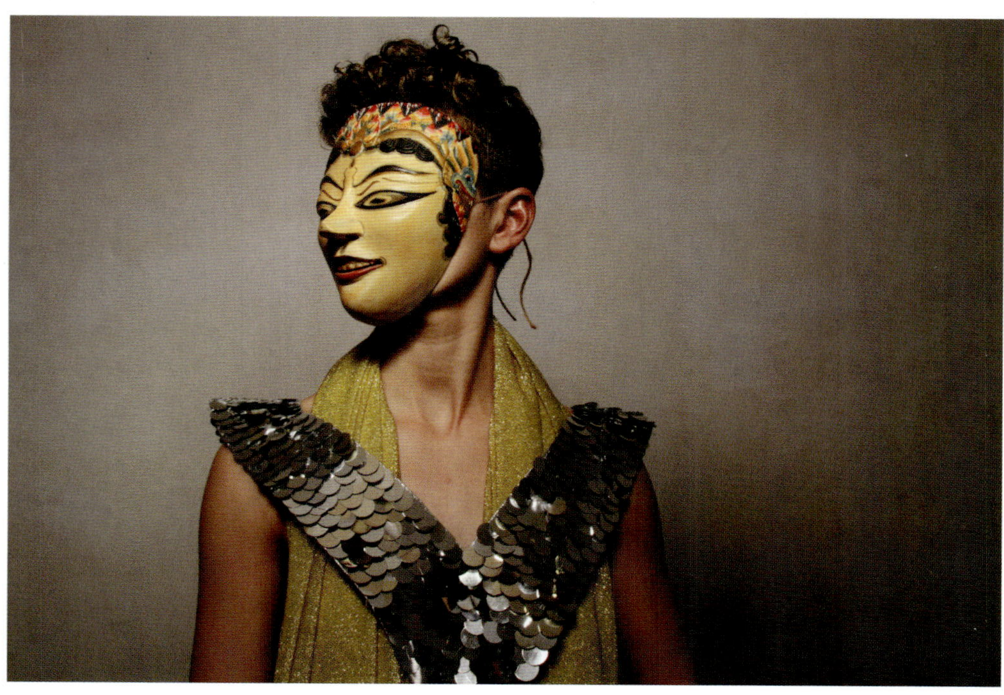

PLATE 29

Zavé Gayatri Martohardjono (Canadian/American, b. 1984)
Brother Honeyqueen's Dance of Darkness (studio costume photo), 2013

10-minute performance, April 5, 2013, Boston Center for the Arts—Mills Gallery
Courtesy of the artist
Photo: Syd London

PLATE 30

Maya Mackrandilal (American, b. 1985)
Sheath IV, 2013

Inkjet print on paper, acrylic, and acrylic paint pen (edition of ten)
31 x 26 in. (79 x 66 cm)
Courtesy of the artist

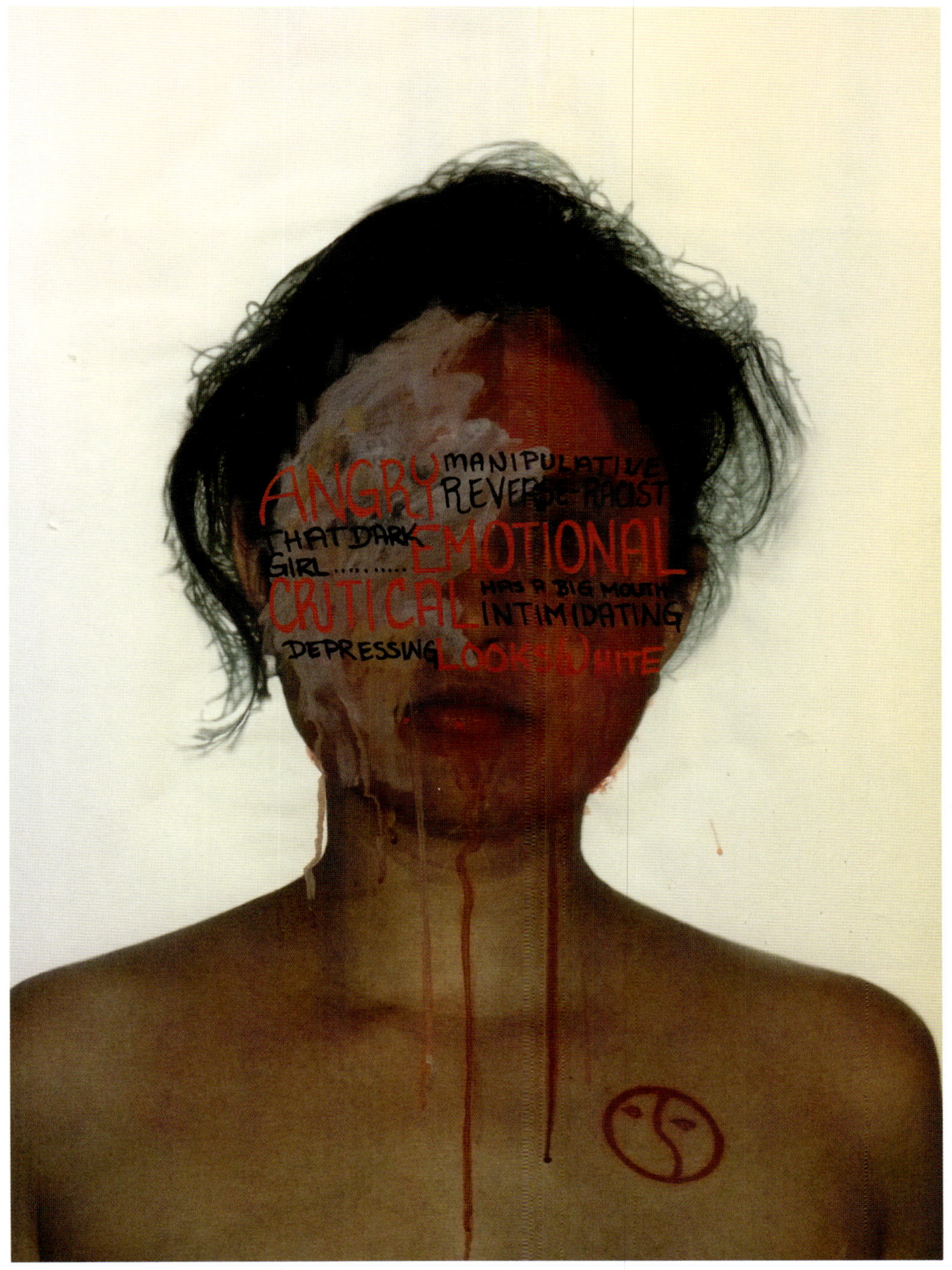

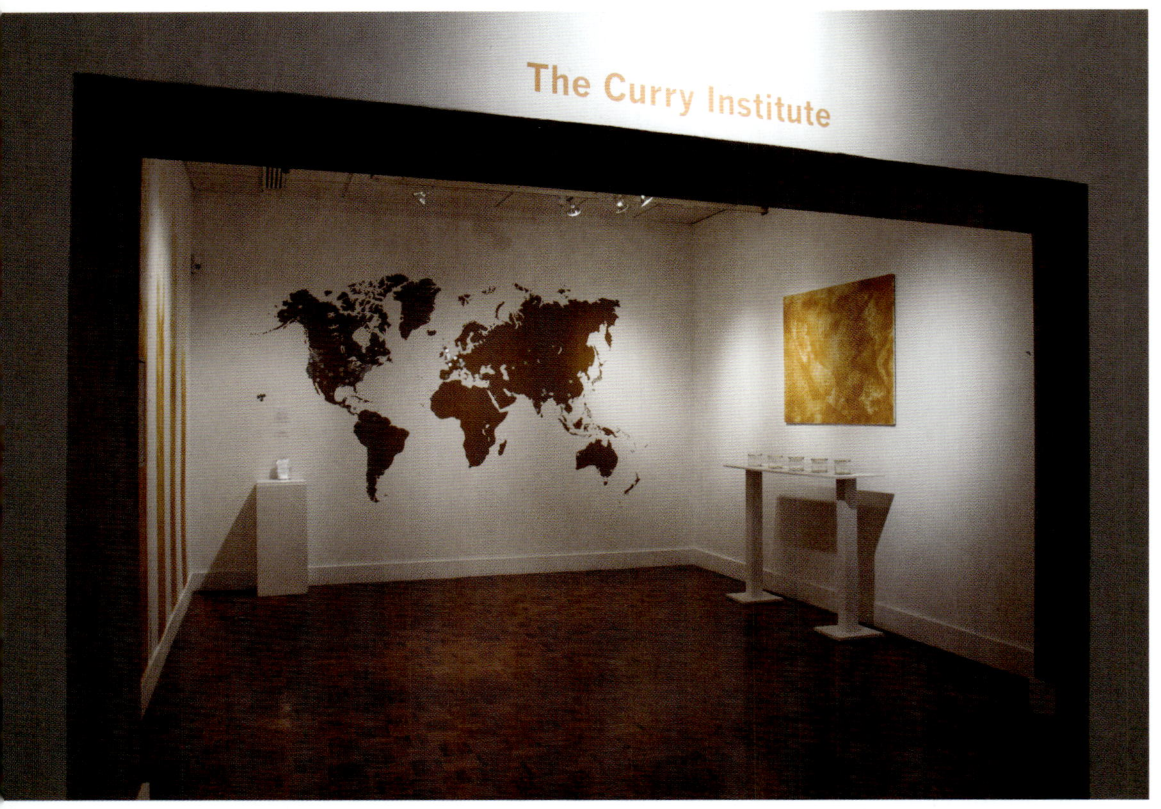

PLATE 31

Sita Kuratomi Bhaumik (American, b. 1981)
The Curry Institute, 2011

Curry powder, adhesive, scent, containers, stickers, Behr UL 160-1 Curry Powder house paint.
Site-specific installation, Sheehan Gallery, Whitman College.
Courtesy of the artist

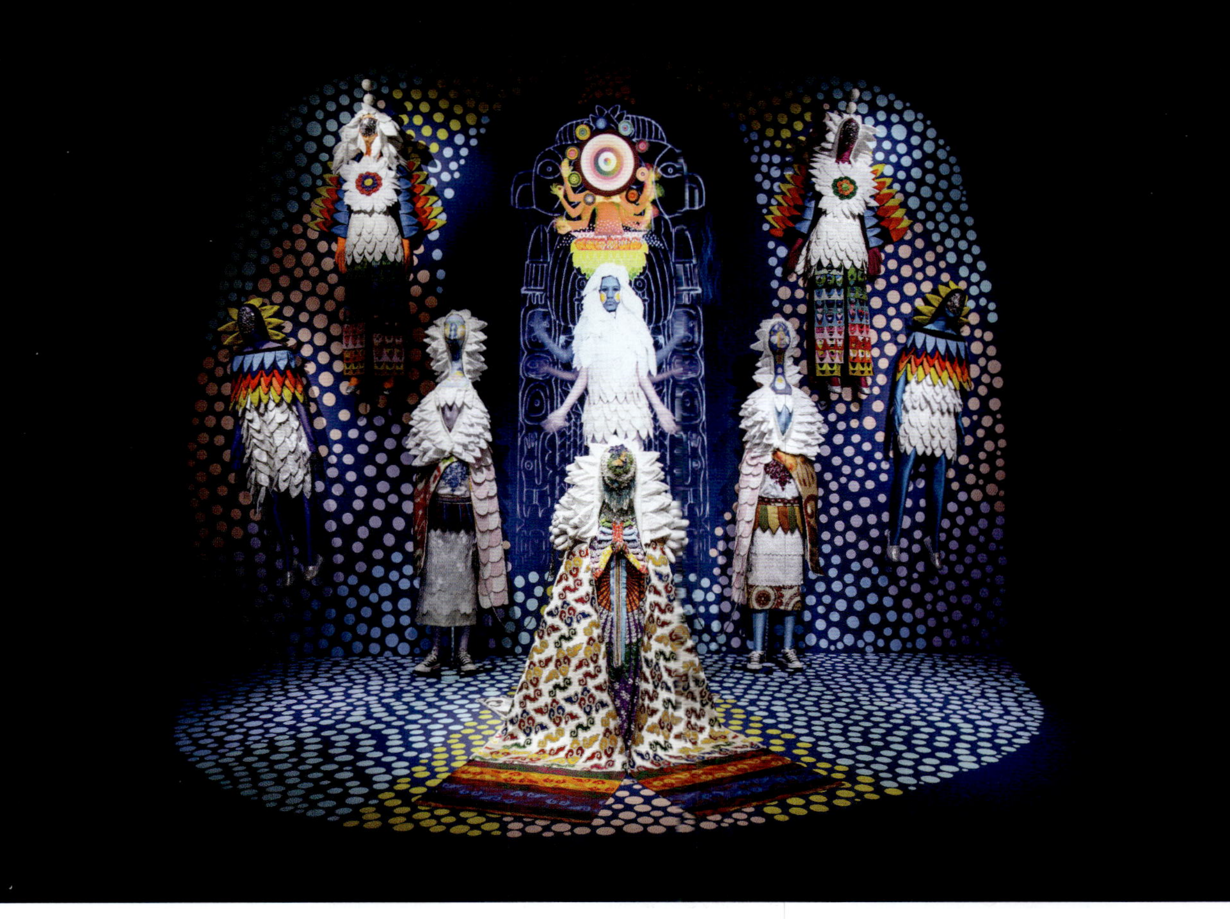

PLATE 32

Saya Woolfalk (American, b. 1979)
Chimera, 2013, from the Institute of Empathy project

Digital video and mixed media installation installed at MOCA Taipei, Taiwan
Courtesy of the artist and MOCA Taipei

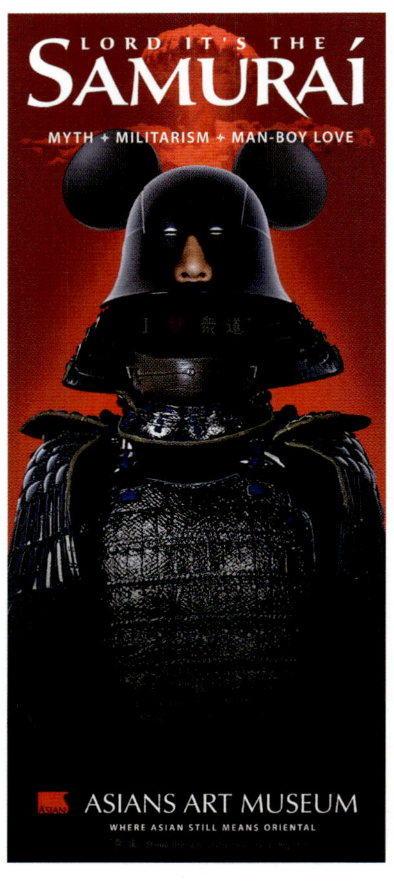

RIGHT

PLATE 33

Scott Tsuchitani (American, b. 1962)
Lord, It's the Samurai, 2009

Rack card
9 x 4 in. (23 x 10 cm)
Courtesy of the artist

BOTTOM

PLATE 34

Gaye Chan (American, b. 1957)
Share Seeds (Model: Nomad), implemented at Oahu Farmers Markets, 2012–ongoing

Repurposed wood and envelopes, seeds
10.5 x 15.5 x 6.75 in. (27 x 39 x 17 cm)
Courtesy of the artist

Photo: Eating in Public

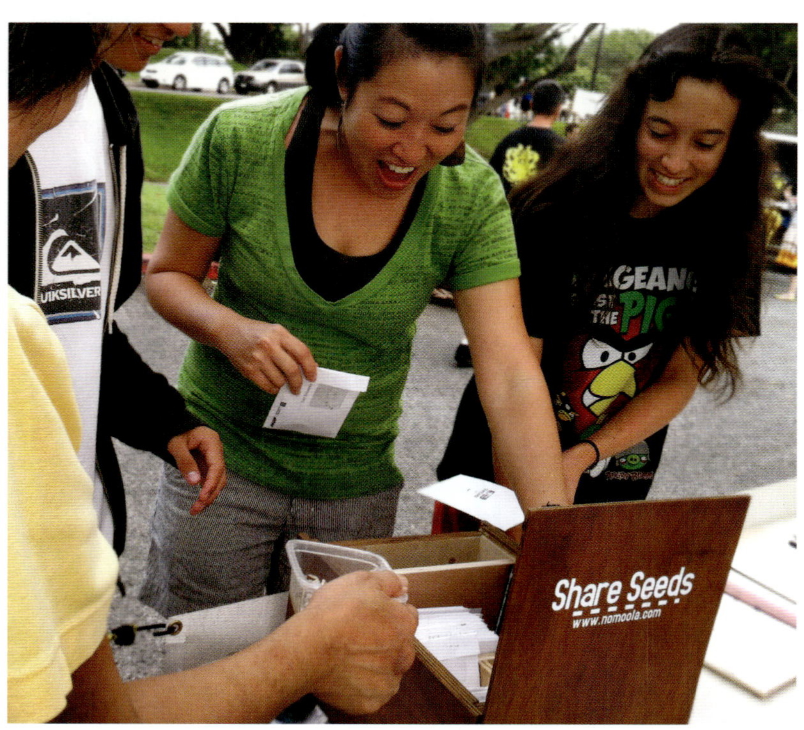

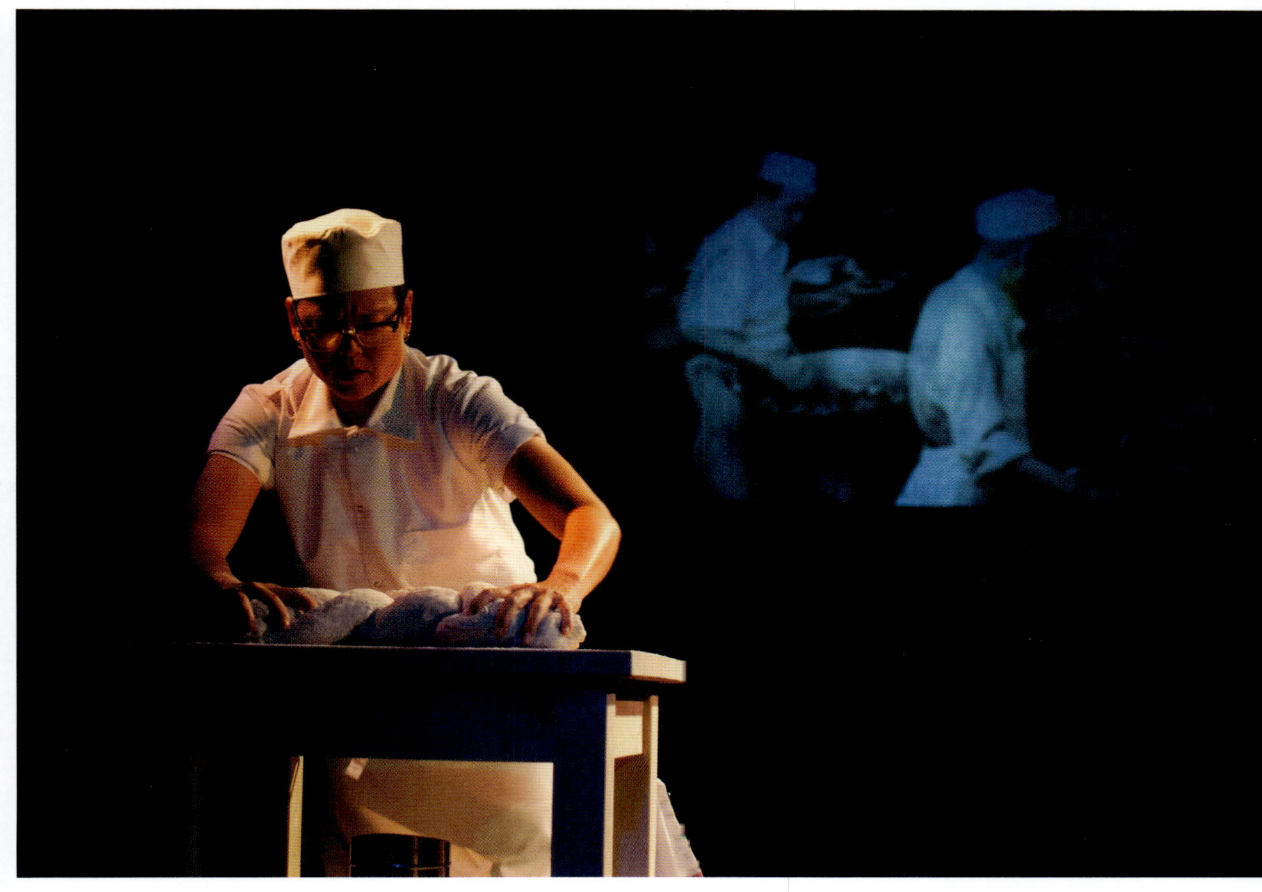

PLATE 35

Tina Takemoto (American)
Video production still from
Looking for Jiro, 2011

DVD, 5 min., 45 sec.
Courtesy of the artist
Photo: Maxwell Leung

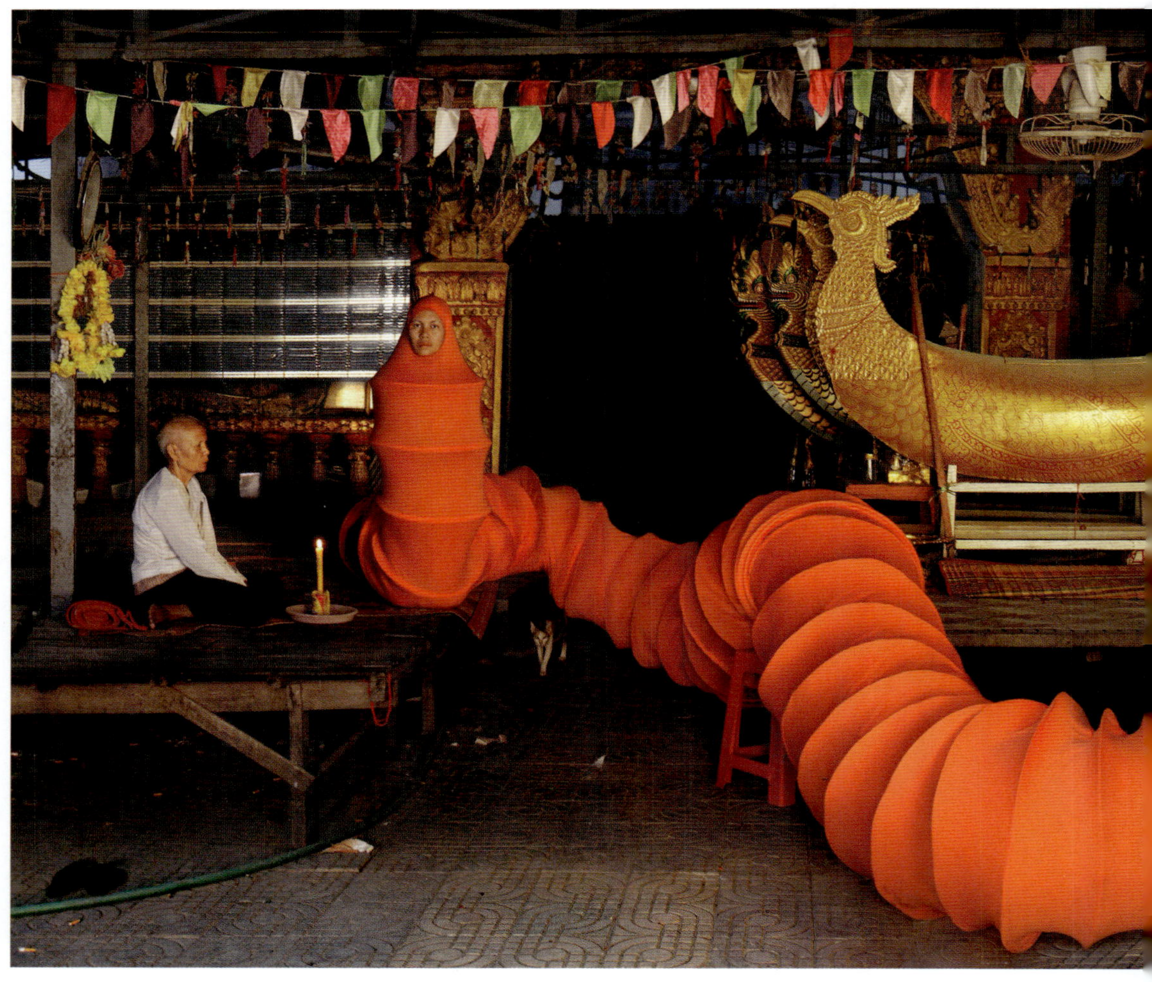

PLATE 36

Anida Yoeu Ali (Cambodian/American, b. 1974)
Off the Golden Ship, from *The Buddhist Bug Project*, 2013

Digital C-print
95 x 39 in. (242 x 100 cm)
Courtesy of Studio Revolt

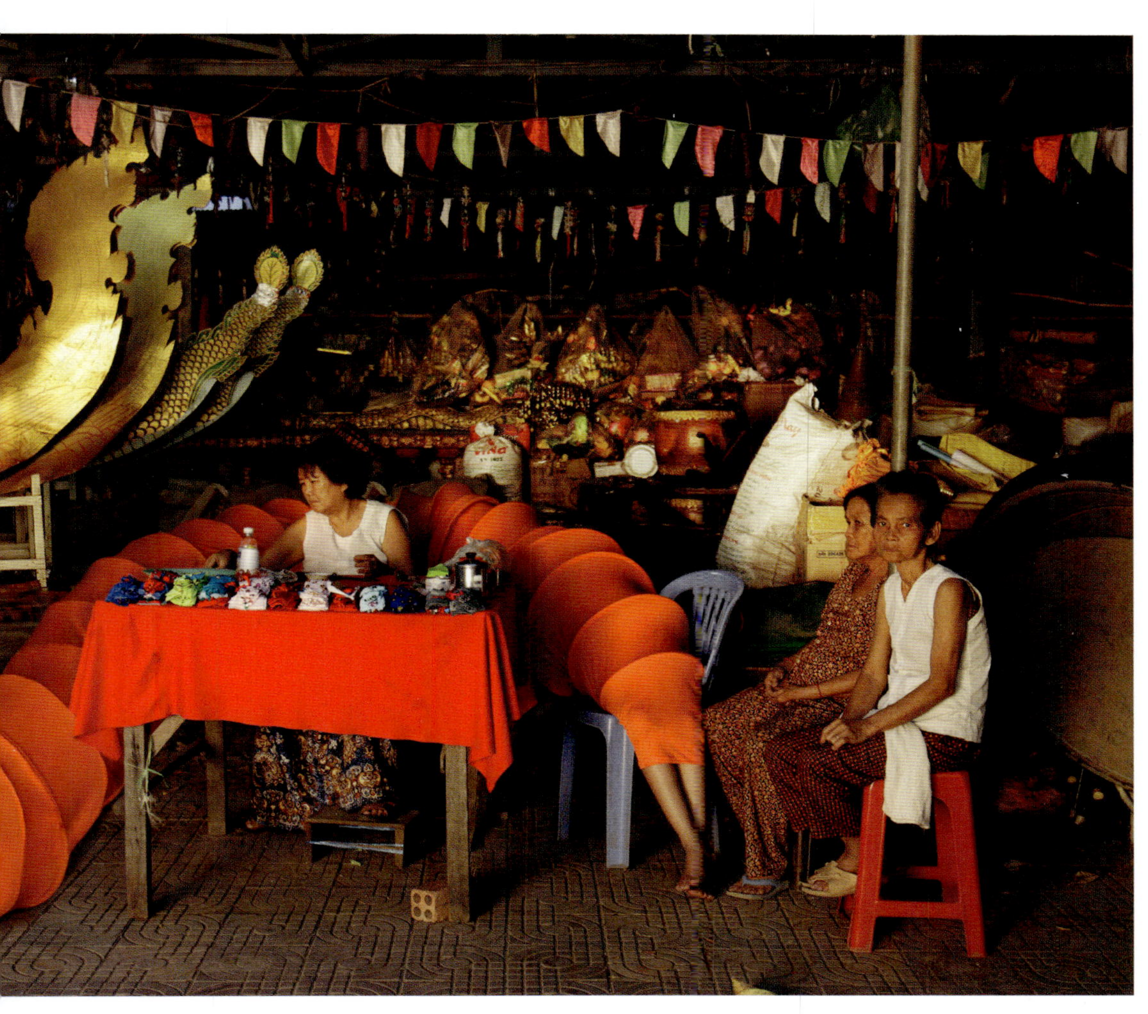

Chapter 2

Queering Time

Pacific Standard Time: Queering Temporality in Asian American Visual Cultures

MARIAM B. LAM

Among the most penetrating afterlives of US imperialism and other global empires are their reach on the regulation of our disciplinary formations, their visible institutional interventions, and their potential life spans. The effects of such hegemonic academic politics have manifested in the development of Asian American visual arts practices and criticism as a whole, as they have in Southeast Asian American visual arts in particular. Perhaps more saliently than some other Asian American ethnic populations in recent historiography, Southeast Asian American visuality is inextricably and temporally linked to diaspora, transnationalism, and Asian regionalist colonial legacies, as well as to Western imperialisms. As a result, common themes in art production and scholarship regularly include trauma and war, migration and refugee passages, history and memory. These foci are at once generative and polemical.

Southeast Asian American artists themselves roam more widely and wildly across the Pacific and the West, with multivalent considerations of their own northern spaces and the Global South and with the discrepant historical narratives told of them. David Eng has argued that the liminal position of Asian Americans more generally vis-à-vis the US nation-state renders them "queer as such."[1] By focusing on constructions of both racialized and queered gender and sexuality, on transnational identifications and on sociocultural marginalization, this essay examines the ever-evolving functions of Asian American visual arts—liminal yet ubiquitous—in articulating queer connections across historical temporalities and geopolitical spatialities.

At the same time, for many art critics as well as many of the artists, a queering of the putative field of Southeast Asian American arts is perhaps at once premature and long overdue. This querying may be premature, because "the field" has only just begun constructing itself as such in recent decades, as global multicultural neoliberalism has turned its gaze toward Southeast Asia as a region of growing importance (once again) and toward its large, increasingly networked diasporic populations across the world. On the other hand, this may be precisely the already past imperfect moment at which the field needs to confront any potential self-orientalizing discursive practices. Contemporary visual artists are using aesthetic forms that betray or deviate from normative conceptions of time, queering them by racializing, transgendering, and sexualizing time and historiography intersectionally. Such new considerations can compel arts criticism to move Asian American studies as a whole toward alternative terrains, temporalities, and analytics. This mobility likewise will help to evolve Southeast Asian American studies by formulating varied critical apparatuses of Asian American racialized, queer temporality and spatiality that modify Southeast Asian American studies orthodoxies, including familiar tropes of trauma, memory, and the refugee.

Here I address how contemporary visual art challenges what Laura Kina and Jan Christian Bernabe have called "normative Asian American temporality," or a kind of Pacific Standard Time. I deploy the video installation and mixed media work (2005–2010) of collaborative artists Lin + Lam, experimental filmmaking by Nguyen Tan Hoang, and the work of artists Eliza O. Barrios and Việt Lê to reveal nuances of media arts activism that magnify 1) the polemical perpetuation of traditional art historical genres as they are embedded in attempts at new field formation, 2) the complex pedagogical and scholarly (il)legibility of such a transnational body of work for consumers and connoisseurs, and 3) the newer exhibitional geopolitical mappings across which Asian American studies will need to travel to appropriately conceptualize and build a field like Southeast Asian American visual arts.

QUEER TEMPORALITY AND BEYOND

To begin, it may be useful to articulate my particular usage of queer temporalities as complement and supplement to existing theories.

At the 2015 annual international conference of the Association for Asian American Studies section-sponsored roundtable "Southeast Asian American Studies Today: Methodologies, Race and Space," cofacilitators Emily Hue and Pahole Sookkasikon expressed anxieties about the pressure to "do" ethnography, to "do" trauma, and to "do" critical refugee studies. Sookkasikon, in particular, had researched the historical scholarship on refugee studies with the working assumption that he needed to fit, however uncomfortably, his own scholarship on Thai diasporic and transnational cultural history into these rubrics in order to be legible within the field of Southeast Asian American studies and thereby legible within Asian American studies more generally. While it was somewhat unusual self-policing, given that Thailand is the only

Southeast Asian nation never formally colonized by a Western imperial power and that Thais in the United States did not follow the same post–Vietnam War refugee migration waves that Vietnamese, Cambodians, Laos, and Hmongs traversed, it was clear to everyone in the room that this academic pressure did exist to some extent, experientially.

This vague but present pressure stems in part from the history of Asian American studies field formation, with its initial sociological and historical bent and its later acceptance of and appreciation for humanistic and aesthetic discourses, often accompanied by a reactionary distrust of theoretical scholarship as somehow less politicized. This Asian American temporality, this version of its historiography, is insufficient for welcoming the next generation of scholars and artists practicing today and needs to be both queried and queered.[2]

For this project, I insist on an institutional *willfulness* and a transformative phenomenological practice of queer temporality for Asian American studies. In accordance with Sara Ahmed's formulations of the former, "the very labor of transforming institutions, or at least aiming for transformation, is how we learn about institutions *as* formations. We can thus think of diversity work as a 'phenomenological practice,'" following Edmund Husserl, and be the "willful subjects" that recognize the need for a theorization without abstraction that can and does indeed benefit the field of Asian American studies as a whole.[3]

What follows is an elaboration of this methodological practice in theoretical terms and concrete visual arts critique. In their preface to *Q & A: Queer in Asia America*, David Eng and Alice Hom describe the cover photograph by I. H. Kuniyuki as one that "neither prescribes nor mandates how we should see and interpret the convergence of sexuality and race for Asian Americans," with "enigmatic figures" that "emerge and fade—together yet apart . . . at once but not altogether in the same ways, in identical patterns, or in similar directions," providing "ample room to question to wonder, to admire."[4] Similarly, Judith Halberstam contends that "part of what has made queerness compelling as a form of self-description in the past decade or so has to do with the way it has the potential to open up new life narratives and alternative relations to time and space." Further, "queer subcultures produce alternative temporalities by allowing their participants to believe that their futures can be imagined according to logics that lie outside of those paradigmatic markers of life experience—namely, birth, marriage, reproduction, and death."[5] To this list of the generalized empirical everyday, I would add common collective markers for Southeast Asian Americans, such as migration, war, refuge or asylum, trauma and community.

I combine Ahmed's insistence with Halberstam's reminder that "to define queerness as a temporality—'a moment,' 'it is also then a force; or rather it is a crossing of temporality with force' . . . ; [Eve Sedgwick and others] summarize these currents in terms of a 'moment,' a 'persistent present,' or 'a queer temporality that is at once indefinite and virtual but also forceful, resilient, and undeniable.'"[6] Asian Americanist arts critique must sift and push through thick rhetorical layers and "imperial debris" about war, trauma, refugees, and migration to move aesthetic and cultural politics beyond that which is already familiar and licensed within the scholarly field.[7]

Much like Kuniyuki's enigmatic figures and similarly for Elizabeth Freeman, "queer time elongates and twists chronology," "appears haunted" with a "yearning queer archivalism"; in Freeman's words, "Even non-nationalist cultural belonging is a matter of affects that inhere, in many ways, in shared timings, and I stake my claim for a counterpolitics of encounter in which bodies, de-composed by the workings of experimental film and literature [and art], meet one another by chance, forging—in the sense of both making and counterfeiting—history differently."[8] I have written elsewhere about the crucial function of traumatized archives and strategic affects in the precariat reckoning of Vietnamese and diasporic cultural production, so Freeman's references to archives and affects are particularly salient within this context.[9]

It is precisely within these concurrently competing nationalist and transnational/diasporic contexts that these Southeast Asian American and "other works confront, on an affective register irreducible to traditional historical inquiry, what has been forgotten, abandoned, discredited, or otherwise effaced," "touches that are both painful and pleasurable break open the past, slicing it into asynchronous, discontinuous pieces of time."[10] Together, intended or not, they synergistically, competitively, and provocatively create a racially globalized and domestic queer temporal counterpolitics and alternative counterpublics.

Even Halberstam's and Freeman's incisive and productive conceptualizations of queer time's potentialities leave room for more enunciative formulations of race, ethnicity, transnation, and "disidentification."[11] Because Asian Americans and Southeast Asians in particular (along with other racialized minorities) have been "forgotten, abandoned, discredited, or otherwise effaced" by both history and disciplinary formations, their criticism cannot unfold at an abstract or "purely aesthetic" level; such abstraction has perpetuated their absence or invisibility in the US black/white racial binary and in arts criticism.[12] Such abstraction has also left the work, the labor, of critique and drawing visibility to these minoritized artists in the hands of minoritized art critics. Bliss Lim conceptualizes "a form of temporal translation that renders supernatural agency in secular terms while also exposing an untranslatable remainder, thereby undermining the fantasy of a singular national time and emphasizing shifting temporalities of transnational reception."[13] If queer temporality is tuned to frequencies that register and confront racial, ethnic, and transnational markers and discursivity, it has the potential to temporally/historiographically/sociologically/aesthetically translate the "untranslatable remainder" left behind by more "mainstream" arts critique, such as that of Southeast Asian American visual arts and cultures.

LEGIBILITY, GLOBALITY, AND THEMATIC GENRE

To briefly address the pedagogical history of this academic remainder relative to mainstream arts criticism, I refer to the historical analysis of Asian American arts curatorial history in the United States juxtaposed against the minimal attempts at Asian American arts education within and against such a history.[14] In order to rehistoricize and transnationalize or geopoliticize such a pedagogical history, I analyze the works of Lin + Lam and Nguyen Tan Hoang through a racialized and globalized lens of queer temporality.

For pioneer Asian American artist and arts critic Margo Machida discussing Asian American collectivist artists of the 1990s, it is crucial to invest in an "integrative view of the artist as a social actor, whose role was not simply to produce work but also to act as a theorist, educator, and organizer," to use Machida's approach of "oral hermeneutics" in order to recognize that the "passion of these calls for collective expression and empowerment, as well as for resistance and social justice, likewise inflects [Machida's] view of art as an epistemic asset for minoritized groups as they seek to more fully apprehend the conditions and the experiences they may share, and hence to envisage new cultural paradigms and forms of affiliation."[15] Here, however, to complement and queer the chronological history laid out by Chang, Johnson, Karlstrom, and Spain with Machida's auteur-driven approach, I shift the focus from the artists' own articulations or self-narrativizations of their work and the widely varying degrees of oral hermeneutical prowess of contemporary Asian Pacific American artists to the function of academic audience reception and critical scholarship of such artists and art practices to do the work or queering of such art historiography, so that it does not rest in the hands of minoritized ethnic artists and academics alone.

Machida captures one of the biggest problems facing this remainder when she writes, "Embracing relativism, indeterminacy, and a performative construction of the self, identity, and culture, many artists and critics today instead invoke postidentitarian rhetorics to signal a perceived rupture with any form of politics based on strong assertions of otherness."[16] The Asian American artists who choose this path often do so to (non)racially "pass" as the legible and the legitimate in an imagined "postracial" modern arts industry. Some resist doing the labor of what is deemed to *need* translation by domestic cultural others out of frustration and resistance, while others are not versed enough in that historical remainder to attempt such cultural translation.

But if we follow Denise Ferreira da Silva's analysis of the racial as the guiding critical framework for the entire field of modern representation, then racial knowledge and the power of racism and racialization produce all modern global spaces.[17] Global arts and American visual arts cultures and communities are equally saturated and compelled by racial politics, even while they may deem aesthetics colorblind and postmodern to a large extent. The racial *is* the queer temporal signifier of globality, and global arts criticism requires an analytics of raciality and historicity.

Even within the field of Asian American studies, South Asian, Southeast Asian, Pacific Islander, and increasingly today Middle Eastern scholarship has lagged in academic development after East Asian American history, sociology, immigration and labor studies, and certainly visual arts field formations. One could argue this is simply a product of immigration history rather than global racialization within the field, but one need only look at early immigration Filipina/o American history to see the subsequent struggles with inclusion/exclusion within the putative field of "Asian American studies," a field formation that carries a spectral parenthetical *Eastern* prefix. The earliest transnational Asian / Asian American artists are then documented or curated with chronological historical scholarly approaches that tend to perpetuate the same internal racial demographic coverage, often completely unintentionally by the curator or academic but nevertheless grounding such an intentionality.

For example, the scholarly initiative funded by the J. Paul Getty Trust, *Pacific Standard Time: Art in L.A., 1945–1980,* attempted to historicize the contributions of Los Angeles–based artists, curators, critics, and others and took nearly a decade to plan, granting nearly sixty organizations throughout Greater Los Angeles County a total of $10 million to produce events and exhibitions between September 2011 and April 2012. As a multicultural and multiracial endeavor that saw some of the most exciting exhibitions, such as that of African American arts, it nevertheless showcased primarily early Japanese and Chinese American artists in painting, lithography, and photography genres.

Even the excellent National Endowment for the Humanities–convened 2012 summer program on Asian Pacific American visual arts designed for teachers, scholars, and program builders (at which most of the contributors to this anthology met and during which time our coeditors conceived of this anthology's potential contribution) included a flexible canon of sorts that covered two weeks on early Chinese and Japanese artists and one week for all the others, including queer, mixed race, South Asian, Southeast Asian, and experimental artists. Our charge to grow the field was therefore very tangible and the work ahead monumental.

In the particular disciplinary field of Southeast Asian American visual cultures, familiar discursive methodologies include dominant thematic genres: trauma and war, refugee migration and resettlement, memories and fragmentation, and comparative immigration generations (pre-1965, post-1965, labor and professional classes, refugees, pre-1975, and post-1975). Indeed, Margo Machida's *Unsettled Visions: Contemporary Asian American Artists and the Social Imaginary* (2008) already does an excellent thematic survey and rich sociohistorical analysis of orientalism, social memory, trauma, rupture, and migration in the work of Southeast Asian American artists such as Marlon Fuentes, Pipo Nguyen-Duy, Hanh Thi Pham, and Long Nguyen.

Below, I hope to problematize the categorization of Southeast Asia American visual arts by reframing and queering, or by moving through and then beyond, the popular tropes of war and migration to other potentially complex and less visible tropes of critical regionalism, as opposed to nationalisms and East/West binaries, to enable us to question the category and borders of Asian American arts altogether. By engaging in larger global de-imperial conversations and tracing alternative geopolitical mappings, by placing in the foreground questions of race, gender, and sexuality, by highlighting the pedagogy of mixed media, performance, and collaboration, by queering the temporality of field historiography, the following artists resist the incorporation or absorption of Asian American visual arts critique into pervasive neoliberal statist projects.

Lana Lin and H. Lan Thao Lam's collaborative works *Even the Trees Would Leave* (2005), *Unidentified Vietnam* (2006), and *Tomorrow I Leave* (2010) succeed in all of the above. In the first photo and text narrative piece project, *Even the Trees Would Leave* (2005), Lin + Lam document how former refugee camps in Hong Kong have been transformed into golf driving ranges and family BBQ recreation centers. The Pillar Point refugee camp in the New Territories had closed in 2000, but the state still had not removed the bus stop sign with the name "Pillar Point Refugee Camp" on it even five years later. By the time Lin + Lam returned to Hong Kong in 2010, they learned of reunion tours in which former refugees returned to visit their camps, and they visited Lam's former refugee camp in Pulau Bidong, Malaysia. A project like *Even the Trees Would Leave* shifts the seemingly indelible and timeless image/sighting/siting of the Vietnam War from a Vietnamese jungle battle zone, napalm and Agent Orange victims, refugee exodus, and American assimilation to present-day Malaysia and Hong Kong as contemporary sites of upwardly mobile, middle class Vietnamese diasporic refugee tourism, thanatourism (death tourism), and global ruin porn. Lam confirms her discomfort with the resonant spatiality and temporality of common Vietnam War discourses in Lin + Lam's interview in this collection, when she explains that because the Vietnam War is such a contested space, she represents the past not as history has been written but to instead "find some crevices," and that perhaps, "this is what queering it has meant for me—to find a different place rather than the binary opposition . . . the residue, the marker of time, history and experiences can be seen but also not seen until you focus on it," the ruins of Pulau Bidong buildings once prohibited to refugees now welcomed spaces. And nevertheless, they insist that it is a space that *was* and *is* a place "even the trees would leave." For Lin, the ruin carries the present and the past simultaneously and is thoroughly charged with that history, but can also serve potentially very different purposes in the current moment and space. The Malaysian sites "seem more layered because there isn't a huge commercial production going into reconstructing those sites or marketing them," while Lam explains that one of the sites is now a semivacant parking lot and another in total ruins, which nature had reclaimed "in this incredible way that bore little resemblance to what" her twelve-year-old self knew and remembered. In Hong Kong, however, the refugee sites have become a space "that is reclaimed for Hong Kong people." The many registers of *reclamation* in their interview alone are fascinating, from refugees to nature and Hong Kong.

When Asian Americanist scholarship articulates notions of reclamation for the Vietnamese diaspora, they often look toward the homeland and notions of diasporic loss, exile, memory, and reconciliation, but at Pillar Point in the New Territories space of Hong Kong, reclamation takes on a very different character with very different cross-purposes, purposes that harken back to regional and racist geopolitical antagonisms between various East and Southeast Asian nation-states during the late 1970s and throughout the 1980s with boat people refugee flight. Lin + Lam's project takes on at once an imaginative archival creativity and a future prognosis of commodified refugee ruination, global commercial enterprise, and international historiographical fleecing.

The artists continue their reverse archeological and archivist urge in the *Unidentified Vietnam* (2006) series (plate 8, figure 2.1). According to their website, the project takes its name from over a dozen South Vietnamese propaganda films archived at the Library of Congress and labeled only "Unidentified Vietnam":

> These 1960's films—made with U.S. support—call into question the policies and politics of nation building. With exacting attention to the material artifacts and architecture of the archive, *Unidentified Vietnam* simultaneously expands and contracts the space of history, offering a view of the present moment through the lens of past events. At the center of the installation, a card catalogue contains photographs of Library of Congress interiors and empty film cans. On the reverse of the cards are excerpts from interviews about the propaganda films conducted by the artists. In their video re-enactment of archival footage, former leaders of the failed republic refute Graham Greene's implication that Vietnam is "invisible like peace." Also on view, enlarged photographic stills of transitional moments in the films connote absence, stasis and movement. Employing irony, humor and melancholia, Lin + Lam expose the force of bureaucracy, the dangers of nationalism, and the ramifications of U.S. foreign intervention. Recognizing the contingency of democratic discourse, they ask viewers to consider the viability of and possibilities for ethical interaction between nations and peoples.[18]

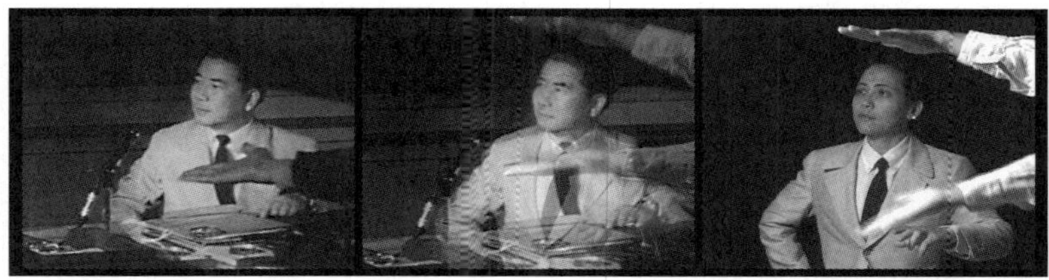

FIGURE 2.1

Lin + Lam (Lana Lin, American, b. 1966; H. Lan Thao Lam, Canadian, b. 1968)
"Invisible Like Peace" (a component of *Unidentified Vietnam*), 2006

16mm film
Courtesy of the artists

They worked with drag in "Invisible Like Peace," with Lam reenacting different female and male roles, such as those of Ngô Đình Diệm (pictured) and Madame Nhu, from these propaganda films. They wanted to deploy both a "conventional sense of drag but also a temporal drag," explains Lin, as evident in the overlaying of the drag performance and the political leader, while Lam adds that though she does self-identify as queer, they haven't made any explicitly queer art and don't find that they are showing or exhibiting in the queer community either. For a Vietnam War scholar, such overlaying also returns the viewer to superficial orientalist criticisms of Republic of Việt Nam president Ngô Đình Diệm as a weak puppet government leader relative to the United States. The drag performance forces the spectator to consider that racialized gendered position, and its limitations as well as its potentialities in the global political sphere. Further, Lam doesn't think it would be possible for her to claim one identity, asserting that she doesn't necessarily identify herself as an Asian American or even Asian Canadian artist. For Lin + Lam, their work mode is project specific, research driven, informed by the material, the research gathered, and their conversation with each other in such a way that they are also "queering collaboration" because they have an "open relationship" when it comes to collaboration.

In the multimedia installation *Tomorrow I Leave* (2010) (plate 9), Lin + Lam include a music video installation of the classic Vietnamese song "Biển nhớ" (Sea, Remember) with its central refrain: "Ngày mai em đi, biển nhớ tên em gọi về" (Tomorrow [you/I] leave, sea, remember [your/my] name and beckon [you/me] home).[19] Written in 1962 by the famous antiwar composer Trịnh Công Sơn and sung by the antiwar vocalist Khánh Ly, his one-time lover who rose to fame in the 1960s, the available music videos for the song today appear to be much more contemporary productions of the now septuagenarian celebrity diasporic singer on what looks to be a California beach as she looks longingly out at the ocean. This song played regularly over refugee camp intercoms as people entered and left makeshift sites like Pulau Bidong, Malaysia. For Lam, it is "a heart-wrenching emblem of Vietnamese 1970s pop music, and was banned after the war ended; it's about a calling, a recognition and letting go, and yet thinking about the ones left behind."

However, this song resonates very differently for various demographics—for those who came of age during the war with vexed romantic departures, such as Trịnh Công Sơn and Khánh Ly (Lam's parents' generation), for the refugees who heard the song played in camps each day as someone left, as described by Lam above, and for the diasporic youth of Lam's and my own generation who grew up with it as a household reminder of parental nostalgia. In fact, though Khánh Ly is often cited as the songwriter's muse, old schoolmates of the now deceased Trịnh Công Sơn claim it was written for an early love of the composer, Bích Khê, upon their departure and return to Huế. The diversity of possible and simultaneous receptions by different generational participants or subjects of this war history and the multiple temporal moments it conjures perform a generative queering of the archive, as well as anchoring forms of interpersonal, intergenerational, and geopolitical gravitas.

Many linguists and literary scholars of Vietnamese have declared the language's exquisite beauty to be a product of its monosyllabic, multitonal phonetics, which roll rhythmically off the tongue, like rain droplets skipping off river stones or a thunderous cacophony of war bombing. The less obvious beauty of the Vietnamese language is its nonrequisite temporality. Past, present, and future verb tenses are not required in Vietnamese grammatical forms, with communication clearly rendered from context clues of the past imperfect or subjunctive future. The exhibit layers this sonic register with additional experimental visual displays in video, sculptural, and photographic forms.

Lin + Lam continue playing with notions of return and tourism by making postcards from the photographs they took at former refugee camps in Malaysia in 2010 and then sending them to the future exhibition at 1-A Space, a gallery in the Cattle Depot Artist Village of Hong Kong. They intentionally utilized postcards as a touristic medium facilitated by the national and international postal service. Postcards were the quickest mode of communication for many Vietnamese refugees to convey safe escape or passage to their loved ones in other global spaces or in international waters. Asian American studies often forsake this thick transnational past in favor of contemporary American domestic struggles. According to Lin, "In thinking about the ways in which people are returning, it's thinking about a time in the past but which always held this promise for the future—this hope to be leaving and finding a home somewhere else. The project speaks to this duality, or maybe even more than duality, between present, past, future—this multiplicity in temporality."

SCHOLARLY TRAJECTORIES, REJECTIONS, AND ERECTIONS

Southeast Asian art has also been mired in a particular temporality, a pastness, specifically in the tradition of Asian civilizations and archeology, with diasporic arts projected to occupy a later present and future additive and diluted representational space. Such representational tendencies are evident at the Los Angeles County Museum of Art (LACMA) and the smaller Ivy League university gallery collections, for example. Subsequent contemporary scholarship has again followed generic parameters despite strong contributions, including performance, film, theater, and visual art.[20] The next generation of Southeast Asian and diasporic arts scholars come from training in extremely diverse disciplines—art and art history, film and visual cultures, American/ethnic studies, Asian area studies, literature, and creative writing. So where would a disciplinarily liminal artist such as experimental film and video artist Nguyen Tan Hoang fit within such a scholarly trajectory?

Americanist and Asian Americanist critiques of Nguyen's films often deploy them as interventions in the contemporary mainstream heteronormative visual arts industry and culture. Meanwhile, Asianists warn us that scholarship on media flows often assigns "cultural stasis to receiving media populations portrayed as waiting impotently to be culturally colonized," insisting instead that even when media texts are produced in Western spaces, "they are adapted, appropriated, reconfigured, and indeed rejected as they circulate" and asserting the critical significance of Asia and Asians in transnational media traffic as "another set of nodes for production and circulation."[21] Therefore, I build upon both Elizabeth Freeman's loving queer temporal reading of pre-AIDS white urban gay male porn and sex without latex scenes in Nguyen's film *K.I.P.* (2002) and Mimi Thi Nguyen's close textual analysis of the refugee figure and autobiographical diasporic identitarian politics in Nguyen's film *PIRATED!* (2000) (plate 10), including another of Nguyen Tan Hoang's earlier films, *Cover Girl* (2000), to extend the potential queer and racialized transnational temporal critique available in Nguyen's repertoire.

Freeman's analysis of *K.I.P.* emphasizes how the "temporal reshufflings particular to the fragmented sex scene between the two hunky actors actually came from a specific history of consumption," and then focuses on Nguyen's personalized or individualized revision or re-envisioning of *that* primarily white historiographical scene.[22] By depicting the reflection of Nguyen's own racialized, marginal open-mouthed countenance in the television glass as it screens 1960s/70s porn star Kip Noll's best scenes, Freeman writes, "*K.I.P.* suggests, the medium of video, and especially the genre of pornography, produce powerful sexual disorientation . . . , dis-integrating the so-called sex act . . . , [a] derangement of bodies and pleasures." She invests in this "logic of fragmentation and remixing to open up gaps in the sexual dyad, inviting in . . . any number of viewers or even participants," and describes how such a "hiccup in sequential time has the capacity to connect a group of people beyond monogamous, enduring couplehood—and this awareness . . . is crucial to revitalizing a queer politics and theory that until fairly recently has focused more on space than on time."[23] For Freeman, the "mourning and lusting spectator, who seems to want to have sex with history—with dead men, with men older than he, with an era and place barred by both linear time and racial politics" becomes "more than a gay-affirmative experimental film: it is also a queer hauntological exercise" "by centering on erotic pleasure." Freeman then concludes, "Too young, too racialized, too 'foreign' . . . Nguyen could not have literally joined the pre-AIDS white urban gay male scene for which *Kip Noll, Superstar* is a metonym. But by superimposing his own image as spectator onto a scene already containing a trace of earlier spectators, with that trace in turn present only in the negative as gaps and repetitions, Nguyen figuratively joins a community of past- and present-tense viewers, some of whom we can presume died in the AIDS epidemic or are now seropositive. R.I.P., or 'Rest in Peace,' indicating both the desire to enliven the dead and the understanding that this is never wholly possible."[24]

My critical investments are respectfully different from Freeman's. What if they, Kip Noll's queer temporal crew, instead joined Nguyen's gawking spectator in 2002? In terms of hauntological gaps of historicity, sociocultural omissions, and desired emissions, what if the open-mouthed spectator's masturbatory subjective desire is for Kip Noll to instead join this young diasporic Vietnamese American gay man in rickety refugee fishing boats, in gay threesomes with Thai pirates and swashbuckling British pirates, with Asian American techies in Silicon Valley, in gay Los Angeles Asian American arts scenes, in transnational cosmopolitan Việt Nam? What if we imagined instead the Spivakian (third) "worlding" of American 1960s/'70s gay sex and porn cultures? What if Kip Noll instead joined in Nguyen's revival of Norman Yonemoto and other early Asian American porn historiographical interventions? How would *K.I.P.*'s champagne wishes and fishy caviar sticky rice dreams intervene if the subjective gay communal referents were even more minoritarian? How did the AIDS epidemic affect the Asian American and other racialized gay minority communities? How globally did Kip Noll's popularity sell then, and what would such access and circulation mean in Southeast Asia or to Southeast Asians today?

Indeed, Nguyen often plays with other media favorites, such as the sampling of popular Vietnamese songs and musical figures in his two 2000 films, *Cover Girl* (his curious and ironically obsessive fangirl homage to Dalena, the blond, blue-eyed white American singer of Vietnamese diasporic community fame), and *PIRATED!*. "Biển nhớ" is sampled in both 2000 films, as is a well-known Vietnamese cover of Nancy Sinatra's "Bang Bang" (1966), also banned during the war, to which I will return in the discussion of Việt Lê's work. In elevating Dalena's popularity to diasporic celebrity sensation status, Nguyen's imagined spectator's desire manifests the possibility of full immersion of mainstream Americans into the hearts and minds of Vietnamese diasporic communities. Dalena is reported to have subsequently had a long romantic relationship with Henry Chúc, her occasional singing partner and producer of many years, following in the footsteps of an earlier, slightly older, blond, blue-eyed beauty of Australian origin, Lynn, of Công Thành and Lynn, another singing duo of Vietnamese diasporic fame. While the kitsch inherent in these women's popularity is amusing, the artist's potential subjective identification with these love objects (if read in the same way as Freeman's articulation of the spectator's/artist's desiring gaze at Kip Noll and his queer temporality) represents a racialized and global-diasporic queer temporal departure or detour.

Kobena Mercer reminds us that "migration throws objects, identities and ideas into flux," "but what often arises is a largely de-historicized outlook that tends to identify cross-cultural aspects of the visual arts with the limited shelf-life of 'the contemporary.'"[25] Similar to postmodernist abstraction's tendency to flatten differences of race, class, gender, and so on, global arts criticism often treats diasporic and transnational cultural production as vague but pleasant contemporary commercial multiculturalisms with very little explication of deep geopolitical diversity and historiography. Freeman asserts, "Longing produces modes of both belonging and 'being long,' or persisting over time . . .; desire is 'historiographical,' a way of writing that object into the present"; "naked flesh is bound into socially meaningful embodiment through temporal regulation: binding is what turns mere existence into a form of mastery in a process I'll refer to as *chrononormativity*, or the use of time to organize individual human bodies toward maximum productivity . . . people are bound to one another, engrouped, made to feel coherently collective, through particular orchestrations of time."[26] Southeast Asian American studies has somehow developed a *chrononormativity* around refugee studies and trauma studies, if we recall Pahole Sookkasikon's Asian Americanist anxieties.

"Erotics, on the other hand, traffics less in belief than in encounter," proffers Freeman. When the protagonist of Nguyen's film *PIRATED!* confesses, "At last, I too found myself. Not among the rice paddies of my ancestors. But on the High Seas: In the arms of Pirates and under the bodies of Sailors," he disrupts every single popular and scholarly imagistic aspect of Vietnamese American diasporic and refugee exodus, trauma, and return in his eroticization of the historical pirate figure in that historical context. The voice-over further cements, "Remember, you're on a pirate ship, in pirate waters, in a pirate world. Ask no questions. Believe only what you see." [27] Read in a critical refugee studies disciplinary light, this at once ominous and tongue-in-cheek warning almost ironizes that field's own historiographical urges and desires; the field itself is being pirated and parodied by this experimental film's queer temporally charged pastiche.

Mimi Thi Nguyen has described *PIRATED!* as "a polyvocal and perverse refugee autobiography, which is both singular and quasi-ethnographic," focusing on the multiple generic interventions where the idea that "classic cinematic images of manly men might also inspire homoerotic desires in young boys is complicated . . . by the racialized geopolitics of danger and rescue, of invasion and imagination, which are enacted in the globalization of the Hollywood film industry and histories of French colonialism and US intervention in Southeast Asia."[28] The erotic desire in the film complicates far beyond Western orientalist investments in white love to even the disciplinary desires for coherence and consolidation of refugee experiences of loss, and disrupts the relevant complex diasporic cultural codes even in its references to Thai pirates, if we are to consider Sookkasikon's other potential Thai and Southeast Asian cultural historical research possibilities. The protagonist can be always already the refugee, the pirate and the sailor in one. Even the shakiness and blurriness of the pan-racial pirate romance and sex acts footage, as seen in the still image, capture an attempt to racialize differently, to historicize queerly, and to make transnational the complex and fuzzy interstitial subconscious of the queer desire and temporality in *PIRATED!*. The Asian bottom refugee/sailor/pirate pictured wears a facial expression of pronounced pain, pleasure, fear, danger, ecstasy, history and memory, trauma and refugee studies, all simultaneously. It is in the ass grabs, gropes, and gasps that the spectator both grasps aghast and delights in the possible perversions of history and queer temporalizing within Nguyen Tan Hoang's body of work.

TRANSNATIONAL ARTISTS AND EXHIBITIONAL POLITICS

I conclude this chapter with a discussion that builds upon the 1997 art exhibit *Memories of Overdevelopment—Philippine Diaspora in Contemporary Art* by examining the ways in which artists working in installation art, performance, and video art negotiate aesthetics and politics in today's rapidly developing Southeast Asian region and its diasporas against deeply layered and contested geopolitical terrains, architectural markers, and spatial histories. These artists handle the architectonics of such fabricated, reprocessed, and reborn histories and memories provocatively to address diverse concerns with transnational and diasporic arts, protest politics and critical cosmopolitanism. Their works at once bear witness to historiographical iconography and attempt to encourage their audiences to act as the "emancipated spectator."[29]

The visual and performance art of Filipina American Eliza O. Barrios stands in rather stark contrast to her collaborative work in the collective Mail Order Brides (M.O.B.). While the latter's efforts are more loudly satirical and oppositional (in performance and even in still photography), Barrios's solo work reveals quieter moments of sociopolitical critique and queer temporalizing.

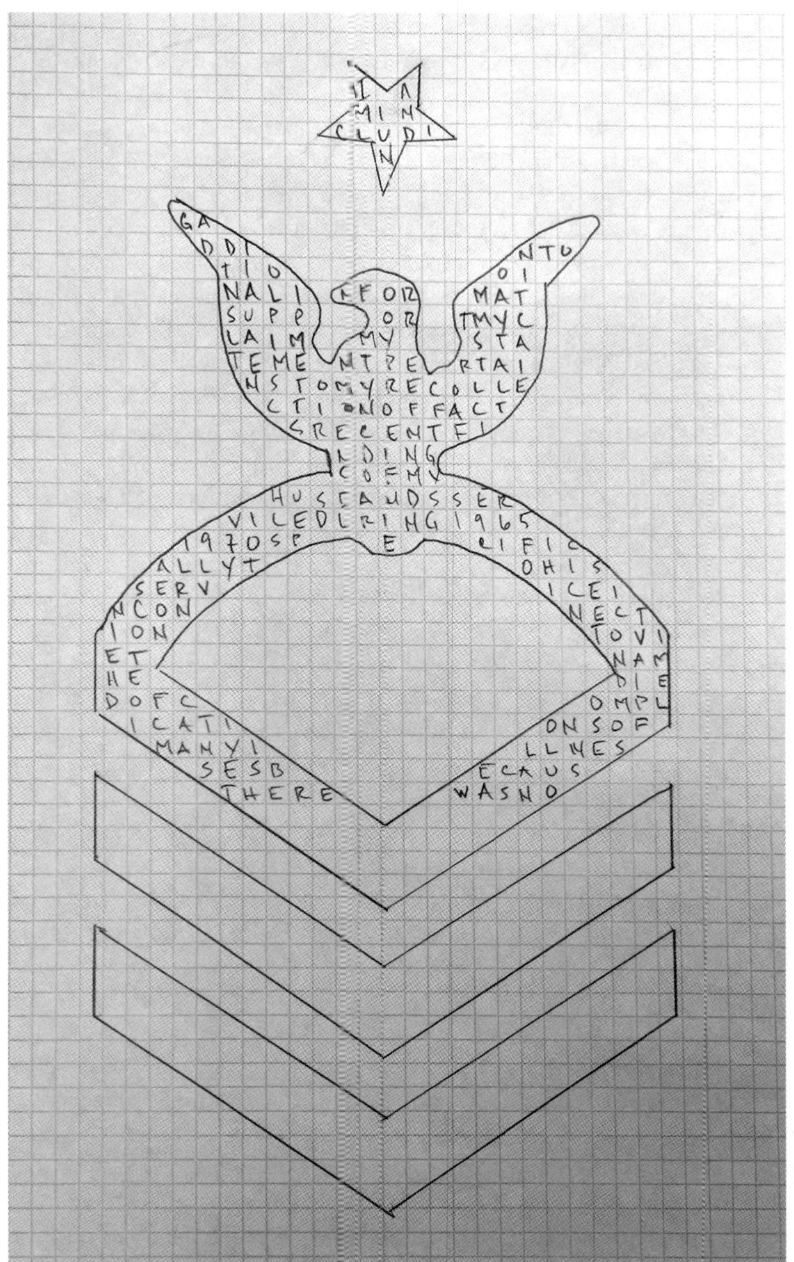

FIGURE 2.2

Eliza Barrios (American, b. 1968)
D.K.C. 3, 2013

Graphite
14 x 9 in (36 x 23 cm)
Courtesy of the artist/dedicated to E. R. Barrios

In a series of six drawings in graphite on paper called *D.K.C.* (figure 2.2), Barrios incorporates the text of her family's letter to the Department of Veteran's Affairs requesting support due to her father's tour of duty in Vietnam. It was only after the death of her father on February 23, 2013, that the family discovered he had served five tours of duty in Vietnam and had slowly suffered the effects of Agent Orange. He had lived most of his life keeping the secret of his active duty of over twenty-five years and had never sought treatment, which most likely contributed to his alcoholism. *D.K.C.* was a personal homage to him after his death. Machida has explained, "The central purpose of most exhibitions in history and anthropological museums is to make what is depicted more accessible to the general public," while a work like Yong Soon Min's *DMZ XING*, and I would add Barrios's *D.K.C.*, "avoids any clear-cut resolution and asks more of the viewer" and "coupled with a discontinuous, fragmentary visual-discursive strategy toward historical narrative and inter-Asian relations, a far more dedicated level of engagement is required."[30] Barrios's work queers the Vietnam War historiography as a transculturally inter-Asian project that includes Filipino Americans, Japanese Americans, Koreans, Pacific Islanders, and so on, and activates the queer temporality of active Pinoy servicemen as a pervasive nineteenth-, twentieth-, and twenty-first-century global phenomenon.[31] It also begs the causal questions regarding her father's resistance to disclosure. Are there aspects even of Asian American pan-ethnicity that may serve as policing mechanisms in the aftermath of multicultural, international sociopolitical upheaval? A work such as this and an exhibit such as *Sulat sa Pader/Writing on the Wall*, where *D.K.C.* was displayed, commands rather than demands a high level of critical historiographical participatory engagement.

Machida further describes Elaine H. Kim's work on comparative exhibitional politics, emphasizing "the historical focus of Asian American studies on the West Coast (whereas the eastern seaboard is the larger locus of artistic and critical activity)," noting that many scholars "find visual culture and visuality itself highly suspect because it has long been recognized as a tool of suppression and stereotyping for Asians in this nation" and that "equally problematic is the history of the entrenched elitism and exclusionary practices of the art world, especially in regard to artists of color."[32] Barrios's *D.K.C.*, however, almost intentionally offers an extremely aesthetically accessible form and reception, both at the level of textual content and meaning and in terms of its production, construction, and installation. Written in graphite on commercially available graph paper, Barrios handwrites the text, letter by letter, in the individual squares with an almost dyslexic writing/reading of letters or appearance of reversed writing in a number of the individual pieces. The iconic outlines, too, clearly represent military uniform insignias and iconography, but despite the ease of accessibility and apparent clarity, this personal familial and global political historiography has to be pieced together letter by letter.

In the larger project from which this chapter comes, I offer a comparative survey of East Coast and West Coast Asian/American US arts development, visibility, framing or lack thereof, and programming. More specifically, I explore the divergent/diverse access opportunities to archives, materials, audiences, and exhibition spaces that artists have on the East Coast in relation to those accessible to Asian American visual artists on the West Coast, an exploration of exhibitional activism. For example, one discussion examines a historical case study of anticommunist protests against Vietnamese American art exhibits of the past four decades by forcing into dialogue local community politics and global political shifts and alignments.

This last point shifts our locale attention to Cambodia and Việt Nam, where exhibitional spaces in both Hanoi and Ho Chi Minh City, for another example, face differently configured forms of postsocialist censorship and protest politics. My investment revolves around the sociocultural and political economic embeddedness of the visual arts currently "surfacing" and circulating in the multiple imagined and geographical spaces. Artist and academic Việt Lê says of his skillfully crafted "time traveling, trans, love triangle," the 2012 music video *Love Bang!* (plates 11, 12), "It's not necessarily a linear teleological time but it's disjunctured time; in the video the characters move back and forth in time; the main character, she's a nightclub singer but she imagines her ideal lover, who is fighting this war back forty years ago—and they reunite in the future" (chapter 2 interview). The video interjects the drag musical performance and rap sequence with footage of an aestheticized lone soldier in battle, half-hero/half–water buffalo slaving in the Khmer countryside, high fashion catwalk shoots in a gorgeous incomplete 1970s modernist architectural structure in Phnom Penh by Khmer "starchitects" such as Vann Molivann, and Khmer dance choreography. Lê explains that in the singer's version of the song "Bang Bang," it is a metaphor for war, her lover, and the violence of war, but that Lê himself is interested in what these songs or this mass media means given that war history.

The terms with which Le describes his project goals—connection/disconnection, congestion and compression of time, developing/developed countries, discrepant modernities, visions/versions of modernization, identify/disidentify, veneer/cover up, third worlds in first worlds, temporal and musical mash-ups, and soft power/soft politics—as well as his comparison to developmental and neoliberal rhetorical tactics for the commodification of sexuality in Singapore,[33] gesture precisely toward the analytical interpretative queering of transnational spaces, time zones, and historiography necessary to combat the superficial international obsessions with cultural development in Southeast Asia in the familiar forms of pan-Asian pop culture, pop music, high fashion, sexuality, and the pseudo-visibility of LGBITQ rights, appearances of "progress" that often coincide temporally with human rights abuses and other forms of censorship and political oppression.

For artist Việt Lê, this provocative creative analytical space can be anywhere—this imaginary setting, this mash-up. But then who does the work of answering the questions he poses in our interview: "What are the ruins when you think about discourses on modernity? What happens after social political change? What happens when regimes change and these discourses shift?" I imagine an exercise in oral hermeneutics between the artist Việt Lê and the academic Việt Lê. Discussions of perceived critical mass, strategic affect, performance and political performativity, neoliberal disciplining, censorship, and cultural economic development necessarily pervade the longer monograph from which this chapter comes, in order to make sense of these changing geopolitical and racialized historiographical contexts. As Lana Lin recalls in her own reference to the song "Bang Bang," "[Lin + Lam] like to cite or to appropriate because we are interested in notions around translation, which parallel the idea that memory isn't fixed—that there are different translations, different interpretations of the past and present." To queer temporality in Asian American visual cultures, then, is to do the heavy critical work of articulating that seemingly ever "untranslatable remainder," and to recognize that there is at once *no* Pacific *Standard* Time and that *Pacific* Standard *Time* is always already *everywhere* across the globe.

Promiscuous Time Traveling (on Leaving and Returns): A Conversation with Lin + Lam and Việt Lê

LAURA KINA

On August 6, 2014, Laura Kina talked with the New York–based artist collaborative Lin + Lam (Lana Lin and H. Lan Thao Lam) about their 2010 installation Tomorrow I Leave *and San Francisco–based artist Việt Lê about his 2012* Love Bang! *music video. Their discussion explored queering time and their proximity to and distance from Vietnamese history and memory.*

LAURA KINA: Can you each introduce yourself?

H. LAN THAO LAM: Lin + Lam was "born" in 2000, so we are teenagers!

LANA LIN: We began working together as a multidisciplinary collaborative in New York City.

HLTL: When we met in 2000, a conversation began, and we found that we share similar interests and politics having to do with feminism, postcoloniality, and critical discourse. What cinched our collaboration together was the way in which our varied backgrounds overlap, inform, and fill each other's gaps. I studied architecture, and then I switched over to sculpture/installation, completing my MFA at CalArts in 1998. My practice has been interdisciplinary, but I hadn't ventured into time except using some sound work in my installation. I hadn't used moving images. Working with Lana helped me understand that relationship much better since her background is in experimental film and video. Currently, I teach at Goddard College MFA in Interdisciplinary Arts program.

LL: We shared a lot of mutual friends as well from going through the Whitney independent study program, which we did at different times. The first collaboration was what became *Unidentified Vietnam* (2006), which was based on these propaganda films in the South Vietnam Collection at the Library of Congress. That work was in progress when I received a Fulbright Grant to make a project in Taiwan, which ended up being called *Departure* (2006) and was based around three postcolonial cities: Taipei, Shanghai, and Hanoi.

HLTL: I was born in 1968 in My Tho during the Tet Offensive. We moved around a tiny little bit; the last place we lived was Saigon. I left Vietnam with my father and three sisters in 1980. We landed in Malaysia, Pulau Bidong. Then we were transferred to Kuala Lumpur. We then settled in Vancouver, Canada. In 1986, my mother and my younger sister joined us in Vancouver. We then moved to Toronto, where the rest of my family still is.

LL: I was born in Montreal, Canada, in 1966. When I was two years old, my family moved to Naperville, Illinois, which is a suburb of Chicago. I went to University of Iowa in Iowa City for my undergrad. In 1988 I came to New York and was working for the Merce Cunningham Dance Foundation on a documentary, and I did some film production assistant jobs. Then I decided to go to Bard College to study film, where I earned my MFA in 1996. I was studying psychoanalysis for a number of years at a psychoanalytic institute, and I wanted to bring that into my art and research. I am currently in the doctoral program in media, culture, and communication at New York University. I've also been teaching at Vermont College of Fine Arts since 2006.

LAURA KINA: How did the two you of meet Việt Lê?

HLTL: We met Việt through Yong Soon Min when they were curating *TransPOP: Korea Vietnam Remix* [an international traveling exhibition, which included work by Lin + Lam and opened first at ARKO Arts Center, Seoul, Korea, 2007].

VIỆT LÊ: I'm an artist, academic, and curator. I was born in Sài Gòn or Hồ Chí Minh City, in Việt Nam in 1976 and then immigrated to the United States around 1980. I was a "boat refugee." My dad went to the United States to study, and then my mom and I escaped on our own and joined him in Orange County after we left Thailand, where we were at an educational camp for six months. I did my MFA at University of California, Irvine, in 2001 and was teaching there for a bit in the studio art department and did some residencies. I earned my PhD from the University of Southern California in 2011 from the Department of American Studies and Ethnicity. I was living in Asia for a while—five or six years—[and] Europe for about a year. Part of it was for research. I was in Việt Nam for a Fulbright, then Cambodia at the Center for Khmer Studies and in Taiwan for a postdoc at Academia Sinica. I recently moved to San Francisco, for the past two years, to teach at the California College of the Arts. I'm in the visual studies program and the visual and critical studies graduate program.

LK: I found it interesting that in all of your biographies, it's transnational. There are multiple countries you have each lived in and many different ways you could position yourselves. I'm curious how each of you identifies at this moment in time?

HLTL: It is a seemingly simple question, but it is also deeply complicated. I don't think I can identify myself as Asian American because I'm not an American citizen. I'm a Canadian citizen. I'm not a Vietnamese citizen anymore, but I never feel connected to the Canadian Asian community either. Queering is very much the way I negotiate the spaces of the politics of nationality and identity.

LL: In terms of nationality, I identify as Asian American or Taiwanese American, though I recently did recover my Canadian citizenship because I was born in Canada. In terms of gender, I identify as queer. In terms of practice, I identify as an artist/scholar. But identity is very fluid and constantly changing.

LK: Lana and Lan Thao, earlier you mentioned that feminism was a connection for your practices. Is that something you form your own identity around as well?

LL: If asked, I would always claim being a feminist. But I don't identify, for instance, as a feminist artist. Nor do I identify as a queer artist or an Asian artist. I like to think about these terms more independently, and my art practice and scholarship independently from the other identities that I have and occupy.

HLTL: Yeah, I don't think it would be possible for me to claim one identity. I also don't identify myself as an artist as Asian American or even Asian Canadian. In my work I don't find that I am showing in the queer community either.

VL: I'm always thinking through identifications, plural, and disidentification à la José Muñoz and thinking about my subject position.[1] As a cultural arts organizer, I also think about how cultural producers or academics position themselves or get positioned. It's something I am constantly questioning or queering. Depending on the situation and location, I do identify as a queer Vietnamese, or Vietnamese American, artist-scholar-cultural activist. It changes. It's fluid and morphing. In Việt Nam, I and other Southeast Asian artists are called to represent a geographic location (i.e., Việt Nam or Cambodia). There are a lot of artists who were educated in the United States or born in the United States who move elsewhere and get positioned as a representative of that country. Sometimes that happens to me. Sometimes I'm seen as Vietnamese. Sometimes I'm Vietnamese American. In terms of my academic work, a lot of the work deals with trauma and modernization—the traumas of history and modernity. Although I address gender in my academic work, I deal more with queer issues in my creative work. There's a sort of bifurcation there. I'm also questioning the politics of identity and having to negotiate that; what institutions and structures situate you—it's something that I'm always "queering," and also resistant to.

LK: I want to talk about queering time and ask about your artwork: Việt, your 2012 music video *Love Bang!* (plates 11, 12), which you have described as a "time traveling, trans, love triangle," and Lin + Lam, your 2010 work *Tomorrow I Leave* (plate 9), which is about thanatourism (death tourism) but the title is also based on a song. I think there is a connection between your works in terms of music and how that relates to time.

VL: *Love Bang!* comes from some of my curatorial work and also my academic work, trying to figure out what is the gap between historical trauma and pop culture, particularly pan-Asian popular culture. It seems like many people don't talk about past wars, but there is such an obsession with pop music, and I was wondering what was the relationship. I had been making these faux Asian boy band posters [*boy bang / gang band* series] looking at desire, transnational audiences, and (homoerotic) affect. To echo anthropologist Lisa Rofel, what is the relationship between national and consumer desires?[2] What's the connection between the body and the political body? Baudrillard's "hyperreal"—more real than the real—meets realpolitik.[3]

So I decided to make a real fake music video trilogy. This is the first installment. It's trilingual "hip pop"—a fictitious cross between hip hop and pop. The allegorical characters represent the triangulated relationship between Vietnam, Cambodia, and the United States. I was thinking about how time and space is compressed and there are these ever-present pasts. Even though the video is a very fluffy pop video, these traumatic vestiges are still there. I was reading "Bliss" Cua Lim and thinking about conceptions of time and "Jack" Halberstam's conception of queer time—it's not necessarily a linear teleogical time, but it's disjunctured time.[4]

In the video the characters move back and forth in time. The main character, she's a nightclub singer but she imagines her ideal lover, who is fighting this war back forty years ago—this year is the fortieth anniversary of the Việt Nam War—and they reunite in the future. It's this congestion and compression of time that I think happens in both developing countries and developed countries—also thinking about discrepant modernities and how that works. There's not one vision or version of modernization.

LK: Việt, could you describe the narrative arch and the aesthetics of the video? I'm particularly interested in the "Charlie's Angels (of History)" scene and poster for the video (plate 11).

VL: *Charlie* was a term for a communist that was used by US soldiers during the Vietnam War. I was thinking about the seventies television show and of Benjamin's "angel of history"[5]—how do we think about history in the present moment? He talks about this wreckage of the past. There are these trans performers at my favorite nightclub in Phnom Penh, Cambodia, Classic Night, and they do a sort of ethnic play—so they're Khmer performers but they sometimes perform in Vietnamese, South Asian, or Thai costumes or outfits. I was just thinking about how this play or "drag" is rehearsed and how people identify or disidentify. There are a lot of Chinese as well as Vietnamese, Americans, Thai, Australians, and Koreans, among others—living, working, and investing—in Cambodia. I am compelled by the interrelated relationships between these countries, transnationally and regionally.

In terms of the visual, I was interested in developing this hyper pop, saccharine aesthetic to talk about this overlay of popular culture but then using humor or parody or play as a strategy to think about the twin traumas of history and rapid development of a society. It's a sort of veneer. For instance, in Vietnam there are all of these "propatainment" films that are about sexy supermodels or love stories and are "innocent," but they really talk about some other issues with these moralistic story lines. The video is intentionally disjunctured so there is not a real narrative. When I was working to come up with an original song with the songwriter—the music producer—I told him it was basically a love triangle narrative. The Khmer performer has a Vietnamese club manager (a cameo by yours truly) who is abusive, and she thinks about the past and this ideal dream lover, and they all reunite. It's this disjunctured narrative. I was thinking about how people think about their place living in Asia or even here in the United States—everything butts up against each other. There is no "this is the past, this is the present, this is the future." I think it's all in one space—third worlds exist in first worlds, etc. I was really interested in that mash-up. It's a temporal mash-up and musical mash-up. I use different songs . . . Khánh Ly—this Nancy Sinatra song she covered in French in Vietnamese and other different covers—Stevie Nicks, that kind of stuff.[6]

LK: And the video is in three different languages.

VL: I directed it in Cambodian, in Khmer—the rap part is in Khmer. The first opening sequence is in Vietnamese, this Vietnamese song. The refrain is in English. Part of the beat is from a Stevie Nicks song from the seventies. It talks about this transnational movement of culture, memory, cultural production—how it gets absorbed and then reconfigured.

LK: The "ideal lover" is this figure with horns right?

VL: Yeah, ideal or imaginary or past. It's a metaphor for the relationship between those countries and the relationship between the past, present, and future and trying to reconcile that.

LK: The video is shot in several different settings, and one of them is this amazing architectural space (plate 12).

VL: That is actually supposed to be this sci-fi space. It was built by this Japanese architect, and it is this library that is housed on the grounds of a Buddhist temple. There is this traditional temple and then this space, and it's actually not being used as a library—other people use it as a space for rehearsal, things like that. Parts of it are still unbuilt. It was built in seventies. So there are a lot of modernist gems in Phnom Penh by Khmer "starchitects" such as Vann Molivann. So thinking about that past, this idea of the vision of the future back then in the seventies and what modernism meant and this building boom and then looking at it now—what this idea of futurity means. It's an amazing building. Parts of it were filmed in the nightclub. Parts of it were filmed in Koh Pich, "Diamond Island," where there is the sand and it's also being developed—that part. Thinking about trauma—people being displaced to have these mega high rises and strip malls built.

HLTL: I was actually really curious about the architecture because of this kind of modern ruins.

VL: It's also this projected fantasy space. For me, the architecture and settings were also characters—the nightclub or this space; you can't pinpoint what it is. I wasn't interested in saying, "This is Cambodia or Vietnam." It can be anywhere—this imaginary setting. What are the ruins when you think about discourses on modernity? What happens after social political change? What happens when regimes change and these discourses shift? I was interested in thinking about that as well. This idea of ruins is also relevant in Lin + Lam's pieces *Even the Trees Would Leave* (2005) in these former refugee sites, and *Tomorrow I Leave* as well. I was wondering about the relationship of modern ruins in your practice.

HLTL: We are both really drawn to it. It's a kind of space that the residue, the marker of time, history, and experiences can be seen but also not seen until you focus on it. At the refugee camp on Pulau Bidong, with all of those ruins, we were actually able to enter the buildings, which, from what I could surmise, were houses reserved for the Malaysian officers—spaces where Vietnamese refugees were not permitted. Now that they are ruins, I can enter.

LL: What's interesting to me about the ruin is that it carries at least two different temporal positions—both the present and the past simultaneously. When we go to these sites of ruin, they are so charged with history, but we are there in the present moment documenting their current space.

VL: And it's interesting that these are also trauma tourist sites. I haven't been back to the refugee camp where I left, but Lana, I think you were talking about thanatourism [at a lecture at Vermont College of Fine Arts], and then oftentimes in these sites. . . . Other people have written about how the past or the politics of the past get evacuated, like the Củ Chi Tunnels, so it becomes this site in some ways for people who didn't go through that trauma, a site of spectacle or of projection. I'm not sure what you feel about these thanatourism sites or that discourse around trauma?

LL: I think that's absolutely true about those certain sites like the Củ Chi Tunnels because they definitely are marketed as tourist sites. The ones that Lan Thao and I have visited are a little more complicated because they are not so explicitly marketed as tourist sites, though there are reunion tours returning to former refugee camps in Malaysia. But they seem more layered because there isn't a huge commercial production going into reconstructing those sites or marketing them. The former refugee camps in Hong Kong are tourist sites for a different purpose. They've been transformed into golf driving, recreational centers.

HLTL: It becomes more of a space that is reclaimed for Hong Kong people. At Pillar Point, which is in the New Territories area of Hong Kong, it seems to me to be very complicated. One of the reasons why we wanted to visit these former refugee camps is to see what they are like now, while also looking for what was there. For *Tomorrow I Leave*, the notion of returning and tourism was very much on our minds. We made postcards from photographs we took at former refugee camps in Malaysia and then sent them back to the exhibition in Hong Kong. In that way, we utilized this touristic medium of the postal service, before e-mail and Twitter and Facebook was popular. Also that was a mode of communication for some Vietnamese refugees. It was the quickest way to let people know you have safely escaped.

The other component in the installation is the video, which includes Khánh Ly singing "Biển nhớ." This song played regularly over the camp intercom as people left and arrived on Pulau Bidong. From my research, it seems like other camps in Malaysia also used that tune. It's such a heart-wrenching emblem of Vietnamese 1970s pop music and was banned after the war ended. The first line of the song is "Ngay mai em di," or "Tomorrow I leave." It's about a calling, a recognition and letting go, and yet thinking about the ones left behind.

LK: You created this installation in 2010. Where was the exhibition at?

LL: It was at 1-A Space in Hong Kong. That's where we sent the postcards from Malaysia, to this gallery space, which is part of the Cattle Depot Artist Village in Hong Kong.

LK: What inspired you to make this piece as a collaborative team? I know you both have independent practices as well. How do you know when it needs to be a piece you make together?

LL: We had already made a piece called *Even the Trees Would Leave* (2005) that Việt referred to, which documented how former refugee camps in Hong Kong have been transformed into driving ranges and family barbecue recreation centers. That came about just because we were in Hong Kong in 2005 and somebody had told us that the Pillar Point refugee camp in the New Territories had closed in 2000. We were really curious, and we made the trip out to the New Territories, and we got off at the bus stop where the bus stop sign still had the name "Pillar Point Refugee Camp" on it even though it had been closed for five years. That project was a photo and text narrative piece. When we had the opportunity to come back to Hong Kong in 2010, we had read about the reunion tours where former refugees were returning to visit their camps. So we thought we would visit Lan Thao's former camp in Malaysia. That's how that project came about. In terms of "queering time," we gravitated towards the title *Tomorrow I Leave* because in thinking about the ways in which people are returning, it's thinking about a time in the past but which always held this promise for the future—this hope to be leaving and find a home somewhere else. The project speaks to this duality, or maybe even more than duality, between present, past, future—this multiplicity in temporality.

LK: Lan Thao, what was that experience like returning to the refugee camps, and do we see your personal perspective on that in the installation?

HLTL: Because we did a lot of research online, gleaning from people's blogs about their experiences of returning to the camps or seeing for the first time the camps where their parents were interned, I don't think it was emotional for me in the same way because I was already thinking about these issues, and I wasn't there that long. I was at each of the camps just a few months, although it was a very formative experience for me. I did learn a lot about community organizing and activism. Seeing the island from the other side, seeing Pulau Bidong from the main island, that was actually probably the strangest experience because of the distance and also proximity to the past. Also it was strange knowing I was on the other side looking at this side some thirty years ago. I arrived on the island late May 1980 and we were there in June 2010, so it was almost an anniversary.

There were a couple of things that happened when we were in Malaysia. We tried to contact the tour operator to take us to Pulau Bidong, but just the two of us wouldn't be worthwhile for them to take us. Also we needed more time on the island. The tour would be a package with snorkeling and lunch somewhere else, but all we were interested in was Pulau Bidong. In Kuala Lumpur, by chance we met one of the architects who built some of the structures at the transit camp, Sungei Besi, in Kuala Lumpur. At that time, during the eighties, he was an architecture student. He made some drawings for us of what he could remember of the corrugated-metal two-story housing that was the main mess hall, where we had the kitchen cafeteria and community center. He was in his late eighties and a retired architect that we just happened to meet through word of mouth when people were asking us why we were in Kuala Lumpur but not interested in other tourist sites. We ended up hiring a cab to drive us around to look at these empty parking lots with a lot of jackfruit trees that have grown around the perimeter, and they were just ripe and for the taking and I was like, "But we have to shoot the video!"

LK: You were twelve years old when you left. How long were you there?

HLTL: For each camp, a few months. We got to Canada in the fall of 1980, so maybe six months.

LK: Did seeing the camps thirty years later change your original memories?

HLTL: No, because one is now a parking lot that is hardly used. The other is in total ruins that I couldn't navigate. We could only get to certain parts—nature had reclaimed the island in this incredible way that bore little resemblance to what I knew. Being a twelve-year-old, I remember snorkeling and seeing the fish.

LL: Certain continuities remain. There were some things that remained the same, from what you've told me, like the seashells. We actually collected some of the seashells and rocks from the island for the installation.

LK: In seeing the ruins overtaken by the jungle, I'm wondering if you had any feelings about your own age and mortality and how much time has passed?

HLTL: We made two or three trips to Pulau Bidong. We hired a local fisherman with a little motorboat to take us there and back, and we paid him for his time. On that last trip, the weather was perfect—clear skies—but then they raced around and looked for us and told us a storm was coming. We quickly wrapped up our gear, put it into waterproof bags, and got back on the boat. The sea did change. The weather got windier, the waves got really rocky—we felt every single wave and bump, and I remember hanging onto the boat and thinking, "If I die here, it'd be really absurd and I'll be really, really mad! Here again, thirty years later, I'm just here to do an art project and what would happen if the boat flipped, and we are both not strong swimmers." That moment of mortality was very clear to me.

LK: Việt, can you address how your work challenges representations of contemporary Vietnam in relation to the Vietnam War?

VK: This year is the fortieth anniversary of the Việt Nam War, or the American War. I grew up with all of these stereotypes of the Việt Nam War because I don't actually have any memories, only embodied memories, of the war. My memories are from American films about the war—*Apocalypse Now*, *Deer Hunter*, that kind of stuff. As Marita Sturken writes about it, for a lot of North Americans and a large part of the world, those depictions are engrained in popular consciousness.[7] Living in Việt Nam and then having to come back and thinking about the communities that have left and returned, I'm thinking again about this idea of return. I was interested in what that looked like. In my video piece, which is also an installation, I really wanted to play with these expectations of what this topography would look like—rethinking what love, "trauma," and popular culture would look like and also playing with form.

We were talking about Khánh Ly—the original song was a cover of Nancy Sinatra's "Bang Bang" (1966), but in her song it's this metaphor for war, this lover of hers and the violence of war. That song was also banned. It's called "Golden Music"; thinking about the communities who would listen to that song when it was banned during the war but then subsequently in diasporic communities and what these songs or this mass media means—it's a connection but also a disconnection. I also think about the Việt Nam War, other past wars and US military occupations, our current wars in the Middle East and their overdetermined connections (between Việt Nam and the Middle East). US military engagement and occupation—past and present—and those connections are something I really ruminate on besides the hypervisible representations of people suffering and dying—this spectacularization of violence; thinking about the mundane or other sites of these traumas we don't normally think about—popular culture, and the different audiences for them.

LL: Việt, it's really interesting that you used "Bang Bang," because we also used it in our earlier work *Unidentified Vietnam* (figure 2.1, plate 8).

VL: I think Nguyễn Tan Hoàng, the experimental filmmaker, has also used Khánh Ly's "Bang, Bang" and "Biển nhớ"—it's a popular genre.

HLTL: In *Unidentified Vietnam*, we use the version by Thanh Lan, and she sang it in French. We also used Cher's cover. Her music video was filmed on the Intrepid in New York, which is so bizarre.

I guess I can't really speak so well or as fluently as Việt on contemporary Vietnam. I came back once during the time we were in Southeast Asia in 2005. When we were working on *Departure*, I went to Hanoi and Saigon and visited family. I think my position as an artist has been that when I make a work about the Vietnam War—it is such a contested space—that I'm not representing the past as the history has been written but to find some crevices. Maybe this is what queering it has meant for me—to find a different place rather than the binary opposition.

LL: Lan Thao, your work *Tracing Echoes* (1998–2008), a solo piece, really brings up this notion of how memory is variable and contested, so that there is no one memory that captures the authoritative version of the past. Just to add to the use of the song "Bang Bang," similarly we like to cite or to appropriate because we are interested in notions around translation, which parallel the idea that memory isn't fixed—that there are different translations, different interpretations of the past and present.

LK: Việt, earlier you talked about the veneer of pop, and in Lin + Lam's *Tomorrow I Leave* there is a look of anthropology with the display of artifacts. Việt, you distribute your video on YouTube, so if someone just stumbled across it, they would probably just consume it at face value. I also saw it as part of an installation in *Past, Present, Future Imperatives: Queer Space Time* at Sabina Lee Gallery in 2012 in Los Angeles. What experience are you hoping to elicit from your viewers?

VL: I'm interested in questions of audience and questions of translation, so like the multiple platforms and reads that it has, so some people who don't have access to Khmer or Vietnamese on a certain level can have a take on what it is, and I was hoping that on YouTube it would go viral and function as a straight-up music video. In film festivals, it's done a lot of experimental, queer film festivals, and that's a different read, and thinking about this idea of queer or queering Asian / Asian America or Asian Canada, I was thinking also about how the term *queer* and gay identities are situated within Southeast Asia or Asia and coupled with national discourse, and how that rises and its development, especially thinking about Western queer identity shifts in different other contexts in Asia and Southeast Asia. It's a different form of identification than what we think of as these identities that we have now in terms of queer politics—that there are these multiple identifications.

LK: Việt, you used the phrase *drag* earlier in reference to the three trans characters in the video. Can you tell me what terms you would use to describe them?

VL: Well, I was talking about ethnic drag, mainly. They take on different ethnic identities. That was just a way for me to think about the interrelated investments. In Cambodia, Koreans are the number one tourists in the region, and there is Japanese and Vietnamese investment, as well as Americans spending dollars, so these regional/transregional interactions. Of course, I'm interested in trans and queer identities/identifications, but I'm also thinking about transformation and change within the region as well.

LK: Is there anything culturally specific I need to understand—is this burlesque, is this drag, or a whole other thing?

VL: When you speak to the performers, they might identify in different ways. You know in Vietnam or the Philippines there isn't this "gay, straight, queer," there's *bakl̂a*, some people do identify as queer or gay, but then in different contexts they identify as different things. This discourse around visibility and rights may shift. In Cambodia there is a lot of queer LGBT visibility, and some of that is through NGOs, but there is also resistance to it. There is this discourse of this Western gay/lesbian hegemonic identity that's being imported, so discussions around that and what does that mean? What does that look like? Being careful to think about the situated politics in the region—that's not one thing, that's multiple and shifting. And other people have written about it. Eng-Beng Lim writes about Singaporean queer identity as being this pink capital that is being used by the state to cover other human rights discourses.[8] Việt Nam is similar. Over ten years ago, gays were officially seen as a "social evil," along with gambling, prostitution, AIDS, things like that. But now there is an embrace of LGB, queer, and trans identity to embrace the pink dollar and pink capital, and also to address human rights discourse. Going back to this veneer, what are these discourses around sexuality, gender, pop culture—what does it cover up? It's a sort of soft power or soft politics.

LK: Lan Thao, you were saying earlier that your queer identity isn't present in your collaborative process, but it's more about a strategy or process or intellectual engagement.

HLTL: We haven't made any explicitly queer art. I do self-identify as queer.

LL: We worked with drag in *Unidentified Vietnam*. Lan Thao reenacted different female and male parts from these propaganda films. We thought of this in the conventional sense of drag but also a temporal drag.

HLTL: The way in which we work is very project specific and research driven, so decisions about the ways in which we form the project are informed by the material, by the information that we gather, and then our conversation with each other and also with the material. In that way, I think we are also queering collaboration too, because we have an open relationship when it comes to collaboration. At every beginning of a project, or a kernel of an idea, we check in with each other, and there is a discussion if the other person is interested—whether, in fact, this is a Lin + Lam or a solo project. So I'd never expect that Lana will be working on something that I find more interesting.

LK: Do you collaborate with other people?

LTL: I have in the past but not since I met Lana and we've been working together.

LK: So maybe it's a "common law" collaboration at this point?

HLTL: Yes, I guess we are not so promiscuous!

Chapter 3

Queering Affect

Filipino Diasporic Queer Killjoy: Recuperating Failure in Jeffrey Augustine Songco's *Guilty Party* and *BOMH* Series

JAN CHRISTIAN BERNABE

IN THIS BOOK I HAVE TRIED TO RESIST THE AFFIRMATIVE TURN IN QUEER STUDIES IN ORDER TO DWELL AT LENGTH ON THE "DARK SIDE" OF MODERN QUEER REPRESENTATION.

Heather Love, *Feeling Backward* (2007)

SOMEONE TOLD ME I SHOULD TRY A REALLY GOOD EXERCISE, "JEFF, WHY DON'T YOU JUST MAKE SOME REALLY POSITIVE ARTWORK AND JUST TRY TO GET THAT PART OF YOU OUT?"

Jeffrey Augustine Songco, interview (2014)

By all accounts, San Francisco–based multidisciplinary artist Jeffrey Augustine Songco experienced a fairly conventional and normative upbringing, perhaps to be expected growing up in *the suburbs*.[1] Born and raised in Livingston, New Jersey, to Filipino immigrant parents, Songco, as he describes his childhood, "grew up in a very suburban, white town. It was very American."[2] Outside of attending Catholic Mass every Sunday, Songco's connections to Filipino diasporic culture or identity (or to the Philippines) were tenuous at best. He notes, "My parents didn't really raise me with a strong Filipino background culture." Of the umbrella label *Asian American*, which he is also reluctant to claim as an identificatory marker, he states, "I don't really understand it quite as much as I do *being American*." He gravitated to American popular culture, which he consumed from television. For queers of color growing up in the suburbs, television, as queer cultural studies scholar Karen Tongson points out, "remains a significant medium for 'creative appropriation' for the queer of color suburban artists and figures."[3] Indeed, Songco's visual oeuvre, one could argue, is marked—whether overtly or subtly—by his love for television, a pastime that he has carried with him since his childhood in Livingston. Coupled with his experiences working as a child actor, Songco's formative years were always connected to television in one way or another. If television provided both an escape from the homogeneity of suburban geographies like Livingston (especially for queers of color like Songco), it also ensured that normativity—whether class, gender, race, or sexual orientation—among those living in these suburban spaces was sustained.

I am particularly drawn to Songco's courtroom-like chalk pastel sketches—portraits of prisoners depicted with gift boxes that hide their faces, indeed their heads—from his 2014 *Guilty Party* series (plate 13). I read the four portraits that compose the series as capturing the tensions embedded within the practice of identifying that emerge from Songco's youth in the suburbs and the ways in which the weighty demands of identification become more intense for Songco as a queer person of color in the urban setting of San Francisco, a city in which he currently resides. These tensions are made manifest by what I call Songco's *affective oscillations,* which draw my attention to the ways in which Songco pictures and scrutinizes *the body*, his own or other bodies that might stand in as a *proxy* for his own, in his artwork. By proxy, I deliberately suggest that bodies in works that do not reveal Songco's face or any other distinguishing markers of his identity are still intimately tied to his corporeality, indeed to his racially marked queer identity, however much Songco chooses to disidentify on normative identificatory practices.[4] "To disidentify," as queer performance studies scholar José Muñoz reminds us, "is to read oneself and one's own life narrative in a moment, object, or subject that is not culturally coded to 'connect' with the disidentifying subject."[5]

The affective oscillations produced by Songco's *Guilty Party* give us a sense of how the artist navigates racial difference as it intersects with gender, sexuality, and more broadly, sociality (ideas of citizenship and belonging) in his artistic practice. Songco's choice of subject matter—that is, his interest in prisoners and other failed bodies in society—captures a particular type of Filipino queer negative affect that brushes against neoliberal discourses of privacy and political inclusion, and stands in contradistinction to heteronormative social cohesion. *Guilty Party* does not stand alone in calling attention to Songco's affective oscillations. Earlier work gives viewers a taste of Songco's progression as an artist influenced by the complexities and ironies of neoliberal suburban culture, especially as they shape the artist's views on individualism, choice, and consumerism—and most importantly, his sense of identity and sociality. These influences are seen in the *BOMH* series (2009; *BOMH* is an acronym for "Bag Over My Head") (plate 14) as well as in other pieces created prior to *Guilty Party*. *Guilty Party* represents a potential challenge to the visual expectations of viewers, or more broadly the Filipino diasporic and queer communities at large, conferred upon queer artists of color like Songco.[6] I contend that suburbia has created Songco as *the killjoy*—a *Filipino diasporic queer killjoy artist*, to be more precise. Describing the feminist killjoy subject, queer cultural studies scholar Sarah Ahmed writes, "Certainly to be a good subject is to be perceived as a happiness-cause, as making others happy. To be bad is thus to be a killjoy."[7]

What is at stake if Songco's art fails to represent and conform to the visual expectations of the community or communities in which he is supposedly located, especially through his recuperation of failure (or failed bodies)? I am taken by queer studies scholar Jack Halberstam's take on failure, which as he notes "allows us to escape the punishing norms that discipline behavior and manage human development."[8] Might Songco's turn to failure in his art serve as a critique of the larger forces that discipline the psychic and somatic bodies of queers of color in the United States? What might we glean from Songco's artwork and his exploration, to borrow literary and queer studies scholar Heather Love's term from this chapter's epigraph, of the "'dark side' of modern queer representation"? Before moving forward to explore Songco's killjoy conceptualism and aesthetics in *Guilty Party*—and before entering the darker side of race and representation—I would like to time-travel back to Songco's childhood in suburbia, where Songco would unsuspectingly hone his killjoy tendencies. I would like to revisit Livingston, New Jersey, where the impressionable Songco spent countless hours watching and dreaming about television, wondering all the while where he fit in the larger American popular cultural landscape.

QUEER BROWN BOY IN SUBURBIA

From his childhood television viewing practice and his experiences trying to succeed as a child actor, Songco learned early on about his racial minority status. On being a child actor, he states, "I quickly understood that there weren't a lot of minority roles in media, and I wasn't getting any of these other roles." Despite feeling rejected for roles designated for nonminority (i.e., white) children, Songco speaks about his suburban upbringing as unremarkable, with nary any racial or antigay antagonism directed at him.[9] If casting calls informed the young artist of racial stereotypes deployed on screen, Songco always had the suburbs to retreat to; Livingston anesthetized him and others from experiencing racial and, more broadly, social marginalization. Songco admits that the suburbs conferred upon him a degree of privilege as a minority subject. He states, "I grew up pretty privileged, and I didn't experience issues of prejudice growing up." If racism, classism, sexism, homophobia, or other social ills were thought to thrive in the urban domain—New York City, after all, is only about thirty miles from Livingston—or in the imaginary plotlines of television shows, life in suburban Livingston seemingly shielded Songco (and his family) from confrontation: "The postwar suburbs would serve as sanctuaries for the good life where racial and economic homogeneity guaranteed 'safety.'"[10] While Tongson's description is ostensibly about suburban white

Americans, the sentiment uncannily holds true for immigrant families who aspire for the suburban lifestyle. Indeed, the pull of *the good life*, with good schools and a healthy distance from social maladies thought to be endemic to urban settings, has become an all-too-common narrative of validation (aspirational or not) for the suburban lifestyle for middle-class immigrant families.

The oscillations between the realities of racial marginalization from which Songco was shielded as a youth living in the suburbs (a space that insulated him from those realities except during casting calls) and representations of race and racial marginalization that he gleaned from television shows speak to Songco's affective ambivalence and negotiation over claiming racial categories, which continue to this day. I am interested in Songco's affective oscillations, which I contend are symptomatic of the consequences of neoliberal imperatives on Filipino diasporic queer bodies. That is, I read Songco's sentiments against present-day neoliberal discourses of democratic inclusiveness, privacy, and consumption that conspire to produce *postracial* and *homonormative* citizen-subjects.[11] Songco's ambivalence stands betwixt normative imperatives of identifying or, more specifically, speaking for or representing the communities in which he is claimed or that he claims. How might we read Songco's affective oscillations about race and sexuality in light of neoliberalism, which ultimately comes at a social and political cost to some of the very communities in which Songco would find himself? How might we read Songco's artistic practice as a means to visualize his affective oscillations—indeed, imaging his racial anxieties, nervousness, and ambivalences? These affective trajectories index, in part, the continuing aftermath of US empire and its fraught relationship with the Philippines and the Filipino (queer) diaspora at large.

Suburban culture—within which the desire for domestic privacy, political participation, and capitalist consumption are to be found—epitomizes in many ways the domestic goal for many racial minority families and LGBTQ communities in the context of neoliberalism. We cannot dismiss the suburb of Livingston and all that it afforded (or denied) to Songco or its continued influence over his creative projects at present. That is to say, Songco's biography in the suburban space of Livingston becomes a critical archive and lens to comprehend the aesthetic, material, and political stakes of transgressing (hetero)normative aesthetic expectations and the desires of and for queer artists of color like Songco. His childhood suburban experiences are never far from his artistic practice, even after several relocations to study art. Indeed, the underlying conceptualism of his work and the queer forms and affects generated by his art were born out of the suburb of Livingston.

Songco states pointedly, "There's always a specific role for me as a brown child." In many ways, the Songco of today continues to see the world in the same way as the brown child actor from suburban New Jersey, full of nonminority children who get cast for television shows and nonwhite kids like Songco who are relegated to the sidelines. Songco's use of *brown child* unwittingly recuperates the Filipino "little brown brothers," a popular gendered and desexualized or even hypersexualized representation of male Filipinos that was readily disseminated in American culture during the American colonial period in the Philippines (1898–1946). The Philippine Reservation at the 1904 Saint Louis World's Fair only heightened the image of America's "little brown brothers" and the US empire's rhetorical deployment of the stereotypical image for its colonizing mission. Patronizing in usage, the term signifies failed bodies that could be rescued through American intervention, especially education projects. Songco's recuperative speech act, bringing the brown brother figure back from the archives of American empire to the contemporary moment—and in so doing, bringing back the iconographical history and the processes that had shaped its existence—serves as a tactical aesthetic strategy, what I have described elsewhere as an *archive imperative*: a decolonizing artistic praxis performed by Filipino diasporic artists.[12] Indeed, in his pithy statement, he creates a linkage between the visual history of the little brown brother and his own personal history to foreground the strange, if not queer, relationship between Filipinos and US empire. Much like the artists and performers that Asian American literary scholar Sarita See surveys in *The Decolonized Eye*, Songco "respond[s] to the positioning of Filipino America as 'foreign in a domestic sense.'"[13] That is, Filipino America is always already queer in relation to US empire, which produces what See calls "contradictions of a subjectivity"—and this, for Songco, facilitates the affective oscillations captured in his artwork. Songco negotiates this macro queer Philippine–US relationship on a micro level by inserting himself as the brown child, who, rather than accepting his failure, seeks to find resolution despite perhaps the instability of such a task, or even the impossibility. Referring to his creative process, Songco admits, "I always have some kind of worry or nervousness, like some kind of weird feeling, strange, queer feeling, if you will, that I need to resolve." The "weird, strange, and queer feelings" produce desire for closure, yet are often left open ended without any quick and easy answers.

LIVINGSTON IS IN THE HEART

From Livingston, New Jersey, Songco moved out of the suburbs to attend Carnegie Mellon University to get his BFA, with a focus on printmaking. Between his time in the suburbs and moving to the urban setting of Pittsburg for school, he came out as gay. The distance from Livingston undoubtedly influenced critical reflection on the time that Songco spent there as a child. It comes as no surprise, then, that Songco's early work captures the artist grappling with his suburban upbringing and his relationship to it; the suburbs would be Songco's strongest reference point for his work. We see recurring religious themes (influenced by his Catholic upbringing) playing out in his early digital prints. And with his newly proclaimed gay identity, Songco explores the contours of gay of color masculinity through performance and self-portraiture practices. Indeed, in many of his early digital prints, Songco is not the only "Filipino" or racialized minority whose body is pictured. His interrogation of race, gender, and sexuality while at Carnegie Mellon would rely on creating a fictional brotherhood, the Society of 23, whose membership comprised solely himself.

In digital work, Songco reduplicates his body in various staged scenarios. While this process of digital manipulation, of inserting multiple images of himself within his digital prints, might be reduced merely to the narcissistic tendencies of a college-age art student, to do so would be dismissive of Songco's interrogation of his racial and queer identity and his reflection on his experiences in Livingston, a town that he describes as very white and very American. In creating the Society of 23, Songco asserts the centrality of his existence, indeed his very presence, and privileges his brown body over the white ones with whom he grew up and with whom he associated frequently. Influenced by fraternal sociality, Songco notes, "I [was] very interested in group dynamics and social psychology." While the noticeable lack of white bodies in his early work might indicate his disinterest in whiteness, whiteness is never far away. That is, Songco's work captures Livingston's synecdochic relationship to whiteness.

In a 2005 digital print called *growing up catholic*, a Christ-like Songco clad in white rises eerily above the central table as the other sitting Songco bodies gaze up at him. In this and other early digital prints, Songco produces scenes where the artist plays all the characters. No longer on the sidelines during casting calls, Songco becomes the lead actor as well as the supporting cast in all of his work. He admits, "I love acting. I love acting in front of the camera." The attention to the multiple configurations of his body and performances in his practice would continue well after his time at Carnegie Mellon. After his BFA, he moved to San Francisco to pursue an MFA in new genres at the San Francisco Art Institute, working with Allan deSouza among others, and yet he really never leaves Livingston behind.[14]

Even after receiving his MFA, Songco was keen to recuperate his own personal and family histories to create his artwork, much like in his early work. Specifically, television culture becomes an integral repository for Songco to cultivate ideas for his work. Television and his love for it as a child and as an adult provide compositional material, including iconographical details taken from beauty pageants, soap operas, home shopping networks, reality television, and the like, which he is quick to appropriate and employ in his art. As an example, the digital print *The Real World: Pittsburgh* (created between 2007 and 2008) depicts Songco in multiples, again playing all the roles. The work itself references MTV's long-running *Real World* series as a source of inspiration *and* a source of anxiety. If Songco's work—its references to white suburban spaces and his psychic, temporal, and spatial navigation thereof—captures the affective oscillations of identity, his appropriative techniques also cause him affective ambivalence. How might feelings of anxiety drive the production of his artwork? What are we to make of the anxiety of the artist caused by the burden of representation and the weight of racial belonging? As an artist, Songco is well aware of issues of anxiety generated by his artistic practice. In the case of *The Real World: Pittsburgh*, his anxiety stems from both the weighty demands of identificatory practices *and* his appropriative compositional strategies. The affective dimensions of his art will ironically be televised in *The Real World: Pittsburgh*. Songco is keen on creating narratives, often writing elaborate movie and television scripts that relate to his artwork. In these narratives, Songco reworks tropes and motifs from movies and television that work in tandem with his artistic practice in his interrogations of race, gender, and sexuality.

This is especially true for the *Guilty Party* series, which Songco produced long after he finished his graduate studies. Reworking news coverage of actual courtroom dramas by sketching portraits of four prisoners, Songco images affective oscillations that move between humor and seriousness, sentiments that reverberate in other pieces. In *Guilty Party*, we find Songco returning to television, news and educational programming specifically, and recuperating failed bodies, much like the brown child who was objectified by the US empire to justify the occupation of the Philippines at the turn of the twentieth century—or the failed child, sidelined on casting calls. Songco's recuperation of failed bodies in the *Guilty Party* is laden with racial and sexual anxiety and ambivalence, giving viewers pause. While Songco's work is emotionally charged, the portraits become archives of his emotions. Indeed, Songco's art practice becomes a mode of transferring his affective oscillations onto his audience, instantiating the making of Songco as a Filipino diasporic queer killjoy artist.

GUILTY PARTY, *BOMH*, AND SONGCO AS A FILIPINO DIASPORIC QUEER KILLJOY

Inspired by courtroom sketches that are often substitutes for actual footage of real courtroom cases on the news, the *Guilty Party* series draws in viewers by the iconography of prison attire, but more pointedly by the oddly positioned gift boxes that cover the prisoners' faces in the four portraits. By calling the series *Guilty Party*, Songco intentionally puns on the word *party*.[15] The iconic orange jumpsuits link the four individuals and signify their status as prisoners. And the gift boxes that cover the prisoners' heads beckon viewers to partake in another type of "party." As viewers, we are all invited to the prisoners' parties, but they are not happy parties, as their fates have already been decided—they are all guilty, after all. The work inspires both unease and discomfort in its viewers. Do we laugh at the portraits for the strange juxtaposition of gift boxes over the prisoners' heads? Do we approach the portraits with seriousness, since these portraits are supposedly drawn from the courtroom? As we linger in front of the drawings, we can sense the artist's anxious hand in the hurried pastel lines that compose the sketches. This anxiety is transferred to viewers, and we, too, become anxious, uneasy with the sketches, and confounded by the artist's reconfiguration of signifiers in the work.

The portraits produce Songco as a Filipino diasporic queer killjoy, a troublemaker, a queer artist who is drawn to and images bad subjects. His work facilitates the production of affective oscillations, feelings of negativity, ambivalence, and anxiousness coupled with humor through the absurdity of the juxtaposition of signifiers in the portraits. Inspired by Sarah Ahmed's definition of the feminist killjoy, one who "refuses to convene, to assemble, or to meet up over happiness," I read Songco's pastel drawings of prisoners as unhappy Filipino queer beings, who are part of and yet not recognized or acknowledged within the broader Filipino diasporic social, cultural, and intellectual web.[16] Songco as a queer killjoy artist refuses to bow in his artwork to the pressure to recuperate images of happy, good, or heroic Filipino subjects. Rather, Songco's *Guilty Party* performs another type of cultural and epistemic work through his recuperation of failed bodies. That is, through the artist's act of recuperating failed bodies, Songco poses a challenge to the ways in which we think about the larger forces that work to create Filipino diasporic sociality; to the structures that shape our forgetfulness or ignorance of the US empire's role in forging narratives of success (the project of benevolent assimilation, for example); to those who continue to embrace narratives of success and happiness while eschewing failure or failed bodies and missing the opportunity to nuance and show the affective stakes in identificatory practices of racial *and* sexual minorities. While the *Guilty Party* series is overt in its focus on the failed body as the primary subject matter, the series is not Songco's first attempt as a killjoy.

I mark the prisoners pictured in *Guilty Party* as "Filipino" and "queer" for several reasons. On the level of iconography, we might connect the *Guilty Party* prisoners in their orange jumpsuits to the video of 1,500 Filipino inmates in the Cebu Provincial Detention and Rehabilitation Center performing Michael Jackson's "Thriller" music video. The video and the prisoners (including others made after "Thriller") became a worldwide viral phenomenon, with over 54 million views since 2007. We might also associate the iconography of the covered head with the circulation of the Abu Ghraib pictures in 2004 of tortured and abused hooded prisoners—with the violence of the US empire in the Middle East, which uncannily resembles the violence of the US empire in the Philippines at the turn of the twentieth century. These images and videos of prisoners certainly resonate in the *Guilty Party* series. And given Songco's love of television, we might likewise view the success of the television series *Orange Is the New Black* as having an impact on the association of the orange uniform with the incarcerated (queer) body and Songco's use of the television series as a reference.[17]

On the other hand, I am more inclined to return to Songco's earlier work, before *Guilty Party*. Songco uses his body quite deliberately and liberally throughout his artwork, performing multiple roles by duplicating his image multiple times in the mise-en-scène of his digital prints, including self-portraits. On self-portraiture, Songco notes, "I took self portrait photography for a very long time. . . . I love acting in front of the camera. . . . [I]t was very natural for me to pose and take a photo."

We find Songco performing the role of the killjoy in works that predate *Guilty Party,* through his appropriation of negative signifiers to picture his Filipino queer self. In *GayGayGay Robe* (2011) (plate 15), for example, Songco transforms rainbow-colored fabric (iconic for the gay pride flag) into a Ku Klux Klan robe and hood that the artist wears during a gay pride event. The iconographic references to the white KKK hood and white apparel are also found in the digital prints *Hosanna* (2012), *God Bless (Miss) America* (2012), and *Confessional* (2014). The three prints were inspired by movies and television shows, and they image Songco performing whiteness—as the star of a home-shopping TV show, a beauty pageant winner, and a reality TV housewife, respectively—by wearing all-white clothes with white shopping bags over his head. The bag shape has an uncanny resemblance to a KKK hood. Adjacent to the portraits of the characters is tongue-in-cheek text that provides context for the mise-en-scène.[18] The three digital prints, through the juxtaposition of the white characters and the absurd text, illuminate the affective oscillations of the artist. By appropriation of television characters and provocative staging of whiteness, the artist recuperates the failed bodies of the KKK, intentionally or not, and their negative associations as a means of negotiation of whiteness and white privilege through his resignification strategies. On his attraction to the white race, Songco states, "I think it's a super interest in power." The artist's use of his body to perform each role in the work creates a profound conceptual connection between his (failed) body and the prisoners pictured in the *Guilty Party* series. Songco's embrace of these failed bodies in his art is an integral component of his conceptualism, which targets the affective dimensions of failed or negative signifiers and indexes his ongoing negotiation of race, masculinity, hetero- and homonormativity, and sociality.

In the digital prints *Hosanna*, *God Bless (Miss) America*, and *Confessional*, Songco's face remains unseen because of the white shopping bag that hides his head. The iconography of the covered head first appeared five years before the *Guilty Party* series. In 2009, Songco created the *BOMH* series, an acronym for "Bag Over My Head." The eleven prints of the *BOMH* series are self-portraits, with the artist shown in various scenes with a variety of shopping bags covering his head. Again, Songco acts the main role in each portrait, but the bodies are faceless. In their faceless states, Songco disrupts the desire to identify and to be identified, which are at the core of the sense of belonging to a particular community. He kills the joy in the process of knowing the pictured bodies and locating them to their proper communal spaces through disidentification.

Songco's visual oeuvre is tinged with racial anxiety and other affective oscillations about race, gender, and sexuality. This is particularly true in the

BOMH series, which is not grounded in self-hatred per se; rather, the racial anxiety stems from Songco's direct interrogation of his body and his attempts to locate himself within the larger Filipino diasporic social and cultural web. His is a Filipino queer body in the portraits, unhappily cast as foreign and imprisoned by the shopping bag, and consumerism writ large, within the neoliberal domestic landscape. Ahmed writes, "Unhappy subjects hence feel alienated from the world as they experience the world as alien."[19] Referring to the *BOMH* series, Songco states, "I had really bad acne and I just thought . . . no one wants to buy a photo or no one wants to see a photo of someone with a lot of acne because you don't see that in media. . . . On the very base level, it sort of started out as, 'I want to take a portrait of myself but I don't have the face, I don't have the proper skin.'" From his statement, Songco the brown, television-watching child actor reappears and examines the world from the periphery. Disgruntled for not having the "proper skin," he strips away markers of identity by hiding his face, conveying a cognizance of the normative processes that produce social cohesion and standards of beauty. What does it mean for a Filipino queer artist like Songco to disidentify with identificatory practices? Covering his face with a bag becomes Songco's trademark killjoy act—an act that he returns to repeatedly after the *BOMH* series.

Instead of the realism produced by digital photography (and exploited by the artist in his meticulous work of inserting multiple Songco figures within the digital frames), the portraits in the *Guilty Party* series are figure studies of Songco as a prisoner. Songco's anxieties over race and sexuality culminate to produce the quintessential negative, repellent subject. This negative racial and sexualized subject formation begs the question of what Asian American studies, and more specifically, Filipino American studies, would look like if we took a step away from the drive for cultural and racial cohesion by recuperating bodies tainted by failure from what Ahmed calls the "unhappy archives."[20]

(UN)HAPPILY EVER AFTER

The Filipino queer artist as killjoy, I argue, is a critical subject position that Songco embodies and embraces in his work. It is through the negative, failed, or queer bodies that he inhabits and the affective oscillations or dissonances from the killing of joy that we, as viewers, might gauge the limits of heteronormative *and* homonormative sociality within the current neoliberal moment. If happiness, as Ahmed says, is "a form of world making," we might also think about how recuperating what she calls "troublemakers, dissenters, killers of joy" from the "unhappy archives"—may create alternative worlds that allow us to see, feel, and imagine the constraints of heteronormative and homonormative sociality, especially inside racial minority communities.[21] The worlds that Songco creates as a Filipino diasporic queer killjoy artist allow for the production of alternative affective structures and social modalities. His attraction to and imaging of prisoners may even throw a much-needed wrench into the methodologies we use in our own intellectual labor. How might we understand Asian America using negativity and failure as our critical lens?

"To kill joy," Ahmed writes, "is to open life, to make room for life, to make room for possibility, for chance."[22] Indeed, to read Songco's *Guilty Party* as well as his other works as art produced by a killjoy artist is to create opportunities for dialogue and spaces that embrace difference within otherwise restrictive social, cultural, and intellectual geographies during these neoliberal times.

Negotiating Desire and (Queer) Masculinity: An Interview with Kenneth Tam

JAN CHRISTIAN BERNABE

On June 6, 2014, Jan Christian Bernabe interviewed Kenneth Tam in his Los Angeles studio to talk about his sculptural work Blue Pillow with Stand *(2013) and HD video* The Compression Is Not Subservient to the Explosion; It Gives It Increased Force *(2011). Tam spoke about his encounters with strangers met on Craigslist who feature in his video work, including one piece that conveys a (queer) negotiation of masculinity. His work adds to ongoing discussions about race, masculinity, and sexuality as they are expressed in sculptural and video art.*

JAN CHRISTIAN BERNABE: I happened upon a review of your installation [*Blue Pillow with Stand*] (plate 16) in *ArtForum* in 2013. I kept looking at the image of the blue cushion against the black backdrop. I read it in very sexualized manner. Not to sound too crass, I thought, "Oh, that's an asshole."

KENNETH TAM: Yeah, totally. Or a used condom.

JCB: I remember that desire, sex, and perversion were not even mentioned in that review.

KT: Right, it's kind of perfect that it continues to be repressed in that way.

JCB: That was my introduction to your work. I started to see a reoccurring motif of orifices and phallic symbols.

KT: Well, can I ask if you've seen any of the videos?

JCB: No, that's what I was going to ask you about.

KT: I feel like that's a pretty big part of what it is that I do. I wasn't sure what exactly you have seen of mine.

JCB: I've seen video screen shots.

KT: I think it's pretty important that we watch it then. I feel like [*The Compression Is Not Subservient to the Explosion; It Gives It Increased Force* (2011) (plate 17)] foregrounds a lot of everything. My body of work consisted of sculpture and video. Video for a while was the only thing I was doing, so I didn't bracket it as one particular body of work. I was making videos with individuals off of the Internet, particularly Craigslist. But it's not important where they come from. These are people I don't know who, sometimes I pay, sometimes I don't, but with whom I have no previous relationship. We do these things in front of a camera in their home, just us two. It's about this intimacy. It's about awkwardness, about this random encounter with people. I've been doing them for a number of years now.

They have become more explicit in their content, in what I'm willing to do, which makes sense as you're building up the confidence and the comfort of exploring the things I'm interested in. This particular video [*The Compression Is Not Subservient to the Explosion*], which you said you saw a still of, is with an individual. Typically I post ads on why I'm looking for people to work with, a pretty generic advertisement. And this individual, we actually won't see in the video, he responded. He had his own desires for me. This is interesting because this has never happened to me before. People usually just respond and say, "Yeah, I'll do what you want." But this guy had his own agenda for me. And long story short, the video that you'll see here is actually this sort of document of the negotiations through his desires and what I wanted to do and also was willing to do for him. So the video is actually this compromise. It's an ongoing negotiation.

JCB: Did that take you off guard?

KT: A little bit, sure. I wasn't expecting it, but at the same time, it definitely piqued my curiosity. I explored it and I pursued it. This is essentially the product of that encounter. And [the title of the video] is a quote from Bataille if that matters.[1] We can talk as we're watching it.

JCB: Do you know the name of the man in the video? Or is it totally anonymous?

KT: Yeah. It's rarely a totally anonymous encounter. We've met each other, more or less.

JCB: You've edited it down?

KT: Oh yeah. This is about a three- or four-hour encounter.[2]

JCB: Did he want to be in the box?

KT: No, that was my idea. So this setup was essentially my idea.

JCB: And he has a box cutter in there?

KT: Yes.

JCB: Is he naked in there?

KT: No.

JCB: Did you know he was into men?

KT: Oh, of course. He is a photographer, and he wanted me to do a nude modeling session.

JCB: So, how are you feeling during this whole thing?

KT: I was pretty nervous. I didn't know exactly where things would go. We talked about a general understanding of the arc. When I make these videos, I have to be cognizant. I'm the director, but also a participant at the same time. I was pretty nervous.

JCB: Did he actually reach out and grab you?

KT: Yes. And, you know, the other videos I've made are not nearly as explicit as this one. There are a range of interactions. But almost all of them involve another man. I mean, I have made some with women, but I think my interest is dealing with complications of homosocial relationships. And I think this was definitely the most erotic of all the things I've done.

JCB: Speaking from the standpoint of being queer, I'm going to borrow a term from one of the participants in the book, Tina Takemoto, who uses the term *queer speculation*—or the speculative queer dimension that one who is queer looks for. And so, not even knowing how you identify, I just thought, "Oh, this is really a butt, and it's queer." Then I saw the still of *The Compression Is Not Subservient to the Explosion*, and I thought that was just an extension of your negotiation of identity, because you're implicating yourself in there.

KT: Yeah.[3]

JCB: There's this unknowing. Even after watching that, I'm thinking, "Well, is Kenneth queer?" That's why I asked you, "How did you feel in that moment?" Was there an attraction? Or was that piece about a negotiation of your own masculinity or identity?

KT: I think definitely more the latter. It's evolved quite a bit, since I've been doing them for a number of years now, but I was always thinking about it originally as "the potentials" that can happen when two people come together and explore intimacy.

JCB: With respect to how one locates him- or herself, in terms of being gay, being straight, being white, being black.

KT: I think that's unavoidable. But at the same time, it's not what drives the encounters necessarily. I like what you said about how even after seeing that, you're still not sure what I am. I think that's important because I'm not making these videos as necessarily an exploration of identity and how perverse things can get or how confusing or how ambiguous things can become. [I am not] clearly stating [my] relationship to the other person. [You are] understanding it from just what I'm giving you. It's always about this sort of strange potential that can happen between two people.

JCB: When you start negotiating even before an encounter, does your race matter?

KT: It matters in the fact that I can't hide who I am. I'm not expressly marketing myself as an Asian individual in my ads either.

JCB: I've seen your ads. They're very generic. You don't say your race or anything. But I wonder whether, especially in that encounter, he knew what you looked like before you entered that room?

KT: I'd been in that room a few times before the video was made. And so he definitely knew who I was. I knew who he was. We'd seen each other in person. There was an understanding of who I was, where I was coming from, where he was coming from, some of the expectations that were going to be explored, what he wanted to do. Ultimately, I didn't consummate the thing that he wanted from me. He was very explicit about direct physical intimacy, almost to the point of being manipulative. The box was kind of a safety mechanism for myself: a prop. But also this thing that limited what could happen. But [it] also added to the tension.

JCB: You had a lot of control in the video in that you could just walk away.

KT: And I'm ultimately the one editing this.

JCB: I wonder whether your sense of control was influencing his desire to get to you.

KT: Essentially, I think this whole thing was probably a huge turn-on for him. Even though he didn't get exactly what he wanted, the strangeness of the encounter and the fact that I was being so willing must've been very exciting. And to have it recorded was probably another dimension.

JCB: There is an affective dimension where it is about desire. It is about the unexpected. What do you get out of it outside of making the art?

KT: I don't know if I get anything necessarily [personal] out of the art. I don't like to think of these as personal videos. I put myself in them in order to create the video. I think these are probably learning experiences for myself. What you said about negotiating my masculinity and seeing the limits of that and testing those—I think that has been helpful and interesting. But I think it's ultimately about the creation of the video. About setting the stage for this sort of encounter and do[ing] something interesting for the camera.

JCB: I like the idea of ambivalence projected in the video. You're stringing your viewer along, but the viewer never gets the final piece.

KT: Correct.

JCB: And that, to me, is very queer. There's a certain level of expectation that we have when we watch a linear video. There's a beginning, middle, end. For whatever reason, you deny us a huge piece of that ending. For me, that's frustrating but also cool because it opens up more questions. There's a queer aesthetic that you're projecting by trying to play with viewers' expectations.

KT: The things I choose [to do] have an overt sexual connotation. At the same time, I would hope that you can't locate [me] precisely, like you can't say, "Oh, this is the product of a gay artist or a straight artist." I think that would be really unfortunate.

JCB: To reduce it to that level?

KT: Absolutely. Or to be able to think that you know what this is immediately. If you could locate that so quickly, I think that would be a sort of failure on my part as an artist. At the same time, the goal of the work is not to remain sexually ambiguous. I think there are other things I'm trying to explore.

JCB: Right. "Oh, you're Asian or Asian American." And so there's an expectation that your pieces are going to be about that identity. I didn't even think of that because the first piece I saw was *The Blue Asshole*. The challenge of a critic writing about Asian American art is how to avoid being identitarian. Do you think about issues of being Asian American?

KT: You know, I do and I don't. I don't in the sense that there's no overt sort of identity politics in my work, or at least that's not why I'm producing the things I am producing. I wouldn't know how I would fit into any sort of larger discussion of contemporary Asian American art other than the fact that I am that artist.

JCB: There are particular ways desire and sex get amplified once you unveil or show or expose your race.

KT: I definitely understand that being an Asian person has its own baggage in terms of the erotic.

JCB: I wonder whether that factored into the box video because you were wielding the power. Because you are Asian, you were subverting that erotic baggage.

KT: I'm the one who's setting up the situation and controlling it. But it's not just me who's "on top." I think there's this constant negotiation of power and desire.

JCB: How would you compare that box video to your videos with women?

KT: If there's a woman who is equally desiring of me, or who was in that box, it could be very similar.

JCB: But it was important for you, right? You sought him out.

KT: No, he sought me out.

JCB: Oh, he did?

KT: Yeah. But like I said, he responded to my ad with his own project. I had an idea, but he wasn't interested in it at all. He proposed his own project.

JCB: Where did you place the ad?

KT: It might have been "Casual Encounters" [on Craigslist], one of the few times I posted there. It's pretty much just erotic encounters.

JCB: But for men looking for men?

KT: I don't remember. It was probably generic. I probably did either/or. But he responded with his own counterproposal and took it from there. I think what was important was that it did test my idea of masculinity in a way that a woman couldn't. I wanted a tension, that's the charge. The violation would feel different from a woman.

JCB: Was there pleasure to be gained for you during that encounter?

KT: Probably very little. Probably next to none. This is information that you would never get from just watching the video. The whole thing was not about pleasure for myself. I think there was very little that was pleasurable except knowing that I got this very bizarre document.

JCB: Okay.

KT: The next video that I'm working on right now, it's going to be with my father. And I feel like there must be some level of wanting to learn from that.

JCB: And why with your father?

KT: Because I have a fraught relationship with him. I got a small grant and [I proposed producing] videos with individuals who would play my father, and we would create these intimate activities exploring masculinity, with the idea that masculinity was a concept learned, passed down from father to son. I wanted to play with that relationship. [So] why don't I actually just work with my father? It seems like a much more intense, fraught encounter than working with other individuals. I don't have a great sense of physical intimacy with my father. He wasn't necessarily around during my upbringing. It was mostly my mother. He was overseas working. He was doing other things. I never developed this physical closeness with him that probably other people will have had in a more adjusted sort of father-son relationship. That is possibly the whole impetus for starting this project—a way to understand what I've been doing [up to] now. Why this fascination of working with men? [I'm] thinking maybe it is to do with my father.

JCB: Did you tell your father about this project? How did he respond?

KT: I asked him, and he was fine with it. But I haven't given him any specifics. I think he sees it as an opportunity to bond with me or something. I think he's kind of excited by that prospect.

JCB: So if you don't mind me asking, is your father an immigrant?

KT: He didn't grow up in the States. He came from Hong Kong. But he's been here for quite a while.

JCB: This leads me to a question that I've been holding off until now: how do you identify?

KT: Chinese American, straight.

JCB: How do you react to people reading you as queer? Or reading your work as queer?

KT: To the casual observer, they probably do think I'm a gay man doing this work. But I think that's interesting. That adds another layer of complication that I self-identify as hetero, making work that is so loaded with homo.

JCB: Eroticism, right?

KT: Yeah. At first I was very apprehensive about that. Getting into these more curious areas of Craigslist. It really made me question my identity in a way like, "What am I getting myself into? Do I really want to go down this path? Am I prepared to do this?" Clearly I've become more and more comfortable with it. I embrace all the complexities and the problems of this sort of thing.

JCB: I read this ambivalence as queer.

KT: Absolutely. Well, what is being straight? Does it even matter ultimately? Going back to what you were saying about identifying as Asian American and whether or not I foreground that in my work, I'd say, define what Asian American even is. I find that term to be so problematic and so fluid. It encompasses so many things that maybe other minorities don't have to contend with. If you're going to, let's say, curate a show about Asian Americans, and you put me in there as someone who doesn't foreground their identity, you kind of have to figure out what that even means to you.

JCB: Right. The very premise of the show should establish that.

KT: So I would hope. It shouldn't just be a given that Asian American is a static identity, when it, in fact, encompasses a multitude of backgrounds.

JCB: Where did you grow up? Where were you educated?

KT: I grew up in Queens, New York. And I pretty much lived there my entire life until I came out to LA for graduate school. I went to the Cooper Union for my undergrad. I graduated in ’04. I came out to USC [University of Southern California] and I graduated in 2010.

JCB: What do you call yourself: a sculptor or an artist or . . . ?

KT: People just ask me what I do, and I tell them I make sculpture and video.

Chapter 4

Queering Methodology

Queer Zen: Unyoking Genealogy in Asian American Art History

ALPESH KANTILAL PATEL

My interest in exploring Asian American art history through a queer methodological framework has surprisingly led me to abstract works from the 1960s by an artist who is not of Asian descent—Cy Twombly (1928–2011)—and his interlocutors, especially Roland Barthes (1915–1980).[1] Given that much work remains to make visible the artworks of US-based artists of Asian descent—lesbian, gay, bisexual, trans, questioning, queer, and intersexual (LGBTQI) identified or not—my approach appears at best peculiar and naïve and at worst flippant and irresponsible.[2] This chapter, stripped from the context of this volume, could indeed lean toward the latter and be construed as a hyperbolic provocation that masks its shortcoming. However, I want to underscore that my essay should be read *relationally* with and through the other interviews, artist statements, and scholarly essays in this book, which do make visible the work of artists of Asian descent that are LGBTQI identified. Moreover, this chapter challenges how one might approach visibility and inclusion, especially in the context of LGBTQI-identified artists of Asian descent and their artworks, which are largely absent from narratives of mid-twentieth-century American abstraction. I suggest that what counts as evidence in art history has to be rethought—a point to which I will return later in this essay—and that Asian American art history has to be recast as *not* only tied to genealogy.

Indeed, binding or yoking Asian American art history to genealogy is what has led to the occlusion of artworks exploring LGBTQI themes and created by LGBTQI-identified artists of Asian descent in the first place. Sexuality is at best a secondary area of interest for this subdiscipline of art history. For instance, the 2008 publication of *Asian American Art: A History, 1850–1970* was a watershed moment for making visible the contributions of a broad range of artists of Asian descent. The volume includes 150 artist biographies and

400 reproductions. However, a quick glance at the book's index reveals that words such as *gay*, *lesbian*, *queer*, *bisexual*, *transgender*, *gender*, and *sexuality* are missing. Supplementing art history is an important but always already fraught exercise. Jacques Derrida's writings on the supplement are instructive in this regard. As he writes, "[The supplement] adds itself [and] is a surplus, a plenitude enriching another plenitude. . . . But the supplement supplements. It adds only to replace." Supplementing art history is a frustrating task that can "never fully . . . deliver on its promise of inclusivity."[3]

I suggest that we shift attention from authorship or "roots and routes," around which my discussion above pivots, to an equally valid (and flawed) subject, namely Asian American art history as a category of discursive knowledge that may or may not involve artists of Asian descent.[4] The latter is along the lines of how Kandice Chuh suggests we should approach Asian American studies in *Imagine Otherwise: On Asian Americanist Critique*. Chuh is concerned with literature rather than artworks, but her point is transferable to Asian American art history. She writes that rather than evincing a "desire for subjectivity," the field of Asian American studies should be "subjectless."[5] She notes that a "strategic *anti*-essentialism," rather than bounded notions of identity, is what coheres Asian American studies.[6] Indeed, it is ironic that despite postmodernism's troubling of the author as the repository of meaning, as crystallized in Barthes's proclamation of the "death of the author," the author still remains quite important in art's histories.[7]

Thus I precariously linger at the edges of a more specifically *queer*, or troubled, Asian American art history. *Queer* signals the importance of sexuality to my analysis. Indeed, as I intimated earlier, Asian American art historical scholarship has hardly focused on themes of sexuality. Moreover, a decidedly Asian American framework ensures this discussion of sexuality is transnational.[8] Scholars such as Margo Machida have already laid the groundwork for the importance of thinking beyond the frame of nationality, and that transnationality—and by extension transregionality—is embedded in an Asian American framework.[9] In addition, I mobilize *queer* as not just a noun but a verb: it is a destabilizing force that cuts across various categories of identification but still in relation to Asian American sexualities and sexual identification broadly construed. A *queer* and *Asian American* framework for my investigation demands that we think about nationality, sexuality, and genealogy as slippery pivot points rather than fixed categories.[10]

I make one more important digression before explaining how Twombly's artworks and the writings about them became central to this project. I briefly explore discourses of identity in artistic meaning in the post-2000 period to further ground and situate my points above in the context of the art world. A good place to begin is Thelma Golden's use of the phrase *post-black* to describe her 2001 *Freestyle* exhibition at the Studio Museum in Harlem. For Golden, the term was used to refer to work of artists of the African diaspora. More specifically, it primarily served as a generational and formal marker that distinguished the work of artists who came of age in the heyday of identity politics in the late 1980s and early 1990s from those who came of age in the late 1990s and early 2000 period.[11] For *New Yorker* critic Peter Schjeldahl, however, the term signaled the end of an era in which identity was important in the art world. Ironically, he relegates identity to the past as a historical formation and reintroduces the importance of disembodied "form" as crucial to artistic taste.[12] In other words, a curious—though not conscious—alliance formed between Golden, who is sympathetic to identity politics, and Schjeldahl, who has always been suspicious of artistic meaning being tied to any notion of identity.

Both agree that we are in a "post-identity" era: Golden does so to distinguish between different waves of artistic production concerned with primarily racial, gendered, and sexual difference, but seems to fall back on conceptualizing identity as positional or fixed; while Schjeldahl suggests that we are post or over identity, but only to return artistic value back to a disembodied art object.[13] What follows is an attempt to avoid both of these positions while not removing the activism that underpins the production of Asian American art histories. I will proffer a model for exploring identity (broadly construed) through Zen Buddhism, or more specifically, *queer* Zen Buddhism.[14]

QUEER ZEN

This approach is inspired by art historian and queer studies scholar Jonathan Katz's groundbreaking work in which he theorizes that the abstract works of Agnes Martin from the 1960s can be read as expressions of a queer-inflected Zen Buddhism.[15] I was first introduced to Katz's work on Martin through a YouTube video of a lecture he gave on this topic as part of a symposium connected to an exhibition he co-curated with David C. Ward at the National Portrait Gallery in Washington, DC, in 2010, *Hide/Seek: Difference and Desire in American Portraiture*.[16] I think highly of Katz's scholarship; however, my immediate reaction was skepticism. I thought it was a stretch to discuss sexuality in the context of Martin and her work, given that she never publicly identified as a lesbian, and especially considering the nonrepresentational character of her artistic practice. Katz, though, was careful not to focus on authorial details as "truths." As Katz perspicaciously notes in his article on Martin, sexuality does not necessarily come in forms that are legible: "Where would we be if we made acknowledgement the truth test of art-historical knowledge?"[17] Moreover, Martin's works have often been linked to Zen Buddhism, which was important to a number of American artists not of Asian descent whose works emerged in the 1950s and 1960s.[18] Alexandra Munroe's 2009 groundbreaking exhibition *The Third Mind: American Artists Contemplate Asia, 1860–1989* at the Guggenheim Museum in New York City explores this topic in some detail.[19] Katz makes convincing parallels between the nondualistic conception of identity often associated with Zen and queer as an unstable signifier of sexual identity. Through Martin's work, he radically reworks her negation of identification as a lesbian into an expression of identity that uncannily prefigures queer understandings of sexual identity.

Expanding upon Katz's brilliant work, if sexuality is a referent for queer, then I suggest that the region could be one for Zen since the East and Asia are frequently associated or conflated with it. Moreover, this opens an avenue to mobilize queer Zen to explore similarly pared-down artworks by artists of Asian descent. In the same way that Martin's abstract yet embodied artworks prefigure theories of sexuality as queer or unstable, can the latter foreshadow contemporary theories of Asian American identity as transnational, or blurred across regions or nations? My initial approach to this essay was to explore abstract artworks by artists of Asian descent to answer this question, but then I came across the writings of Roland Barthes on the works of Cy Twombly.[20] They were intriguing for two reasons. Firstly, Barthes is not known for his writing on artworks, so why did Twombly seek him out as he did to write about his artworks?[21] What did Twombly's work *do* that compelled Barthes to accept his invitation? Secondly, Twombly had attended lectures of the Buddhist monk D. T. Suzuki at Columbia University in New York City in 1951 and a number of Cage's legendary performances in the summer of 1952 at Black Mountain College.[22] In contradistinction to Cage, whose indebtedness to Zen Buddhism and Suzuki is explicit, however, how these lectures affected Twombly's artistic practice is unclear. So, why did Barthes turn to Zen when writing about his artworks?

I will argue first that Barthes's writing and Twombly's artworks suggest a queer understanding of sexuality that is integral to answering the questions I have posed. I am not interested in "outing" Twombly and Barthes or gauging intentionality (which, of course, is mediated, too). What I am interested in, though, is how Barthes's writing and Twombly's work might suggest a queer approach to sexuality, just as Katz argued that Martin's work did. Secondly, I reread Barthes's writing to suggest that it prefigures (if implicitly) Katz's writings on queer Zen in ways that move beyond discussions of sexuality as unfixed. That is, I argue that Barthes's writings indicate that Twombly's works gesture toward the notions of regionality and nationality as always already queer, or unstable.[23] Therefore, Twombly's work and Barthes's writing can help think through queer notions of nationality, as well as sexuality, that are important for the construction of a queer Asian American art history.

TWOMBLY'S *FERRAGOSTO* SERIES

To further animate my points above, I begin by exploring the five works that compose Twombly's *Ferragosto* series from 1961, and then filter my findings through Barthes's writing as well as other interlocutors of Twombly's larger body of work. Each canvas of the *Ferragosto* series is roughly the same size (5½ by 6½ feet) and constructed of the same materials—oil paint, lead pencil, and wax crayon. The corporeal body is evoked in several ways. Body parts—penises, ass cheeks, and breasts—hover somewhere between representation and abstraction throughout the entire series. Intense colors such as pink, red, and brown are suggestive of flesh, blood, and excrement, respectively.[24] (Art historian Elisabeth J. Trapp even suggests that "one can smell the decay" of trash rotting in the summer months of August during which Twombly made these works.)[25] Also, Twombly's handprints are visible—such as in *Ferragosto IV* (plate 18)—indexing a trace of the artist's body on the canvas. By *Ferragosto V*, he begins to work over the entire canvas with smears of paint, and there is more evidence of the artist's direct use of his fingers rather than brushes to paint. Finally, while there is an economy of paint early in the series, such as in *Ferragosto II* (see plate 19), by *Ferragosto V* the generous amounts of thickly applied paint give the works a tactile quality. Claire Daigle's description of *Ferragosto V* captures the work's dynamism and corporeality: "A thickly encrusted palette of brown, pink and red takes on a viscerality paired in the work with a body parcelled into pictograms: pendulous breasts, erupting penises, scatological posteriors."[26] Perhaps more than the tactility, though, I argue that Twombly's complex smudging, smearing, and scratching onto his large canvases beckon the viewer.

The artworks' size and materiality coupled with the semi-abstracted body parts rendered in colors evoking the body blur the boundaries between viewer and artwork. Given that male and female sexual organs (albeit abstracted) populate each of the canvases of the series in varying degrees, this intertwining can be considered erotically charged, even if ambiguously so. Of course, it cannot be so easily coded as heteroerotic or homoerotic, especially given that I am arguing the works elicit an embodied relationship with a contingent viewer.

Barthes writes that "whatever is scribbled it [the work] comes as an enigmatic supplement."[27] At least implicitly, Barthes is invoking Derrida's aforementioned supplement: Twombly's works in his estimation effectively act as supplements: meaning is never complete. For Barthes, Twombly's works produce a gap between sign and signified—and this space is one in which connections can be made and unmade. Following Barthes's description of Twombly's painting as producing gaps, the *Ferragosto* works could be said to engender a productive space of possibility for reworking norms of sexual identity as queer.

This reading gains more traction when Barthes writes the titles of Twombly's paintings. The often semilegible inscriptions found on them function as citations. That is, their meanings are identified through the very act of naming. Art historian Rosalind Krauss expands upon Barthes's thinking by invoking J. L. Austin's notion of the performative, in which to say something is also to do something.[28] The classic example of the performative is the utterance "I now pronounce you man and wife" in a marriage ceremony, which "hails or interpellates" the two individuals as a married couple.[29] In other words, speech acts simultaneously do what they say. Krauss writes that "it is thus a linguistic operation in which reference is suspended in favor of action."[30] Barthes, too, notes that Twombly's work "does not derive from a concept (*mark*) but rather an activity (*marking*)."[31] Trace is the record of a gesture, and "line is visible action."[32] Thus, the title *Ferragosto* does not illustrate the content of the work but refers to the action of naming it as such.[33] Krauss's essay appears in the September 1994 issue of *Artforum*, a little less than a year after Judith Butler's "Critically Queer" appeared in *GLQ: A Journal of Gay and Lesbian Studies*. Whether or not Krauss was aware of the latter is unclear, but given that performativity—and its productive misfires—is the bedrock of queer theory, it seems that extending the discussion above to gender and sexuality is appropriate.

For Barthes, though, deconstruction was not enough to describe Twombly's works. He turned to Zen. For instance, Barthes observes that Twombly's mark-making is similar to the Japanese Zen notion of *satori*: "A sudden (and sometimes very tenuous) break in our causal logic."[34] Interestingly, this has parallels with Butler's theorization of the break in a performative that can redirect norms. Of more importance is that, for Barthes, the works engendered an affect that he felt was possible only outside the West: "If we required some reference for this [Twombly's] art, we could go looking for it only very far away. . . . outside the West."[35] Therefore, we can argue that Barthes via Twombly's work does not so much contain Zen to the East as position it as neither Eastern nor Western: it is effectively transregional. His essay suggests a queer relation not only to sexuality but also to regionality.

BRIEF NOTES ON QUEER METHODS

As intimated at the beginning of this essay, a queer exploration of sexuality and regionality would necessarily involve exploring silences and literally what is not said. That is, it is important to note that my investigation requires methods beyond a formal analysis of Twombly's works or a recontextualizing of the writing about them that I do above. These methods can only be described as queer or unusual for art history. I utilize evidence that is often anecdotal or not written, said, or known. For instance, Barthes had the perfect moment to "out" himself when he wrote the preface to Renaud Camus's sexually explicit *Tricks*, but he refused the call to do so. In his preface he writes: "Ultimately, the attribute is of no importance; what society will not tolerate is that I should be . . . *nothing*, or more precisely, that the *something* that I am should be openly expressed as provisional, revocable, insignificant, inessential, in a word irrelevant."[36] I will return to Barthes's poignant entreaty to a specifically activist "society," but for the moment what is of interest is the refusal to identify or to be "interpellated" per Louis Althusser as anything but "*nothing*."

In a related manner, hardly anything exists regarding Twombly's sexuality. However, what does exist is innuendo or gossip, especially regarding a romantic relationship with the artist Robert Rauschenberg.[37] Irit Rogoff notes how exploring gossip in visual studies can be productive: "In Foucauldian terms it [gossip] serves the purpose through negative differentiation, of constituting a category of respectable knowledge. . . . In Derridean terms gossip allows for the formal boundaries of the genre and its outlawed, excessive and uncontrollable narratives."[38] Rogoff compellingly argues that a consideration of gossip can be useful in reassessing the mechanisms that bound and define certain knowledge as "true" or "acceptable." Drawing on Rogoff, Gavin Butt uses gossip to reexamine art world practices in the 1950s and 1960s, especially in relation to homosexuality.[39]

My point here is that innuendo is all the evidence that may be available given that any discussion of Twombly's sexuality would have understandably fallen outside of Cold War–era America as a (drawing on Rogoff) "category of respectable knowledge." The intellectual history regarding the links among the Cold War, sexuality, and artistic practice can be traced back to a prescient article written by Moira Roth in 1977.[40] What is important to note is that this category of respectable knowledge was consolidated through not only an active homophobia but also xenophobia. Indeed, "homosexuals and Communism were quickly conflated" by McCarthyism, as the State Department's own archives now readily admit.[41] Moreover, the Japanese internment camps were still fresh in the minds of many Americans of Asian descent.

TWOMBLY'S DOUBLE GESTURES: TOWARD BARTHES'S TRANSNATIONAL ZEN

More recently, Jonathan Katz has expanded on Roth's groundbreaking work to explore the activist potential of silence.[42] This is important as I shift my focus to what Twombly has said about his artworks, or rather what he has not said. That is to say, Twombly was largely reticent about his work. Katz writes that silence can be "performative" by removing "claims to meaning which are usually recognised and solidified through language and speech acts. Silence therefore allows us to reflect upon the ways in which we create and construct meanings and possibilities, and this reflective process involves the recognition that our socio-cultural constructions are always situated, conditional and partial."[43] In this way, I will consider what Twombly says as "partial" and take his performative silence as an opportunity to extrapolate a range of different possible meanings.

Twombly gave only two interviews during his lifetime, one conducted by David Sylvester in 2000 and the other by Nicholas Serota in 2007.[44] Indeed, when Nicholas Serota writes about the "rare opportunity" he had to interview Twombly, he is referring to Twombly's long-standing refusal to speak about his work; however, the subtext is the importance of getting Twombly to speak—as if his words would complete the meaning of his works.[45] At the end of his interview with Twombly, Serota says, "Cy, I think we've got plenty," to which Twombly replies: "You've got enough. And if there's something I didn't say, you could make it up."[46] Twombly's response could be read as indifference, cynicism, or a defensive posture regarding art historical writing and criticism in general. Given the manner in which his works had been excoriated both within the art world (consider the vitriolic response to his 1964 Castelli Gallery exhibition)[47] and without the art world (the characterization of his artistic practice as akin to the scribbles of a child),[48] this is certainly reasonable. However, his statement could also be considered evidence of the artist downplaying the weight of his spoken words in his works' meaning. Then again, he does not necessarily completely negate the importance of his words either, which could just as well signal to Serota that he should not "make it up."

More to the point, Twombly's response produces a chain of meanings, which mirrors the functioning of his *Ferragosto* works, as I explore in the next section. Twombly manages to deflect attention from himself and his work to his interviewer. That is, though he literally gets the last word, he does so in a manner that delays it from ever arriving. This double gesture of the artist—providing insight into his practice and simultaneously erasing its potential influence on the meaning of his works—produces a Derridean supplement that "is in reality différance," the simultaneous process of difference and deferral, which prevents the definitive closure of the meaning of Twombly's work.[49]

Again, it is important to underscore that for Barthes, deconstruction was not enough to characterize Twombly's works. He turned to Zen. For instance, Barthes ends both of his essays on Twombly's work with the following quotation from the Tao Tê Ching, which seems to resonate with the double gesture I have just outlined:

> *He produces without taking for himself;*
> *He acts without expectation;*
> *His work done, he is not attached to it;*
> *and since he is not attached to it,*
> *his work will remain.*[50]

In so doing, a queer relation not only to sexuality but also to the region—specifically the East or Asia, the referents for Zen—becomes possible. To be sure, Barthes's writings on Zen at first glance veer toward orientalism, the most egregious example of which is as follows: "If we required some reference for this [Twombly's] art, we could go looking for it only very far away, outside painting, outside the West, outside the historical period, at the very limit of meaning."[51] The West/non-West dualism is simplistic and reductive, as is the implicit signification of the non-West as geographically ("very far away"), temporally ("outside the historical period"), and discursively ("outside painting" and therefore art history) distinct from the West. The characterization of the non-West as being outside of "meaning" suggests the non-West is where rationality dissolves. The West is rational and the non-West is not.

Rather than accusing Barthes of orientalism, it is perhaps more appropriate to write that his xenophilia is what is problematic. At the same time, viewing the above through the lens of his preface to Camus's *Tricks* could yield a more sympathetic, nuanced reading. Barthes was often seen as a traitor to the gay rights movement because he refused to identify as gay; in this way, this text can be seen as a defense against activists who wanted him to identity as something (rather than nothing). Meanwhile, academia often undercut the seriousness of his scholarship because he was nonetheless coded as gay. Harvard scholar and poet Helen Vedler, for instance, notes that she was once chastised for liking Barthes, who she writes was referred to as "that silly homosexual" by an otherwise esteemed colleague of hers.[52] In this way, it is not surprising that he would not want to be in the West, where he is identified in categories. Indeed, Nicholas de Villiers provocatively writes that Barthes has been closeted rather than that he was closeted. He recasts Barthes's silence as a queer tactic of "opacity" in which his relationship to the closet is a productive inscrutability.[53]

Per de Villiers, Barthes's philosophy of identity was effectively queer and at odds with his lived reality. When Twombly invited him to write an essay for the catalog accompanying his retrospective at the Whitney Museum of American Art exhibition in 1979, it seems that Barthes might have found an analogue for his more nuanced approach to identity in Twombly's work. One imagines his artwork evoked an affect that resonated with the queer way Barthes lived and that he could describe only through Zen. His mention of Zen as being "at the very limit of meaning" might be not where rationality dissolves—as I previously suggested—but perhaps where meanings do not cohere into recognizable entities. That is, Twombly's works blurred East and West so that Barthes—at least while experiencing the paintings—need not go to the East. The works effectively brought a Zen-like affect to the West, thereby decoupling Zen from a stable, regional referent.

The majority of Twombly's works do not reference the East. However, Claire Daigle suggests that Twombly's references to the classic polytheistic tradition can be linked to the East through what Barthes's says about the signifiers of Japan: "They are empty because they do not refer to an ultimate signified, as our [the West's] signs do, hypostatized in the name of the God, science, reason, law, and so forth."[54] Twombly could be said to do the latter, but through the polytheistic tradition of the West, which also had no singular "ultimate signified."

Twombly's work can be read as explicating a mode of identity that is effectively queer, and his interlocutors' reliance on performativity and Zen add a specific traction by gesturing toward a queering of both sexuality and the region or nation, both core concerns for this book. This, of course, only became possible by shifting attention away from an essentialized understanding of Asian American art history. Perhaps more provocatively, by recalibrating the lens through which one views the hegemonic canon or archive of art history—the one that includes Twombly and Barthes and Krauss—it becomes clear that retrospectively art history has always been concerned with queer notions of sexuality and the region.

To conclude, I consider Alex Juhasz's conceptualization of "queer archive activism," a term she coined to describe her practice of editing her AIDS video archive so that it maintains "an indexical trace of the past but creates the possibility for an anticipated trace of the future."[55] Similarly, I contend that both Twombly's artworks and Barthes's writing as "trace[s] of the past," per Juhasz, contain the seeds of the "trace of the [queer] future." Their works portend the limits of conventional identity politics and suggest that it remains more important than ever to look backward to look forward. Drawing on Juhasz, Anne Cvetkovich notes that the "radical potential" of LGBT archives can be activated by taking "an activist relation to the archive that remains alert to its absences and that uses it to create new kinds of knowledge and new kinds of collectivities."[56] My approach to the extant archive of art history aims "to create new kinds of knowledge" that radically rethink hegemonic mid-twentieth-century art history.

The following by Barthes on the work of Twombly (whom he refers to as "TW") indicates how I believe art historians should approach Asian American art history: "Of writing, TW retains the gesture, not the product. . . . [E]ven if TW's productions link up with (they cannot escape) a History and a Theory of Art, what is *shown* is a gesture. What is a gesture? . . . [I]t seeks only to provoke an object, a result."[57] My hope is that my writing (by focusing on absence, invisibility, and the performativity of silence) still manages to retain the activism (as a kind of "gesture") that underpins the field rather than (only) the conventional goal ("product") of such activism: inclusion. At its best, the history I write is a provocation of my objects of study: Asian American art history and art history more generally. "Queer" is crucial in this regard in that it redirects our attention to what Asian American art history "does" rather than what it "is."

Pin@y Projections: Urban Spaces, Digital Ephemerality, and Planned Obsolescence: An Interview with Eliza Barrios

JAN CHRISTIAN BERNABE

On October 10, 2014, Jan Christian Bernabe interviewed Eliza Barrios by phone about her digital projections Solace *(2010) and* Sustain *(2010), and her* QR Series *(2010–present). Barrios speaks about her collaboration with Mail Order Brides/M.O.B under the name E. Neneng Barrios, and how technology has shaped her artistic practice and the spaces in which she works.*

ELIZA BARRIOS: I was born in San Diego, California, in 1968, and was a "military brat." My father was in the navy. I moved to the Bay Area, San Francisco, in 1990, where I received my Bachelor of Arts from San Francisco State University in photography, then my Masters of Fine Art at Mills College in sculpture and photography.

JAN CHRISTIAN BERNABE: How do you identify? Do you see your work participating in how the anthology is conceptualizing "queer"?

EB: I am hyperaware of all the layers there are in identity and identifying. It's such a fluid question, and my answer depends on who I'm talking to. For instance, I have two careers, my artistic as well as my day job as a technician. I'm totally into motherboards and fixing machines and working with software and doing all those geeky things. When I find myself in the corporate realm, I find myself identifying as an artist. Whereas when I'm with artists, I identify my day job as a technician. I find it creates another dialogue, a way to extend the conversation and a way to know that everyone has multitudes of identities.

In relation to this question, while working for the past fifteen years in collaboration with the Mail Order Brides/M.O.B., we'd often talk about issues of queerness.[1] Even though Jenifer [J. "Baby" Wofford] and Reanne [R. "Immaculata" Estrada] are straight (in a heteronormative way, they are both partnered with the opposite sex), I'd consider us queer; there's an aesthetic and a sensibility that makes us queer. By this, I mean our trajectory and our pieces tend to move past binaries. For example, the *Mananganggoogle* project (plate 21) is our corporate selves, whose mission is to organize the world and make it universally accessible and useful.[2]

If you had asked us, "How do you identify?" in the nineties, I'm not sure if I would have defined us as such. In the nineties, both my collaborative practice and individual practices were not consciously participating in the anthology of "queer." I think I was from that camp that defining identities were restrictive, but would accept it if folks felt strongly about a specific project being queer. Let's just say I was not very rigid about identifying as queer, though as the years go on I realize the importance of identifying my work as such. Thus far, queer to me means that you are open to anything that sort of pushes your own and society's boundaries; it is not a purely sexual term.

JCB: What you are saying is that in the nineties one had to say, "I'm a gay artist" or "I'm a Filipino American artist." And now, I'm hearing that things may have changed where there's more fluidity in that proclamation of identity. What do think about that? Is identity politics still relevant today?

EB: I do think identity politics is relevant on many tiers, with the caveat that when one defines anything, it will or may change, which then needs to be allowed for. Identity is important to oneself. It's relevant for oneself. For example, people coming out may need guiding points of knowing where they're at and where they want to (or not) go. But when you ask if it's still relevant, are we talking about it in academic terms? Or are we talking about it in a museum/art gallery area?

JCB: I'm thinking about it in the art historical sense—where it was something that was used in the early nineties to incorporate difference in shows: artists of color, queer artists, what have you. There was a deliberate attempt to incorporate those differences without much regard to why. I'm wondering if that still happens today. Does the art world still harbor those sentiments? Or has it sort of moved on? Do gallerists really care anymore that an artist is of color or queer or whatnot?

EB: I know for a fact that it's still relevant in that I was fast-tracked into a show recently because I was a woman of color. One of the curators looked at the roster of artists that were included and noticed that they were all white. But for me when I create work, it has never been too important. I feel there are some works that are overtly queer. Though I would often ask myself, "Why am I not using apparent iconography or obvious mediums to sort of push the identity envelope?"

JCB: I like your statement that there's no overt iconography of identity in your pieces. That's a challenge for critics. It used to be, and it may still be, that Asian American art was about, or is about, looking for those iconographies that claim a particular ethnicity or region or culture. What draws me to your work is that you may be addressing identity, but you're not hammering it on our heads.

EB: I do struggle with myself because of that. I suspect the reason why I avoid obvious iconography and identifiers is because I'm drawn to the subtle nature of complex visual cues.

JCB: I want to go into some of your artworks. I'm fascinated by your use of projections in public spaces, and I want to talk about why you do these projections in the first place and how you choose your spaces. I'm thinking about your pieces *Solace* (plate 20), *Sustain,* and the *QR Series.*

EB: Those projections go back to [my early work], literally the nineties ('92, '93), when I was playing with a slide Kodak projector. I always wanted to go bigger and larger. I've always been curious about systems of belief and about ephemerality, which seem to go hand in hand with projection. The projection is an image—it's there, very tangible in a visual sense, but it does not leave a mark. It leaves an indelible mark in your mind but not in the space. Those are qualities about projection that have always intrigued me. It's this weird ephemerality of the medium itself and the potential of working in various scales. As far as the specific pieces, when I was creating them, I was mainly in urban spaces. I was looking at projection as a vehicle to sell product (like advertising—the blinking and moving lights in a public space), but with *Sustain*, the basis was meant to project an idea rather than a product. *Sustain* was projected on the side of a large condominium building in the midst of the hustle and bustle of the Tenderloin, deep in the heart of an urban center. It was a way to offer respite from this bustling area. There's a lot of street activity day and night, always movement. I found it pretty appropriate to share that visual or that sequence.

JCB: Was that a renegade sort of project?

EB: Yeah, it was. For about a year and a half, I was the curator of the Luggage Store Gallery's *Luggage Store Projection Series.* It was a pilot program started in summer 2010. We were doing that on Market Street. So the projection on the rooftop in Tenderloin was like that—it was renegade. If you happened to be there that night, you got to see the projection. That's how I liked it. I liked doing the sort of throw ups. It sounds funny, right? But that's my dream, to acquire the control to do that, to do projections in the city, anywhere, everywhere. But *Sustain*—or all three of them (*Sustain* fell into the *QR Series*)—was [created] while I was a curator for the Luggage Store project. Essentially having access to equipment made all of that happen.

JCB: I was rewatching *Solace* this evening and thinking about your projections in relation to space, but I was thinking about it more broadly in terms of San Francisco—in terms of its history of AIDS. I was like, "Wow, this is really an interesting commentary on the urban history of San Francisco." I don't know whether that was your intent. I was thinking about this idea of life and death and San Francisco. There is a very overt phenomenon of displacement going on because of the tech industry.

EB: Around the time I created the second iteration of *Solace*, I had a friend whose father was going through pancreatic cancer. I was doing a whole series on our thinking about your choice of life depending on your health and what the environment offers you as well as how choosing to end your own life is such a political and business issue. I think if *Solace* had been projected in a natural setting or somewhere really far away, it would take on a whole different meaning. It might be perceived as a commentary on the automatic occurrence of life and death in nature. But here in the city, it's a little grittier because there's a lot more at stake. There's a lot more money at stake.

JCB: I want to linger on that point. I see an obsession with temporality in your pieces, and I think it goes with the technology.

EB: It really, really does. I could talk about it on different levels. I mean, on the technology level, it's all about planned obsolescence. In our history, we're putting things in the cloud, like our memories, our thoughts, our pictures, everything. What happens if we run out of electricity? Remember Zip drives as storage? I had some really valuable journals on my Zip drive, and now that history of myself is gone. The progression of technology is almost like the planned obsolescence of us as a species. I think art in itself is also temporal; the meaning of a piece that you come back to every year or even every minute changes.

I just finished a huge project with YBCA [Yerba Buena Center for the Arts] called *Projecting SoMA: Elders and Youth's Voices*. A project was funded by the Irvine Foundation to look at ways to engage art "in community." The final project/exhibit was to take place within the SoMA community. SoMA has been rife with gentrification due to the tech companies moving in and creating condos, potentially displacing the Filipino community who have been living there for years. The final result after close to two years working with the youth and elders of the community was a large-scale projection using stories and words from the community describing their SoMA. Again using the tool (advertisement) to make the public know that there are people and communities that exist and that big tech money does not necessarily mean progress—though some elders welcomed the change, ironically enough.

Queer Traveler–on Desiring and Failing Sublime Landscapes: An Interview with Kim Anno

JAN CHRISTIAN BERNABE AND LAURA KINA

On May 5, 2014, Jan Christian Bernabe and Laura Kina e-mailed a set of questions to San Francisco–based artist Kim Anno, followed by another set of questions in spring 2016. In her responses, Anno describes her multimedia methods and how her multiracial identity, queer sexuality, and environmental concerns have always been intertwined as she explores the "tyranny of the picturesque" in her Grand Tour *series.*

JAN CHRISTIAN BERNABE / LAURA KINA: Please introduce yourself. Where were you born? Where did you grow up?

KIM ANNO: I grew up next to the ocean. I was born on the west side of Los Angeles and came of age in the 1970s at a moment when California, and the whole country, was in flux. This was a time of social upheaval and personal liberation. My parents rebelled as beatniks and civil rights activists; my father took me to see Martin Luther King. Mass gatherings were common, whether cultural, like folk or rock-and-roll festivals, or political, such as the Chicano moratorium, Cambodian bombing protests, or the UFW's [United Farm Workers'] Gallo boycott. As a response to California drought, on the LA's Westside Dogtown Z boys were inventing skateboarding as a sport, including Peggy Oki and Jeff Ho's surf shop gang, who made up the Zephyr surf and skate team.[1] The electricity of the time ignited my creativity. It's the current running through my work all the way to the present.

My Hapa father was half Polish and half Japanese. His family was severely impacted by Executive Order 9066, which mandated Japanese Americans to be relocated to concentration camps during World War II. The family changed its Japanese name and lived in hiding to avoid incarceration. My father tried to blend in and make something of himself as a physicist. His evacuation plan for the area around Three Mile Island would become well known. My mother's parents had grown up in a boxcar in Oklahoma. My maternal grandfather, a Choctaw/Irish man, was the only plumber for the African American community in a small West Texas town. My parents found their way to college at the University of California, Berkeley, where they met and married in 1955.

LK/JCB: How do you identify? Please feel free to address themes of "queerness" and/or "queering Asian American" identity and whether they inform your artistic practice.

KA: My queerness was always defined by the intertwining of race and sexuality. Even in high school, I was a queer person with a keen interest in social issues. Despite the fact that my parents chose complete assimilation, I was passionate about the nuances of my multiracial heritage, particularly the Japanese and Native American histories. My first art education came through the Feminist Studio Workshop at the LA Woman's building in downtown LA, where I studied performance art. The majority of the students and teachers were Caucasian with little relationship to the Latino Boyle Heights neighborhood that the workshop was situated in. This irked me, but my questions were not taken seriously. Feminism would later confront this dynamic through the scholarship of bell hooks, Deborah Willis Thomas, Angela Davis, Barbara Smith, and others. When my father refused to pay for my art education, I moved north to San Francisco to finish school on my own. I enrolled in San Francisco State University and, later, the San Francisco Art Institute. The artistic counterculture milieu drew me in. I was too young for Woodstock, but I made sure I did not miss the effervescence of the San Francisco Bay.

JCB/LK: How do you see your identity as an Asian American and as a queer-identified person intersecting, and how does this affect your artistic practice as well as your political imagination?

KA: In San Francisco, queer activism captured my imagination. Along with a collective of artists, in 1983 we formed a queer artists' festival called Mainstream Exiles. From our living room, Mainstream Exiles would produce exhibitions, performances, and concerts at various venues in San Francisco, most of us living and working on Valencia Street in storefronts down the street from Punk clubs like Valencia Tool and Die, where the Dead Kennedys performed. The social milieu was avant-garde, theatrical, communal, celebratory, and hilarious. At one point, we sang Broadway show tunes with rewritten lyrics to denounce our greedy gay landlords in the Castro. Although *intersectionality* was not yet a term, that is what we were experiencing. The racism of the queer community was well known to us, and yet we were carving out our own places. On the one hand we were giddy with reinvention, and on the other hand, the pressures of family and society were palpable. The silence and politeness of our Asian fathers was restrictive, and in reaction we had to amplify our actions. In New York, Godzilla East opened the *Curio Shop* exhibition, and in San Francisco, Godzilla West created exhibitions as well. The Asian Women Artists Association emerged in 1989.

In college I became serious about making objects. The San Francisco Art Institute (SFAI) was a place that taught me to become fearless, a wild thing.

At SFAI there was a natural continuum between the avant-garde and the contemporary moment of pop culture. Queerness gave me two things: a harbor and a sailing vessel. The nurturing of cultural communities gave me the moxie to step out of the boundaries of categories. My interests steered away from an identity-based context and toward an expanded audience.

JCB/LK: You work across a range of mediums, from painting, photography, video, to artist books. Can you talk about how switching methods and mixing mediums have impacted what you are trying to say?

KA: For the past twenty years, I've been an abstract painter and an installation artist. Abstraction was a way to establish an intimate and collaborative dialogue with a viewer, who completed the aesthetic experience in my mind. More recently, I altered my process, strategy, and aesthetic destination. I became a much more interdisciplinary artist, while still practicing painting. Since 2009 I have made over twelve short films and video installations and several series of large-format photographs—all of them saturated with painterly effects. Filmmaking and photography opened an entirely new horizon for me as an artist; this wind of change slapped me into a kind of clarity. I want to reach a different, younger audience. I look squarely at my own time: the shifting form of books, news, the dramatic climate changes, the joy and consequences of technology, the tragedy of environmental injustice. I want viewers to find the meaning between empathy, subversion, and irony.

JCB/LK: We are intrigued by your recent body of work, *The Grand Tour*. Please tell us about the series and how the process of making it questions dominant ways of thinking about bodies of knowledge, history, and culture.

KA: My new paintings reflect on the tyranny of the picturesque. What is the nostalgia for the pristine land we once traveled to? Why do we need to capture and package it, as if archiving it for the future? Domestication of nature now requires a spectacle for us to experience it. The colored light projected at night on Niagara Falls, a transnational border monument, leaves us in awe of the natural beauty despite the destructive effects it has on the falls themselves. Governments spend millions of dollars cementing in the falls, keeping the wonder of the world intact, as on an old picture postcard.

This current project consists of large-scale paintings of iconic views such as Yosemite, Santa Monica, Las Vegas, thus recreating "the grand tour" of picturesque wonders. Young men and women made such a tour to the capital cities of Europe to learn about the world. I realized that I am no different than any other romantic traveler. I, too, covet and want to possess the place I travel to; therefore, I touch it too many times. I am reminded of stalactites in a cave that grow black from being touched by tourists. Our attachment to the picturesque became a tyranny of nature that the planet's inhabitants cannot afford.

We artificially distance ourselves from our garbage, or "unscenic nature,"[2] and for this we will pay a heavy price. There is a "*no going back*" to how it "*was.*" As an artist, I can imagine the consequences, both the antipathy and the empathy present in an image, present in a mark made by the hand. I want the sublime memory of the nineteenth-century landscape painters; only I want to turn it on its head and use irony, allowing desire and failure to intertwine.

JCB/LK: We want to return to your comment about your work being "saturated with painterly effects." The *Grand Tour* series uses postmodern strategies and aesthetics. You combine black-and-white landscape photography with some element of visual distortion or deterioration. At times your marks reference abstract color field paintings, but at other times the blurs and computer-generated geometric gradient shapes recall glitch art genres. The rainbow color schemes are also a reoccurring motif, which we read as literally queering the landscape. Can you talk about these aesthetic choices?

KA: I made the choice to print sublime images of landscapes on aluminum and use the paint as an antiheroic gesture. The paint is marring the landscape, disturbing its romantic pristine loveliness. This is quite a departure for a painter who has revered the lavishness of paint for two decades. It caused me to reconsider the entire strategy of my painting. The digital photograph is the nostalgia. Old photographs are both lovely and historically problematic and revealing. Sometimes I take the photograph, and sometimes I appropriate an old one. This is reversing a colonial gesture. I am an Asian artist culturally appropriating a Western source, instead of vice versa. I am the Asian tourist who is grabbing the Western picturesque for her own means. I, too, love these landscapes and want to interact with them, but as an artist I can use them to make something else out of them

I wanted to implicate my own desire for travel. I have a carbon footprint *and* a desire to see the world simultaneously. I do want to walk in the shoes of the "European young Men of means" at the turn of the century. Making the grand tour requires a complicit action of revering Western capital cities and landscapes. I hope to update this by revering Asian heritage sites as well. For example, *Kyoto* is also a painting of mine. Everyone idolizes Kyoto, including myself. Thus I paint, and mar, the picturesque image of Kyoto in the series. I sacrifice my own desire for the spiritual awakening and gentleness of Kyoto.

Disturbing the photography, which I do through various software—distorting it, glitching it—is an interruption in the mediated image of nature in my paintings. It is a human-generated interruption. It is another way to problematize our picturesque tyranny of nature. We have our blue-sky postcards from our favorite natural environments. These are collected as memories of a real place. These postcards contribute to a stance against an actual experience of nature and for a domesticated yet possessed nature. Selecting these aesthetic strategies and painting with and against them is a sense of queering. I like the flexibility of the term *queering*.

The rainbow in my work can be seen as both queer and utopian. The rainbow emerged from the 1970s as a symbol of LGBT identities. Young hippie communities in the sixties had tie-dyed rainbow T-shirts to distinguish themselves from the formalness of subdued color—thus the association with a utopian, collective, rebellious worldview. Aesthetic hunger to let people fly their "freak flags free" was in the air. The sexual liberation movement was a powerful incubator for culture in general.

I use this rainbow as a motif in multiple disciplines of my work. For example, I am working with the song "Somewhere over the Rainbow," which I am also queering and commissioning singers to interpret in decidedly *queerish* ways. The song has been associated with the queer community for generations. I disrupt the structure and melody of the song entirely and make it considerably more abstract. In my paintings, I let the paint flow over the printed image: it takes over a little, it melts into itself—it fails. The queer rainbow references the utopian gesture and conflates the two. Queer utopia acknowledges our thriving existence apart from suffering. The Asian quality about these paintings is the space and the verticality of landscape. I have been studying the reduction and vertical space of Chinese and Japanese painting for decades and allowing their aesthetics to influence my work in general. I have to give respect to both Japanese and Chinese painting for giving vertical space to the Western world, for birthing minimalism, too.

JCB/LK: Earlier you said you "covet and want to possess" the places you travel to, and that this caused you to "touch it too many times." Can you expand on this and your interest in irony and how you allow "desire and failure to intertwine"?

KA: Think about the glorious Yosemite Valley and then the yellow haze that hangs in the air there—it is overrun by tourists. We rush to gaze and touch heritage sites and then watch them deteriorate as we get there. We want to capture our picturesque and put it in our pockets. We gave rise to the thing that Las Vegas is, where we can travel the world in a single day, walking through from one simulated capital to another, watching the simulated rainstorm at the Paris hotel to quench our thirst.

This hunger to travel, but yet at our convenience, is a tyranny. Certainly the part of the world that makes up Asia can speak about this as well. Orientalism is still alive and well in the ravenous travelers on the planet. We contribute to the horrific deterioration of the populations of people, places, and animals in Asia, as our consumerism drives our appetites. How many ornate statuettes of ivory do we need carved by Chinese artisans, after exporting the tusks of Africa's animals and leaving them writhing in the dirt?

Desire and failure wrestle in my work. They are both multilayered. When you are willing to implicate yourself, examining your own excess, your own material exploitation, it's confrontational. Painting is inherently confrontational with the self anyways. You cannot hide anything there; it is all out there for viewers to devour. I sometimes want to present the image as falling apart. I want to make books that look like they are falling apart, because books are failing now too. The physical book is a ghost. My generation is madly trying to save them as well. I am also keen on making more artists' books for this reason. The patina of age is both a failure and desirable. Handmade things are sexy as well. Then when you combine these two, then the real irony comes into play, and the questions begin to proliferate.

JCB/LK: As in the nineteenth-century landscape paintings that inspired your work, representations of the human body are notably absent in your paintings. In *Niagara* (plate 22), your gaze appraises the transnational border monument, but your body is present only behind the viewfinder, and it is markedly different from the presumably wealthy European participants of the grand tour rite of passage tradition. Can you expand on this presence and absence of your Asian, female, queer body in your work or in Western art history more generally?

KA: It was relatively recently that the contemporary art world acknowledged the contributions of Asian artists in museums, galleries, universities, and media. While working through identity issues in my own abstraction over the years, I realized I wanted a broader audience than design trade clients whose desires may be motivated by orientalism. As I began to achieve some success, with museums and other public collections acquiring my work, I began to examine everything in my practice with new eyes.

The solution has been to embrace social critique by being more subversive and ironic. I am asking myself who my audience is and evolving and expanding the intended audience. For this reason, I am not only painting but also making films and photography. The venues for my projects are varied. In my films I am working with teenagers and twenty-year-olds as musicians and actors. I want more queer and Asian audiences, too. My body is the subversive, the social commentator, and the arbiter of culture.

Chapter 5

Queering Subjectivity

Risky Subjectivity: Select Works by Korean Adoptee Artists

EUN JUNG PARK

In a photograph taken of artist Kate Wall at an orphanage in South Korea (figure 5.1), she stands in awe of a place where her origin narrative comes to an unsatisfactory end that is forever incomplete. Kate Wall is a Korean American artist based in Los Angeles who recently started to search for her birth mother in South Korea. Art by Korean adoptees dramatizes the production of nothing: empty rooms, silences, and accumulations toward oblivion. For adoptees, the loss of stories sharpens the hunger for them, tempting them to fill the gaps, to fabricate a witness to a birth not much noticed. *Personhood*, *consciousness*, and *agency* are words often synonymous with subjectivity. Besides one's current affiliation with a community of choice, justification of subjecthood often rests in the past, in the histories, the familial alignments—things that are often located in an archive. In other words, one usually finds a sense of self and empowerment in the past. But what if your past has been eradicated? Eradicated by what, by whom? Who or what has the power to eradicate a past? These questions are similar to those posited by literary scholar Saidiya Hartman, who asks, what

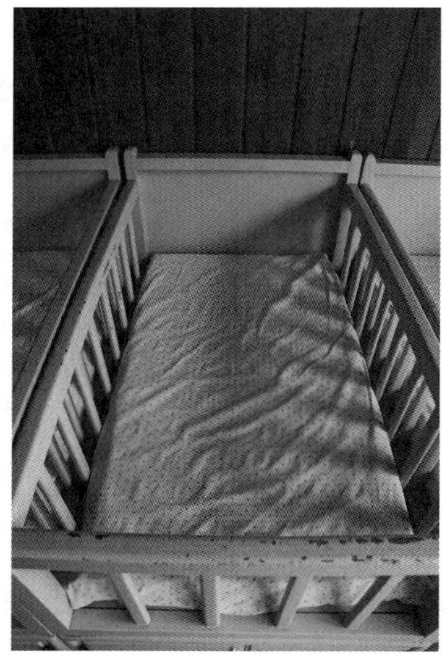

FIGURE 5.1
Untitled, 2012
Digital file; dimensions n/a
Courtesy of Kate Wall

does it mean to think "historically about matters still contested in the present and about life eradicated by the protocols of intellectual disciplines?"[1] This is how the archive is central to subjectivity; if there is no archive, does it mean that there is no subjecthood? The answer to that question is where I found the conceptual relationship between adoption subjectivity and queer subjectivity: in what Michael Warner calls a "subjectless critique," which he defines as a site of social violence where normalization occurs to create the neoliberal subject.[2]

My interpretation delineates several conceptual crises within traditional terrains of subjectivity and interpellation that are posited by the artworks of Kate Wall, Deann Borshay Liem, and Mihee-Nathalie Lemoine. These three artists deliberately denaturalize origin narratives and reconceptualize the social contingency of subjectivity. *Subjectivity* is often defined as the "will to power" or point of view; however, *subjectivity* is continuously redefined through otherness and alienation in the visual or carnal experience of others and is specific in its definitions. The works of these artists show engagements with normative pressures—pressures that are constitutive of a neoliberal subject, such as family, nation-state, religion, and sexual orientation.

This past decade has seen several notable contributions to the study of Korean adoptees from fields such as sociology, anthropology, history, and literary theory. These investigations engage with the epistemology of the Manichean logic, the rhetoric of the Cold War, and the ontology of subjectivity.[3] Anthropologist Eleana J. Kim, Soo Jin Patae, and literary studies scholar David Eng have established a foundational understanding of collective identity formation produced through group art exhibitions that feature Korean adoptees. Kim, for example, posits that these group exhibitions are a socializing apparatus. Furthermore, Kim argues that "the resignification of the cultural meanings of oversees adoption and the shifting receptions and representations of transnational adoptees are suggestive of the degree to which neoliberal rationalities have made kinship relations and social belonging acceptable sacrifices in the pursuit of human capital investment, liberal self-actualization."[4] This chapter builds on their research, but rather than focusing on the social apparatus of group shows under the banner of Korean adoptee art, I examine individual works by Korean adoptee artists in order to delineate the ways in which these artworks evoke a further refinement of what constitutes subjectivity.

Although only a few artists are analyzed in this essay, many notable artists who identify as Korean adoptees engage with many important issues, including kate hers RHEE, Maya Weimer, and KimSu Theiler. For example, KimSu Theiler's film *Place-Names: New York City* (2011) accentuates the gap between memory and nonplace. Theiler's film highlights a journey with no origin and no destination. This work illuminates the regimes of sensible intensity as it drafts trajectories between the visible and the sayable and the invisible and unsayable, relationships between modes of being and the negation therein, creating lines of fracture and disincorporation into a self-reflexive loop. Along with Deann Borshay Liem's film *First Person Plural* (2000), kate hers RHEE was part of a first wave of influential artists making work about Korean transnational adoption. It is worth noting that RHEE does not want to be defined as an adoptee artist.[5] She is just one of the many Korean adoptees who have dealt with adoptee issues in past works and would rather not be identified as such because the description of an adoptee artist binds her to a limited set of perceptions. To that end, it is important to note that the definition of subjectivity will continue to evolve, as the analysis of "queer diasporas" emerges as a concept that provides new methods of contesting existing definitions, according to David Eng.[6]

IRRECONCIBLE ENCOUNTER: KATE WALL, DEANN BORSHAY LIEM, AND MIHEE-NATHALIE LEMOINE

A characteristic element in origin narratives is an articulation of the place where one grew up. Extending the trope of family photographs, Kate Wall's installation, *When the peaks of our sky come together, my house will have a roof* (2008) (plate 23), documents her adopted family's empty house in upstate New York after their move and interrogates the concept of home. The installation documents the emptiness of pictures that used to hang on the walls, marks where furniture used to occupy rooms, and suggests the silences that have become amplified through silent expressions of bodies that used to occupy that space, where she could have come out to her adopted parents but didn't, where she could have asked questions about her biological mother but couldn't. Each photograph in the installation is uniformly bordered by a simple white one-inch frame. Creating an abstract pattern of squares and rectangles of varying sizes, not all of the photographs hang on the wall; some rest on the floor, leaning against the wall. The documented emptiness in Wall's 2008 photography installation highlights the gaps between a sense of home and an origin that lacks a fixed referent and is missing her adoptive mother, who has since passed away. The conceptual crisis posited through Wall's installation deliberately denaturalizes origin narratives and reconceptualizes the social contingency of her existence as a Korean American adoptee.

In addition to showing the complexity of the ideological state apparatus of the family, Korean American adoptee artists also illustrate the ways in which official government documents encourage sanctioned assimilation. *Practical Hints about Your Foreign Child* (2005) (figure 5.2) by Deann Borshay Liem is an installation that includes a projection of historic footage of children interacting with US troops during the Korean War. The piece sardonically juxtaposes didactic verbiage from official brochures produced by the International Social Services Office for potential adoptive parents with sayings like "Your adopted child might hoard food," "Korean children are eager to please and most will learn quickly," or "Soon he will join the ranks of other happy American children." Through these quotes, Borshay Liem highlights assimilationist fallacies that are at the heart of the model minority myth.

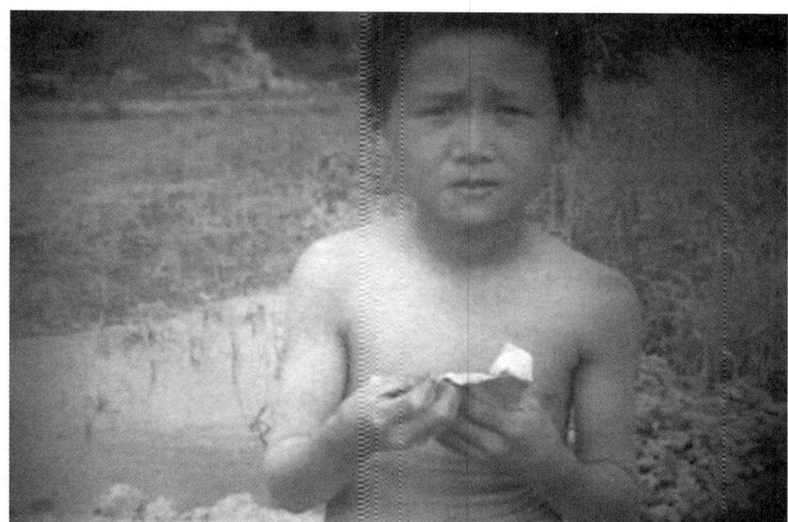

FIGURE 5.2

Deann Borshay Liem (American)
Practical Hints about Your Foreign Child, 2005
Video, 3 minutes, 36 seconds
Courtesy of the artist

Practical Hints widens the schism between official documents and personal experience to traverses the terrains of government documents, surveys, and brochures in the context of parental expectation.[7] Concordantly, the use of official documents to imagine otherwise exposes the artifice of their origin, which relies on interpellated modes of behavior.

In addition to works that appropriate official documents, artworks by Korean adoptees frequently integrate kinship with the history of struggle of other disenfranchised groups in the United States. Belgian Korean adoptee Mihee-Nathalie Lemoine created *Who Are You? 2014: 60 Years of Korean Adoption* (2014), a video that consists of black-and-white images of one hundred Korean adoptees from adoption profiles for prospective parents. The video shows photographs of infants and toddlers superimposed over an RGB screen that recalls the colors of traditional Korean blankets. The soundtrack for the video is the politically and historically charged Korean song "Arirang" dubbed over a speech and television interview with Malcolm X from 1964:

> Who are you? You don't know. Where were you and what did you have? Who are you? You don't know. What was your name? It could not have been Smith, Jones, or Bud Joe Powell? They don't have those kinds of names where you and I came from, no what was your name? Why don't you know now what your name was then? Where

> did it go? Where did you lose it? Who took it and how did he come? What tongue did you speak? What language did you speak then? What was your name? Why don't you know what your name was then? What tongue did you speak? How did the man take your tongue? Where is your history? How did the man wipe out your history? What did the man do to make you as dumb? Who are you? You don't know.

A second or so after this speech, a recording of Malcolm X's voice continues:

> But if a Chinese person were to say his name was Patrick Murphy, you would look at him like he's insane, because Murphy is an Irish name—a European name—or a name that has a Caucasian or white background. And a Chinese is a "yellow man" and he has nothing to do—or no connection whatsoever—with the name Murphy. And if it doesn't look proper for a person who is yellow—or Chinese—to be walking around named Murphy, or Jones, or Johnson—or Bunche or Powell . . .

Malcolm X's voice fades, and the wailing sounds of a woman's voice repeating "Arirang" are heard for a few seconds, then Malcolm X's voice returns with the same question: "Who are you? You don't know." In addition to the connection between one's name and one's ethnic affiliation, this video is compounded with another socially assimilationist imperative. According to the artist, 10 percent of the infants and toddlers featured in this video are queer; she equates the imperative of a moral correction that she correlates with the sentiment that most of the families who adopted these children were operating under an evangelical purpose.[8]

Another work by Lemoine that further complicates positionally is *100 Me (Baek Me)* (2003) (plate 24), which features digitally manipulated photographs of the back of her head. In a deliberate negation of identification, images are placed along a central axis pointing toward an empty void at the center. Along and in between the digitally altered images are words that read centrifugally:

> *Did you know that*
> *I had to turn*
> *my head*
> *my heart*
> *and my back*
> *to forget that*
> *my life is*
> *just to gain*

balance between
my past and a
reason to live
a happy life

Baek is Korean for one hundred. I interpret the title as referring to a traditional Korean birthday celebration called *tol,* for babies who have survived the first hundred days of life, signaling that the dangers of infant-related death and disease are over. The image resembles a mandala, a cosmic map of subjectivity in a suggested dispersal into myriad versions of the same subject in a mise-en-abyme. This mise-en-abyme is constructed through a production of agency that is enacted through negation: the presentation of the back of her head in a non-gender-specific hair style negates racial and gender identification. This presentation disperses competing identities that yield an accumulation beyond the subject's discursively rendered desire to be positioned and challenges the rigidity of the politics of cultural identity. *Baek Me* is a representative example of the ways in which the artworks by Korean adoptees are highly charged with what art historian Amelia Jones has called "intersubjective contingency," which complicates the centrality of the subject, particularly in terms of a self-portrait like this one.[9] According to Amelia Jones, intersubjective contingency is the collapse of distinctions between subject and object, self and other, public and private, where artistic engagement is a means of claiming immanence that yields a productive ambiguity and exposes the artist-as-subject as both destabilized yet irreducibly embodied.[10] The work reflects and exaggerates synchronous multiplicity; *Baek Me* refutes the Hegelian concept that "what I am" is bound to "what I am not," as it proliferates the multiple contingencies of subjectivity from nationality, ethnicity, gender, sexuality, and religion.[11]

INTERPRETIVE ANALYSIS: RISKY SUBJECTIVITY

The description of the artworks above shows resistance against the sites of social violence, including government and adoption agency documents, such as those in Borshay Liem's and Lemoine's work; family, as presented in Wall's installation with the sense of home and place in terms of geography as a marker of identity formation; and the normative imperative of heterosexuality, as implied by Lemoine's explanation of *Who Are You?*

According to literary theorist Anne Anlin Cheng in *Melancholy of Race,* "It is precisely that move of replacement—*from object-relation to an imagined relation to one's self*—that gives identification, personal or social, its hold."[12] The archive, in the form of a self-portrait, a family photograph, or adoption agency paperwork, is turned on its head; for example, the title and visual presentation of Lemoine's *Baek Me* suggest a nonportrait; Wall's documentation of the family home lacks any figurative subjects; Borshay Liem's and

Lemoine's adoption brochures and government paperwork are deliberately presented as ironic. This engagement intersects with the technology of the self as representation (e.g., self-portraits, family photos, and official government documents) that presupposes an ontological imperative; however, the analysis these artists present is an altogether different way of conceptualizing embodiment. In the context of Asian American art history, self-portraits are often interpreted as a synecdoche of nationhood and culture, among other trappings of identity politics. Mise-en-abyme is a shattering of the reflection in the mirror; in the case of Korean adoptees, these self-portraits are a synecdoche of the mise-en-abyme, that is, the self positioned between multiple mirrors in which the reflections of the self are multiplied into infinity toward oblivion. This multiplication of self goes to the heart of what I call "risky" and refers to the following: first, the risk of rehearsing and thereby concretizing strategic gestures that confirm notions of identity politics under the burden of representation; and second, subjectivity at risk of passing because of the very institutional forces that lead to artworks by Korean adoptees being exhibited: gatherings sponsored by the South Korean government, which are always already determined by the interpellated modes of exhibition, reception, and interpretation. Gatherings often include and even feature art exhibitions by adoptees. Eleana Kim describes these gatherings as the production of a normative adoptee identity through a syllogism that enacts a strategic essentialism.[13] Accordingly, she describes the gathering conferences as "rites of institution" that attempt to enforce an ontological reality and yield a neoliberal subject. The artworks presented in this essay refuse this positioning through the construction of imagined territories and deconstruction of origin narratives, as they deliberately traverse traditional terrains of subjectivity and interpellation in order to evade and challenge them.

A productive paradigm in art history both from inside and outside art history reexamines mainstream ways of looking, gazing, and spectatorship, and the problems of the anachronistic eye. Eleana Kim analyzes the multivalent rhetorical positions of nation, race, and family that are rehearsed and concretized, where adoptees are perceived as honorary ambassadors of their adopted countries and vice versa.[14] In this way, adoptees are processed through gathering-like events sponsored by offices in the South Korean government and the tourist industry. Anthropologist Alfred Irving Hallowell writes that "the self is a social product more accurately characterized as also a cultural product."[15] He posits that we live in a "culturally constituted behavioral environment." Therefore, applying Hallowell's aforementioned logic, these artists and their works are at risk of becoming socially constrained constructions, where shame and frustration are culturally and institutionally configured through the rhetoric of these gatherings. These figured worlds are thoroughly imagined (defined, narrativized, and embodied) by discursive forces and produce constantly practiced emotions and experiences that are always already framed. Therefore, adoptees must appear to accept the rhetoric in order to enter the configured space. Adoptees are scripting themselves and being scripted within a discursive milieu constructed by the program that produces and reinforces the desire to become a neoliberal subject.[16] However, working against the grain of these forces, the artists described here are in positions where, in the words of Gayatri Spivak, they "cannot not want."[17] Emotions are created by both the complex interaction of interpersonal negotiations and the subjective experience of a social structure that follows the Foucauldian microphysics of power relations. Therefore emotions are laden in ideology, history, and ethnotheoretical ideas about the nature of self and social interaction.[18]

Faced with the mechanisms of subjecthood described above, Korean adoptee artists are aware of the levels of double consciousness. The marked difference is between being positioned by others and the acknowledgment that how they are seen is different from how they see themselves. These events position them in ways they might not choose, but they willingly play the part in order to enter this space and exhibit artwork that might be antithetical to the imperative to be neoliberal subjects. Accordingly, this chapter's title, "Risky Subjectivity," also comes from deducing the characteristics described by anthropologists, namely, trying to be normal after being hailed as abnormal. Risky subjectivity refers to the constant construction and reconstruction of perpetual struggle that deliberately fails at a normative imperative. Therefore, in the context of these dominant discourses, the artworks posit the nuances of the mise-en-abyme of subjectivity, which I interpret as the transformation of the individual into a formal yet contradictory subject. This particular kind of subjectivity has much in common with Saidiya Hartman's concept of reading against the grain and resisting the impulse to archive, which aptly describes the ways in which these artworks present a position that is between an articulation of a subjectless subject and subjecthood-in-formation. In other words, the artworks presented in this essay show how art functions to interrogate epistemological limits by emphasizing absence and negation as the subject matter that underscores the relationship among visual analysis, subjectivity, and knowledge production. In this way, these works are an embodiment of the elusion of rhetorical capture that elucidates productive tactics for resisting interpellation in an irreconcilable encounter of origin myths, nationality, and other trappings of identity formation.

Therefore, rather than obsess about what art is, the more productive approach is to look at what art does in the context of discursive frameworks. The art of Korean adoptees functions as an estuary of productive voids for locating the mechanisms of constraints that I have outlined regarding subjectivity.[19] The most productive approach in my mind is to concentrate on what art does to the discursive bind. Paraphrasing the advice of the late Karin Higa, progressive and radical art historians should function as termites eating away at the boundaries of epistemology.[20] The artwork of Korean adoptees and individuals in the interstices is potentially at the forefront because it provides opportunities for intervention between representation and meaning in order to prevent the always already diagnosed predicament that the artworks and individuals are at risk of being imprisoned in. Namely, the artworks present the ways in which normative appropriation by the artists fractures subjectivity. These artists denaturalize various origin narratives by contesting traditional family structures and reorganizing nationality based not on origin but on destination. These artworks render the reconciliation between the biological origin and the socialized self as undermined by the incompleteness that the artworks seek to overcome against the grain of normative discursive formations.

Dazzle: A Conversation on Transgender Subjectivity with Greyson Hong and Kiam Marcelo Junio

JAN CHRISTIAN BERNABE AND LAURA KINA

On June 10, 2014, in Chicago, Laura Kina and Jan Christian Bernabe sat down in person with Chicago-based artists Greyson Hong and Kiam Marcelo Junio to talk about subjectivity in relation to Hong's 2013 new media project Funereal Archive, *Junio's Jerry Blossom persona and 2012–14 multimedia series* Camouflage as a Metaphor for Passing, *and their identities as queer, trans Asian Americans.*

KIAM MARCELO JUNIO: My name is Kiam Marcelo Junio. I was born in 1984 in Quezon City in the Philippines. I grew up in the Philippines as well as in Japan and in Southern California before I joined the US military after high school. I graduated with my BFA from the School of the Art Institute of Chicago in 2013, and I currently live and work here in Chicago.

GREYSON HONG: My name is Greyson Hong, and I was born in 1982 in Chicago. We eventually moved to Atlanta and are still there now. My parents are both South Korean, and I was surprised to find a huge Korean population in Atlanta. So I grew up in a large Korean American community. At eighteen, I went to the Naval Academy in Annapolis, Maryland. I left the Naval Academy after my first year and attended the School of the Art Institute of Chicago (SAIC) for my BFA, and then in 2014 I completed my MFA at Bard College in upstate New York.

LAURA KINA: How do you know each other?

GH: It's a small community [Chicago's queer community].

GH: I found out you were a student at SAIC.

KMJ: And we kept running into each other.

LK: I want to follow up on this mutual navy connection. What caused you both to join?

KMJ: I was born in the Philippines. My biological mother passed away when

I was five, and since then the process had been for my aunt, my mother's sister, to adopt me. Her husband was in the US Navy. When I was ten, I was officially adopted by my aunt and uncle and went to live with them in Japan. So early on that was my connection with the military. After high school, I was persuaded by my family to also join. Having and seeing no other way outside to be able to live on my own and be independent, I decided to also join the US Navy.

GH: How long were you in the navy?

KMJ: Seven years.

JAN CHRISTIAN BERNABE: We actually attended the same high school, Nile C. Kinnick in Japan.

GH: These are inevitable possibilities of diasporic narratives. The overlaps are very consistent of us all being of some sort of Asian descent. It's inevitable that the military is involved.

JCB: Greyson, why did you go to the Naval Academy?

GH: In hindsight, I thought it was my only way out. I needed to go to college, but what was my strategy? Not only is it a full scholarship school with a fancy reputation, but it also secures a job as soon as you graduate as a naval officer. I only applied to West Point and the Naval Academy. I knew that as a female, Asian, athletic, well-performing student the odds of getting in were pretty high.

JCB: Why did you leave there, given your expectations? It sounds like you strategized.

GH: I think at the time I didn't realize that it was such a strategy. [The school] just didn't fit, and I finally, for whatever reason, felt like I could handle doing something outside of that . . . which was to come home for a year, work full time at some random job, and save up to go to the Art Institute.

LK: I know that since the early twentieth century Filipinos could become US naturalized citizens by serving in the navy. In your case, what was the circumstance?

KMJ: In the military they don't necessarily have a requirement for you to be a US citizen, in the enlisted side at least. Definitely officers have to be citizens, but in my case it was always presented as an option to encourage US service members to become citizens—there would be commercials on TV about how to get your citizenship. It just seemed like an inevitability for me at that point to become a US citizen. My name has changed throughout my life, but it was when I got US citizenship that I changed my first name Kim to Kiam, adding the *a*. Thinking back now, I consider that my first piece of performance art—this changing and reclaiming this name that was given to me and adding the *a*, the alpha, the beginning, a new beginning inside the old name.

LK: Could you both talk about your identity and your names? Kiam, I know you also go by the plural *they* and Jerry Blossom.

KMJ: I go by the pronoun *they* as a personal and political act. I don't identify with the imposed definitions of gender, and I often feel that I am or can be different people at once—hence, the plural *they*. I am a Filipino American, immigrant, queer, gender nonconforming, visual and performance artist, veteran, and many other names. These identities all have different lenses with which I see or experience the world. As Jerry Blossom (and their "evil" twin Jeri Withers) (plate 25), I illustrate aspects from all those dimensions, past histories, and possible futures—combining, mixing, remixing those images, and imagining new ones to embody in the present moment.

GH: Naming is such an important part of queerness. Whether it's a nickname or in terms of a trans individual—if you think about the naming of something or someone and the naming of oneself, as opposed to the name that was given to you by your parents, it really does break a kind of genealogy or the passing down of a name in terms of heteronormative family structures. It's a really critical moment, the renaming. Working with the legal system to do that is such a strange thing. It brings an intentionality reserved usually for new parents, newlyweds, divorcees, and of course immigrants.

My birth name is Caroline. So it's 1982, and it was right around the time when Grace Kelly died and her daughter Princess Caroline of Hanover is all over the media. So if you think about it, both my mom and dad are watching television and hearing the name Caroline a lot. This is how I'm imagining these things. If you think about Grace Kelly, femininity, Westernization, and Western ideals, and you think about Europe and she's a princess. Not surprisingly, I know several Asian women in my age group with the name Caroline. After a lot of deliberation, I settled on Greyson. I went through the whole legal process of changing it. That was a rebirth, of course—people like to think about this as ritualistic and ceremonious. My middle initial is still *C*, so there actually is no middle name. There is just the letter *C* to reference back. It's this uncomfortable thing—when you have a relationship with your parents, who went through this process of naming their child, it's almost offensive to rescind that. I was trying to find a meaningful way to retain that history. My mom raised my sister and me as a single mom. The idea of woman, of being raised as the first daughter, is an important concept that I struggled with for a long time.

KMJ: Gender and names are really fascinating to me, especially because the origin of my birth name, Kim, is still really murky. I remember a story that my biological mother was dating a Korean or Chinese man named Kim, and he left her and broke her heart, and she ended up meeting my biological father, who was already married at the time, and they had an affair. The other story is that my mother really wanted a daughter and she wanted to name the daughter Kim, and I ended up being assigned male at birth but still received the name Kim. That name growing up has always been uncomfortable because I felt that it was based on a broken heart or failed expectations. That has always stuck with me. I didn't really want to leave it, either, because I thought that was part of who I am and who I had come to be at that point. In claiming a new citizenship, I also claimed a new identity by adding a new beginning.

JCB: Were you comfortable in your new name?

KMJ: I was, and still am. I love my name! I remember feeling like the name change was a discovery rather than a choice. It felt so right. This is me.

LK: It's literally "I am." You have a middle name you go by, too?

KMJ: Marcelo—that's my mother's maiden name. I also dropped Gregor from my name, which is attributed to my biological father, Gregorio. I used to be Kim Gregor Marcelo Santos, and then Santos came off and became Junio, and then Kim Junio, and then I dropped the Kim and became Kiam Marcelo Junio.

I just remembered that I had changed my name already when I was in the military. I came in as Kim. However, since we primarily used last names, it wasn't really a big deal for me to start using Kiam. I never really had to use it anyway, so I had years to kind of sit with the name.

LK: Were you Marcelo?

KMJ: I was just Junio.

JCB: I think this shows these very interesting negotiations we have to make as queer folk, whether it's immediate or over time. I'm just wondering what you think of these transitions and negotiations?

KMJ: Negotiation is a really good way to talk about that. I see identity as a moment-by-moment negotiation. Which part of myself am I using at this point? What am I showing? Who am I at this time? It's always an internal negotiation for me.

JCB: How did Jerry Blossom evolve?

KMJ: Jerry started primarily as a burlesque character or burlesque name. I was taking burlesque classes with Vaudezilla when I first moved to Chicago. I wanted to come up with an Asian name or an Asian-themed name because I knew I wanted to represent my heritage but also critique orientalism by being cheeky and campy. Jerry relates to Sailor Jerry [a tattoo artist famous for tattooing sailors in a now-iconic style]. It's also both masculine and feminine.

JCB: Jerry Blossom has a very distinct look: you wear a long, flowing blond wig and sing karaoke. Why?

KMJ: Why not?! Originally the image developed as this critique on whiteness and growing up Filipino—like the prize of whiteness and the beauty and the allure, the social class and privilege of whiteness. What is the most transgressive kind of combination I could personally embody? For me that was a male body, Filipino, brown skinned with blond hair. I ran with that primarily as a joke and as a critique of that desire for status and image. Jerry originally started out as more masculine and gradually evolved into this high femme persona that then became related to my experience, my research, and what I remember from my childhood of the *baklâ*, which itself has a lot of deep history of gender and labor performativity in Filipino culture.

JCB: Feminine, *baklâ*, kind of accepted . . .

KMJ: Yeah, *baklâ* has places within the society, similar to the *hijra* in Indian culture.

JCB: or *fa'afafine* in Polynesia—a third gender.

JCB: I'm curious how this non-normativity gets transmuted into your works? Greyson, in your PDF artwork *Funereal Archive* (plate 27), is that a direct response to your identity and to being trans?

GH: I would say that all of my work is like that to some degree. I'm really interested in the archive and the historical right now and what would it mean to "queer" history (and I'm using this playfully). History is so linear and so much about the "winners," power, and who is recording. I'm really trying to question issues of subjectivity in terms of how we are always looking into the individual and what is our identity as an individual isolated from everything else. Rather than looking inward, I am considering how subjectivity is shaped by our environment and by our understanding of these things. That project was a lot about dealing with personal grief but also how grief is related to this pathological understanding of melancholy and then trying to depathologize it through this seemingly arbitrary archiving process that lives on the Internet—this intangible space.

I wanted to move away from the storytelling, confessional structure and play with that so it's not just about our own individual histories but rather how they overlap. *Funereal Archive* is in response to my grandfather's passing. It got me thinking about genealogy and kinship. In terms of the cultural thing, how colonialism and postcolonialism and the notions of race, class, and gender have affected my relationship with my grandfather. The fact is there is no affect there or very little affect, so I'm finding other ways to create meaning in this tenuous relationship.[1]

JCB: Was your presence at the funeral an issue for you or your family?

GH: I think they weren't paying attention. I'm not very close to my grandfather, so all of the community that came don't know me. It is a little bit tricky because the program says I'm my mother's daughter, and then I'm in a suit. I'm very much passing as male but I'm not a pallbearer. Everyone is kind of looking at me because I'm obviously standing with the family but I'm not participating in one of the male roles. It was very awkward and painful, actually. Those are the moments where these breaks happen—that this ritual that shouldn't be that important unexpectedly has so much meaning. For some reason I had this strong desire to be a pallbearer and I'm not allowed to be.

KMJ: It's interesting how you can cross borders within yourself and within a society you are part of, yet in going back to a different one, or previous one, those boundaries are not yet crossed.

JCB: Kiam, do you have that sort of relationship with your family, of this negotiation of your identity?

KMJ: Not really. I've always been very independent, and I feel tensions differently. Having grown up in multiple homes throughout my childhood, the word *ambivalence* stands out to me. My biological mother, before she passed away, was a nurse in Saudi Arabia, and for the first years of my life I was raised by our landlady. My biological father was there, but I hardly ever saw him because he was working. From there I went to live with my aunt, and then to various other relatives around the Philippines. Until the age of eleven, when my aunt (my mother's sister) adopted me, I had lived with different families, moving every year or so, and because of this, I feel that I grew up with a type of destabilization which influences or mirrors my own queer subjectivity. Early on, I realized that nothing is permanent, and that definitions of family, home, and identity are highly malleable. Now I've taken quite strong control of my own identity. I didn't ask my parents if I could change my name or even what they thought about it. I just did it. Moving here [Chicago] was also my choice, even though my mom wanted me to move back to California.

GH: That's so different from the role of family for me and how it's shaped my decision making. In terms of Korean culture, it's such a huge responsibility.

JCB: Kiam, would you say that you have found and redefined family for yourself?

KMJ: I have. Especially coming to Chicago and finding a beautiful community of queer artists and queer beings and the love and support that we all give to one another. I love my family. I love my three sisters, all younger. I stepped away, however, from this expectation of me as the eldest brother: to be a provider and the example I'm "supposed" to set. I'm setting a different example from what is expected of me, of resistance and forging your own path.

JCB: Kiam, your *Camouflage as a Metaphor for Passing* (plate 26) is about an absent presence and camouflaging oneself. Can tell us about this series?

KMJ: I was working on a screen-printing project in which I picked plants from all around downtown Chicago and used the live plants as stencils, playing around with the layering and the color. I quickly realized it began to resemble a woodland camouflage pattern I was familiar with from the military. From this initial experiment, it exploded into all the different ways to look at camouflage personally or more as a social commentary.

GH: So what are your thoughts on passing?

KMJ: I was coming from the perspective of passing in the military as straight, heteronormative, as one cog in the system, but then pulling outside of that and delving into queer theory and passing in society and gender presentation and what that means to pass as a perceived gender in order to navigate the world, to survive in a society that does not promote being original or showing who you are. Additionally, the theme of camouflage is very charged in the Filipino experience, as we have often been called "the invisible minority." Visibility and representation within the larger society is still a very important aspect of Filipino identity and a source of pride. With my series *Camouflage as a Metaphor for Passing*, I'm seeking to ask to what extent we make ourselves visible and invisible in order to survive. Specifically with the mirror pieces, the viewers see themselves reflected back in the piece, allowing them to interact with the theme of camouflage in their own way. How are they passing or not passing? How are they visible or invisible?

LK: Can you talk about the red silk and camouflage military jackets in this series?

KMJ: I have two series within *Camouflage as a Metaphor for Passing*: *Crypsis* and *Mimesis*. *Crypsis* is a type of camouflage employed evolutionarily by animals in the wild, where they hide by mimicking their surroundings. The use of camouflage in the military to hide within the natural environment is highlighted by the use of camouflage gear. The jackets were modeled after camouflage jackets I actually wore in the military. I used oriental silk brocade, a lush, beautiful, red, rich fabric evocative of orientalism and femininity, to recreate this military jacket. When it's hanging on a gallery wall, there is an absent body that's implicated by this coat hanging unworn. The *Crypsis* series has to do with stand-ins and the use of materials to evoke a body or make apparent the absence of a body. They also serve to reverse the purpose of the original jacket, which was meant to obscure. In my series, they become art objects that are meant to be seen and displayed.

Mimesis is a type of camouflage when an animal mimics another type of animal or plant, or an orchid mimics a bird—those kinds of ways where impersonating something is a way for those species to evolutionarily be successful.

JCB: When you were talking about passing in this heteronormative, cis-normative, environment, do you have any thoughts on passing in the queer community as, for example, in the Jerry Blossom persona.

KMJ: Jerry Blossom is a declaration of anti-passing, of being *very* visible: the use of very bright colors, for example, to draw attention rather than to hide. Jerry is about claiming space and being as fabulous, loud, and unapologetically sexy as I want, as I'm, or have been, told *not* to be.

JCB: Do you think anti-passing is a survival tactic? It's sort of the opposite of being camouflaged, right?

KMJ: Actually there is a third type of camouflage called dazzle, which is when an animal or print will move so quickly that it confuses a predator's visual field. I consider this my lived camouflage. Movement is important. As queer people, we have grown in opposition to the normative and oppressive, which is always changing. What does that mean for us? This brings in a discussion of homonormativity. Gay culture was once counterculture, and now it's becoming a part of the norm. It's more discussed in media around issues of gay marriage and assimilation. As a queer community, who are we, and who do we represent? As we become more visible in the larger media, at what point do we stop resisting, or do we continue to resist? When is the battle done? For me, I choose to continue to resist and evolve, because there is still much more work to be done. Equality is nowhere near here. For a lot of people, once they have reached a point where their difference has become normalized, then there is a privilege there that people can stay with and be comfortable with and stop fighting for the rest of the community. I am just now coming out again, choosing to identify as transgender, as I feel that I am neither man nor woman but rather something that is always moving and changing and shifting depending on context. *Gender-fluid*, *gender-nonconforming* are some of the terms to describe this. There are a lot of dissatisfactions in the transgender and trans community about feeling left behind by the gay agenda. Trans identity and trans rights are issues that have largely been ignored till recently, and there is much more that needs unpacking

GH: The coming-out story holds a lot of importance, and there is always that post-coming-out adolescent period, no matter what age you are. Being in Chicago for the past ten years and in and out of the queer community, I think it's really important to distinguish what is queer culture and what is queer politics and what it means to be queer. I think queer is about antidogma and anti-ideology, but I fear there are dogma and ideology coming from the contemporary queer agenda. That's why so many people are feeling left behind and the community is so divided, including myself. I'm very wary of this language of queer individualism. Passing ties into privilege, race, class, and access. Passing could be a privilege and also a necessity in some contexts. To oversimplify these things is something we need to reevaluate. What is the gay agenda versus the queer agenda versus the trans agenda? We need to be wary. If we think about queerness, I think of it as a positioning of yourself against normativity. I want to think about this in terms of failure. How do we queer something and fail at it? Like Halberstam suggests, we do failure really well.[2] I love that idea. I love dealing with failure as a kind of strategy. The queerer-than-thou attitude is really problematic, and it's happening right now.

JCB: That idea of failure is very interesting when you tack on the Asian American experience and the immigrant experience, because it's all about succeeding.

GH: As the model minority.

JCB: Recuperating these narratives of failure is really important because it broadens what it means to be part of not just a queer community but also a racialized community.

Chapter 6

Queering Mixed Race

Liminal Possibilities: Queering Mixed-Race Asian American Strategies in the Art of Maya Mackrandilal and Zavé Gayatri Martohardjono

LAURA KINA

The 2000 US census, which was the first to allow individuals to self-identify as more than one race, increased the visibility of multiracial populations, who have been lauded as both signs of "melting pot" racial progress and as potential "threats" to existing "normative" monoracial categories. At the same time, there was a neoliberal and conservative postidentitarian/postracial push posed against the putative ossification of multicultural racial identity constructs. Curatorial frameworks and studio practices centered on race as a locus of investigation were challenged if not rendered invisible and seemingly obsolete. And yet race and attendant cultural issues remain pertinent for artistic production and analysis. A double tension results in moves to recognize the continuing importance of race as well as the critical push to reframe and disarticulate categories that cannot contain the complexity of increasingly miscegenated peoples, histories, and subjectivities.[1]

Maya Isabella Mackrandilal and Zavé Gayatri Martohardjono are two artists for whom race and cultural negotiations remain heated points of departure. Mackrandilal is a Chicago-based sculptor who works across a range of media, including performance. With a mother of multiracial Indian/black/white heritage from Guyana and a white father from Belgium, she identifies as "politically black and politically queer." Martohardjono is a New York performance artist who identifies as a "queer, transgender, mixed race, Indonesian American." His mother is Javanese from Indonesia, and his father is Italian American from a suburb outside of Boston. As mixed-race millennials who embrace the creative potential of their queer liminal positionalities, they both entered their teenage years during a "postracial" era of wider, albeit colorblind, acceptance of multiraciality, when the moniker *Asian American* was a distant mirror more associated with East Asian American multicultural identity politics than with its Third World, collective, antiwar, civil rights, and community activist roots, which would have reflected the sense of solidarity these two young artists share as self-described people of color.

Through the artwork of and interviews with Mackrandilal and Martohardjono, this chapter builds on the book's trajectory of interrogating Asian American *identity* and its sister concept of *subjectivity*.[2] In mapping their practice through the lens of biography, I am reminded of Asian American author Frank Chin's polemical warning in "Come All Ye Asian American Writers of the Real and the Fake" against the underlying Christian confessional mode of autobiography and Western ideals of individualism.[3] My intent in using oral history methodology is to give the artists dialectic agency on the terms of their visibility as multiracial and queer subjects who use postmodern strategies of mixing forms and genres and share an interest in veiling/masking the face—the primary site on the body in which we are accustomed to reading race.

THE SIMULTANEOUS INVISIBILITY AND HYPERVISIBILITY OF MIXED RACE

Miscegenation has a long history in literary and cinematic representation, usually in the trope of the tragic mulatto—an illegitimate offspring caught between black and white worlds—but there remains scant analysis of mixed race in visual arts. Even less has been written critically on mixed-race Asian American art and visual culture.[4] The mixed-race body, which was once tragic or invisible, in the 1990s became hypervisible as marketers such as United Colors of Benetton used racial ambiguity to signal "progressive" cosmopolitan politics, and Nike sought to corner the multicultural market during the "Cablinasian" years of golfer Tiger Woods's career. Since the new millennium, we have seen the turn in hypervisible representation of the multiracial person to what University of Washington communication scholar Ralina Joseph has termed the "'Exceptional Multiracial' who is the unifying, post-racial, U.S. ideal" (e.g., President Barack Obama).[5]

In her 1991 essay, "Optical Illusions: Images of Miscegenation in Nineteenth-and Twentieth-Century American Art," Judith Wilson notes that "race is a peculiarly optical system of classification. . . . In the English-speaking world, it is a concept that characteristically stresses a single feature of color-value—and is structured by polarities: 'white' and 'black,' 'white' and 'non-white,' 'the white race and the 'the darker races' or 'white people' and 'people of color.'"[6] Michael Omni and Howard Winant, in their seminal 1994 text, *Racial Formation in the United States*, trace the emergence of notions of race from biblical times, and the optical system of classification of race from eighteenth-century Enlightenment sciences and subsequent nineteenth-century ideas of race as a biological concept. Race is also enmeshed in European colonial projects on a global scale and specifically in the United States with the systematic enslavement and dehumanization of African peoples. Omni and Winant note that today "the social sciences have come to reject biologistic notions of race in favor of an approach which regards race as a social concept."[7] As a sociohistorical concept rather than a biological pathology, mixed-race studies in the United States grew out of the multiracial movement that emerged in the late 1970s and 1980s. These initial discussions and communities were formed around heterosexual interracial relationships, gaining social acceptance and offering support networks for interracial families and peoples. As my co-authors and I wrote in introducing the 2014 inaugural issue of the *Journal of Critical Mixed Race Studies*, "By the 1990s, one of the multiracial movement's key initiatives was to bring about changes in standards of official racial data collection in the US census. The goal was to facilitate the expression of a multiracial identity in contrast to existing policies that required individuals to identify with one racial background as part of the enforcement of monoracial norms."[8]

Despite the hypervisibility of the multiracial body in marketing of the 1990s, in the new millennium the dominant discourse on multiraciality has decidedly *not* been framed around the visual, and certainly not around art, but rather within the civil rights bookends of the 1967 *Loving v. Virginia* Supreme Court case, which federally overturned antimiscegenation laws, and the aforementioned 2000 US census. The 2008 election of President Barack Obama was heralded as the resolution of Martin Luther King's dream: here was the first black president, the first biracial president. We no longer needed to *see* race. As David L. Eng cautions in *The Feeling of Kinship: Queer Liberalism and the Racialization of Intimacy,* this "refusal to see difference—to acknowledge race—marks the politics of colorblindness in our 'post-identity' U.S. nation-state, which is characterized by the persistent disavowal of race in the name of freedom and progress."[9] This chapter echoes Eng's critique of "queer liberalism" in which LGBTQ rights and representation in our current neoliberal framework of civil rights, of seeking legitimacy from the state—rights to love and marriage, to property and inheritance, to be counted accurately on the census, to citizenship, and to immigration—once achieved, assimilate the "non-normative" body (be that queer, multiracial, or interracial) into the nation-state and do very little to change the state itself.[10] Legal frameworks and state-sanctioned legitimacy do much to describe where we can go, with whom, and what we can have access to, but they do little to describe who we actually are or to remember the messy and complicated origins of our arrival or how we might envision an entirely new future.

This is the realm where the arts can excel. In the most universal sense, art can preserve traditions, transform existing forms and expressions, or seek to create something entirely new. Art can archive affect; generate narratives and counternarratives; create movement; take us through time and space; capture disjuncture; juxtapose, slip, erase, and make visible forms; and engage all of the senses. Art is thus perfectly suited for the job of describing, remembering, feeling, and making visible the complexities of "non-normative" bodies, people, and histories to examine the intersectional confluences, overlaps, and competing pulls of race, ethnicity, class, gender, and sexuality.

Maya Isabella Mackrandilal and Zavé Gayatri Martohardjono both participated in the panel "Miscegenating Racial Representations: Critical Mixed Race Strategies and the Visual Arts," which I co-chaired with Asian American art historian Margo Machida for the 2014 College Art Association Annual Conference in Chicago. We were eager to continue talking to each other about our shared experiences of being mixed-race Asian American artists and had all been struck by a closing comment Zavé made: "How do you claim an identity that does not claim you?"

On June 27, 2014, I met with Maya Isabella Mackrandilal in her Chicago studio/home to look at her 2013 *Seated Woman* sculpture/performance (plate 28), and on July 11, 2014, I spoke to Zavé Gayatri Martohardjono about his 2013 solo Butoh performance *Brother Honeyqueen's Dance of Darkness* (plate 29) and his related 2014 stage play *Brother Lovers* (figure 6.1), which was set to premier the following week at the Fresh Fruit Festival in New York. I followed the same questions we used for other artist dialogues in this book, asking them to introduce themselves, address how they identify, and talk about their artwork in relation to the chapter theme. I asked them to consider several questions: How has being mixed race influenced your studio methodology? How does your work decenter or broaden the way we understand *Asian American*? In what ways does your work engage queerness in either form, content, or studio practice/methodology?

MAYA ISABELLA MACKRANDILAL: POLITICALLY BLACK / POLITICALLY QUEER

Maya Isabella Mackrandilal works in sculpture, performance, installation, drawing, and digital imagery. She describes her work as a "fusion of different signifiers" where she employs a sense of "fracture, pastiche—things getting pushed together." She draws on South Asian iconography and sees this "as a past that is and isn't mine."[11]

She was born in 1985 in northern Virginia to a single mother from Guyana who identifies as Indian with Chinese, black, and white heritage and a white father from Belgium. Her childhood was split between growing up in northern Virginia surrounded by her Guyanese aunts and uncles, traveling to Africa for her mother's work with the World Bank, and living in a predominantly white community in Fairfield, Iowa, while her mother was working on her MBA at the Maharishi University of Management. Maya, who in high school was jokingly referred to as "Windian" (white + Indian), identifies as multiracial and feels like a "liminal person" in terms of "existing in this in-between space." She describes herself as "politically black and politically queer even if, in my desires, that's not necessarily legible. I'm not legibly black and not legibly queer." She is a cisgendered woman who presents as female and is married to a white male partner. How Mackrandilal presents racially is less clear than how her gender presents: "People want to ask, 'What are you?' That question and having to explain this whole history of British colonization and why there are Indian people in South America—that, in many ways, is similar to when people ask your sexual orientation. You have to come out. You explain and justify yourself. To me being politically queer is about wanting a culture that embraces ambiguity and liminal identities regardless of what those are. Being comfortable with being uncomfortable." "Queer" in this sense is not situated in the discourse of queer sex but rather as a way to position the mixed-race subject as willfully resisting assimilation into normative whiteness. And yet the mixed-race body remains as a symbol of "non-normative" sex through its physical recalling of miscegenation—the crossing of monoracial lines through the act of sex. This is not to say that being mixed is synonymous with being queer. What does it mean for a cis multiracial to adopt a queer subjectivity? Is this about being an ally to LGBTQs, or does this choice risk appropriation? In her position as "politically queer," the operative word is *political*. Maya understands her work as queer in that she is deeply influenced by second-wave queer black feminist theoretical discourse and practice that emerged in the 1970s and 1980s, and not as limited to a naturalized a priori identity.[12]

Mackrandilal also notably identifies as politically black, both in solidarity with her darker-skinned family members and as an acknowledgment of the system of white supremacy and her own racial privilege "as a light-skinned person of color. I understand that when I walk into a store, I'm not going to have the same level of scrutiny." Although *multiracial* is her preferred category "when you have to check things," she does occasionally check *Asian American* because "it is the closest." "If someone said, 'that Asian girl,' no one in America would think of a body like mine. They think of East Asians. But if you said that in England, they would think of someone who is Indian or Pakistani. So even that term is not fixed at all. I've always been interested in Asian American cultural production, history, and politics, but I'm also very skeptical of the term because it erases. . . . I tend to use *woman of color* because it's more important to be in solidarity with *all* women of color than specifically Asian women."

She earned her MFA in sculpture in 2011 from the School of the Art Institute of Chicago (SAIC), where she began exploring the concept of a lacuna, which continues to inform her work today. She describes a lacuna as "a gap. An unfilled space or interval, a missing portion in a book, a missing word in a language, a cavity in a bone. It is a thing we know the edges of. It comes to us from the Latin for 'lake' or 'pool,' a sense of the unknown, the hidden—uncertain depths."[13] In 2008, right as Maya began her graduate studies, the

Art Institute of Chicago, which is physically attached to SAIC, opened the Alsdorf Galleries of Indian, Southeast Asian, Himalayan, and Islamic Art. "As a member of the South Asian diaspora, descended from indentured laborers brought to the Caribbean to work the sugarcane plantations after the abolition of British slavery, I was drawn to the objects in the space as a link to a culture I felt both close to and distant from." She initially attempted to find out the provenance of the objects but was met with resistance by museum officials, who told her the records contained "confidential information." She then asked if she could do a performance in the gallery where she would put her own body on display along with the other South Asian female stone sculptures, which seemed to her to be "ripped out of time and context." The museum would not allow her to do this either, so she opted to create digital montages of her proposed performance, placing her body virtually in the gallery. "I became an ethnographer of a territory that exists equally in the minds of others as it does in physical space. The gallery became a nexus of histories, stories, and identities ready to be uncovered, catalogued, laid bare."[14]

Working with these objects motivated her to return to her mother's country of Guyana. "I was trying to find out family genealogical information, and one of the records that I needed was missing from the national archives. . . . [T]hese lacunae, these gaps, keep cropping up in thinking about my identity, my history, and how I interact with the world." She began to think of her art as a "way to inhabit that gap," as a "productive space" to reference "stories or things that may or may not be true in my family history and also the objects and their history, which is a mystery, at least to me . . . what gets recorded and what doesn't get recorded and who gets to make that decision."

In 2013, she was invited to do a performance on the terrace in front of the University of Virginia's Fralin Museum of Art, where a Henry Moore sculpture titled *Seated Woman* had recently been removed. In the lacuna created by the absence of the Moore sculpture, and recalling her proposed Art Institute of Chicago performance, Maya created her own *Seated Woman* to explore "the invisible authority of the museum and the power dynamics of the gaze upon the Other that it engenders."[15] For seven and a half hours, from noon to 7:30 p.m. on April 26, 2013, she sat silently, perched on a plinth in front of the museum. A large white lace veil resembling a Spanish wedding mantilla covered her face. Inspired by the head adornments she remembered from Indian dance lessons she took as a child and from South Asian sculpture, she created a headdress of wrapped gold and burgundy fabric that cascaded from a high ponytail into braids of multicolored sari and batik fabrics resembling dreadlocks running down her back.

> I conceived of the terrace space as a liminal space, both "public" yet very much "owned" by the museum. I would be the trace of the *Seated Woman* who had been there before, a reference to the many bodies that the museum

> puts on display. But I would be more than this, I would be the specter of my miscegenated history, I would be my grandmother's story, I would be "Aaji," a term for grandmother that has fallen out of use, itself both dead and alive. I would be all the women who had survived, planting their babies at dawn, harvesting them at dusk, the former slave who ran away, carrying a half-white daughter in her arms to another country with another language, the little girl kidnapped and sold. The headdress I wear is a kind of protection, a kind of armor, and also a kind of threat. It is the veiled Other, but a miscegenated image, referencing both the East and the West. Because just as I carry in me the legacy of the colonized, I also carry the colonizer. I'm the people who do the collecting, and the people who are collected.[16]

The performance took place on the last Friday in April right before "Fox Fields," a big horseracing event. The museum faces a sports field and is across from a row of fraternities. "People get drunk the day before in preparation of getting drunk the next day. Right next to the museum is another frat, and they played music basically throughout my entire performance." While Maya was channeling "a being that's fallen outside of time" and thinking about issues of agency and the gaze, many pedestrians simply ignored her on their way to other festivities. Some art students and museum attendees stopped to interact or shoot snapshots. But she was Othered enough that it made most of her viewers uncomfortable. She was totally silent and would occasionally move her head to follow people. One woman asked if she was real. A drunk boy with a red Solo cup tottered precariously next to her for some time, ultimately oblivious to her and to his own presence. A young man on the sidewalk shouted out, "You know I can see you?" A pickup truck of middle-aged men stopped to glare. "For me the veil was a protection from the gaze of the viewer. And I think we can talk about being regarded as a mixed-race person—to me the veil was a protection from that. But a lot of people saw it as threatening and ominous. I started to think about the people who would walk by and act very aggressively towards the performance, yell things at me or get visibly angry." She was struck by the varied responses and how the meaning of the performance could only be completed by its relationship to the viewer. "To me, the performance was a kind of offering of the body to History as an act of love, an act of completion that acknowledges the fractures, honors the trauma, tells the stories, but also knows that in the moment of the telling we embrace everything we cannot know, cannot say—the unknown depths we only know the edges of. What I learned was that this kind of offering, this kind of subjectivity, can be in and of itself a threat, that the assertiveness of miscegenated bodies, however subtle, can be incredibly powerful."[17]

Mackrandilal's use of the veil also points to issues of passing and "coming out" that are central to both mixed-race and LBTQ discourse and experience. However, as bell hooks cautions in *Talking Back: Thinking Feminist, Thinking Black*, most people of color do not have a choice to racially "hide, change or mask dark skin." In looking at the binary categories of black/white and gay/straight, hooks warns against the erasure and deflection of the "impact of racial oppression on people of color" by attempting to make the oppressions of blackness and "gayness" synonymous; she urges rather that we find ways in which these experiences "are linked and yet differ."[18] Keeping this in mind, the comparative framework of examining Mackrandilal and Martohardjono's respective biographies and artistic production allows us to see how race, gender, and sexuality come into play in a liminal space or the lacunae between the binaries of black and white (e.g., mixed-race Asian) and between gay and straight (e.g., queer).

ZAVÉ GAYATRI MARTOHARDJONO: "HOW DO YOU CLAIM AN IDENTITY THAT DOES NOT CLAIM YOU?"

Like Mackrandilal, Zavé Gayatri Martohardjono employs strategies of masking, wrapping, veiling, revealing, and inhabiting stories to explore the miscegenated body in his performance work, but whereas Maya's performance is concerned with the language of sculpture and artifacts and remnants of history, Zavé's practice is centered on mythology. Zavé's ten-minute solo Butoh dance performance *Brother Honeyqueen's Dance of Darkness* (2013) is a queer study of the half-human/half-sun deity warrior king Karna from the Hindu epic poem *Mahābhārata*, a character that became fully realized in his eight-act play *Brothers Lovers*.

Brother Honeyqueen's Dance of Darkness debuted at the Boston Center for the Arts as part of an exhibition featuring Southeast Asian artists curated by Edwin Ramoran and titled *Me Love You Long Time* (February 15–April 7, 2013, Mills Gallery). Brother Honeyqueen is Zavé's name for Karna, and "Dance of Darkness" is a literal translation of *Ankoku Butoh*, the Japanese avant-garde dance form. Zavé was drawn to *butoh* because "it's a space for physical transformation and physical possibility outside of human bounds." His use of *brother* and *queen* reference house and ball culture.

Because of his childhood connections to Indonesian performance traditions such as the Javanese gamelan and *wayang kulit* (shadow puppet) theater, Zavé was drawn to the cultural mythology of the *Mahābhārata*, which runs through these performances, and the story of Karna in particular. In his video and performance work, he approaches myth by retelling and reconfiguring the stories of well-known characters and representing his own experiences through them. He finds connections with the possibility for transformation in the "transgender figures, shape-shifters, women warriors in mythology."

> The part of Karna's story that I love the most is one version of the end of his life. According to some stories, he makes a deal with a Brahmin, thinking it will help him defeat Arjuna. The Brahmin tells him he can win a battle with Arjuna, but he has to give up his skin. He was born with this golden armor, physically attached to his body like metal or human skin, and two golden earrings, one in each ear. His armor makes him immortal; it protects him from danger—it makes him invincible. And it's his only protection. I think about this story so much because when he was born, he was a mistake. His mother [Kunti] had been granted a wish, and she could call to the gods only once. She called to the gods, but when the sun god [Surya] arrived, he felt her call was not worthy, so he raped her. Her illegitimate, half-god/half-human child is Karna. Kunti abandons Karna, sending him down a river, and the sun god refuses to recognize the child. So Karna has ordained powers, but the only thing he really has is this skin. His skin is his ultimate protection. I think so much about what it means to give up that skin.

In *Brother Honeyqueen's Dance of Darkness*, Zavé enacts Karna ripping off his skin: "For me there is something in this skin sacrifice related to these questions of identity, and performing identity, and how we are or are not outwardly recognized. Our identities are the only things we have; they define us. . . . What are we without these bodies that carry history? And what are the many burdens that come with our skin?"[19] In his performance at the Boston Center for the Arts, Zavé entered the gallery from behind the crowd wearing an elaborate mask influenced by Javanese mask making and by commedia dell'arte, the Italian mask tradition. He wore a neon yellow ski cap and heavy dark green cloth cloak and trailed a tail of string with paper text tags repurposed as costume from a previous collaborative performance.[20] He carried a boom box playing a mix of romantic songs, house and ball music, gay nineties club hits, electronic music, and Balinese gamelan. In the front of the gallery, lights were projected on his figure, creating shadows that recalled Javanese shadow puppetry. The audience was not privy that this dance was an adaptation of the story of Karna. "I try to leave it in a really body-based place where you are then watching the transformation, watching the reveal and reacting to the experience." As he threw off his cloak and tail of text, he revealed his body wrapped in sparkling gold fabric to reference Karna's golden skin. He slowly unraveled the golden wrap until the dance "ends with me being mostly naked and taking off my face—the mask." He gestures to house and ball dancing with the unwinding of his head and ends by coming out from underneath the costume and mask to reveal himself "as the artist underneath the character." Zavé has little interest in exposing his transgendered body to the audience for the sake of exhibitionist exposure but rather is interested in revealing the processes of physical transformation and "shared vulnerability." Both the Karna/Brother Honeyqueen character and the actors in *Brother Lovers* (figure 6.1) use masks, which "come on and off at specific times to reference putting up your armor versus being vulnerable. It also harkens back to the identities we carry, both physically and superficially." I asked him if these were self-portraits, as the hybrid Javanese and Italian style of masks relate to his own mixed Javanese-Italian heritage, but this was not something Zavé had thought of consciously.

Zavé Gayatri Martohardjono's own body presents as racially and gender ambiguous. He spoke about his love for his biological family and his queer artistic family, and how he has come to understand his Indonesian heritage through the performing arts.

Zavé lives in Brooklyn and was born in 1984 in Montreal, Quebec. His mother was born in Jakarta, but her family migrated transnationally to Canada, where his mother's siblings are still based. His father's side is Italian American from Woburn, Massachusetts, a working class suburb of Boston. He grew up and went to school in New York, where he earned his MFA in media arts production from the City College of New York in 2009. Although he had taken Indonesian dance lessons as a child, it was not until 2010 that Zavé started

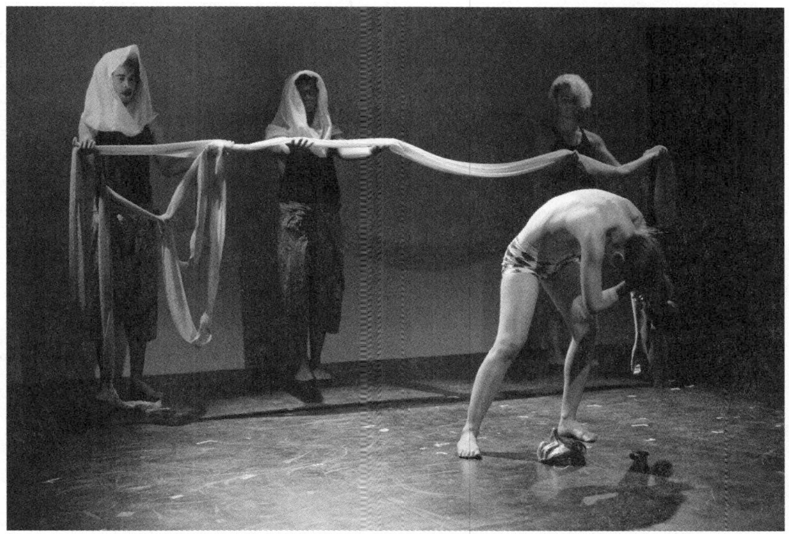

FIGURE 6.1

Zavé Gayatri Martohardjono (Canadian/American, b. 1984)
Brother Lovers, 2014

8-act stage play
Staged at the Wild Project in New York City as part of the 2014 Fresh Fruit Festival in July 2014.
Courtesy of the artist
Photo: Bridget de Gersigny

incorporating dance into his artistic practice, when he joined choreographer Mariangela Lopez's project *Accidental Movement*. He later met choreographer J. Dellacave, who gathers together queer performers who voluntarily work for a year on dance, theater, group discussions, and personal storytelling, which they then choreograph into a finished work. These collaborative interchanges continue to inform his practice.

Zavé identifies as mixed-race Indonesian American, queer and transgender, and as a person of color, but "getting to those terms has taken a while." He struggled with how the terms fit or didn't: "It sometimes feels difficult or easy to claim identity markers but even if they are insufficient words, it's just important to name those things. I do identify as 'Asian,' but being mixed race, I have a complicated relationship to that identity. I often talk about being a mixed-race person of color who privileges from passing as racially ambiguous or even white." He often wonders how others identify him. Although he strongly identifies as being of Javanese heritage, growing up in New York, he was usually ascribed as Latino or ambiguously mixed race. "There are so many diasporas in New York, but the Indonesian diaspora is not a highly visible one. I think if I had grown up in Toronto or other parts of Asia, it would have been a really different experience. . . . Indonesians have not been a hugely visible group [in the United States]. . . . Every time I say I'm Javanese, someone says, 'Oh, so you're Japanese?'"

Zavé spoke of being welcomed into "people of color spaces" but noted that the term has become "synonymous with black/brown, and Asians can really be forgotten in that space. How do Asians fit into POC [people of color]? With the burden of the model minority concept, the Asian experience can become invisible in dialogues on antiblack/antibrown racism. By featuring Indonesian tradition and culture or performance in my work, I'm trying to insert it into POC, queer POC and contemporary movement spaces here."

By drawing on Indonesian performance traditions, Zavé is not only inserting this into the POC discourse but also claiming and transforming part of his cultural heritage. In this regard, I asked him to elaborate on what he meant when he asked, "How do you claim an identity that doesn't claim you?"

> In racial terms, I understand myself as white and Asian. Southeast Asian seems to be absent from a lot of Asian subcategories. More and more I think about what it means to claim an identity at all. When I was a lot younger, I felt a great deal of angst and sorrow about not being visibly Asian to others. I went to a school where 60 percent of the population was Asian. There were Asian cliques who bonded together around a shared immigrant experience. I, on the other hand, was in an oddball group—friends who were culturally mixed, racially mixed, queer, or just somehow not easily categorized. We banded

together. Not that there's a lot of conformity in New York, but amidst such tight-knit diasporic communities, I think I really grew up feeling outside of any diaspora claiming me—even if I was part of that diaspora.

I asked Zavé about his journey in coming to a transgender and queer identity.

> When I was a teenager, I struggled more with questions of racial identity than sexual and gender identity. I had as much heated energy about the ways in which I did not feel seen by others as how I identified myself—constantly having to name my race and ethnicity. I really had to insert it, prove it, and lay claim. Also my connection to Indonesia . . . there are other things that stand in between—like my family living in Canada. We wouldn't visit Indonesia that often. It was only when my Oma's [Dutch for "grandma"] health got really bad that we started going on a yearly basis. I understand the language, Bahasa Indonesia, on a very basic level, but I don't speak it. Also my family does speak Javanese and some of my elders speak Dutch.

As cosmopolitan multiracial children of immigrants who came from families that stressed academic achievement and who also possessed the financial capital for international travel, Zavé's polycultural experiences echo Maya's cultural, national, ethnic, and racial connections and disconnections. Both artists had a clear understanding of themselves at an early age as being mixed, but unlike the multiracial trope of having the "best of both worlds," Zavé felt he could have neither. "I think my white family saw me as this sort of a 'beautiful exotic child.' . . . I have this distinct memory of one of my little cousins in Jakarta marveling at my white skin. I always felt white to brown people and brown to white people but never my own thing to everybody and myself. It took me a long time to say, I don't have to be identified for me to identify." His queer and trans identity came later in life "because race was really the primary place where questions came up."

> Once I landed in a self-accepting place around race, queerness, transness just felt obvious! Having a mixed racial identity, understanding being outside of certain bounds while also crossing various categories, I feel like queerness is an extension of that. When I was young, I guess I assumed I was straight, but when I think about it now, most of my friends, people I dated as a teenager, were queer too. We just sort of found each other. If you

looked at us from the outside, you might assume we were normatively gendered or straight, but we definitely did not have simple relationships with each other. Years later, when everyone went to college and came out, it was like, "Oh right, we were just a bunch of queer kids together, obviously!" For me, queerness and trans identity are open and fluid containers of a space, of being, which each seem like the natural resting place for my body.

For the longest time I identified as "gender queer," unsure if that meant "transgender" because I assumed *transgender* meant someone who changes from one binary gender to another. For a long time I felt that I was more Two-Spirit than F2M [female to male]. Now I think having formed and being part of a real network and community of transgender activism and artists, I really understand *transgender* as also a fluid term as well. I think mixed race, gender queer, trans, queer are these kinds of open spaces that contain me. While it took time to get to those terms, it came with letting go of the possibility that anyone can claim identity categories in a clean way. Those things will always be complicated.

◆ ◆ ◆

In unapologetically using figures that are marked as Other, Maya and Zavé have both run into opposition in an art world that remains mired in a neoliberal, color-blind postidentitarian/postracial moment. In her 2013 work *Sheath IV* (plate 30), Maya recounts some of the things people have said to her either behind her back or to her face. She has been charged with being a reverse racist when she raises the specter of white privilege or simply dismissed as looking white or being angry and emotional when she addresses her multiraciality and racism. Zavé initially was hesitant about making work that was so culturally specific. He worried if it would "be interesting or relevant to contemporary performance or movement work, or is it going to get sidetracked?" How artists frame their practice can have a direct impact on their distribution and exhibition opportunities. Zavé debated whether he should show within Asian American art spaces or if he should make the work more visible "as a queer and trans POC Asian mixed-race person. Do I go to a silo where we are only looking at this—it's culturally specific? Or do I say the practice that I've learned really comes out of contemporary dance? Can those things come together? Then I'm like, let me just make the work!"

As multiracial "millennial" artists entering their thirties, they have formed their artistic identities and strategies in an era after the rise of the multiracial movement of the 1990s, in which many mixed-race artists explored documentary and portraiture to racially index and disclose their bodies in a positivist manner (e.g., half black, half white). They are also coming far after the civil rights and multicultural eras with their calls for inclusion and recuperative representation. They must, however, contend with the wake of over a decade of postracialism and have both found a generative home, full of liminal possibilities, in the open and fluid space of queerness.

Chimera: A Conversation on Mixed Race/Mixed Methods with Sita Kuratomi Bhaumik and Saya Woolfalk

LAURA KINA

Laura Kina talked to Sita Kuratomi Bhaumik and Saya Woolfalk via conference call on July 7, 2014, about how being mixed race might decenter or broaden the way we understand "Asian American." We discussed how their hybrid identities have influenced their interdisciplinary studio methodology, and in particular their mutual penchant for forming faux institutes: Bhaumik's Curry Institute *(2011) and Woolfalk's* Institute of Empathy *(2008).*

SAYA WOOLFALK: I am a multimedia artist based in New York City. I live in Brooklyn, New York, and have a studio in Manhattan. I grew up in the New York area, in Westchester, and was born in Gifu City, Japan. I lived in Tokyo until I was two years old. I went to elementary, middle, and high school in Westchester; went to Cornell University [in Ithaca, New York] for my first year of undergraduate as a fine arts major; and then transferred to Brown University [in Providence, Rhode Island] for my second through fourth year as a double major in visual arts and economics. I graduated from Brown University in 2001. In 2002, after taking a year off to live in New York, where I studied at the Fashion Institute of Technology, I went the School of the Art Institute of Chicago (SAIC) from 2002 to 2004 and received an MFA in sculpture and was deeply engaged with performance, painting, fiber and material studies, and also with the film, video, and new media program. I am very interested in interdisciplinary approaches to art, which began when I was an undergraduate at Brown because Brown wasn't really a production-based studio program. Brown was a conceptual program, where we learned to take on whatever materials and methods we needed to address the ideas we were attempting to bring into the world. When I graduated in 2004 from SAIC, I moved to Brazil for two years, first on a Joan Mitchell Foundation grant and then on a Fulbright. I used both fellowships to study folkloric performance traditions in Brazil, in the Maranhão, São Paulo, and Rio. I attended the Whitney independent study program in 2006–2007, and in 2007–2008 I was artist-in-residence at the Studio Museum in Harlem [both in New York City]. The time that I spent in Brazil was when I formulated my first multiyear, multimedia project, *No Place,* which is still the foundation of what I produce today, which are these multilayered narrative projects that are inspired in part by science fiction and anthropology. In 2008, I showed a completed project, *Ethnography of No Place*, which I created with anthropologist Rachel Lears at the final artist-in-residence exhibition at the Studio Museum in Harlem. Since 2008, I've been working domestically and internationally showing my work, both the *No Place* project and my current project, *The Empathics*. I'm currently working on a new project called *ChimaTEK*, which will be premiering in its entirety at the Chrysler Museum in 2014 in Norfolk, Virginia.

SITA KURATOMI BHAUMIK: I am also an interdisciplinary artist and teacher. I was born in the "OC" [Orange County] and raised in Los Angeles in the suburbs. My mother is Japanese Colombian, which means that she was born and raised in Colombia to Japanese parents. My family has been there since the 1920s. My dad is from a small rural village outside of Kolkata in India. Asian parents have a reputation for wanting their kids to be doctors or engineers but they never pressured me. . . . I don't know if they just looked at me and said, "Yeah, that's not going to happen" or what! They sent me to a Montessori school where we all sat on the floor and weren't allowed to have cartoon characters on our lunch boxes. They always encouraged me to be creative. My mother actually moved here [California] to pursue an art degree. I was raised in a climate where my combination of parents wasn't necessarily "normal," but there were a lot of mixed kids, so I think we were more normative in California than in other parts of the country. From there I went to Scripps College [in Claremont, California], which was a very conceptually based program. I had been making my "angry high school" art, and college was where I learned that art could have intellectual tentacles and be satisfying in that way. I had mentors who emphasized photography and mixed media, and I was primarily educated as a photographer there. I don't think people see that thread in my work. But for me, my work is still all about the visual—why we privilege vision, how we privilege vision, and where we privilege vision. From Scripps, I ended up being a corporate event planner for a number of years, which also plays a huge role in my work. I went to California College of the Arts [in the San Francisco Bay Area], where I completed a dual masters in interdisciplinary art [MFA] and visual and critical studies [MA]. The combination of those two was really great in extending my inquiry into "What is the visual?" In my practice I regularly come back to "What is normal?" or "normative," and a lot of that is based on our sense of sight. My work has been moving towards a more event- and experience-based collaborative practice. All of these seemingly disparate parts are coming together in these projects, the most recent of which is *Mamasita's Tiny Tea House*, a fully functioning tiny teashop originally inspired by a photograph I found of my two grandmothers and my mother. I'm working with artists from Dignicraft to create a series of ceramics in Michoacán, Mexico, that I use in the tea stall. I think about this movement of bodies and things, and food is a material that travels with and without bodies. Things like cups can cross the border more easily than humans. Things like spices can be mixed more easily than one person's body can be mixed with another.

LAURA KINA: Sita, you started to talk about your family heritage and the idea of "non-normativity." Can each of you talk about how you identify?

SW: That's a really hard question because I can tell you how I describe myself. My mother is Japanese and my father is African American and white. My father is from the Northeast of the United States, in the New York area. He's from Harlem. His mom grew up in a utopian community, Father Divine's orphanage—she was a white woman who grew up primarily with African American brothers and sisters and married into a black family.[1] My mom is Japanese, from Japan. But when I identify, it's a very slippery thing. Sometimes I use the word *multiracial* to describe myself. That is a phrase that is really useful to help people understand in an instant what they think they know you are. Sometimes I identify as Asian American because visually it's probably the easiest for people to understand me. I also identify as African American, as a community I'm a part of whose intellectual space I generally function in. It's hard for me to identify. That's basically what my work is about: the idea that identity is an ever-shifting thing, ever mutating position, which is relational and not fixed.

SKB: I didn't have the language to put it in those terms, but I did not identify as Asian American until after I graduated from college. At the time I found it limiting. I eventually realized that everyone is limited by the checking of the boxes, not just someone who thinks they can check more boxes than someone else! I remember getting to Scripps, and I got this letter in the mail that said, "Join the Asian American Student Association." The first thought that came into my head was, "Oh my God, how do they know?" I resisted it for so long. It wasn't until I moved to San Francisco and became active with organizations like Kearny Street Workshop and *Hyphen* magazine where I understood how identifying as Asian American could be a strategy or a tool for political agency, community building, and all sorts of things.[2] For practical reasons, I absolutely identify as Asian American. I also identify as an artist, a cook, a political organizer, and queer ally, among many other things. One of the reasons that narrative is so important to my work is that all of us have these incredible narratives and stories that describe us more fully than single words. As a mixed person, how do you mix those words to make the least amount of sense, so someone leaves thinking, "They are more than the thing they just said"? I was just in India visiting my grandmother, who is 104 years old. My husband, who is Mexican, and I are traveling through India—and I could pass as Nepali or maybe Assamese, but most people assume I'm not Indian, which is something ethnic minorities come up against all the time in India. There's an expected phenotype. I'll have a show in the United States with curry powder on the walls, and people will come in and ask me where the artist is because they assume I am not that person. Sometimes it becomes about playing with that intentionally. But as a mixed Asian American, I learned how to navigate other people's confusion from when I was very young.

LK: The two works I'd like you to talk about both have the word *institute* in them: Sita, your *Curry Institute* (plate 31) and, Saya, your *Institute of Empathy* (plate 32). Saya, earlier you were talking about your grandmother growing up in a utopian community, and I was struck with the parallels of that and what you are doing with *The Empathics*. Sita, you are working with curry, and there is a corollary between curry and your Indian and Japanese heritage. Can both of you describe your works?

SKB: Food is one thing and the gallery is another, and they are not supposed to mix; the food is not supposed to be in the gallery and the gallery has nothing to do with the food. What happens when you make a gallery "smelly"? I first began using curry powder by accident. I was part of an Asian American women's artist collective in San Francisco.[3] We would rent a hotel space, create work, and make it in twenty-four hours. During the last twenty-four-hour show, I had run home to get a bag of spices. I went back to the hotel and started making these prints on glue and replaced all the work in the hotel with it. What I was thinking about was how strange it is that we have these spaces—like the museum, the gallery, a hotel room, an office—where everything is supposed to be neutral. What is a neutral smell? It's supposed to be quiet. It's supposed to be as "normal" as possible, just comfortable enough. All of these spaces are institutional spaces. Let's make the hotel room smell. Maybe someone was here cooking up a delicious, homey meal? I left the prints in the hotel space and I went home and looked up *smells like curry* in a search engine. I expected to find at least a few recipes and maybe some obnoxious comments. But it's all people complaining, "Hey, my neighbor smells like curry. What should I do?" This is actually something I found on *Yahoo! Answers*. The "answer" to that was, "Call the INS." I was completely horrified. This was insane that somebody could put a smell together with someone's legal status. For the first time I started to understand how we can be prejudiced with our entire bodies rather than just our eyes. We think of race as this color-coded thing, and it's not—it's much more complicated. From there I basically worked with curry powder for seven years!

Curry is something of an edible self-portrait. I'm both Indian and Japanese, and both Indian and Japanese people eat curry. On top of that, the most popular brand of curry powder is S&B. Those happen to be my initials, so I took it as a sign from the "art gods" that I was supposed to use this material. Curry has a very interesting colonial history. It is truly a global product. The first published recipe for curry powder was in 1861 in *Mrs. Beeton's Book of Household Management*, which is basically a book English housewives were supposed to take to the colonies so they could run a "proper" household. Of course, in India you go and eat all of these delicious things, and none of them are called "curry"; they all have these different names. The British were trying to make sense of this new cuisine. To simplify things, they took a bunch of coriander, turmeric, and other spices and packaged them all together and sold them as "curry powder." That blend of spices was already mixing together old and new worlds. Your average curry powder is spicy because of the chilies that were brought to India by the Portuguese from the New World. It ended up in Japan because it was so popular on British ships that the navy was serving it once a week. Legend has it that there was this British naval ship that docked and a hungry Japanese boy scurried on board, tasted the curry, and went, "This is the most delicious thing ever," and ran back to his family and told them all how to make it. In reality, the restrictions on eating meat were being lifted in Japan at the time. The British were encouraging the consumption of meat in Japan, and this was one of the ways to do it. Of course there is curry in West India, the Caribbean, Vietnam . . . the spice blend is traveling and circulating, much like myself. As a material, people see curry powder and they think "South Asia," and they don't think of anything else, but I see all of these connections that have come together to make this thing. As an installation-based artist, I've poured it on the ground, I've made a perfume out of it; I figured why not let everyone smell like curry, not just South Asians!

LK: Sita, in 2011 you installed *Curry Institute* at the Sheehan Gallery at Whitman College in Walla Walla, Washington, as part of the exhibition *Techniques: Contemporary Asian American Time-Based Art,* curated by my coeditor Jan Christian Bernabe. So why *Curry Institute*?

SKB: Galleries were never meant to deal with smells or touch or taste. I don't think that's an accident. One of the reasons I'm drawn to using these messy materials is because it challenges these art institutions that are rooted in Western philosophy, which privileges vision and eyesight.

The gallery is supposed to be sanitized; curry powder messes with that. I'm inserting this seemingly innocuous thing that turns into a real problem in the gallery space. How are you not going to track it? What about people with allergies? How are you not going to get it all over the other artwork? For centuries these spaces have been devoted to the visual. That's part of what the word *institution* means to me: this privileging of the visual that makes everything else assumed.

LK: And Saya, what about your use of the word *institute*? Can you tell us about your creation of *The Empathics* and their *Institute of Empathy* and how this might relate to your own family history?

SW: My grandmother lived in Father Divine's orphanage, a utopian community where people could become a part of the community and gave up their children to be raised as common . . . as a single family. I knew she grew up in an orphanage, but that was all I knew until I was in my twenties, when my sister, who was a history major at Stanford, was taking a class on African American political history and Father Divine was covered. As she was talking to our father, it was revealed that that's where my grandmother was raised. What's interesting to me is that there is a relationship between my grandmother's history and my project, *The Institute of Empathy*. It wasn't intentional. I kind of forgot about it until later and subsequently have thought a lot about why that might have happened. *The Institute of Empathy* actually emerged more out of working on a project called *The Ethnography of No Place*, which I made with Rachel Lears.

Interestingly, Sita, when you were talking about the flows and movements of food . . . when I was living in Brazil, one of the things I was thinking a lot about was transplantation of different flora and fauna from the "Old World" to the "New World" and from the "New World" to the "Old World." When I started building *No Place*, I wanted the people of that world to be part plant and part human, because there was a porosity of boundaries for this flora and fauna. In many ways there was a lot of migration—forced migration, self-selected migration —between the different parts of the world. The No Placeans were built thinking through that. *The Institute of Empathy* emerged after I had posited this future world of No Place. No Place is not in the present. It's in the future. This anthropologist goes through a portal, which appears in Queens, and enters this other world. The ethnography is a lot about the anthropologist's experience of dislocation and attempting to document something to which she has limited access, but also to which she has a combination of scientific and emotional access. It's not just science. It's also emotional experiences that constructed the knowledge that the "Old World" built about the "New World." There is this subjective/objective combination in the narrative of *Ethnography of No Place*. The *Institute* came about because I had posited this future utopia, which was mapped thinking with dancers, curators, anthropologists, and biologists. Once that had been posited, I started thinking, "What would it be like for this No Place future world to actually come about?" *The Institute of Empathy* became this R&D hub, where people in the present could do archaeological digs and scientific research to develop a series of processes by which people could become more like these part-plant/part-humans in the future. I like the language of the institute because it has a scientific ring.

Right before I started working on this project, I was an artist-in-residence in upstate New York and was looking at the Oneida community, a historical utopian community in upstate New York. I loved the idea that they had organized a community, which was partially a religious community, but they also sell silverware to people all over the world to perpetuate their way of living. *The Institute of Empathy* and now *ChimaTEK* have come out of that investigation. You have this research and development hub, which is the *Institute of Empathy*, which is a nonprofit organization. *ChimaTEK* becomes the corporation that distributes their ideas and products into the homes of everyday people. It also emerged because I was working with scientists who had labs and institutes, and I was thinking about the different ways these individuals were forming groups that weren't just about political mobilization but seemed to be attempting to address something about the truth, whatever that is. I'm not sure there is any such thing as "the truth," but there is a utopianism and dystopianism in attempts at getting to that truth. *The Institute* became the framework for *The Empathics*. *The Empathics* is actually a project in and of itself. *The Institute of Empathy* is their institute. *The Empathics* is actually the title of the project—the culture's name, the group's name, the group's type.

I do find it rather mysterious that my grandmother grew up in a utopian community and I had completely forgotten about it until after I had produced this project.

LK: Saya, looking at the various fabrics you used, many of them look to be Japanese fabrics. You are combining imagery from many different cultures and the fashion world in the structures you are building.

SW: Part of my early education was working with my maternal grandmother making garments because my family in Japan was in the textile industry. One of the things that really impacted me as a teenager was looking at all the hybrid fashions—fashion designers dressing white European models in a combination of a variety of different textile patterns, and then this was critiqued in the 1990s as appropriation. When I started building the *Empathics* project, I wanted to revisit those methods with a different approach—a kind of approach that incorporates the way the Internet functions and how technology has changed the ways people think about authenticity. I love Yinka Shonibare's projects where he creates all of these garments that seem to be African but they're actually Dutch wax textiles that were made and then exported to Africa. Even though we think that African textile is an African textile, it's actually this hybrid object destabilizing the idea that anything happens alone or without a relation to something else. Going back to something that Sita said, in my work I try to always make people feel located and dislocated in the work. It's ideal to me if someone thinks they recognize something but it's actually not recognizable because it's not the thing they thought it might be. That state of trying to understand what they are looking at, what they are experiencing is really important.

LK: Saya and Sita, I see so many parallels between your mutual interest in colonial history and relationship with using the language of institutions, specifically with science. Sita, you worked with a perfumer to create a curry perfume. Saya, I know that part of your fictional narrative is finding and researching this DNA of hybrid plant-humans.

SKB: I worked with perfumer Yosh Han in San Francisco, who does a lot of conceptual fragrances. When I first got into it, I thought, "This is great, I'm going to be a perfumer!" Then I realized that perfuming is a lot about essences, and there is a huge parallel between essentialism (like when you think of race) and essences (like when we create smells). You can never really replicate the smells we have. You are creating a synonym for the thing. I would have people smell the perfume, and they would be like, "This smells more Indian," and you're like, "What is that?" I mean, come on! So I ended up getting a little disillusioned with it because it was about, How do we distill what an entire people eats into a drop of something? For me the challenge was, How do we explode that and complicate it? Saya, what you were saying is so true. How do you create something that people feel connected to enough that they can find a home in it even though they may not recognize the components around it? I like it when someone walks into one of my installations and says, "This reminds me of when my grandmother used to make these cookies," but it is made up of ingredients that are unfamiliar.

As a kid who grew up in Southern California, we also moved every two years. We would travel all the time, and I spent a few summers in Colombia. I think I was always looking for elements of home. I want people coming into the gallery to have this same experience in a way.

SW: For me, the plant-human hybrid produced the necessity to think about genetics. Even though I wasn't thinking about genetics initially, just by looking at *casta* paintings or the history of race mixture in the United States and Brazil and around the world, you start thinking about how much one thing starts making a thing one way or the other. When I began to imagine how people could actually become these plant-humans, the most logical and realistic way for that to happen was through some sort of mutation, a transformation of one's DNA. Things like this do happen in nature: viruses change. Chimerism is a real thing, women who have children will often have their child's DNA floating through their blood system for the rest of their lives. You are part of your child even after they are born. In extreme cases, people have different genetic tissue inside their bodies. They have two different kinds of genetic material. For me, this was a way for me to point to broader conversations around ideas of race mixture. The genealogy projects and the proliferation of DNA testing, Henry Louis Gates's history project about Oprah's DNA—these were popular conversations emerging at the same time I was thinking through *The Institute of Empathy*. It was a very logical approach to making these people become closer to the No Placeans, this slight mutation. What's important in this project is that it is about self-selection and agency. Anyone can choose to become an Empathic. It's not a closed circuit. It's a community that is constantly emerging and evolving because there are more and more people who are able to self-select into this community.

That's the difference between *The Institute of Empathy* and the *ChimaTEK* project, which is a more dystopian project. It's more about the erasure of the agency and the topicality of engaging with ideas of hybridity. The reason I am doing this is because the project has always been a three-part narrative arc where there is the future, the present, and the future future, where it's a utopian future projected, which produces a dystopia. It's all three parts in tandem, which work together to create the story of No Place and the Empathics. It's supposed to be similar to the way our reality has been functioning with our histories, our present present—specifically the history of the United States. That evolution of a utopian ideal into a dystopia is the simple narrative arc of the project, but the temporalities are supposed to be encountered at once.

LK: We've been talking about how you navigate and inhabit multiple identities in your work, specifically as mixed-race Asian Americans. Is there anything else you would like to add to that, and can you also speak to how your work might engage queerness in either form, content, or your studio methodology?

SW: Part of the reason I built a whole other world is because of the limited language around multiraciality. For me, building a whole world has allowed people to enter an entire logic of a place, which would not be something they would have immediate access to without having experienced some of these things through their own bodies. That, I think, is a direct result of being someone who is a world crosser, who is constantly shifting between categories, which could be considered a queering as well, if you'd like.

SKB: I was talking to a filmmaker friend, Kay Cuajunco, about, Is there such a thing as queer food or Asian American food, and what are those things? My friend was like, "If you think about queerness as something that exists beyond binaries, then yes, of course there is such a thing as queer food, or Asian American food, or queer Asian American food, for that matter." For me, that translates into, Why is it that I use these ingredients and materials in my work? What is it that I'm trying to get at? Normativity really hinges on a system of binaries. If you feel trapped within these binaries, that's when you need other possibilities, like the one Saya is trying to create in her work. I don't think it's a mystery why I am drawn to mixed media and installation work. That experience is beyond a visual/no-visual binary. It's about these other senses that occur between smell and touch or between sight and sound that we may not have language for or that science doesn't even have language for. Researchers now think that we have forty-two or more senses instead of just five. I think many of us experience a life where we have more than five senses, or five races, or five ways of doing things. For me it is about creating possibilities. But, as

Saya mentioned with her dystopian project, sometimes it's about creating the world we want to live in, and sometimes you're also really angry and not so optimistic about things. How do those two look together in your work? How do you make work that is critical and challenging but also isn't so unrelatable that it doesn't have a place for you to inhabit? How do I make work that has space for people to inhabit it?

SW: I love what you just said. My original work was much more straight critical. It didn't leave a place for people. The strategy in the last six years has been, How do you build a logic that people can enter so that their perceptions of these things can be transformed slowly through repeat engagement though a narrative arc?

SKB: The other parallel I see is how your projects are really rooted in narrative but not fixed by it. That is also part of this participation. The narrative can shift depending on the people who come, or inhabit it, or contribute toward it or change it. I feel that the story is one of the few strategies I can identify that really represent us as mixed people. Clearly box checking isn't it. Photography has a very long and contentious history with representation. I always come back to the story as a tool that can get at the different things that we are.

LK: In terms of a history of mixed-race artwork, many times it is first-person narrative: I'm a product of . . . , my mom is this, and my dad is that, and telling the story as if somehow we are exceptional. What interests me in both of your works is how you are using narrative not in a way that is based in fact or a documentary impulse but rather in fantasy and fiction.

SKB: I used to have a superiority complex about being more interesting because I had this complicated story. Mixed people are celebrated for that. "Oh, how exotic," right? How interesting. How fantastic that there was a boat that went from Japan to Colombia and there was a plane that went from . . . , and it's like everyone's story—it doesn't have to be dramatic in the distance that's crossed, everyone has a story, everyone. I often have white students who claim they don't have anything to say about their family history. It's a double-edged sword. As mixed people, our elaborate migration stories are part of how we are celebrated, but it also identifies us as other. If I'm unwilling to lose that story about myself, then how can I flip that? How can I involve other people in that story?

SW: I actually have had the opposite experience. I grew up in a place where people fetishized multiraciality but did not celebrate multiraciality, which I think is a pretty big distinction. It was a very different experience for me. I always wanted to just blend in to this very white community I grew up in.

SKB: California in the 1980s is probably not indicative of a lot of places on the planet!

SW: I think about the chimeras, these multipart creatures are in some part camouflage.

LK: Saya, you were in Tokyo until you were two, which you probably don't have any memory of, but then you said you were in Westchester, New York?

SW: I was in Westchester, but I went back to Japan every summer. I spent two months every summer studying Japanese and living with my grandmother.

LK: Both of you are phenotypically relatively dark. I think this may be something worth noting. Saya, I'm wondering how you were racialized in both Japan and Westchester? You mentioned early that when you think of mixed-race Asians, it tends to be Asian-white, and in both of your cases it's a different sort of mix—and as a result, probably a very different sort of experience of how you were accepted or not.

SW: On a global spectrum, I'm not light but I'm not dark. It just depends on whom I am in relation to. In Westchester I was just ambiguous. I was racially ambiguous and moved between different social groups pretty regularly. In Japan, because I'm fluent in Japanese, I actually fit in perfectly. I had no problems. Maybe it was difficult when I was first going to school, but my language skills. . . . Actually that is where I always felt the most comfortable—in Japan. That's kind of an odd reality.

SKB: Language is really interesting. I speak fluent Spanish, and being in Colombia—in a way it's the most I've ever felt at home. We have this shared tongue and shared space. I'm with my family, but we are totally out of place in the country around us. My family is very insular and has been really sensitive to outside criticism. We share a sense of alienation. I think that's what makes me feel at home. Language has directed a lot of what has happened in my life. It's the reason I've traveled to Mexico so many times, the reason why I'm now collaborating with a group of artisans [Dignicraft] there. I'm involved in a lot of groups that speak a lot about family. It's been part of my work more now than it has been before, because I think it's been a little sensitive and painful to think about—and this is something that comes up in queer communities a lot: the family we choose and the family that we are born with and how that supports the world that you create for yourself. I exist in two or three different chosen families and my one giant family split across three continents. I think this may be particular to me, but also to many of us who have chosen each other as well.

Chapter 7

Queering Asian America

Open-Source Identities: Identity and Resistance in the Work of Three Asian American Artists

VALERIE SOE

This chapter looks at the ways in which three Asian American contemporary artists utilize the Internet in sourcing and disseminating their work in order to continue in the tradition of many past Asian American artists and artists of color who employ a socially engaged art practice. By utilizing twenty-first-century online platforms, these artists also expand on the creative strategies of previous Asian American artists, as well as address newer concerns such as the racialization of people of color online.

In an essay from 2000, Japanese American singer and activist Chris Iijima noted, "Asian American artists who are conscious and responding, either through their art or in the process of living their lives, to the racial, gender, class, and other subordination that continues to exist and to the reactionary onslaught that poor Asian and other communities of color are presently facing are, to me, APA [Asian Pacific American] artists who have continued the tradition of what APA culture was originally meant to be."[1] Iijima's statement reflects earlier Asian American artists' concerns with using art as a tool for social change and placing the concerns of the community ahead of those of the makers themselves. It is indicative of the overtly political creative practice of many Asian American artists and other artists of color.

However, when presented with work by artists of color that explicitly challenges structural inequities, the mainstream art world has been less than receptive, often dismissing the art out of hand by denying the relevance of the topics it examined. This widespread resistance to culturally specific art by Asian Americans and other people of color came to a head with the 1993

Whitney Biennial, which met with near-universal derision from the art world, exemplified by *Time* magazine art critic Robert Hughes calling it "a fiesta of whining."[2] In discussing the oddly narrow critical perception of Asian American art from the 1990s, Margo Machida notes, "The supposition, of course, was that the issues addressed by these artists could be meaningful only to other Asian Americans—despite the fact that the exhibition addressed matters of diasporic journeys, displacement, migration, border crossing, hybridity and cultural difference, race relations, and historical connections between the United States and Asia, as well a host of other concerns that could potentially affect everyone. Apparently, though, framing those issues through an Asian American lens continues to be regarded as parochial."[3]

Why such a rush to pronounce the death of artwork dealing with racial politics? This is in part because multiculturalism forced the art world to look at artwork in a broader framework—political, social, cultural, structural—which also brought into focus the complicity of the art market in perpetuating social inequity. Many artists that challenge the status quo also threaten the commodity-based, capitalist model on which the commercial art world is based, since the commercial art world (or more accurately, the art market) and capital are intrinsically entwined.

After the turning back of multiculturalism, exemplified by the hostile rejection of the 1993 biennial, many artists of color who deal with social inequities have changed their approach to dealing with these topics. Nineteenth-century German military strategist Helmuth von Moltke noted, "No battle plan survives first contact with the enemy,"[4] and Asian American artists have continued to shift and change their strategic approaches. As Susette Min states, "What characterizes much of their art, as distinguished from its predecessors in the 1990s, is a freedom to pick, choose, manipulate, and reinvent different kinds of languages and issues, both formal and political."[5]

This essay looks at three Asian American artists—Scott Tsuchitani, Gaye Chan, and Hasan Elahi—who use online platforms, public interventions, and socially engaged art practice to subvert and resist oppressive economic, political, and social systems. Like many earlier Asian American artists, they integrate creative practice with social activism, using their work as a means of actively resisting what they perceive as oppressive or outdated systems of exchange. By utilizing online platforms for sourcing and distributing their work, however, they expand the strategies of earlier social-practice Asian American artists who similarly dealt with themes of race and culture, identity, and self-determination. These artists further explore the connections among corporate, military, governmental, and colonial control and link them with issues of sovereignty and resistance to imperialism by integrating and investigating virtual spaces in their work.

GIFT ECONOMY

Following, in part, the tenets of the Free Art Movement and exchange-based art, which seek to bypass or circumvent capital-based systems of exchange in the distribution of creative work, these artists produce open-source artwork, creative work that is meant to be freely shared and given away without expectation of monetary gain or reward. Their art practice is in part based on the concept of the gift economy, which entails giving goods and services without expectation of return or reward. This notion, popularized by writer and poet Lewis Hyde in his 1983 book *The Gift*, emphasizes that creative work should not be a commodity to be bought and sold but a gift to be given away freely.

However, this concept is not new. Some Northwest Native American cultures utilize the idea of potlatch, customarily a festival of giving and gift exchange that in some cases was the basis for an entire economic system of barter or exchange. As practiced in northern Thailand, Theravada Buddhism includes the concept of merit-making, which emphasizes monetary and food-based gift-giving to increase karma. Among Asian Americans, the practice of sending money or goods "back home" to relatives overseas, as seen in *balikbayan* boxes in the Filipino American community and remittances, also reflects both merit-making and filial piety. The Free Art Movement similarly posits the practice of giving away creative work rather than selling it for economic gain. Of course, these practices do often result in rewards such as increased social status, professional recognition, or karma, but traditionally they are not based on the market-based exchange system of monetary reward.

Perhaps a more relevant recent manifestation of the gift economy can be found on the Internet, where open-source programs such as the Linux operating system, freeware software applications, peer-to-peer file sharing, and the Copy Left and free culture movements all encourage the principle that, in order to create more just and equal social structures, information and knowledge should be freely available to all without cost. As free software activist Richard Stallman notes, "This is a matter of freedom, not price, so think of 'free speech,' not 'free beer.' These freedoms are vitally important. They are essential, not just for the individual user's sake, but for society as a whole because they promote social solidarity—that is, sharing and cooperation."[6]

Although these online gift-based practices are not without flaws, they speak to an urge to challenge or undermine capitalism by refusing to participate in the commodity-based market system. Further, an information-based gift economy can also have a global impact, as seen by the literally earth-shaking effects of WikiLeaks, which has revealed governmental machinations around the globe and resulted in much consternation for the powers-that-be.

The artists here all create work that utilizes the Internet's free exchange of information or ideas, and online platforms are intrinsic to the creation and dissemination of all their work, thus utilizing a borderless, interconnected virtuality that more easily transcends geographical and national boundaries. By interrogating capital-based systems of exchange and by resisting commodification, classification, and control, these Asian American artists are using new strategies in their creative practice to actively oppose the regulation of identity, autonomy, and culture.

Their work also reflects the fact that people of color have been increasingly present on the Internet, in some ways addressing the "digital divide" of the late twentieth and early twenty-first centuries. As Lisa Nakamura notes, "While earlier racial formation theory assumed that viewers were subject to media depictions or racial projects that contributed to racialization, and that these projects were ongoing and differential but nonetheless worked in a more or less one-way fashion, new media can look to an increasingly vital digital cultural margin or counterculture for resistance."[7] However, Nakamura further cautions against a utopic idealization of online spaces, observing, "The multilayered visual culture of the Internet is anything but a space of utopian posthumanism where differences between genders, races, and nationalities are leveled out; on the contrary, it is an intensely active, productive space of visual signification where those differences are intensified, modulated, reiterated, and challenged by former objects of interactivity, whose subjectivity is expressed by their negotiations of the shifting terrain of identity."[8] The artists discussed herein use the Internet advisedly, with full knowledge of the pitfalls and shortcomings of relying on a mediated space in order to source and distribute their work, and they often address the inequities still present in web-based systems, such as the hypersexualized, racialized online iterations of women and people of color.

SCOTT TSUCHITANI: CULTURAL AGENCY

Based in San Francisco, Scott Tsuchitani possesses two patents and several degrees in mechanical engineering, and worked as a documentary film producer prior to becoming a visual artist. Although trained as an engineer, Tsuchitani earns his living peripatetically as a working artist and part-time lecturer, so his interest in critiquing capitalist economic structures is a result of his lived experiences.

Tsuchitani's online and in situ interventions, including *Memoirs of a Sansei Geisha* (figure 7.1) and *Lord, It's the Samurai* (plate 33), critique representations and assumptions about Japanese and Asian culture within the museum system. In his artist's statement, he cites piracy as a means of resistance, noting, "In the same way that colonialism and imperialism are based on histories of *taking* without consent, the piracy or re-appropriation of the visual culture of commerce offers a political praxis through which the marginalized

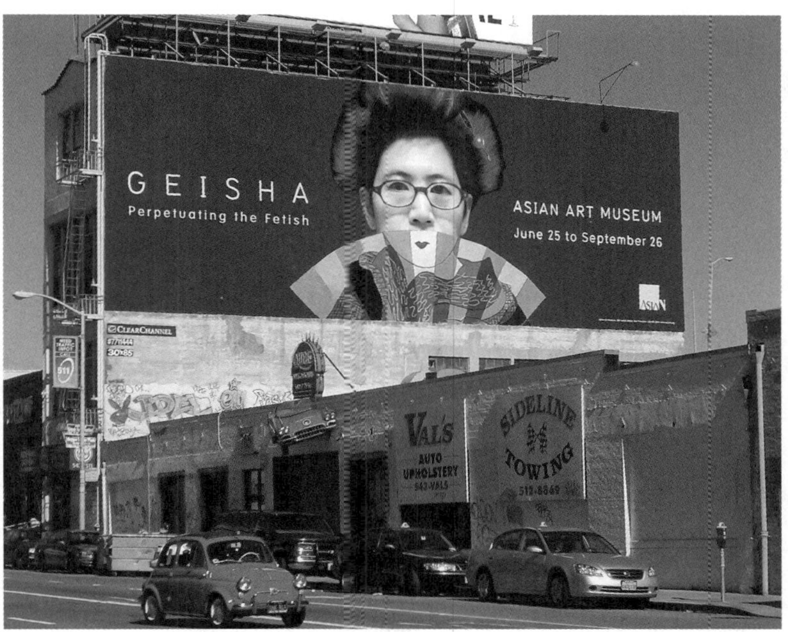

FIGURE 7.1

Scott Tsuchitani (American, b. 1962)
My Geisha Fantasy #1: Billboard Liberation, 2005, from the Memoirs of a Sansei Geisha project

Lightjet Print
11 x 14 in (28 x 36 cm)
Courtesy of the artist

can regain cultural agency."[9] Here Tsuchitani reflects some of the goals of the 1960s Situationist International movement, in which useless products of pop culture are "détourned" for political or artistic purposes, as well as the culture-jamming movement of the 1980s, in which artists and activists appropriated corporate mass-media products, most notably advertising, in order to comment on and deconstruct their meaning and efficacy.

In 2004 the San Francisco Asian Art Museum (AAM) opened *Geisha: Beyond the Painted Smile*, a blockbuster exhibition that drew more than 150,000 visitors in three months. The exhibition poster for *Geisha: Beyond the Painted Smile* featured an Asian woman peering coyly over a gilded fan, the lower half of her face occluded. In response to the poster, Tsuchitani created *Memoirs of a Sansei Geisha*, an intervention begun by photoshopping his own image onto the exhibition's poster and changing the text to read "Orientalist Dream Come True. Geisha: Perpetuating the Fetish." He then printed out the altered posters and posted them throughout San Francisco's Japantown commercial district, oftentimes near or adjacent to the original AAM poster. He furthered the intervention by creating mock flyers of the exhibition and installing them in the information racks in the AAM itself.

Sansei Geisha refers to Tsuchitani's generational status in the Japanese American community as a third-generation (Sansei) American-born person of Japanese descent. The Sansei generation, for the most part children of Japanese Americans imprisoned by the US government during World War II, came of age during the birth of the Asian American movement in the 1960s and 1970s, and many were politically and culturally progressive, becoming active in the antiwar movement and the 1967–68 Third World Strike at San Francisco State University. In contrast to the predominantly assimilationist Nisei generation, the Sansei often engaged in radical politics, and many were in the vanguard of agitating for redress and reparations in the 1970s and 1980s. Historian Jere Takahashi notes, "Unlike the Nisei who submerged their ethnic and racial identity, the Sansei's consciousness took on a definite racial tone as they identified themselves as a racially oppressed group and linked themselves to broader movements for racial change."[10] Tsuchitani's use of the term *Sansei* suggests a connection across generations to the multiethnic coalition-building of 1960s and 1970s Asian American activism. As political organizer Steven G. Louie notes, "One of the hallmarks of the Asian American movement was to 'unite all who can be united,' whether that was within the Asian community or with other communities, especially people of color."[11] Tsuchitani's work reflects this international perspective, including images such as the geisha and the samurai to emphasize his concerns with defining and representing transnational Asian identities.

Tsuchitani also reappropriates the term *geisha*, reclaiming it from the museum poster's orientalist usage. He notes, "Literally translated, the word *geisha* simply means 'person of the arts,' which in my case as a Japanese American artist, includes me. So in détourning of the museum's poster, I replaced the visage of the submissive faux geisha with my own, thereby returning the Orientalist gaze. In doing so, the figure is transformed from passive object into active insurgent artist."[12]

His intervention critiqued the poster, not the show, acknowledging the impact of the mass-distributed image over the museum show. As Tsuchitani notes, "For me, it was the museum's choice of using that image and the presence it had in the visual landscape of the city. . . . It's a loaded image in our culture—perpetuating the imagery of the sensuous Asian woman, the Asian mystique of the East. It's constructing an idealized 'other,' and for what purpose? While the exhibit may have tried to deconstruct that image, the number of people who actually had their minds changed can't compare with the number of those impacted by that image."[13]

While the flyers were created as a spontaneous response to the AAM's omnipresent advertising campaign, with an ephemeral physical manifestation, Tsuchitani used the intervention as a springboard for an extended dialogue on orientalism and the fetishistic representation of Asians in US culture. He created mock flyers for the exhibition and installed them in the information racks in the AAM itself, then followed up the poster and flyer with online and media guerilla work that further extended the dialogue with an e-mail address at the bottom of each poster, which generated several relevant responses. These included a message from Liza Dalby, a US resident who became a geisha in Japan and wrote an essay for the AAM's exhibition catalog. In her e-mail, she noted, "I was in Japantown this weekend and saw your clever satire on the SF Asian Art Museum's 'Geisha' poster. I agree with you entirely about the fetish, which has not much to do with the real geisha and everything to do with Western fantasy."[14] University of California Berkeley professor Gregory Levine wrote, "Congratulations on your provocative and quite impactful intervention in the AAMSF's recent 'Geisha' exhibition. I gather from sources inside the museum that you have really hit a nerve. . . . Your voice is a welcome addition to what should be a larger debate about 'Geisha,' images, audiences, representation, museums, neo-Orientalism, and so forth."[15]

The e-mail address provided a means through which community members could participate in the intervention. One such person used it to warn Tsuchitani that the AAM was on the lookout for him: "FYI, Judy told me that Asian Art Museum has been calling around (Japantown) to find out about the 'Geisha' posters. Just to give you a heads-up!"[16] Tsuchitani had utilized his social capital in the Japanese American community to gain permission to place the altered posters in Japantown storefronts and businesses. The active engagement of community members reflects the collaborative nature of the installation, underscoring Tsuchitani's interest in providing others a forum for speaking out and pushing back against the original ad campaign's retrograde representation of Japanese culture.

In the summer of 2009, the Asian Art Museum in San Francisco exhibited *Lords of the Samurai* in its main galleries. The exhibition showcased works from the Hosokawa family's collection of ceramics, swords, artwork, and other artifacts identifying the samurai clan and, by extension, the code of the samurai. As the AAM's exhibition statement claims, "Elite clans such as the Hosokawa were also great patrons of the arts and learning, and were creators of a highly sophisticated aesthetic world."[17]

Tsuchitani's online intervention, *Lord, It's the Samurai!,* challenges the museum's curatorial assumptions while critiquing the institution's history of orientalism. *Lord, It's the Samurai!* replicated the AAM show's official website with a twist, offering a detailed, pointed, and well-researched deconstruction of the problematic exhibition. The faux site pointed out the less-than-savory aspects of samurai culture that the AAM exhibit conveniently glossed over, including the militarism, slavery, pederasty, and misogyny inherent in the "code of the warrior."

The parody website meticulously recreated the layout of the AAM exhibit's official site and used language similar to the museum's source text. The lead section explained the site's premise: "Enter the world of the samurai, where more than seven centuries of martial rule are reduced to a single Disney-like trope of gentleman-warrior myth. Military prowess meets cultural connoisseurship in an ideal of masculine perfection—selling militarism as beauty in a time of war. Neither harmless nor innocent, it masks a real history of violence and domination that extends well into the twentieth century."

Tsuchitani carefully backed up each of the claims on the faux site with extensive documentation, with dozens of embedded links to scholarly articles that supplemented the website's information. The text of each section mimicked the AAM's breathless orientalist rhetoric. The subsection titled "Precision of the Blade," for instance, read, "Let the gleam of naked sword-blades transport you to a time when samurai used them to slice noses off of an estimated 38,000 victims, buried in this mound in Kyoto, one of at least a couple such 'nose tombs' in Japan."[18] By closely matching the AAM exhibit's official website, Tsuchitani dissected the carefully constructed image of the gentleman warrior that the AAM exhibit extolled.

The ersatz site also commented on the hidden politics of the exhibition, recognizing the dangers of the exhibit's glamorization of violence by noting, "No myth here, and it hasn't changed since the times of the samurai: it's universal and real, how war dehumanizes everyone."[19] The site also made a connection between the museum's soft-pedaling of Japanese nationalism and the US government's interest in remilitarizing Japan, which would aid the United States in maintaining the upper hand in Asia. The faux site noted that this was not the first time the AAM has backed up a superpower's questionable point of view, as seen in *Tibet: Treasures from the Roof of the World*, the 2005 show that gave credence to the People's Republic of China's claim that Tibet is really just the back door of China.

The intervention was multivalent; Tsuchitani took on the persona of a mock artists' collective dubbed the Asians Art Museum and again produced hard-copy flyers that were distributed in public brochure racks in San Francisco's Japantown as well as in the AAM itself. Unlike the *Sansei Geisha* posters, which remained in situ for several weeks, within a few days of Tsuchitani's covert placement of the brochure, the counterfeit flyers were removed and replaced with the AAM's own brochures, and the fake site's initial e-mail address was disabled shortly after sending out its first e-mail blast. The website eventually went viral, with nearly two dozen articles and reviews in books, academic journals, newspapers, and blogs, including *8Asians*, *ArtsJournal*, and *Art Practical*.

When speaking publicly about the project, Tsuchitani used a fictional identity, further extending the parodic aspect of the project. He notes, "I created a public persona as Majime Sugiru (which means "way too serious" in Japanese), Communications Director of the Asians Art Museum, and performed an educational and media outreach campaign in which I conducted interviews with press, blogs, KPFA's 'Hard Knock Radio,' and spoke to a number of local college classes."[20] Ultimately, Tsuchitani utilized multiple strategies, combining guerilla performance, "real life" intervention, the Internet, social media, and traditional media to critique the structural racism of the Asian Art Museum.

GAYE CHAN: WILD AND STRONG

Gaye Chan was born in Hong Kong and immigrated to the United States in 1969. She currently resides in Honolulu, Hawai'i, where she is the chair of the Department of Art and Art History at the University of Hawai'i. Chan's installation *Free Grindz* (2011) is an element of Chan's ongoing collaborative project *Eating in Public,* a collective art project she founded in 2003 with activist and scholar Nandita Sharma that utilizes guerilla plantings, seed sharing, and free goods exchanges to explore issues around land use, centered on retaking the commons from both private and public interests.

In *Free Grindz,* Chan presented a brief history of various edible weeds found on O'ahu, including dandelions, amaranth, and purslane, along with seeds, recipes, and identifying photos. Chan inscribed each recipe on a large rubber stamp and supplied scratch paper on which gallery visitors could then stamp the recipes. She also provided seed packets, filled with weed seeds and stamped with the name of the weed and the exhibition's website, in order to facilitate the dissemination of the seeds into local gardens.

Chan's aesthetic of reuse extended to the installation itself. The entirety of *Free Grindz* was displayed in the reconfirmed shipping crate in which the materials traveled from Hawai'i, which Chan purposely designed to deconstruct into a seed-sharing kiosk. The rubber-stamp recipe station used torn-up sheets of recycled paper, and the project's seed packets were made from repurposed envelopes from various sources, including utility companies, the University of Hawai'i advertising department, and other junk mail solicitations.

In addition, Chan made the seeds and recipes free for the taking, as gallery visitors were encouraged to take as many seeds and recipes as they liked, and to (literally) disseminate the plants and information without cost. Artist Claire Pentecost, who also has worked with seed sharing in her soil-art projects, notes, "The development and exchange of genetic plant material in the form of seeds is perhaps the longest running open-source knowledge network in human history."[21] Chan's seed-sharing projects acknowledge the long history of this form of gift economy, by distributing goods without expectation of monetary gain.

Chan has worked with Native Hawaiian environmental justice organizations, such as Kalihi Ahupua'a Ulu Pono Ahahui and the Malama Learning Center, which integrate traditional Hawaiian cultural practices with land-use activism, and her creative practice reflects this. She recognizes the Hawaiian origins of the seed-sharing project by including pidgin English in *Free Grindz*'s title and signage. *Grindz* indicates tasty local food, while other text states “how fo cook” and “put in dirt/water/pau (finish)”; in addition, Chan presents *Free Grindz*’s project description in both pidgin and standard English on her website. By including both pidgin and standard English, she recognizes the validity of both languages and affirms the cultural diversity of Hawai‘i, acknowledging the ongoing struggle for Native Hawaiian sovereignty.

Chan makes reference to Hawaiian sovereignty on her website, where she discusses the misperception of weeds in both pidgin and standard English:

> In da Oxford English Dictionary I wen look up da word “weed.” It wen say dat weedz are just plants dat no get value, no get beauty. But it also wen say dat weeds grow so wild n strong dat dey can take over “superior vegetation” (da kine stuffs you buy in da supahmahket).
>
> According to the Oxford English Dictionary weeds are plants that are not valued for their use, or beauty. Plants that grow wild and strong. So wild and strong that they can take over the growth of what some call “superior vegetation”—meaning those you buy at garden stores and supermarkets.”[22]

Here she suggests that the vigorous persistence of weeds is a metaphor for the tenacity of indigenous cultures in the face of colonial incursions. She goes on to state, “There many weeds that are edible and many of them taste really good! We are rarely informed about this because being able to get stuff for FREE is bad for capitalism. Freedom from capitalism begins when we diminish our reliance on it.” In these terms, Chan delineates *Free Grindz* and other seed-sharing projects as an explicit resistance against the tyranny of the global market economy.

The in situ iteration of Chan’s seed-sharing project (plate 34) extends her vision of bypassing and circumventing the market economy. Chan distributed prefabricated seed-sharing stations, which are portable, self-contained boxes, without charge to agencies that were willing to display the boxes in a public space. The boxes, complete with seed packets and recipes, ended up in community health centers, elder centers, art galleries, and farmers’ markets around O‘ahu. As noted in the project description, “The ancient practices of seed saving and sharing are currently under threat. Plants carefully cultivated by farmers the world over for millennia—skills and knowledge that belong to no one and everyone—are being claimed as ‘inventions’ and patented by corporations with the support of national states and international bodies, such as the World Trade Organization. Most of these patented seeds are genetically modified. To support corporations, states have made it illegal for everyone else to save and share patented seeds. Saving and sharing seeds is crucial to our freedom, autonomy from capitalism, and crucial for our survival.”[23] In addition, on the project's website Chan offers do-it-yourself instructions for constructing seed stations and creating rubber-stamp recipes, as well as information on foraging edible weed seeds and other information about seed sharing, exemplifying the idea of the free culture movement.

Chan's uses her seed-sharing projects as a way to undermine corporate control and to actively advocate for a more equitable system of food production. Chan is thus actively circumventing the capitalist system of exchange in favor of a gift-based economy where the social benefit comes from sharing rather than hoarding.

Chan's *Barter Baskets* (2012) further continues her interest in undermining monetary systems of exchange. In the project description, Chan discusses the genesis of the piece: "In August 2012 I'd wanted to get a case of tomatoes to make sauce, so I went to visit Annie Moss who owns an organic foods distribution company. While there I noticed heaps of baling straps. These single-use straps are found around nearly every box shipped across the globe. Binding box to box, paper to paper, and everything to pallets. Even though Annie intends to recycle them the waste factor irked me to no end. I gave myself the task of figuring out how to reuse or upcycle them."[24]

Chan taught herself to weave baskets from the baling straps, then proposed to Moss that, in exchange for one of Chan's baskets a week, Moss would give her fruit and vegetable seconds from her distribution company. Chan then redistributed the produce to several local families, while Moss gave the baskets to her workers and suppliers. Chan has since expanded this project to include bartering the baskets for goods and services, including sewing, drawings, homemade jam, clothing, and a few items from a local pharmacy. Chan documented this ongoing process on her Facebook feed, posting images and text from *Barter Baskets* that showed her various attempts at basket weaving, the goods and services exchanged with barter partners (for instance, a pile of organic vegetables, a chocolate cake, photography), as well as photos of each completed basket, noting, "Many baskets later, still not a cent has changed hands."[25] By utilizing Facebook to disseminate information about her projects, Chan appropriates and subverts the social media platform's primary use as a commercial site for social exchange in order to advocate for alternatives to a cash economy.

Sweat (2013) featured the artist in a week-long performance at a storefront in Vancouver's Chinatown, where Chan demonstrated the basket-weaving techniques used in *Barter Baskets*. For several hours each day, Chan wove baskets in the storefront, which was shrouded in a semitransparent cube, with only her hands fully visible from the street. Working within the shrouded cube, Chan obscured her body and brought her hands into sharp focus, addressing the often unseen contribution of laborers, as well as the importance of manufacturing (literally "hand-making") in maintaining global economic flows. Chan harkens back to her own background as a Chinese American and an immigrant from Hong Kong by siting the performance in Chinatown and referencing the sweatshop in the project's title, recognizing the labor of Chinese garment workers both in North America and abroad. In this way, she emphasizes the way her identity as a Chinese American artist informs her activism as well as the interconnectedness of workers worldwide.

On her website and in the exhibition's printed materials (including the signage on the storefront window), Chan includes links to how-to basket-weaving instructions in English and simplified and traditional Chinese. In this way, Chan acknowledges the diversity of the Chinese diaspora by making available the instructions in all three written languages, as simplified Chinese is primarily used in China and Singapore, while traditional Chinese is used by most of the rest of the Chinese-speaking world. Chan provides these basket-weaving instructions free of charge, again emphasizing her interest in freely sharing goods and information without expectation of monetary gain. She also recognizes the global audience accessible via the Internet and the ability of that audience to cross political and geographic boundaries.[26]

HASAN ELAHI: IDENTITY MANAGEMENT

Born in Bangladesh in 1971, Hasan Elahi now lives outside of Washington, DC, "roughly equidistant from the CIA, FBI, and NSA headquarters."[27] His past work has dealt with photographic interpretations of highly politicized sites, such as the Joint Security Area between North and South Korea and Cambodia's killing fields. Hasan Elahi's web-based project *Tracking Transience* (figure 1.1) and the related multimedia installation *Hiding in Plain Sight*

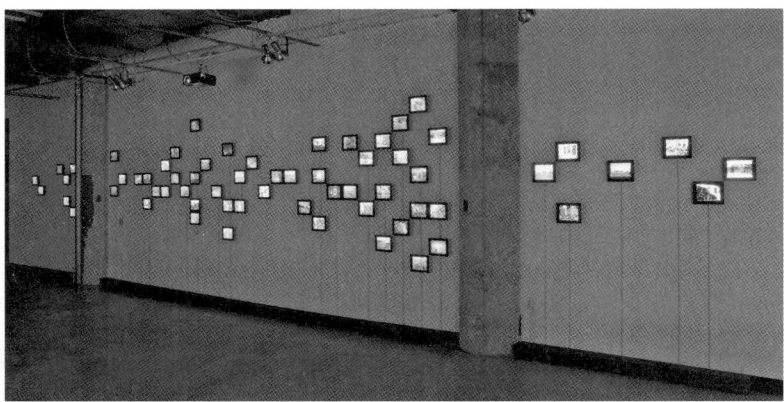

FIGURE 7.2

Hasan Elahi (American, b. 1972)
Hiding in Plain Sight, 2011

24 x 42 x 10 ft (7.4 x 12.9 x 3 m)
85-channel media installation, as installed at Intersection for the Arts, San Francisco, California
Courtesy of the artist

(figure 7.2) present an alternative to the market economy by continually placing minute details of Elahi's everyday life on the Internet for all to access. What's more, the projects comment on Elahi's experiences as a South Asian man living in the United States.

In 2002, shortly after the destruction of the World Trade Center, Elahi was returning to the United States from traveling abroad when he was detained by Homeland Security on suspicion of terrorist activities. After that incident, he began obsessively photographing his everyday activities and uploading the snapshots to his website, trackingtransience.net. The website pinpoints Elahi's location through a GPS that he carries in his back pocket, showing his location on the map as well as a street-level view of the site.
As Elahi noted to the *New York Times*,

> I created a list of every flight I've ever been on, since birth. . . . On my website, I compiled various databases that show the airports I've been in, food I've eaten at home, food I've eaten on the road, random hotel beds I've slept in, various parking lots off Interstate 80 that I parked in, empty train stations I saw, as well as very specific information like photos of the tacos I ate in Mexico City between July 5 and 7, and the toilets I used. . . . I also provided screenshots of my financial data, communications records and transportation logs. . . . By putting everything about me out there, I am simultaneously telling everything and nothing about my life.[28]

For *Hiding in Plain Sight* (2011), an installation of the trackingtransience.net project at the Intersection for the Arts gallery in San Francisco, several dozen small monitors arrayed on the wall of the darkened gallery showed random images, constantly downloaded from Elahi's server, of the thousands of toilets, airports, takeout dinners, cups of coffee, and other bland, quotidian details of Elahi's everyday existence. A bank of larger flat-screen monitors on an adjacent wall scrolled through Elahi's daily bank statements and credit card transactions, while a wall-sized projection of trackingtransience.net played on another wall. The volume and detail of the images and information, uploaded daily by Elahi, documented his every move and cleverly defeated any attempt to imply illicit activities by him, as well as diminishing the worth of his "private" information. As he told the *New York Times*, "In an era in which everything is archived and tracked, the best way to maintain privacy may be to give it up. Information agencies operate in an industry that values data. Restricted access to information is what makes it valuable. If I cut out the middleman and flood the market with my information, the intelligence the F.B.I. has on me will be of no value. Making my private information public devalues the currency of the information the intelligence gatherers have collected."[29]

This statement parallels the anticommodification bent of Chan's seed-sharing project, putting an interesting spin on the idea of the gift economy. In this case, Elahi is sharing thousands of images, bits of data, and other electronic flotsam from his life, over-gifting the viewer with the intimate yet ultimately not very useful details of his daily existence. Here he's using information as the coin to be bartered, yet instead of stingily withholding that coin, he's freely sharing it with whoever cares to sift through it. "It's economics," he says. "I flood the market."[30] In this way Elahi defies the capitalist model of the scarcity value of goods or information.

Elahi also uses his over-the-top data dump as a means of resisting the government's invasive surveillance. He notes, "My activities may be more symbolic than not, but if 300 million people started sending private information to federal agents, the government would need to hire as many as another 300 million people, possibly more, to keep up with the information and we'd have to redesign our entire intelligence system."[31]

Tracking Transience and *Hiding in Plain Sight* make cogent comments about Elahi's life as a South Asian man living in the United States and the conflation of his ethnicity with that of "Arab" terrorists. Elahi recounts, "[The FBI agent] eventually went on to tell me that they received a report that an Arab man had fled on September 12th that had explosives. And that person would be me. Never mind I'm not Arab."[32] Following his initial detainment at the Detroit airport, Elahi took nine polygraph tests and had dozens of interviews with the FBI. "For six months, I had to justify every second [of] my existence, proving to the FBI that I was not a terrorist or a terrorist threat of any kind," Elahi told *ABC News*. "So, after having to recount every detail of my life to the micro level, I said to myself, 'Why don't I just do this myself?'"[33]

Although people of color are often disenfranchised and misrepresented on the Internet, Elahi used this experience to actively retake control of his life and identity, as he explains: "By taking matters into my own hands, I decided that I'm going to define myself based on my own information, not based on what someone else thinks I might be and this is really the center of this project. It's really all about identity management."[34] This reflects the great importance that Asian American activists place on self-determination and self-definition. Despite the FBI's best efforts to pigeonhole him as a terrorist, Elahi uses his art practice to retain control over his identity.

A DECOLONIZING PRACTICE

Despite the mainstream art world's attempts to characterize 1990s multiculturalism as parochial, these three artists affirm the vitality of Asian American art, updating their artistic strategies and exploiting the freeness and accessibility of new media platforms to investigate hegemonic power structures. Although their methodologies rely in part on twenty-first-century technologies, their work follows after many other artists of color who have used creative work as a means of activism. In this way, these three artists are continuing the practice of many earlier Asian American artists, utilizing the open-source framework of the Internet to critique orientalism, racism and racialization, commodification, and ownership, and using their creative work to actively effect social change. By retaking the virtual spaces of the Internet and making it a site for challenging racism, imperialism, and social inequities, these artists have also updated past practices by Asian American artists who have dealt with similar concerns. As they claim an online space for Asian American voices, these artists also counter the objectification, racialization, and hypersexualizing of people of color and women that often occurs on the web.

Cultural critic Sarita See notes, "Identity is a decolonizing practice, one that ironically comes most alive when identity is under erasure."[35] Following in the tradition of earlier Asian American artists, activists, and cultural workers, these three artists use their artwork as a means of decolonizing Asian American identity, integrating creative practice with social activism and critiquing the political, economic, and governmental systems that increasingly bind and restrict us.

Muscles, Mash-Ups, and Warning Shots—Queering Japanese American History: An Interview with Tina Takemoto

JAN CHRISTIAN BERNABE AND LAURA KINA

On April 12, 2016, Jan Christian Bernabe and Laura Kina interviewed San Francisco–based artist Tina Takemoto via phone about her use of queer speculation in her 2009 experimental music video Looking for Jiro *and 2016 experimental film essay* Warning Shot, *as well as the ways in which both videos disrupt and trouble master narratives of Japanese American history.*

LAURA KINA: Several of your recent works are centered on Japanese American history. Can you start with a *jikoshokai*, a self-introduction, and talk about your relationship to Japanese American identity?

TINA TAKEMOTO: I am Yonsei, or fourth-generation American. My father's side of the family was from Watsonville, California, and they were incarcerated in Poston concentration camp in Arizona. My mother's side of the family was from Sebastopol in northern California. They were incarcerated at Amache, also known as "Granada," concentration camp in Colorado. I grew up forty-five minutes inland from the San Francisco Bay Area. Only a handful of Asian American families were living there at the time, so we were quite isolated from the Japanese American community. A few times of year we would go to Watsonville or Los Angeles for Japanese American New Year or Obon festivals. Since my father was the youngest of seven children, our family was probably more disconnected from the "classic JA" experience than the rest of his extended family.

In terms of camp history, I wasn't even aware of wartime incarceration until I was in middle school, when a teacher assigned me that topic for a class presentation. I remember reading the encyclopedia and being appalled by the treatment of Japanese Americans. I asked my father, "Have you heard of these camps where people were kept in horse stalls?" My father very calmly replied, "Yes, we were there." I was really upset because I thought my parents had kept this secret from me. I also didn't understand why they didn't know very much about the camps; my dad was only three years old when his family was imprisoned, and my mom was born in Colorado right after her family left

Amache. No one in our family talked about incarceration until the early 1980s, during the Redress Movement, when Japanese Americans called for an apology from the US government for their unlawful incarceration. My maternal grandmother started speaking about her camp experience for the first time because she was interviewed by Mei Nakano for a book about three generations of Japanese American women.[1] She carried around this book with her for months, proudly showing off the page where she was called a "heroine" for enduring so much hardship at Amache.

LK: What was your grandma's name?

TT: Hannah Yasuda. She was a feisty, outspoken woman, and we had a complicated relationship. I was her first granddaughter and a tomboy. My family was fine with that, but my grandmother really wanted me to act like a girl. I would have to stay in to set the table and wash the dishes while my brothers would be out playing, even though I knew I was better at climbing trees than they were. She was a seamstress and sewed us matching muumuus. Needless to say, I wasn't the perfect granddaughter.

Before I went away to MFA graduate school, my grandmother handed me her photo albums with pictures from Amache. She told me to Xerox the albums so I could make art about her and her experience in camp. She wanted me to make her famous [*laughter*]. I was very resistant but begrudgingly took these photocopies with me. Eventually, I did start making work based on her images, but I focused on my distant and ambivalent relationship to her histories and memories by making paintings that would intentionally fade or deteriorate. I burnt lemon juice on paper and applied heat to old Thermo-fax paper and resin using a small travel iron. The techniques were deliberately imprecise and unwieldy, which also meant that my grandmother often looked quite monstrous. This pleased me quite a bit.

JAN CHRISTIAN BERNABE: How do you relate to the book's theme of queerness, either artistically, personally, or politically? We are using the term *queer* as a framework to explore difference/nonnormativity, whether in practice, how one chooses to identify, or as a critical lens.

TT: Even before I identified as queer, gender queer, gender nonconforming, or an Asian American dyke, my art practice was engaged with the notions of difference and non-normativity. After grappling with camp history, Asian American femininity, and my fraught relationship with my grandmother, I spent ten years examining the relationship between illness, intimacy, and grief through artistic collaboration and queer or nonnormative relationships. When I moved to San Francisco in 2003, I used *Memoirs of Björk-Geisha* to challenge art world orientalism. Most recently, I have been engaged with alternative and experimental approaches to queer perspectives on Asian American history.

JCB: In your 2013 article for *Art Journal*, "Notes on Internment Camp," you write about "affective attachments to the archive." Describe how these attachments "can open up possibilities for engaging with queer history, postmemory, speculation, and desire."[2]

TT: My attachment to the archive began when E. G. Crichton set me up on a "blind date" with Jiro Onuma, a deceased gay Japanese American dandy who came from Japan in the early 1920s. Crichton was an artist-in-residence at the GLBT Historical Society, where she served as a "matchmaker" by asking artists to develop intimate and creative responses to individual collections in the archive.[3] I was immediately enamored with Onuma's prewar pictures of gay Japanese Americans in San Francisco and his collection of homoerotic male physique magazines. When I came across some of Onuma's pictures that were clearly taken in the concentration camps, I realized that I had never considered the possibility of a queer camp experience or what it might have meant for same-gender-loving individuals—like Onuma, who was thirty-eight when he was incarcerated. After I discovered that Onuma's pictures might be the only known images of adult gays in the camps, I dove into archival research in hopes of fleshing out Onuma's history and gaining insight about the queer camp experience. My research took many twists and turns and ultimately led to more questions than answers. I wrote that short piece for *Art Journal,* followed by a much longer piece for *GLQ*, where I consider what it means to engage in queer archival research, especially since it involves so much speculation and desire. For me, postmemory reminds us of the difficulty of remembering in the absence of memory and acknowledges our desire for and the impossibility of bearing witness to queer traumatic pasts in the present.

LK: The first time I met you was in 2012 at Sabina Lee Gallery in Los Angeles's Chinatown. You were showing with Việt Lê, Genevieve Erin O'Brien, and Jai Arun Ravine in *Queer Space Time.* I remember seeing your music video *Looking for Jiro* (2011) (plate 35), along with queer recreations of World War II concentration camp art from your *Gentleman's Gaman* series: a bird pin, soy sauce drawings of guard towers. Can you tell us more about this work?

TT: I began by studying the craft practices that were developed in the camps, known as the art of gaman or the art of enduring hardship using found materials such as scraps of wood and the tarpaper that covered the prison barracks.[4] Many Japanese Americans have small carved wooden bird pins in their family collections; my dad's mother had one, and Rea Tajiri in her film *History and Memory* talks about finding a bird pin in her mother's jewelry box and then seeing a photograph of her grandmother in a carving class in camp. I started thinking about how to queer these craft practices by asking, If Jiro

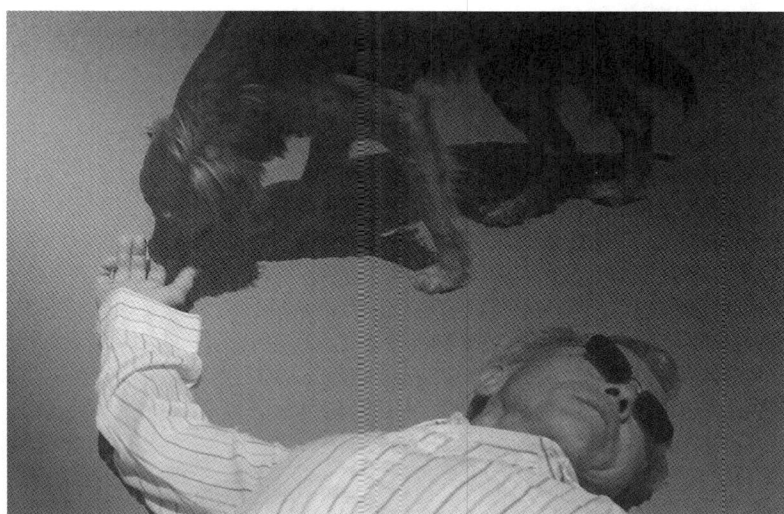

FIGURE 7.3
Tina Takemoto (American)
Video production still from *Warning Shot*, 2016
DVD, 12 min, 30 sec
Courtesy of the artist

Onuma was in the bird carving class, what kinds of pins would he make? I thought, he wouldn't make a broach. He would make cuff links or a necktie clip. I made a series of gay gentlemen's accessories using tarpaper and other found objects. Since Onuma was also obsessed with male physical culture, I made some exercise devices and other homoerotic items that would relate to this aspect of his gay imaginary.

Looking for Jiro started as a live performance or "filmformance" piece in which I perform as Jiro in front of a video projection of appropriated imagery, including US war propaganda footage from the camps. I wanted to come up with an activity that Jiro could do on stage that had a temporal arc to it. Onuma worked in the mess halls at Topaz, and I had found archival photographs of men baking bread in the camps. During the performance, Jiro's character mixes flour and water, kneads the dough, and shapes it into two large, muscular loaves. In the end, he slathers Crisco on his arms and "fists" the bread so he can wear the loaves as muscles while dancing to pop music.

JCB: In your new video, *Warning Shot* (2016) (figure 7.3), you are returning to the subject matter of the forced incarceration of Japanese Americans during World War II. Can you tell us about what drew you to tell this story as a queer "experimental film essay" using the "Rashomon effect"?[5]

TT: When I was doing research on Jiro Onuma and his time at Topaz, I kept coming across the name James Wakasa. He was a sixty-three-year-old bachelor who was shot to death by military police while walking a dog near the barbed wire fence. Wakasa's death is well known in Japanese American wartime history, but many versions of the story still exist in newspapers, government documents, and international conversations between the US government and the Japanese government regarding America's treatment of prisoners of war. Some say Wakasa was justifiably shot while trying to escape. Others claim the shooter accidentally killed Wakasa with a warning shot that was only intended to scare him. Still others assert that because Wakasa was shot through the heart while facing the shooter, his death was second-degree homicide. I decided to approach the story using Akira Kurosawa's strategy, known as the "Rashomon effect," of showing the same crime from multiple points of view.

The opening sequence of my film is inspired by *Rashomon* and Kurosawa's film *Stray Dog*, which begins by showing a dog panting. I think of Wakasa's dog as the only impartial witness to the crime, and I use his expressions to carry some of the emotional weight of the film. I was also influenced by Errol Morris's *The Thin Blue Line* and his use of repetition and constructed scenarios. But unlike Morris's film, *Warning Shot* is closer to an experimental film essay than a documentary. Even though it is based on government documents and court martial hearing transcripts, it is still very speculative and experimental in structure and tone.

LK: In *Looking for Jiro* you deliver a campy drag king performance as Jiro set to a musical mash-up of Madonna's "Hung Up" and ABBA's "Gimme Gimme Gimme (A Man after Midnight)." In *Warning Shot*, your father plays the protagonist, and the feeling of the video is much more ominous.

TT: *Looking for Jiro* uses the Madonna/ABBA mash-up as a way to communicate the character's experience of longing and desire as an adult gay man in the camps, where "time goes by so slowly" when you are waiting for a lover who will never arrive. The video also attempts to convey the psychic and physical labor of compliance and assimilation. The US propaganda footage showing hardworking Japanese Americans was intended to market them as an available and reliable labor force for factory work in the Midwest and on the East Coast. But in the world of the performance, Jiro's character also refuses this labor. As Madonna suggests, he is "fed up" and "tired of waiting on you." Instead, the performance opens a space where Jiro can admire hot mess-hall workers and imagine doing unspeakable things to young military recruits. Through his acts of homoerotic bread making, he can dream of body builders and imagine being and becoming his muscular fantasy.

With *Warning Shot*, I initially thought I could make a campier film. My original plan was to create a Bon Jovi mash-up highlighting the lyrics "Shot through the heart, and you're to blame. You give love a bad name." As I was making the film, the mood became more and more somber. I still think of it as a queer film, but as you suggest, the tone is more ominous and foreboding.

JCB: In Mariam Lam's chapter in this book, she talks about Nguyen Tan Hoang's *PIRATED!* (2000) video, which turns a violent scene of capture into homoeroticism. As I was watching *Warning Shot*, I saw you employ similar techniques in the way you suggestively cut archival footage of American GIs exercising, bending over naked for inspection, and then rough-handling a Japanese American internee. Can you talk about how you change the perspective in this video and about your choice to embody a gay male perspective?

TT: I'm so pleased you noticed those moments in the editing. The military police who were assigned concentration camp duties were generally seen as inferior to the military personnel who saw combat abroad. This hierarchy is apparent even in military police training films, which constantly work to overcome stereotypes of inadequacy. In *Warning Shot*, I try to destabilize and queer this footage by highlighting moments of homoeroticism alongside absurd displays of masculinity. While both of my films clearly gesture towards a gay male sensibility, I would also frame their homoeroticism in relation to gender-queer masculinity and my own positionality as a gender-nonconforming Asian American. In other words, my masculine-of-center approach is probably closer to a gaysian or dyke aesthetics than other frameworks.

LK: Can you talk about the ending of the video? Are you making a social commentary on contemporary events? I was struck by the sad parallel to today's killings of so many unarmed black men and the sense that police brutality too often goes unchecked and justice is not equally applied.

TT: The final section of *Warning Shot* juxtaposes documentary photographs from James Wakasa's funeral, which was the largest Japanese American funeral in the wartime era, with scenes of several other Japanese Americans who were killed by military police in the camps. In every case, the military police claimed that the Japanese Americans were dangerous or were trying to escape, even though the evidence suggests otherwise. I was editing this sequence during the height of the Black Lives Matter movement, and I was struck by the ways police violence continues to go unchecked in the United States. Unless we have constant pressure from activists and scholars, the historical record of police and state violence can easily become obscured. In the case of James Wakasa, one report suggested he was hard of hearing and therefore was unresponsive to the verbal warnings. Even though Wakasa's barrack mate confirmed that Wakasa was not hearing impaired, the US government continues to assert that Wakasa was deaf and his death was justifiable.

LK: In Mine Okubo's *Citizen 13660* (1946), I first saw a drawing of the James Wakasa story.[6] I remember hearing that he was chasing a dog on the other side of the fence and he was deaf and got shot.

TT: Yes, even within the camp, there was a lot of confusion over the case. I know that many of the children at Topaz were told that Wakasa was looking for a flower or a fossil and that his death was an accident. Parents didn't want the kids to worry that they could be shot down at any moment for no reason. The administration also tried to spin a story that Wakasa was insane and desperate to escape camp by any means necessary. But Wakasa already knew that his application for leave clearance had been approved. There would be very little motivation for him to make a suicide escape just weeks before he was scheduled to be released.

LK: That was so beautiful at the end where you have the origami and roses and you talk about his partner from camp, Tatsumi Watanabe. . . . At the beginning of the film, you also draw together a relationship he had with a fellow chef, Milan Jurich, with whom he traveled across the United States. That was something you did in your *GLQ* article with Jiro Onuma's life, and now in this later film you are again building this history of suggested relationships.

TT: I had always intended *Warning Shot* to be a queer film, especially in relation to my use of mash-ups, camp aesthetics, and nonnormative gay editing strategies. But I did have difficulty thinking through the idea that James Wakasa probably wasn't gay. As I was doing research, I came across a letter from Milan Jurich, who met Wakasa in 1915. For twenty-seven years (up until Wakasa was imprisoned), they traveled together from city to city working at different restaurants and gentlemen's clubs across the country. To me, that suggests something [*laughs*].

Although I cannot definitely confirm that James Wakasa was gay, I found some evidence to indicate that he could have been gay. In the film, I try to provide just enough information for the viewers to think, "Oh, he wasn't *not* gay." Sometimes I wonder why we always assume people are straight unless proven otherwise. I would like to live in a world where that wasn't the case. Was Wakasa planning on reuniting with Milan Jurich in San Francisco after he was released? I'm not sure. At Topaz, Wakasa also befriended Tatsumi Watanabe, who presided over Wakasa's funeral and put the first origami flower on his coffin. Watanabe wrote a letter to the Spanish consulate trying to locate Wakasa's family members in Japan so that he could return the ashes. In that letter, he identifies himself as the "most intimate friend" that Wakasa had in this country. In the 1940s, this language of intimate friendship was quite unusual—even remarkable. Again, Wakasa may or may not have been lovers with Jurich or Watanabe, but their intimate relationships offer a vision of homosociality that I want to hold onto.

The Buddhist Bug—Spanning Borders and Bodies: An Interview with Anida Yoeu Ali

LAURA KINA

On July 10, 2014, Laura Kina talked to Anida Yoeu Ali by telephone about her ongoing Buddhist Bug *performance (2011), which combines Muslim and Buddhist iconography to explore her diasporic identity as a Muslim Khmer woman and war refugee returning to Cambodia after three decades in the United States.*

ANIDA YOEU ALI: I am an artist whose work spans mediums, themes, and borders. My work is rooted in performance and often takes the form of installation, photography, and video. I've also done spoken word poetry and more politically charged works. My performances take the love of narrative from my earlier work and put it out into the public in site-specific environments.

I was born in Cambodia, although my family is of mixed heritage. My family went through the genocidal period, which was very volatile and dangerous [Khmer Rouge era, 1975–79] and caused the murder of two million people in Cambodia. We are war survivors. My family left in 1979, when the Khmer Rouge was ousted. We left as refugees, and that experience never left my body and has continued to inform my work.

Works such as *The Buddhist Bug series* use extensive textile material. I like to use textile that I can pack up very easily and then unpack to become something expansive—a soft sculpture that I then inhabit with my body. That speaks so much to my refugee experience—that idea of carrying everything you own; "the clothes on your back" is a line from one of my poems.

LAURA KINA: I've known you for over twenty years. We first met in 1993, when you were a student at the University of Illinois at Urbana-Champaign, and I knew you through your career as a spoken word artist with *I Was Born with Two Tongues* (1998–2003) and as founder of Mango Tribe (2000–2006) and the Asian American Artists Collective–Chicago (2001–2006). You were heavily invested in a discourse on what it means to be an Asian American woman. You are in a very different place today. I know your family landed in Chicago, where you were raised in a Muslim community, after you left Cambodia. Can you talk about your journey in terms of identity?

AYA: My politicization occurred during my formative undergrad college years and happened in being part of the editorial staff for *Monsoon*, which was a literary arts magazine that was inspired by our encounters with people like yourself and Angela "Ging" Mascarenas of Pintig [a Chicago-based Filipino American theater group] and people my friends and I experienced in workshops about this thing called Asian America and this identity called the Asian/Pacific American identity. I always knew I was different, "Other" and Asian—but I didn't know that *Asian* would be a politically empowering term. I knew I was Cambodian and I knew I was Muslim, but it didn't click to me to organize around those identities through shared stories and shared struggles, particularly with other marginalized groups. To paraphrase Arundhati Roy, "Once you see, you can never unsee. Once you know, you can never unknow." That's exactly what happened.

The journey since has been building on that political identity of owning one's history and voice and learning to find similarities in those differences with other groups to make oneself empowered, stronger, and essentially to pull up everybody else in the process. Being rooted in that Asian American identity gave me the sense that I wasn't alone even though being specifically Cambodian Muslim was a very lonely struggle even in that broader umbrella as Asian and as an Asian American woman. What's complicated things is the fact that my family is of mixed heritage from Southeast Asia; that never gets played out because once you are in America, you are flattened to this or that. Even being Asian, in all of its complexities, gets generalized into this category called Asian, which expands to so many geographic countries, languages, ethnicities, and histories.

LK: What is your mixed ethnic background?

AYA: Thai, Malay, Khmer (or Cambodian), and Cham—which is a very specific ethnic minority in Cambodia, many of whom are Muslims. They used to have a nation, a long time ago. They are currently nationless.

Race is seen so differently outside of America: it's not as thought about or not as important. Our specific identities, all these hyphenated identities, they are very important to us because in America it feels like race, gender, class are issues that just bubble up and come to the forefront of almost every encounter you have.

From 2003 to 2007, [I experimented with] studying Butoh with other [dance] movement forms, letting my body not be bound to written or spoken language [Anida was initially known as a spoken-word performance artist and graphic designer]. I was exploring movement arts, costumes, materiality, going back to my love of textile. I was reminded what it felt like as a child to be in love with the dress form and be in that space where you pretend you're a princess wearing this extremely long train dress. I loved that!

LK: I can definitely see that sort of fantasy in your *Buddhist Bug* piece, which is made of saffron-colored fabric to reference Buddhist robes and whose head covering points to the Muslim hijab. In writing about this work, you've referred to the Bug gender-neutrally as "s/he." Do you see the Bug queering a Cambodian, or your own, identity?

AYA: It speaks to the intersection of multiple identities. One can also transcend identity. This piece is rooted in an absurdity. The whole thing was inspired by multiple moments coming together. One is after the birth of my first child, being a mother and a graduate student and an artist; I came into this form, which was a child's play tunnel that looks like a Slinky, where it can collapse and when you unfold it, it takes up this expansive space. I kept looking at this form, and how my daughter was playing with it and having this amazing fun with it. I loved the form so much and said, "I think this is the form for this idea I had." I was trying to create this creature, this entity. From there it intersected with all of those trips I took to Southeast Asia prior to 2008.

In all of those trips to Cambodia, Laos, Vietnam, Thailand, the thing that never left my imagination, as if it's a gate of entry to Southeast Asia, was these saffron robes that the monks wore. When I was on an artists' residency in Thailand, monks journeyed through with us as though they were our guides and protectors. In Cambodia they are everywhere. It's a very important ritual and rite of passage for young men to go through the monkship when they are of age or when a family member passes. I was very obsessed with spotting the monks. I would take these snapshots of monks: whenever I saw a monk like secretly bathing in a waterfall, I would snap a photo. I would see a monk on a cell phone, and I would snap it. I would see a truckload of monks, and I would snap it; monks on a tuk-tuk [auto rickshaw], monks on a boat—you name it and I was there secretly snapping. I would do these selfies (before we called them selfies) with me positioning myself at arm's length and doing this camera thing, and there would be a monk behind me.

I had all of this, coming into this 2008 point, coming into motherhood [Ali and her partner Masahiro Sugano, a fellow Studio Revolt collaborator, were raising three children in Phnom Penh at the time of this interview]. That's when this idea of creating this diasporic body, meaning something that could be multiple things and that could take up essentially multiple points. The entity itself, the Bug, is a tunnel, and tunnels connect two points. It can also be a bridge. It's a being. It's an unidentified creature. The magic is that once we embody it—and I say "we" because it's not just me that's inside of the bug—this magical thing happens with everybody who is around the bug. It is a suspension of disbelief. It is people thinking that s/he is real, and they start to interact with the Bug.

It's hard for me to use a pronoun *he* or *she*. I'm using *she* because I'm referencing it to myself, but when I write it out, it's *s/he*. *S/he* is not gendered or is all-gendered. Even if I personally occupy the bug, and I am "she," the legs aren't always a "she."

LK: Can you talk about the journey of the Bug from Chicago to all of the places it's traveled? It's not just the Bug costume or performance; the series also exists as photographs, and the situation and landscape in the photos seem to have equal importance.

AYA: The photos capture everyday moments in the Cambodian landscape in this specific time. Cambodia is at the intersection of many things shaping it in a rapid urbanization and the way globalization is impacting the country. Everything you see the Bug experiencing now—those landscapes are already changing. Those moments will come to pass. The positioning of the Bug is that s/he makes those moments absurd and a little more surrealistic.

LK: Many of your landscapes are incredibly cinematic, breathtaking landscapes. As you mentioned, many of them are rural places and others are these urban places where you see a mix of old and new, and then there is one in a campus dining room. How did you go about selecting these locations?

AYA: The rural landscapes give the Bug a sense of solitude and a romanticized notion of what a rural space is; it's the postcolonial imagination of those landscapes that people fall in love with when they think of Cambodia. In the first photo shoot in 2012, I was working with my partner, Masahiro Sugano, to capture a narrative voice and find idiosyncrasies within a city context where people and neighborhoods create the scenario or moment. I had set out to capture an urban Phnom Penh that was rapidly changing every day.

LK: *Roll Call* and *Morning Prayers* (both 2014) are not just scenic landscapes, though. In *Roll Call*, the Bug's body wraps around an entire classroom of children, and in *Morning Prayers* you are standing in front of a mosque, again surrounded by children. What was your relationship to those two places? Are you part of these communities?

AYA: These are all of the Bug's communities. It's really important for me that if the work is in any way to represent Cambodia or myself as Cambodian, I'm showing a different part of Cambodia or some sense of Cambodia's multiculturalism, its plurality. Nobody thinks of Cambodians as being Muslims. I want to be with the Muslims. I'm trying so hard, as the Bug, to be accepted in these communities—from the majority here, who are 95 percent Buddhists, to the minority population. This is an ongoing series, and I hope the narrative arc is teased out over time. Right now where I have free passage is the Muslim community where I was born. The 2014 photos are from my birth village, Battambang. *Morning Prayers* is captured in the morning; it is that time period when s/he is outside of the mosque and suddenly this pack of kids comes around the Bug, and they are trying to figure out who s/he is and why s/he has come to their town. Of course, s/he is like, "I belong here. I'm going to go to prayers." "I'm all dressed and ready to go to prayers. Look, no hair showing!" With *Roll Call*, that's the same school in that village, which both Muslim and Buddhist children attend. It's a state-run school and classroom. Again, s/he doesn't know how old s/he is or if s/he belongs in this particular classroom or grade. There was a moment in the *Campus Dining* (2013) photo where s/he thought s/he could blend in with the Royal University of Phnom Penh students, but now (in 2014) s/he is with these primary school kids. You are supposed to question.

LK: These images function so differently. With the kids, s/he is a protector and her body is wrapping around them and guarding them, and she almost looks like a nun behind them. *Campus Dining* made me think of the caterpillar from *Alice in Wonderland*.

AYA: I like that s/he has this versatility in her shape. But s/he's still trying to figure out how to move this extensive body around, how to configure fitting into these spaces. In *The Old Cinema* (2014) piece, that's an abandoned art deco style cinema in Battambang. It's a real nostalgic kind of moment here for anybody that sees this and understands the context of Cambodia and what it went through in terms of the near annihilation of the arts. That Bug being in that dilapidated theater. . . . The shape I've chosen for her is a ship, a boat; s/he is continually on this journey to move through these spaces, not only to discover oneself but also the Bug's roots and eventually home.

LK: Where did you shoot *Off the Golden Ship* (2013) (plate 36)?

AYA: *Off the Golden Ship* is in Phnom Penh, in the city. It was after we photographed *River Landing* and *On the River* (2013), in this Muslim fishing village in Phnom Penh that is all Cham. On the same side of the river, I stumbled on this Buddhist temple that is eerily run by old women. First, if you know the context of Cambodia, old people . . . they are a rarity to find. They are the ones who died during that period [Khmer Rouge]; secondly, women, they are all women in a Buddhist temple. It's a very special place. I saw this ship they made, it's really big. The one in this picture is smaller, but the Buddhist temple itself has this giant golden ship that is the landmark of this temple. When I went in and started asking them for permission, the old woman, the keeper, had to pray to the spirits to ask whether or not we could have permission. We all sat there through the prayer, and she started speaking in tongues and shaking; something was happening to her spiritually. After the whole thing, she comes to me and says, "Lok Ta [the Old Man] says yes. The old man's spirit says yes, you can do this and people can participate." It was really amazing, and the women were awesome to work with, really patient and friendly. This is a panorama shot so it's actually a few images stitched together to create this scene. What I love about it is, do you see the woman on the right on the red stool? That face is piercing. It says to me, "I survived some shit, home girl."

LK: I want to return to some things from the beginning of our conversation. When you started the Asian American Artists Collective–Chicago, it was shortly after 9/11. That was a pivotal moment for you artistically. When you were a graduate student at the School of the Art Institute of Chicago, your thesis exhibit, the *1700% Project*, about the post-9/11 increase in hate crimes against Muslims, was itself subjected to hateful vandalism. In the *Buddhist Bug* piece, you've talked about embracing being Muslim. I'm wondering if you could elaborate on what your Muslim identity means to you in the context of your art?

AYA: *The Buddhist Bug* is such a moment of all of those things coming together, and within this unapologetic identity of being a Muslim, it all surfaces in the Bug in a really odd manner, an odd persona. The Bug is enveloped in this orange. To me that is how I felt coming to this country and experiencing Buddhism in that way—it is the all-encompassing thing here. All the Islamic stuff, it's my way of dealing with religiosity but with a sense of humor this time. Instead of it being politically charged, which was the case in the *1700% Project*—the piece that was vandalized at the School of the Art Institute—instead of taking that serious, politically charged route, this body of work allows me to use humor next to this idea of "Othering" in a way that allows people access to it. What's been so incredible is to witness people's response to this body of work, which is so different from some of my past works.

With this body of work, both in its live performance and its iteration as photos and videos, people can laugh at it openly. They can ridicule it openly. Seeing people smile because they are curious or perplexed or they just find it silly that a forty-year-old grown woman would dress up like a giant orange "bug"—all those things are really important for me in terms of engagement. Whether it's shown in a gallery space, in an art fair, or through its live embodiment, people want to play with this and be playful, and I think those are ways you can start to have encounters and ultimately discuss religion. You cannot deny the religious iconography in this piece, you cannot. There is no way someone could look at this piece and say it's not referencing Islam or Buddhism. I want that to be part of the discussion—the "why?" aspect of it.

LK: What made you make the shift to humor? Was there a moment? Was it after the *1700% Project*?

AYA: The *Buddhist Bug* project I had conceived in 2011 before coming to Cambodia, but I just didn't realize I would be inspired to actualize it here and take the project to its full scope. Anyone who knows my personality knows I'm actually a very funny person and that humor has a very strong place in my personality and in my life. I'm also a huge sci-fi fan. I grew up watching so many lame sci-fi movies as well as really great ones. All of this was something I thought I couldn't touch in contemporary art, let alone in my "political" art. I feel like it was all bubbling up and had to surface. It's like the universe saying to me, "This is who you are. This is part of who you are, and you can make this work for yourself." Cambodia has really allowed me to have the time and space to be an artist and be an artist unapologetically. I feel like I reinvented myself through the *Buddhist Bug* work. I'm not sure if it's an unconscious response to what happened to *1700% Project* or if it's an organic thing that had to happen because it was time for the Bug to come to life.

LK: You said part of it had to do with searching for home, the Bug and you searching for home?

AYA: I think it's part of the diasporic dilemma—this feeling of being an insider/outsider and constantly shifting between those two modes of engagement. Of course, as a diasporic body, it's that corny "search for home, for belonging." It's sort of constant. Now, with a family, I feel like wherever my family is, is essentially where my home is. That's the home we make—but whether or not you feel fully present and culturally part of it, that's where it doesn't hold up weight all of the time.

AFTERWORD

To Be Queer Being to Queer It . . .

KYOO LEE

QUEERING TAKES ON A RELATIONAL POSITIONING BY WELCOMING IDENTIFICATORY MARKERS OF DIFFERENCE WITHIN ASIAN AMERICA THAT CONSTITUTE FOR US THE QUEER HORIZON.

Jan Christian Bernabe and Laura Kina, "Introduction"

Let me go *straight* to the point, something of a meta-queer conundrum, a challenge: how we—whoever you are—relate, "re-relate," to queerness today, its obscure, avant-garde alterities, when the neoliberal-motorized, global transcultural machine is going all over, soaking up all the queer-edgy energy "out there," with its turbo-spongy orderliness, leaving almost all stonewalls touched up, remastered, upscaled. Queer is being normalized and *queer-normativized*, fast, as if, now, norms could outpace themselves.

"Now listen, you queer," just about a few decades ago (1968), some vocal folks such as William F. Buckley would readily liberally threaten some other vocal folks such as Gore Vidal on TV, with this sort of incendiary line, "Stop calling me a crypto-Nazi or I'll sock you in the goddamn face and you'll stay plastered,"[1] and yet, you should not be surprised to hear the same sort of scene popping up today—although, again, it has been already fifteen years since the publication of the ground-breaking *Q & A: Queer in Asian America* (1998), and the Series Q of Duke University Press, another phenomenal success, concluded a few years ago (2012) already.[2] And as you may also have heard, nowadays, marriage is practically just for gay people (at least in the United States) to the point where some sexually active televangelist such as Pat Robertson warns that "gays will force Christians to like anal sex and, eventually, polyamory, and bestiality" (2015)[3]—a worry aired with a comedic twist in another country, in movieland, where a gay man about to get same-sex-married would come "in" out of the closet as a heterosexual kisser as he sleeps with a girl "for the very first time" (*Toute première fois*, trans. *I Kissed a Girl*, 2015). Also, last but not least, these days, no self-respecting queer theory class, undergrad or grad, would be seen without *QCC* (queer color critique) loud and clear, while asexuals too are joining the "Q" fast & furious . . . and now, listen again, you queer.

As Michael Warner observes in his 2012 essay, "Queer and Then?," quite truly, "People seem to long for a present in which they can be postqueer."[4] The invisible through-line is a somewhat utopian, paradoxical imperative: what would be the point of queer, if not, in a sense, to end "it," to reach the world of no-more-*queer*? Such a (death) drive of the unruly, swerving queer present, constantly auto-critiqued and instituted by evolving networks of norm-questioning psycho-sexual, eroto-social, ethico-cultural practices that give themselves their raisons d'être, continues to resonate with the critical-creative query channeled in this anthology.

What this volume of queer synesthesia explores while "*cruising* the corpus of contemporary Asian American art" (Introduction), itself a moving map in the making, is the very conceptual mélange and edges of *serial Qness*, where eclectic synergy brings out the very pulsation of the possible, including the dialogical and intercategorical openness of the *Q & A*. Here, let's say, *Q & AAA* (Queer & Asian American Anonymous/Areal/Abnormal/Anyhow) in trans*it*, transforming "it," whatever it is, originates from and cuts across the specifically "Asian American" context. With originality indeed, the artists and theorists in this assemblage of work on auto-queered/queering "identities," still a dominant category of concern even and especially for those into "disidentitarian" ethos and practices, confront the very interfacial, interstellar twists and turns of *Asian* Americana.

Then what are we (talking about), *Q & AAA*, you ask? What, or who, else continues to queer the "queer Asian horizon" taken as a (w)hole?—if not just "Sum Yung Mahn, perhaps the only Asian to qualify as a gay porn 'star,' variously known as Brad Troung or Sa or Sum Yung Mahn" back in 2000.[5] In search, in various ways, of a way out of *and* across the polarized aesthetic politics, today, of anti-identitarianism, deracialization, and gender-neutralization, etc., etc., forward-looking folks brought here, as the editors put it, to pursue the category-questioning and creative projects that are "recuperative and community oriented" (Introduction) while actively inscribing, for instance, *oldnew* "Asian" American perspectives into canonically "white" materials, as shown in the piece "Queer Zen," by Alpesh Kantilal Patel, for instance.

Just another example: as parodically re-indexicalized by the transnational and transgendering work by Việt Lê, *Love Bang!* (2012), a meta-queer sexperimental embodiment of "promiscuous time traveling" (chapter 2 interview), *Q & AAA* at work becomes a zone where "'hyperreal' . . . meets realpolitik" and "thanatourism" meets real fakery (chapter 2 interview). Areal becomes real, as one acts queer and stays queer, and queerdom stays viral-vital across and beyond, for instance, the "Pacific Standard Time," which Mariam Lam interrogates with an eye for counterpoints of being. In other words, to be queer—identified as such, self-, mis-, dis-, post-, whatever else—is to queer it, "it," the very referentiality of *X-ness* steely-stereotyped into portable or locatable things, e.g., Asian American "stuff" now being stuffed otherwise, queerly.

Quite simply, the impact this volume of query would have on the lives and afterlives of Asian American Studies and Art and beyond is obvious and remains immeasurable. By now, queer or not, you will have read it—or else read it right now!

NOTES

Notes to Introduction

1 Love, *Feeling Backward*, 1.
2 David L. Eng et al., eds., “What’s Queer in Queer Studies Now?” 1.
3 Ibid.
4 For an overview on antinormativity in queer theory, see Wiegman and Wilson, “Introduction.”
5 Kay Ulanday Barrett, “Brown Out Shouts!,” K. website, accessed May 31, 2015, www.kaybarrett.net.
6 We began conducting interviews in the summer of 2014, and this introduction evolved through the fall of 2015. This has been a time marked by assaults on black bodies and political consciousness. Widespread racial unrest came into the headlines following the senseless deaths, caused by excessive use of police force, of four unarmed black men: Eric Garner in Staten Island, New York; Michael Brown in Ferguson, Missouri; Walter Scott in North Charleston, South Carolina; and Freddie Gray in Baltimore, Maryland. Then, on June 17, 2015, the nation was rocked once again by the brutal hate crime slaying by a white man, Dylan Roof, of nine black church members at Emanuel African Methodist Episcopal Church in Charleston, South Carolina. Much less covered by the mainstream press was the continued rise in hate crimes against Muslims—including the tragic slaying of three Muslim university students in Chapel Hill, North Carolina, in February 2015. In June 2015, we saw the Confederate flag come down from the South Carolina state capitol, and the rainbow flag was raised across the nation in celebration of the US Supreme Court ruling on same-sex marriage. It has been a contradictory season, where the media celebrated Bruce Jenner’s transgender transition to Caitlyn Jenner on the cover of the July 2015 issue of *Vanity Fair* yet continued to turn a blind eye to the violent attacks against transgender women of color in what the *Huffington Post* named a “State of Emergency for Transgender Women of Color” (September 16, 2014, www.huffingtonpost.com/addison-rose-vincent/state-of-emergency-for-tr_b_5792722.html). To reckon with Asian American representation, we must take into consideration our relative privileges and vulnerabilities

in terms of race, religion, gender, class, and geographic location.

7 In 2015 ABC debuted a series *Fresh off the Boat,* the first Asian American sitcom on a major network since Margeret Cho's 1994 failed series, *All American Girl,* which played with and off of the FOB stereotype.

8 See Jack Halberstam, *The Queer Art of Failure.*

9 See Wu, *The Color of Success.*

10 Description of Fannie Wong, Former Miss Chinatown 2nd Runner Up, accessed March 8, 2015, http://kristinawong.com/projects/. "Breaking the bamboo ceiling" is a term coined by Jane Hyun in the book of the same title.

11 Swati Khurana, "Unsuitable Girls," accessed May 31, 2015, http://swatikhurana.com/portfolio/collaborative/unsuitable-girls.

12 Ibid.

13 Ibid. Emphasis added.

14 "Asians Fastest-Growing Race or Ethnic Group in 2012, Census," June 13, 2013, www.census.gov/newsroom/press-releases/2013/cb13-112.html.

15 "The Future's Asian," *Economist,* June 6, 2015, www.economist.com/news/united-states/21653646-futures-asian.

16 Lowe, *Immigrant Acts,* 2.

17 "Press," Jeffsheng.com; for example, see Laurie Winer, "He Asked. They Told," *New York Times,* March 17, 2010, www.nytimes.com/2010/03/18/fashion/18sheng.html?_r=0.

18 The third part of Sheng's series focuses on LGBT military servicemen post-DADT and highlights marriage equality, a political issue that is at the vanguard of the LGBT rights movement.

19 Puar, *Terrorist Assemblage,* 9.

20 Ibid.

21 See, for example, "5 Most Disappointing Things We Learned About HRC's 'White Men's Club,'" *Advocate,* June 4, 2015, accessed June 5, 2015, www.advocate.com/human-rights-campaign-hrc/2015/06/04/5-most-disappointing-things-we-learned-about-hrcs-white-mens-cl. Human Rights Campaign is the largest political lobbying group in the United States, and the report points to patterns of homonormativity that value gay white men and disenfranchise LGBTQ of color. See also chapter 1 in Muñoz, *Cruising Utopia.*

22 Hong and Ferguson, *Strange Affinities,* 2.

23 Edelman, *No Future,* 2–3.

24 Ibid., 3.

25 Muñoz, *Cruising Utopia,* 11. Emphasis added.

26 Ibid.

27 Much like Muñoz, we have conceptualized *cruising* as a queer practice that is not limited to sex acts, but rather is a search for that which holds promise and potential for our project and which is never distanced from the political. Ibid., 18.

28 Ibid., 1.
29 Ibid., 16.
30 O'Brien, *For the Love of Unicorns.*
31 While the unicorns are fictional, they are part of everyday popular culture, or what Muñoz has labeled an ornament. Muñoz reads Andy Warhol's Coke bottles, for example, as an ornament. He writes, "Part of what Warhol's study of the Coke bottle and other mass-produced objects helps one to see is this particular tension between functionality and nonfunctionality, the promise and potentiality of the ornament." The ornament in our reading is precisely the unicorn for the tensions between its utilitarian and non-utilitarian ontology. Muñoz, *Cruising Utopia*, 7.
32 Ibid., 1.
33 Sanam Malik, "Asian American Immigrants in the US Today," *Center for American Progress*, May 21, 2015, accessed November 29, 2015, www.americanprogress.org/issues/immigration/news/2015/05/21/113690/asian-immigrants-in-the-unites-states-today/.
34 Lee, *Picturing Chinatown*; Johnson et al., eds., *Asian American Art.*
35 Shah, "Knowing 'The Unknowns,'" 126.
36 "Chitra Ganesh: Eyes of Time," Brooklyn Museum, Elizabeth A. Sackler Center for Feminist Art, accessed May 30, 2015, www.brooklynmuseum.org/exhibitions/chitra_ganesh/.
37 Shah, "Knowing 'The Unknowns,'" 126.
38 Puwar, *Space Invaders*, 8.
39 Chui and Genocchio, "Book Overview," *Contemporary Art in Asia*, https://mitpress.mit.edu/books/contemporary-art-asia; see also Chui, *Chinese Contemporary Art.*
40 Alexandra Chang, *Envisioning Diaspora*, 1.
41 See Chang, Cornell, and Johnson, eds., *Asian/American/Modern Art*; Chui and Genocchio, eds., *Contemporary Art in Asia*; Johnson et al., eds., *Asian American Art.*
42 Machida, *Unsettled Visions*, 8.
43 Pelaud et al., eds., *Troubling Borders.* Chapter 1.

Notes to Chapter 1: Queering Surveillance

1 Elahi, "You Want to Track Me?," http://elahi.umd.edu/elahi_ny_times.php, accessed on August 6, 2014.
2 Ibid.
3 Ibid.
4 Ibid.
5 Chen, *Animacies*, 104.
6 Chuh, *Imagine Otherwise*, 34; see also Lowe, *Immigrant Acts*.
7 Mann et al., "Sousveillance," 336.
8 Robertson, "Try to Walk with the Sound of My Footsteps," 32.

9 Ibid.
10 Mann et al., "Sousveillance," 347.
11 Magid, *Evidence Locker*, "Letter 30," private e-mail received May 13, 1014.
12 Virilio, "The Visual Crash," 109. Emphasis in original.
13 Rancière, *The Emancipated Spectator*, 113.
14 Foucault, *Discipline and Punish*, 198.
15 Melamed, *Represent and Destroy*, 151.
16 Tadiar, *Fantasy-Production*, 117.
17 Edelman, *No Future*, 127.
18 Downey, "The Lives of Others," 78–79.
19 Edelman, *No Future*, 17.
20 Ibid., 27.
21 Ibid., 29.
22 Jack Halberstam, *The Queer Art of Failure*, 109–10.
23 Muñoz, *Cruising Utopia*, 19.
24 Ibid., 95.
25 Available online at http://liverpool.gov.uk/crime-prevention-and-emergencies/cctv/.
26 "Please register," *Evidence Locker*, www.evidencelocker.net/register.php. Accessed on August 6, 2014.
27 "Evidence Locker," Jill Magid website, www.jillmagid.net/projects/evidence-locker-2.
28 "Prologue," *Evidence Locker*, private e-mail received May 11, 1014.
29 "Letter 3," private e-mail received May 11, 1014.
30 "Letter 5," private e-mail received May 11, 1014.
31 "Letter 8," private e-mail received May 12, 1014.
32 "Letter 10," private e-mail received May 12, 1014.
33 Ibid.
34 Morrison, "Performing Citizen Arrest," 242.
35 Ibid., 246.
36 Ibid., 251.
37 Jovana Stokic, "Jill Magid by Jovana Stokic: Spy Agencies, Multinational Corporations, and the Exchange Of Information." *BOMB—Artists in Conversation*, May 13, 2014. http://bombmagazine.org/article/1000125/jill-magid. Accessed August 6, 2014.
38 Morrison, "Performing Citizen Arrest," 252.
39 Magid, "Letter 15," private e-mail received May 12, 1014.
40 Robertson, "Try to Walk with the Sound of My Footsteps," 35.
41 Sarah E. K. Smith, "Captured and Controlled," 54–55.
42 Ratnam, "Art and Globalization," 278, 280.
43 "Questions and Answers," *Evidence Locker*, www.evidencelocker.net/question.php. Accessed August 7, 2014.

1 "Hasan Elahi: Privacy Artist," Ted.com, accessed July 12, 2014, www.ted.com/speakers/hasan_elahi.

2 Kapadia, "Up in the Air and on the Skin."

3 Bilal's family fled Iraq following the first Gulf War.

4 Elahi tells the full backstory in his 2011 TEDGlobal talk, "FBI: Here I Am": "It all started in 2002, when Elahi was detained in Detroit after a flight from the Netherlands, suspected of hoarding explosives in a Florida locker. Though lie detector tests subsequently cleared him, Elahi . . . was subjected to six months of questioning about his extensive international travels. Figuring once in the system, never out, he decided to turn the tables and cooperate—with a vengeance." "Hasan Elahi: Privacy Artist."

5 Bernd and Hilla Bechers were post-World War II German social realist Neue Sachlichkeit (New Objectivity) photographers who taught at the Kunstakademie Düsseldorf (Dusseldorf Art Academy). Their influence in the mid-1970s on artists such as Andreas Gursky, Candida Höfer, Thomas Ruff, and Thomas Struth is referred to as the Düsseldorf School.

6 Barthes, Camera Lucida.

7 The camera caused constant pain, and Bilal's body rejected one of the three surgically implanted camera posts. Despite this, he continued the project with the two remaining posts, also tying a camera to the back of his shirt collar. Catherine Smith, "NYU Professor Wafaa Bilal's Body Rejects Head-Cam Implant," Huffington Post, February 10, 2011, www.huffingtonpost.com/2011/02/10/wafaa-bilal-body-rejects-head-camera_n_821271.html

8 Mirzhoeff, "The Death of the Death of Photography."

9 Richard F. Grimmet, "Instances of the Use of the United States Armed Forces Abroad, 1798–2009," Congressional Research Service Report for Congress (2010), p. 2, http://fas.org/sgp/crs/natsec/RL32170.pdf.

10 See the NSA's Domestic Surveillance Directorate (https://nsa.gov1.info/utah-data-center/); James Bamford, "The NSA Is Building the Country's Biggest Spy Center (Watch What You Say)," Wired, March 15, 2012, www.wired.com/2012/03/ff_nsadatacenter/.

11 In June 2014, the Islamist militia Islamic State of Iraq and al-Sham (ISIS) staged a jihadi uprising consolidated control over large areas of western Iraq and eastern Syria.

12 Bilal and Lydersen, Shoot an Iraqi.

13 "Wafaa Bilal's brother Haji was killed by a missile at a checkpoint in their hometown of Kufa, Iraq in 2004. Bilal feels the pain of both American and Iraqi families who've lost loved ones in the war, but the deaths of Iraqis like his brother are largely invisible to the American

public. ' . . . and Counting' addresses this double standard as Bilal turns his own body—in a twenty-four-hour live performance—into a canvas, his back tattooed with a borderless map of Iraq covered with one dot for each Iraqi and American casualty near the cities where they fell." ". . . and Counting," Wafaa Bilal website, http://wafaabilal.com/html/andCounting.php, accessed July 12, 2014.

Notes to Chapter 2: Queering Time

1 Eng, *Racial Castration*, 18.

2 For an extended discussion, see the introduction to Pelaud et al., *Troubling Borders*.

3 In the conclusion of Sara Ahmed's *On Being Included*, she explains based on Husserl's redescription of the phenomenological method in his 1935 Vienna lecture: "An attitude is thus not simply a reflection on the world but it is worldly: an attitude could even be thought of as institutionality, in which a norm is also prescribed as a style of life. A norm is how we are immersed in a life. . . . The phenomenological attitude in reflecting on the previous attitudes is thus a new style; a theoretical attitude is new in relation to what already exists because *in* reflecting on what exists, it withdraws from an immersion, such that an existence is transformed" (quoted in Ahmed, *On Being Included*, 174). Therefore, Asian American studies requires continuous theorization if it is to remain relevant, vibrant, and productive. Theorization is not something to necessarily disdain or fret over. Also see Ahmed's *Willful Subjects* for excellent and accessible analyses of the role of willful subjects, the notions of good will and the general will, and of willfulness and its call to arms. And finally, for a strong partial discussion of abstraction and embodiment in Asian American visual arts, see Sarita See's concluding chapter, "Reanne Estrada, Identity, and the Politics of Abstraction," in *The Decolonized Eye*.

4 Eng and Hom, *Q & A*, xi.

5 Judith Halberstam, *In a Queer Time and Place*, 1–2.

6 Ibid., 8, 10–11.

7 See Stoler, *Imperial Debris*.

8 Freeman, *Time Binds*, xi.

9 See Lam, *Not Coming to Terms*.

10 Freeman, *Time Binds*, xiii, xii.

11 See Muñoz, *Disidentifications*.

12 Freeman, *Time Binds*, xiii.

13 Felicidad Lim, *Translating Time*.

14 See Chang et al., *Asian American Art*.

15 Machida, *Unsettled Visions*, xvi–xvii.

16 Ibid., xviii.

17 See Silva, *Toward a Global Idea of Race*.

18 "Unidentified Vietnam," Lin + Lam website, www.linpluslam.com/index/Unidentified_Vietnam.html, accessed March 24, 2015.
19 "Biển nhớ," 1962, www.youtube.com/watch?v=ZDK24S_Mgwo, accessed March 24, 2015. English translation of the song "Biển nhớ" is my own.
20 See Noszlopy and Cohen, *Contemporary Southeast Asian Performance*; Ingawanij and McKay, *Glimpses of Freedom*; Diamond, *Communities of Imagination*; Taylor and Ly, *Modern and Contemporary Southeast Asian Art*.
21 Mankekar and Schein, *Media, Erotics, and Transnational Asia*, 8.
22 Freeman, *Time Binds*, 2.
23 Ibid., 3.
24 Ibid., 13.
25 Mercer, *Exiles, Diasporas and Strangers*, 7.
26 Ibid.; Freeman, *Time Binds*, 3.
27 Nguyen Tan Hoang, *PIRATED!* Beta-SPVideo. Atlanta, GA: Kimchi Chige Productions, 2006.
28 Nguyen, "In the Arms of Pirates," 69.
29 See Guerin and Hallas, *The Image and the Witness*; Rancière, *The Emancipated Spectator*.
30 Ibid.; Machida, *Unsettled Visions*, 167.
31 For more images and a brief discussion of Eliza Barrios's and Yong Soon Min's recent work, see Lam, "Cartographies."
32 Ibid.; Machida, *Unsettled Visions*, 2.
33 See Felicidad Lim, *Translating Time*.

A CONVERSATION WITH LIN + LAM AND VIỆT LÊ

1 Muñoz, *Disidentifications*.
2 Rofel, *Desiring China*.
3 Baudrillard, *Selected Writings*.
4 Felicidad "Bliss" Cua Lim, *Translating Time*; Judith Halberstam, *In a Queer Time and Place*.
5 Benjamin, "Theses on the Philosophy of History," 279.
6 Khánh Ly is a famous Vietnamese singer known for her renditions of antiwar songs by the late composer Trịnh Công Sơn.
7 Sturken, *Tangled Memories*.
8 Eng-Beng Lim, *Brown Boys and Rice Queens*.

Notes to Chapter 3: Queering Affect

1 While the narrative of the American suburban homogeneity ("racialized, classed, sexualized") still pervades, Karen Tongson argues in *Relocations: Queer Suburban Imaginaries* for a counternarrative of inclusion of those otherwise thought to be unwelcome within American suburbia (p. 3). While Tongson's intervention in shaking the myth of suburban homogeneity may befit the demographic composition of Southern

California, which is the geographic focus of *Relocations*, suburban landscapes throughout the United States are as diverse as urban ones. That is to say, a comparison between Livingston, New Jersey, and Orange County, California, may not reflect demographic and cultural similarities. Indeed, according to the 2010 US census, in Livingston those identifying as "White" composed 76.2 percent of the population, versus "Filipino," who represented 2 percent of the township's population. "DP-1—Profile of General Population and Housing Characteristics: 2010 for Livingston Township, Essex County, New Jersey," *United States Census Bureau*, http://factfinder.census.gov/faces/tableservices/jsf/pages/productview.xhtml?src=bkmk. Accessed July 31, 2015.

2 Jeffrey Songco, interview with the author, July 14, 2014. All quotes from the artist, unless otherwise noted, are from this interview.

3 Tongson, *Relocations*, 23.

4 While one's identity may be gleaned from body parts other than the face, I am inclined to return to scholarship on nineteenth-century photographic practices that discusses photographic viewing practices facilitated by notions of facial legibility, especially to determine inner character. The legibility of the face (or lack thereof in Songco's work discussed in this chapter) underscores my argument about Songco's affective oscillations. See, for example, Alan Sekula's seminal essay, "The Body and the Archive"; also Shawn Michelle Smith, *Photography on the Color Line*.

5 Muñoz, *Disidentifications*, 12.

6 While Songco's larger visual oeuvre relies largely on representing the body or bodies rather than relying on the language of abstraction, the point I make here is that the illegibility of these bodies' faces potentially causes pause in Filipino diasporic and queer viewers precisely because the identities of these bodies are unknown. This sentiment of not being able to locate Songco's work within the particularities of social groups is similar to Sarita See's discussion of the turn to abstraction by Filipino American contemporary artists Reanne Estrada and Paul Pfeiffer: "Void of unambiguous, overt signs of things Filipino, their art is perceived as having nothing to do with being Filipino." See *The Decolonized Eye*, 128.

7 Ahmed, *The Promise of Happiness*, 20.

8 Jack Halberstam, *The Queer Art of Failure*, 3.

9 As Songco remembers, "I had a lot of friends growing up, and there was no bullying or anything like that."

10 Tongson, *Relocations*, 2.

11 See Manalansan, "Race, Violence, and Neoliberal Spatial Politics in the Global City"; Puar, *Terrorist Assemblages*; and Duggan, *The Twilight of Equality?*.

12 Bernabe, "Queer Reconfigurations."

13 See, *The Decolonialized Eye*, xi.

14 I mention Songco's relationship with Allan deSouza as I believe that deSouza's artistic practice and focus on his postcolonial South Asian body and identity has influenced on Songco's artistic trajectory and nurtured Songco's understanding about the multiple markers of identity, including but not limited to race.

15 Sarita See has argued that the deployment of jokes, including puns, by Filipino American artists, performers, and Filipino audiences is a means by which "Filipino American expressive culture has organized its own semiotics and aesthetic of violence," which in itself is imbued with "textual ambivalence" (with regard to textual ambivalence, I refer specifically to See's read of *lengua*, meaning both "tongue" and "language," in the title of Manual Ocampo's painting *Heridas de la lengua*, 1991). See, *The Decolonialized Eye*, xvii, 24. Similarly, Songco's play on *party* in the *Guilty Party* is exemplary of the textual ambivalence described by See and its decolonizing potential. I would also add that Songco's use of the pun also gestures at the affective ambivalence, or what I have called the affective oscillations throughout the chapter, to being Filipino and queer in suburban American spaces.

16 Ahmed, *The Promise of Happiness*, 65.

17 The first season was produced in 2013, only a year prior to the creation of the *Guilty Party*; given Songco's strong interest in television culture, the reference to the *Orange Is the New Black* would not be surprising.

18 In *Confessional*, for example, the text adjacent to the image of the reality TV housewife character reads: "She's a hot mess. You know what I had to tell her? 'Keep your hands off my man.'"

19 Ahmed, *The Promise of Happiness*, 11.

20 Ibid., 18.

21 Ibid, 13.

22 Ibid, 20.

AN INTERVIEW WITH KENNETH TAM

1 Bataille, *Eroticism*, 65.

2 At this point in the interview, Tam starts *The Compression Is Not Subservient to the Explosion* on his laptop as we continue to discuss his work.

3 By this point the video has ended.

Notes to Chapter 4: Queering Methodology

1 I delivered an early version of this chapter at the College Art Association's annual conference in 2014 for the panel "Abstraction and Difference," cochaired by David J. Getsy and Tirza T. Latimer. The paper was titled "Queer Zen and the Networked Body: Abstraction and Identity in the 1950s and 1960s." My thanks to the coeditors of this volume

for their feedback on drafts of this essay. In my forthcoming book from Manchester University Press, *Productive Failure: Writing Queer Transnational South Asian Art Histories* (2017), I expand on this essay by exploring the work of Twombly in tandem with that of New York City–based, Indian-born Natvar Bhavsar.

For an excellent discussion of the writing about Twombly's work in relation to his practice, see Susik, "Cy Twombly."

2 I do not mean to elide the vertical, differential power dynamics among these categorical identifications that my horizontal listing of them might signify. Also, I do not mean to minimize the importance of other identifications, such as two-spirit identity, when I use LGBTQI. Indeed, this is the endgame that I am trying to move away from in this chapter, to explore identity that both moves beyond and yet still references these categories.

3 Derrida, *Of Grammatology*, 144–45.

4 I am invoking British sociologist Paul Gilroy's alternative to diaspora that privileges "roots" (where one is from) at the expense of "routes" (where one has been). Gilroy, *The Black Atlantic*, 133.

5 Chuh, *Imagine Otherwise*, 151. I thank Laura Kina for informing me of this important book.

6 Ibid., 10. Emphasis in original.

7 Barthes, "Death of the Author."

8 *Transnational* is used in favor of *diaspora*, given the less than desirable implications of the classical notion of the latter, which Paul Gilroy notes assumes an "obsession with origins, purity and invariant sameness." See Edwards, "The Uses of Diaspora," 63. At the same time, it is not my goal here to set up a Manichean debate between *diaspora* and *transnational*. The genealogy of the latter is already deeply intertwined with that of the former. Other scholars have also theorized diaspora in a manner that addresses the implications of fixed origins and destinations, which Gilroy references. For instance, British cultural theorist Stuart Hall defines *diaspora experience* as determined not through "return" and "not by essence or purity, but by the recognition of a necessary heterogeneity and diversity; by a conception of 'identity' which lives with and through, not despite, difference." See Hall, "Cultural Identity and Diaspora," 235.

9 Machida, "Reframing Asian America." See also the journal *Asian Diasporic Visual Cultures and the Americas* (ADVA)—launched in 2015 and edited by Alexandra Chang and Alice Ming Wai Jim—which focuses on the transnational or more specifically hemispheric: North, Central and South America, as well as the Pacific Islands and the Caribbean. See www.brill.com/products/journal/asian-diasporic-visual-cultures-and-americas, accessed May 7, 2015.

10 As queer theorist and gender studies scholar Jasbir K. Puar notes, queer and transnational do not necessarily "sustain a more perfect union or,

in this case, a more perfect oppositionality." See Puar, "Transnational Sexualities," 409.

11 Golden et al., *Freestyle*, 14; Finkel, "A Reluctant Fraternity, Thinking Post-Black."

12 Schjeldahl, "Breaking Away."

13 I certainly do not mean to create an equivalence between Golden's usage of the term *post-identity* and Schjeldahl's. The former is of course one that aims to complicate thinking about identity (particularly blackness) in art criticism and art history that had largely become stagnant or shoved aside important concerns. For an expanded discussion of this topic, see Jones, *Seeing Differently*, especially chapter 4, "Multiculturalism, Intersectionality, and Post-identity."

14 Recently, art historian Majella Munroe has explored in her analysis of the work of Mira Schendel how Zen can be a useful intellectual framework to explore transnationalism. See Munroe, "Zen as a Transnational Current in Post-War Art."

15 See Katz, "Agnes Martin." Also, he has done much of the work of reimagining the works of a number of important peers of Martin—such as John Cage, Jasper Johns, and Robert Rauschenberg—through a queer framework. See Katz, "John Cage's Queer Silence." This is reprinted alongside many of his other essays that are germane to this topic on the Queer Cultural Center website, www.queerculturalcenter.org/Pages/KatzPages/KatzIntro.html, accessed May 8, 2015.

16 See Katz, presentation on Agnes Martin for "Hide/Seek" Exhibition Symposium, www.youtube.com/watch?v=BbFLur5zdAI&feature=youtube_gdata_player, accessed May 7, 2015.

17 Katz, "Agnes Martin," 173.

18 See, for example, Pearlman, *Nothing and Everything*. I thank Hrag Vartanian for referring me to this book.

19 Munroe, "Buddhism and the Neo-Avant-Garde."

20 Artists whose works I plan to explore include Leo Amino, Chen Chi, Genichiro Inokuma, Seong Moy, Win Ng, Kenzo Okada, Ansei Uchima, and Natvar Bhavsar. For a catalog exploring abstraction in works by artists of Asian descent in the United States, see Wechsler, *Asian Traditions/Modern Expressions*. I am referring to two of Barthes's essays: "Cy Twombly: Works on Paper," originally written in 1976 and titled "Non Multa Sed Multum," though not published until 1979 in volume 6 of Yvon Lambert's *Catalogue Raisonné of Works on Paper* [Milan: Multhipla, 1979], 7–13); and "The Wisdom of Art." Originally published in *Cy Twombly, paintings and drawings, 1954–1977*: Whitney Museum of American Art, April 10–June 10, 1979 (Whitney Museum of American Art, 1979), 9–22].

21 This is noted by Daigle, "Cy Twombly," full article available at www.tate.org.uk/context-comment/articles/lingering-threshold-between-word

-and-image, accessed May 7, 2015. However, there is also evidence that Yvon Lambert had approached Barthes after having been turned down by Michel Foucault: see Leeman, "Roland Barthes et Cy Twombly," 61n1.

22 This information is based on information provided by Twombly to Achim Hochdörfer. Hochdörfer, "Blue Goes Out, B Comes In," 22, 39n13.

23 It is worth noting that Twombly, too, is a transnational artist. He lived primarily in Italy after 1957. Claire Daigle, "Biography," *Cy Twombly*. Accessed May 7, 2015. www.cytwombly.info.

24 Under the biography section of Cy Twombly's official website, Claire Daigle notes that in in the upper third portion of *Untitled*, 1962 (not illustrated, unfortunately), there is a veritable legend of sorts for Twombly's color scheme/graphite marks: a white circle swirled with pink is labeled "blood" and an aggressive red *X* reads as "flesh," for instance. The fixity of these meanings seems discordant with how I will describe Twombly's work in this chapter; I offer this information merely as an interesting counterpoint to my argument.

25 Trapp, "Cy Twombly's Ferragosto Series," 39.

26 Daigle, "Cy Twombly."

27 Barthes, "Non Multa Sed Multum," 32. This is the only place where I do not draw on Richard Howard's translation of the original essay. Instead of "enigmatic supplement," Howard refers to an "enigmatic surplus." See Barthes, "Cy Twombly," 176.

28 Austin, *How to Do Things with Words*; Krauss, "Cy Was Here."

29 Althusser, "Ideology and Ideological State Apparatuses."

30 Krauss, "Cy Was Here."

31 Barthes, "Cy Twombly," 173. Emphasis in original.

32 Ibid., 170.

33 Interestingly, embedded within the genealogy of the word *Ferragosto* is an illustration of how performativity as well as history and power operate. Originally a day to honor Diana, the goddess of fertility, it has become transformed ironically to honor the assumption of the Virgin Mary. The pagan-turned-Roman-Catholic holiday illustrates how (as Krauss notes via Michel Foucault) "sequestered within every seemingly neutral historical narrative was the discursive axis of the performative's relations of authority." Moreover, Krauss's reading of Barthes via Twombly's works differs in that Krauss argues that the present tense of the performative gives way to the unequivocal "past tense of the index." Krauss, "Cy Was Here." Barthes, however, suggests that the "*past tense* of the stroke can also be defined as its *future*." He further notes that "TW's work seems to be conjugated in the past tense or in the future, never really in the present." Barthes, "Cy Twombly," 167. Emphasis in original.

34 Barthes, "Cy Twombly," 161.

35 Krauss, "Cy Was Here."

36 Barthes, "Preface to Renauld Camus's *Tricks*," 291–92. Emphasis in original.

37 See Katz, "'Committing the Perfect Crime,'" 39n1. Also available from www.queerculturalcenter.org/Pages/KatzPages/KatzIntro.html. Katz "recovers" via poet and art critic John Yau a series of letters between poets Charles Olson and Robert Creeley that indicate "matter of factly" that Twombly was in a romantic relationship with Robert Rauschenberg. Twombly and Rauschenberg attended Black Mountain College when Olson was the director.

38 Rogoff, "Gossip as Testimony," 272.

39 Butt, *Between You and Me.*

40 See Roth, "The Aesthetic of Indifference." This has been reprinted in Roth and Katz, *Difference/Indifference.*

41 Department of the Bureau of Diplomatic Security of the United States Department of State, "History of the Bureau of Diplomatic Security of the United States Department of State," 128 (see figure 7 caption).

42 See Jonathan D. Katz, "Passive Resistance: On the Critical and Commercial Success of Queer Artists in Cold War American Art," *Queer Cultural Center*, accessed May 3, 2015, www.queerculturalcenter.org/Pages/KatzPages/KatzLimage.html. Originally published in *L'image*, no. 3 (Winter 1996).

43 Katz, "Performative Silence and the Politics of Passivity," 101.

44 Sylvester, "Cy Twombly (2000)"; Serota, "History behind the Thought."

45 Serota, "Interview."

46 Serota, "History behind the Thought," 53.

47 Kennedy, "Cy Twombly, Idiosyncratic Painter, Dies at 83." He notes that even "artist and writer Donald Judd, who was hostile toward painting in general, was especially damning even so, calling the show a fiasco. 'There are a few drips and splatters and an occasional pencil line,' he wrote in a review. 'There isn't anything to these paintings.'"

48 By the time Twombly had his retrospective at the Museum of Modern Art in New York City, his reputation had certainly been cemented. Even so, the exhibition curator's title of an article for the museum's bulletin is telling. See Varnedoe, "Your Kid Could Not Do This, and Other Reflections on Cy Twombly." Art historian Jon Bird notes that Twombly's work turned Barthes the critic into an artist—well, at least for a brief moment, in which he discovers that mark-making is less straightforward than he might have thought. See Bird, "Indeterminacy and (Dis)order in the Work of Cy Twombly," 487. He further writes that "the critic turns artist in the forlorn attempt to comprehend what his critical tools have failed to provide—an interpretation adequate to its object."

49 Derrida, *Speech and Phenomena*, 88; see also p. xliii.

50 Barthes, "Cy Twombly," 176; Barthes, "The Wisdom of Art," 194 (in italics in the original).

51 Barthes, "Cy Twombly: Works on Paper," 175.

52 Vendler, "The Medley Is the Message."

53 Villiers, *Opacity and the Closet*, 118. See especially chapter 4, "Unseen Warhol/Seeing Barthes."

54 Barthes, "'*L'Express*' Talks with Roland Barthes," 98, quoted in Daigle, "Reading Barthes/Writing Twombly," 225.

55 Juhasz, "Video Remains," 326. Derrida also notes that the archive is as much about the past as it is the present and future. Derrida, *Archive Fever*, 29.

56 Cvetkovich, "Queer Art of the Counterarchive," 32. Cvetovich is referring to the absence of lesbian paraphernalia in archives dedicated to LGBTQI subjects, whereas I am referring to a very different kind of archive. My aim is similar to hers: not to create a new fixed meaning but to maintain a connection to the activist potential of Asian American art history.

57 Emphasis in original. Barthes, "Cy Twombly," 160.

AN INTERVIEW WITH ELIZA BARRIOS

1 The Mail Order Brides/M.O.B. describe themselves on Jenifer Wofford's website http://wofflehouse.com/mob/ as a trio of Filipina-American artists engaged in an ongoing conversation with culture and gender. While other mail order brides are conventionally perceived as ideal obedient domestics, it has not escaped this trio's attention that, acronymically speaking, "Mail Order Brides" abbreviates down to a more sinister acronym that informs the darker subtext of their operations.

Taking matters into their own well-manicured hands, the Brides deploy their innate charm, guile, and fine fashion sense to gently pry open the eyes of the closed-minded. Enforced enlightenment has arrived in the form of karaoke videos and museum makeovers, in photographic psychodramas and parade performances, in bridesmaid entrepreneurships and corporate dominations.

2 For more information on *Manananggoogle* project, see http://manananggoogle.com.

AN INTERVIEW WITH KIM ANNO

1 *Dogtown and Z-boys* is a 2001 documentary film by Stacy Peralta. It profiled the infamous Skate and Surf team on the Westside of Los Angeles and Santa Monica.

2 Saito, "The Aesthetics of Unscenic Nature."

Notes to Chapter 5: Queering Subjectivity

1 Hartman, "Venus in Two Acts," 10–11.

2 Michael Warner, quoted in "What's Queer about Queer Studies Now?," ed. Eng, Halberstam, and Muñoz, 3.

3 Eng, "Transnational Adoption and Queer Diasporas"; Eleana Kim, "Human Capital"; Pate, "Genealogies of Korean Adoption," 205–49.

4 Eleana Kim, "Human Capital," 317.

5 kate hers RHEE, e-mail message to author, August 19, 2014.
6 Eng, "Transnational Adoption and Queer Diasporas."
7 A direct presentation of the fallacy of official documents is further examined in two autobiographical documentaries by Deann Borshay Liem, *First Person Plural* (2000) and *In the Matter of Cha Jung Hee* (2010). Both have been thoroughly reviewed and analyzed by Eleana Kim and David Eng (Eng, "Transnational Adoption and Queer Diasporas"; Eleana Kim, "Human Capital").
8 Mihee-Nathalie Lemoine, e-mail message to author, August 16, 2014.
9 Amelia Jones quoted in Smith and Watson, *Interfaces*, 20.
10 Ibid.
11 Paul Redding, "Georg Wilhelm Friedrich Hegel," The Stanford Encyclopedia of Philosophy (2013), ed. Edward N. Zalta, http://plato.stanford.edu/archives/win2013/entries/hegel/.
12 Cheng, *The Melancholy of Race*, 164.
13 Eleana Kim, "Human Capital."
14 Ibid.
15 Hallowell, *Culture and Experience*, 81–87.
16 Eleana Kim, "Human Capital"; Pate, "Genealogies of Korean Adoption."
17 Gayatri Spivak, quoted in Eng, Halberstam, and Munoz, eds., "What's Queer about Queer Studies Now?," 3.
18 Lutz, *Unnatural Emotions*, 10.
19 This is not to belie important socio-historical conditions. For example, the age group of artists reflects the height of adoption between 1971 and 1988 (1988 being the year of the Seoul Korea Olympics and the political turn of South Korea in the international arena), as well as the fact that many of the artists are women, a reflection of the oppressive Korean patriarchal system that often results in daughters being relinquished for sons. Pate, "Genealogies of Korean Adoption."
20 Karin Higa, "At the Margins of American Modernism: Los Angeles, Little Tokyo, and Japanese American Artists, 1919–1945," lecture at the Asian/Pacific/American Institute, New York University, July 10, 2012.

A CONVERSATION WITH GREYSON HONG AND KIAM MARCELO JUNIO

1 *Funereal Archive* lives as a PDF on *ImageFilePress*, an online zine/gallery. Hong chose this everyday form because of its accessibility across digital platforms and for its symbolic democracy. The PDF begins with an artist statement (an excerpt of which is reprinted below), after opening with a reproduction of Hong's grandfather's Presbyterian Christian funeral program, which combines both English and Korean text. Jungshik Yoon, his grandfather, was a longtime member and an elder in the church. The front of the program features Jesus in heaven welcoming Yoon. The back of the program lists Yoon's timeline of family lineage. To

queer this heteronormative timeline, Hong has included a screen shot of an editing timeline from a previous performance in which Hong wrestles with female subjectivity. He includes his birthdate, that of his mother, and that of his paternal grandmother (to reflect the patriarchal dominance in Korean) with events from popular culture and history relating to the relations between the United States and South Korea at the time. The PDF also includes a documentary image of the traditional upright Korean American funeral floral arrangements, a link to an audio file of Hong attempting to read his grandfather's biography aloud in Korean, a screen shot of a black-and-white photograph of a young Korean woman from the 1920s and hyperlink to "the most popular song in Korea in 1925 [the year Hong's paternal grandmother was born]. Its title roughly translates to 'in praise of death.' After it was released, the singer committed suicide with her lover on the way back to Korea from Japan. This is followed by a series of screenshots of free online translators translating the funeral program and a link to the national anthem for the Provisional Government of the Republic of South Korea 1919–1948. It was originally sung to the tune of "Auld Lang Syne" and was the anthem that Hong's grandfather heard when he served in the military under Japanese occupation. The PDF closes with a reproduction of flag folding from "Art of Manliness" (www.artofmanliness.com/2012/06/29/how-to-fold-the-american-flag/). Hong writes in the image caption, "In 1947 my grandfather enlisted in the Korean military. In 1954, when the Korean War broke out, he fought for the south and was nearly fatally injured. In 2001, I joined the United States Navy and subsequently resigned shortly after 9/11. I hadn't made this connection until recently. I still know how to properly fold an American flag." In his artist statement, Hong reflects, "In September [2013], my maternal grandfather passed away in Philadelphia. I didn't know him well. His was the first family funeral I'd ever attended. I want to believe that our estrangement had something to do with that fact that he was my mother's father, and from what I understand, traditionally children are encouraged to be close to their father's side of the family. Until the funeral, I had not even known his full name, Yoon Jungshik. I was unexpectedly moved; my paternal intervention had arrived. His funeral was restricted to men and held entirely in Korean. As his granddaughter, I was not allowed to participate as a pallbearer. I wore my best black suit and took my place with the rest of the women in the family while the men processioned. My Korean is terrible, and I struggled to understand what was being said. My only record is this program. On the back they had written a short biography: the year he was born, the year he graduated from high school, when he married, when he enlisted, when he left the military, when he arrived in the United States, when he became a church elder, and when he died."

2 Jack Halberstam, *The Queer Art of Failure*.

Notes to Chapter 6: Queering Mixed Race

1 Laura Kina and Margo Machida, "Miscegenating Racial Representations: Critical Mixed Race Strategies and the Visual Arts," abstract for our cochaired panel at the College Art Association Annual Conference, Chicago, February 12–15, 2014.
2 Identity is understood in psychology as the ongoing production of how an individual understands, constructs, expresses, and performs his or her sense of self; subjectivity in social and cultural theory refers to an individual's relation to power structures and how these external forces make one a subject.
3 Chin, "Come All Ye Asian American Writers of the Real and the Fake."
4 See Kina and Dariotis, *War Baby / Love Child*; Nishime, *Undercover Asian*.
5 Joseph, *Transcending Blackness*, 4.
6 Wilson, "Optical Illusions," 88.
7 Omni and Winant, *Racial Formation in the United States*, 60.
8 Daniel et al., "Emerging Paradigms in Critical Mixed Race Studies," 6.
9 Eng, *The Feeling of Kinship*, 2.
10 Ibid., 23–57.
11 Maya Mackrandilal, interview by author, Chicago, June 27, 2014. All quotes by the artist, unless otherwise noted, are from this interview.
12 See Harris, "Queer Black Feminism."
13 Maya Mackrandilal, "Lacuna," paper presented at the College Art Association Annual Conference, Chicago, February 15, 2014.
14 Ibid.
15 Maya Mackrandilal, "Artwork," Mayamackrandilal.com, accessed August 9, 2014, http://mayamackrandilal.com/artwork/3136198_Seated_Woman_Sundial.html.
16 Mackrandilal, "Lacuna"
17 Ibid.
18 hooks, *Talking Back*, 125.
19 Zavé Gayatri Martohardjono, interview with the author, July 11, 2014. All quotes from the artist, unless otherwise noted, are from this interview.
20 From his Autogeography: Word Play, participatory installation created with Lily Mengesha (2012).

A CONVERSATION WITH SITA KURATOMI BHAUMIK AND SAYA WOOLFALK

1 Father Divine was an African American religious leader who came to prominence in New York in the 1930s. Originally dismissed as a cult leader, his Peace Mission and advocacy for racial and economic equality is hailed by many as a precursor to the civil rights movement.
2 The Kearny Street Workshop was founded in 1972 in San Francisco "during the height of the Asian American Movement" and "is the oldest

Asian Pacific American multidisciplinary arts organization in the country," according to its website. See http://i52611.wix.com/kearnystreet. *Hyphen* magazine is a San Francisco–based Asian American arts and culture magazine founded in 2002. See http://www.hyphenmagazine.com/.

3 The 24hourshow was an Asian American women's art collective active from 2005 to 2011 that included Sita Kuratomi Bhaumik, Elokin, Jiz Lee, Mia Nakano, Christine Pan, Han Pham, Elizabeth Sy, and Shawn Tamaribuchi. See the archive at http://femalefighterproject.com/archive-the-24-hour-art-show/.

Notes to Chapter 7: Queering Asian America

1 Iijima, "Chris Iijima, Lawyer, Singer, and Songwriter," 322.

2 Robert Hughes, "Art: The Whitney Biennial: A Fiesta of Whining," Time, March 22, 1993, www.time.com/time/magazine/article/0,9171,978001,00.html.

3 Machida, *Unsettled Visions*, 50.

4 Helmuth von Moltke, Militarische Werke, vol. 2, part 2, pp. 33–40.

5 Min, "The Last Asian American Exhibition in the Whole Entire World," 36.

6 Richard Stallman, "Why Open Source Misses the Point of Free Software," GNU Operating System website, accessed June 24, 2013, www.gnu.org/philosophy/open-source-misses-the-point.html.

7 Nakamura, *Digitizing Race*, 18.

8 Ibid.

9 Tsuchitani, "Making Art, Making Change," 28.

10 Takahashi, *Nisei/Sansei*, 155.

11 Louie, "When We Wanted It Done, We Did It Ourselves," xv.

12 Tsuchitani, "Making Art, Making Change," 28.

13 Annie Nakao, "Memoirs of a Geisha Guerrilla," *San Francisco Chronicle*, December 5, 2004, www.sfgate.com/living/article/Memoirs-of-a-geisha-guerrilla-2667123.php.

14 Scott Tsuchitani, Memoirs of A Sansei Geisha project description, Scott Tsuchitani website, www.scotttsuchitani.com/geisha/dialogue.html.

15 Ibid., www.scotttsuchitani.com/geisha/dialogue2.html.

16 Ibid., www.scotttsuchitani.com/geisha/dialogue4.html.

17 "Who Were the Samurai?," Asian Art Museum blog, accessed June 27, 2013, http://blog.asianart.org/samurai/aboutsamurai.htm.

18 "Index," Asianart.org, accessed June 17, 2013, www.asiansart.org/index.html.

19 Ibid.

20 Tsuchitani, "Making Art, Making Change," 32.

21 Claire Pentecost, "Fields of Zombies: Biotech Agriculture and the Privatization of Knowledge" in agriART: Companion Planting for Social

and Biological Systems, exhibition catalog curated by Ryan Griffis and Mark Cooley, Fine Arts Gallery, George Mason University, 2009, www.yougenics.net/agriart/pentecost.html.

22 Gaye Chan, Free Grindz project description, Gaye Chan website, www.gayechan.com/projects-gallery/free-grindz/statement.html.

23 Gaye Chan, Share Seeds project description, Nomoola website, www.nomoola.com/seeds/index.html. Accessed July 25, 2016.

24 Gaye Chan, Barter Baskets project description, Gaye Chan website, www.gayechan.com/barter/. Accessed June 27, 2013.

25 Ibid.

26 China, of course, is notorious for the "Great Firewall of China," (aka the Golden Shield Project), which officially blocks Facebook, Twitter, and other popular social media sites, but Chinese netizens have developed several workarounds to this. According to GlobalWebIndex, there were 35 million Twitter users and 65.2 million Facebook users in China in the second quarter of 2012.

27 Hasan Elahi, "Artist's Statement," Hasan Elahi website, http://elahi.umd.edu/. Accessed June 27, 2013.

28 Hasan Elahi, "You Want to Track Me? Here You Go, F.B.I.," New York Times, October 29, 2011, www.nytimes.com/2011/10/30/opinion/sunday/giving-the-fbi-what-it-wants.html.

29 Ibid.

30 Clive Thompson, "The Visible Man: An FBI Target Puts His Whole Life Online," Wired, www.wired.com/techbiz/people/magazine/15-06/ps_transparency, retrieved. Accessed June 27, 2013.

31 Elahi, "You Want to Track Me?"

32 Michel Martin, "Artist Takes FBI Surveillance a Step Further," NPR website, www.npr.org/templates/story/story.php?storyId=10540966. Accessed June 27, 2013.

33 Rebecca Lee, "'I Became My Own Big Brother,'" ABC News, http://abcnews.go.com/WN/story?id=3228016&page=1#.UcnhH-ure2w. Accessed June 27, 2103.

34 Ibid.

35 See, *The Decolonized Eye*, 2.

AN INTERVIEW WITH TINA TAKEMOTO

1 Nakano and Shibata, *Japanese American Women*.

2 Takemoto, "Notes on Internment Camp," 57.

3 See E. G. Crichton, Lineage: Matchmaking in the Archive, 2009–present, https://egcrichton.sites.ucsc.edu/projects/matchmaking-in-the-archive/.

4 See Hirasuna, *The Art of Gaman*.

5 Described in the press kit for Warning Shot: The Killing of James Wakasa, a film by Tina Takemoto.

6 Okubo, *Citizen 13660*, 180–81.

Notes to Afterword: To Be Queer Being to Queer It . . .

1 Televised debate between Gore Vidal and William F. Buckley on August 27, 1968, at the Democratic convention in Chicago.

2 Eng and Hom, eds., *Q & A*.

3 Curtis M. Wong, "Pat Robertson: Gays Will Force Christians to Like Anal Sex and, Eventually, Polyamory and Bestiality," *Huffington Post*, April 3, 2015, www.huffingtonpost.com/2015/04/03/pat-robertson-gay-anal-sex-_n_6999832.html.

4 Warner, "Queer and Then?"

5 Fung, "Looking for My Penis."

BIBLIOGRAPHY

Ahmed, Sara. *On Being Included: Racism and Diversity in Institutional Life*. Durham, NC: Duke University Press, 2012.

———. *The Promise of Happiness*. Durham, NC: Duke University Press, 2010.

———. *Willful Subjects*. Durham, NC: Duke University Press, 2014.

Althusser, Louis. *For Marx*. Translated by Ben Brewster. New York: Verso, 2006.

———. "Ideology and Ideological State Apparatuses." In *Lenin and Philosophy, and Other Essays*, translated by Ben Brewster, 127–86. New York: Monthly Review Press, 1972.

Austin, J. L. *How to Do Things with Words*. Cambridge, MA: Harvard University Press, 1962.

Baerwaldt, Wayne, ed. *Memories of Overdevelopment: Philippine Diaspora in Contemporary Art*." Winnipeg, Canada: Plug In Editions and University of California, Irvine, Art Gallery, 1997.

Barney, Matthew, dir. *Drawing Restraint 9*. Restraint LLC, 2005.

Barthes, Roland. *Camera Lucida: Reflections on Photography*. New York: Hill and Wang, 1981.

———. "Cy Twombly: Works on Paper." In *The Responsibility of Forms: Critical Essays on Music, Art, and Representation*, translated by Richard Howard, 157–76. New York: Hill and Wang, 1985.

———. "Death of the Author." In *Image, Music, Text*, 142–49. New York: Hill and Wang, 1977.

———. "'L'Express' Talks with Roland Barthes." In *The Grain of the Voice: Interviews 1962–1980*, translated by Linda Coverdale, 88–108. New York: Hill and Wang, 1985.

———. "Non Multa Sed Multum." In *Cy Twombly: Fifty Years of Works on Paper*, 23–40. Munich: Schirmer-Mosel, 2004.

———. "Preface to Renauld Camus's *Tricks*." In *The Rustle of Language*, 291–95. Translated by Richard Howard. Berkeley: University of California Press. 1989.

———. "The Wisdom of Art." In *The Responsibility of Forms: Critical Essays on Music, Art, and Representation*, translated by Richard Howard, 177–94. New York: Hill and Wang, 1985.

Bascara, Victor. *Model-Minority Imperialism*. Minneapolis, MN: University of Minnesota Press, 2006.

Bataille, Georges, *Eroticism: Death and Sensuality*. San Francisco: City Lights Books, 1986.

Baudrillard, Jean. *Selected Writings*. Translated by Mark Poster. Cambridge, MA: Polity, 1998.

Benjamin, Walter. "Theses on the Philosophy of History." In *Reflections: Essays, Aphorisms, Autobiographical Writings*, 279. New York: Harcourt Brace Javanovich, 1978.

Bernabe, Jan Christian. "Queer Reconfigurations: *Bontoc Eulogy* and Marlon Fuentes's Archive Imperative." *Positions: Asia Critique* 24, no. 4 (2016).

Bilal, Wafaa, and Kari Lydersen. *Shoot an Iraqi: Art, Life and Resistance under the Gun*. San Francisco: City Lights, 2008.

Bird, Jon. "Indeterminacy and (Dis)order in the Work of Cy Twombly." *Oxford Art Journal* 30, no. 3 (2007): 484–504. doi:10.1093/oxartj/kcm024.

Borshay Liem, Deann. *First Person Plural.* DVD. Berkeley, CA: Mu Films; and San Francisco, CA: Center for Asian American Media, 2000.

———. *Practical Hints about Your Foreign Child.* DVD. Berkeley, CA: Independent film, 2005.

Butler, Judith. "Critically Queer." *GLQ: A Journal of Lesbian and Gay Studies* 1, no. 1 (1993): 17–32. doi:10.1215/10642684-1-1-17.

Butt, Gavin. *Between You and Me: Queer Disclosures in the New York Art World, 1948–1963*. Durham, NC: Duke University Press, 2005.

Camus, Renaud. *Tricks*. Paris: Persona, 1979.

Chang, Alexandra. *Envisioning Diaspora: Asian American Visual Arts Collectives*. Beijing: Time Zone 8 Editions, 2009.

Chang, Gordon H., Daniel Cornell, and Mark Dean Johnson, eds. *Asian/American/Modern Art: Shifting Currents, 1900–1970*. Berkeley: University of California Press, 2008.

Chang, Gordon H., Mark Dean Johnson, Paul J. Karlstrom, and Sharon Spain, eds. *Asian American Art, 1850–1970*. Stanford, CA: Stanford University Press, 2008.

Chen, Mel. *Animacies: Biopolitics, Racial Mattering, and Queer Affect*. Durham, NC: Duke University Press, 2012.

Cheng, Anne Anlin. *The Melancholy of Race.* New York: Oxford University Press, 2000.

Chin, Frank. "Come All Ye Asian American Writers of the Real and the Fake." In *The Big Aiiieeeee!: An Anthology of Chinese American and Japanese American Literature*, edited by Jeffery Paul Chan et al., 1–93. New York: Meridian, 1991.

Chuh, Kandice. *Imagine Otherwise: On Asian Americanist Critique*. Durham, NC: Duke University Press, 2003.

Chui, Melissa, and Benjamin Genocchio, eds. *Chinese Contemporary Art: 7 Things You Should Know*. New York: AW Asia, 2008.

______. *Contemporary Art in Asia: A Critical Reader.* Cambridge, MA: MIT Press, 2011.

Come See the Paradise. DVD. Directed by Alan Parker. 1990. Beverly Hills, CA: Twentieth Century Fox Home Entertainment, 2006.

Cvetkovich, Ann. "Queer Art of the Counterarchive." In *Cruising the Archive: Queer Art and Culture in Los Angeles, 1945–1980*, edited by Sarah Kessler and Mia Locks, 32–35. Los Angeles, CA: ONE National Gay & Lesbian Archives, 2011.

Daigle, Claire. "Cy Twombly: Lingering at the Threshold between Word and Image." *TATE ETC* 13 (2008): 62–69.

———. "Reading Barthes/Writing Twombly." PhD diss., City University of New York, 2004.

Daniel, G. Reginald, Laura Kina, Wei Ming Dariotis, and Camilla Fojas. "Emerging Paradigms in Critical Mixed Race Studies." *Journal of Critical Mixed Race Studies* 1, no. 1 (2014): 6–65.

Department of the Bureau of Diplomatic Security of the United States Department of State. *History of the Bureau of Diplomatic Security of the United States Department of State*. Report prepared by Mark Hover. Washington, DC: Global Printing Solutions, 2011. www.state.gov/m/ds/rls/rpt/c47602.htm.

Derrida, Jacques. *Archive Fever: A Freudian Impression*. Translated by Eric Prenowitz. Chicago: University of Chicago Press, 1996.

———. *Of Grammatology*. Baltimore, MD: Johns Hopkins University Press, 1976.

———. *Speech and Phenomena: And Other Essays on Husserl's Theory of Signs*. Translated by David B. Allison. Evanston, IL: Northwestern University Press, 1973.

Diamond, Catherine, ed. *Communities of Imagination: Contemporary Southeast Asian Theatres*. Honolulu: University of Hawaii Press, 2012.

Dinshaw, Carolyn, et al. "Theorizing Queer Temporalities: A Roundtable Discussion." *GLQ* 13, nos. 2–3 (2007): 177–95.

Dogtown and Z-boys. Directed by Stacy Peralta. 2001. DVD. Culver City, CA: Sony Pictures Home Entertainment, 2005.

Downey, Anthony. "The Lives of Others: Artur Zmijewski's *Repetition*, the Stanford Prison Experiment, and the Ethics of Surveillance." In *Conspiracy Dwellings: Surveillance in Contemporary Art*, edited by Outi Remes and Pam Skelton, 67–91. Newcastle upon Tyne: Cambridge Scholars Publishing, 2010.

"DP-1—Profile of General Population and Housing Characteristics: 2010 for Livingston Township, Essex County, New Jersey." *United States Census Bureau*. http://factfinder.census.gov/faces/tableservices/jsf/pages/productview.xhtml?src=bkmk.

Duggan, Lisa. *The Twilight of Equality? Neoliberalism, Cultural Politics, and the Attack on Democracy*. Boston: Beacon Press, 2012.

Edelman, Lee. *No Future: Queer Theory and the Death Drive*. Durham, NC: Duke University Press, 2004.

Edwards, Brent Hayes. "The Uses of Diaspora." *Social Text* 19, no. 1 (2001): 45–73. doi:10.1215/01642472-19-1_66-45.

Elahi, Hasan. "You Want to Track Me? Here You Go, F.B.I." *New York Times*, October 29, 2011.

Eng, David L. *The Feeling of Kinship: Queer Liberalism and the Racialization of Intimacy*. Durham, NC: Duke University Press, 2010.

———. *Racial Castration: Managing Masculinity in Asian America*. Durham, NC: Duke University Press, 2001.

———. "Transnational Adoption and Queer Diasporas." *Social Text* 21, no. 3 (Fall 2003): 1–37.

Eng, David L., Judith Jack Halberstam, and José Estaben Muñoz. "What's Queer about Queer Studies Now?" *Social Text* 84, nos. 3–4 (2005): 1–17.

Eng, David L., and Alice Y. Hom. *Q & A: Queer in Asian America*. Philadelphia, PA: Temple University Press, 1998.

Finkel, Jori. "A Reluctant Fraternity, Thinking Post-Black." *New York Times*, June 10, 2007, www.nytimes.com/2007/06/10/arts/design/10fink.html.

Foucault, Michel. *Discipline and Punish: The Birth of the Prison*. Translated by Alan Sheridan. New York: Vintage, 1975.

Freeman, Elizabeth. *Time Binds: Queer Temporalities, Queer Histories*. Durham, NC: Duke University Press, 2010.

Fung, Richard. "Looking for My Penis." In Min Song and Jean Yu-Wen Shen Wu, eds., *Asian American Studies: A Reader*. New Brunswick, NJ: Rutgers University Press, 2000.

Gilroy, Paul. *The Black Atlantic: Modernity and Double Consciousness*. Cambridge, MA: Harvard University Press, 1993.

Golden, Arthur. *Memoirs of a Geisha*. New York: Vintage Books, 1997.

Golden, Thelma, Christine Y. Kim, Hamza Walker, and Franklin Sirmans. *Freestyle*. New York: Studio Museum in Harlem, 2001.

Grewal, Inderpal. *Transnational America: Feminisms, Diasporas, Neoliberalisms*. Durham, NC: Duke University Press, 2005.

Guerin, Frances, and Roger Hallas, eds. *The Image and the Witness: Trauma, Memory and Visual Culture*. London: Wallflower Press, 2007.

Halberstam, Jack. *The Queer Art of Failure*. Durham, NC: Duke University Press, 2011.

Halberstam, Judith. *In a Queer Time and Place: Transgender Bodies, Subcultural Lives*. New York: New York University Press, 2005.

Hall, Stuart. "Cultural Identity and Diaspora." In *Identity: Community, Culture, Difference*, edited by Jonathan Rutherford, 222–37. London: Lawrence & Wishart, 1990.

Hallowell, Alfred Irving. *Culture and Experience*. Philadelphia: University of Pennsylvania Press, 1955.

Harris, Laura Alexandra. "Queer Black Feminism: The Pleasure Principle." *Feminist Review* 54 (1996): 3–30.

Hartman, Saidiya. "Venus in Two Acts," *Small Axe* 12, no. 2 (June 2008): 1–14.

Higa, Karin. "At the Margins of American Modernism: Los Angeles, Little Tokyo, and Japanese American Artists, 1919–1945," lecture at the Asian/Pacific/American Institute, New York University, July 10, 2012.

———. "Inside and Outside at the Same Time." In *The Sculpture of Ruth Asawa: Contours in the Air*, edited by Ruth Asawa, Daniell Cornell, M.H. de Young Memorial Museum, Japanese American National Museum (Los Angeles, CA), 30–41. Berkeley: University of California Press, 2007.

Hirasuna, Delphine. *The Art of Gaman: Arts and Crafts from the Japanese American Internment Camps 1942–1946*. Berkeley, CA: Ten Speed Press, 2005.

History and Memory: (for Akiko and Takashige). Written and directed by ReaTajiri. 1991. DVD. New York: Women Make Movies, 2008.

Hoang, Nguyen Tan. *PIRATED!*. DVD. Originally published by Beta-SP Video, 2000. Atlanta, GA: Kimchi Chige Productions, 2006.

Hochdörfer, Achim. "'Blue Goes Out, B Comes In': Cy Twombly's Narration of Interminacy." In *Cy Twombly: States of Mind: Painting, Sculpture, Photography, Drawing*, 12–39. München: Schirmer/Mosel Verlag, 2009.

Hong, Grace Kyungwon, and Roderick A. Ferguson. *Strange Affinities: The Gender and Sexual Politics of Comparative Racialization*. Durham, NC: Duke University Press, 2011.

hooks, bell. *Talking Back: Thinking Feminist, Thinking Black*. Boston, MA: South End Press, 1989.

Hyde, Lewis. *The Gift: Imagination and the Erotic Life of Property*. New York: Vintage Books, 1983.

Hyun, Jane. *Breaking the Bamboo Ceiling: Career Strategies for Asians*. New York: HarperBusiness, 2005.

Iijima, Chris. "Chris Iijima, Lawyer, Singer, and Songwriter." In *Yellow Light: The Flowering of Asian American Arts*, edited by Amy Ling, 319–22. Philadelphia: Temple University Press, 2000.

Ingawanij, May Adadol, and Benjamin McKay, eds. *Glimpses of Freedom: Independent Cinema in Southeast Asia*. Ithaca, NY: Cornell University Press, 2011.

Johnson, Mark, Gordon H. Chang, Paul J. Karlstrom, and Sharon Spain, eds. *Asian American Art: A History*. Stanford, CA: Stanford University Press, 2008.

Jones, Amelia. *Seeing Differently. A History and Theory of Identification and the Visual Arts*. London: Routledge, 2012.

Joseph, Ralina. *Transcending Blackness: From the New Millennium Mulatta to the Exceptional Multiracial*. Durham, NC: Duke University Press, 2012.

Juhasz, Alexandra. "Video Remains: Nostalgia, Technology, and Queer Archive Activism." *GLQ: A Journal of Lesbian and Gay Studies* 12, no. 2 (2006): 319–28.

Kapadia, Ronak K. “Up in the Air and on the Skin: Wafaa Bilal, Drone Warfare, and the Human Terrain.” In *Shifting Borders: America and the Middle East/North Africa*, edited by Alex Lubin, 147–63. Beirut: American University of Beirut Press, 2014.

Katz, Jonathan D. “Agnes Martin: Sexuality of Abstraction.” In *Agnes Martin*, edited by Lynne Cooke, Karen J. Kelly, and Barbara Schröder, 170–97. New Haven, CT: Yale University Press, 2011.

———. “‘Committing the Perfect Crime’: Sexuality, Assemblage, and the Postmodern Turn in American Art.” *Art Journal* 67, no. 1 (March 2008): 38–53. doi:10.1080/00043249.2008.10791293.

———. “John Cage’s Queer Silence; Or, How to Avoid Making Matters Worse.” *GLQ: A Journal of Lesbian and Gay Studies* 5 (1999): 231–52.

———. “Performative Silence and the Politics of Passivity.” In *Making a Scene*, edited by Henry Rogers and David Burrows, 101–23. Birmingham: ARTicle Press, 2000.

Kennedy, Randy. “Cy Twombly, Idiosyncratic Painter, Dies at 83.” *New York Times*, July 5, 2011. http://artsbeat.blogs.nytimes.com/2011/07/05/cy-twombly-idiosyncratic-painter-dies-at-83/?_r=0.

Kim, Elaine, Margo Machida, and Sharon Mizota, eds. *Fresh Talk/Daring Gazes: Conversations on Asian American Art*. Berkeley: University of California Press, 2003.

Kim, Eleana. “Human Capital: Transnational Korean Adoptees and the Neoliberal Logic of Return.” *Journal of Korean Studies* 17, no. 2 (Fall 2012): 299–328.

Kina, Laura, and Wei Ming Dariotis. *War Baby/Love Child: Mixed Race Asian American Art*. Seattle: University of Washington Press, 2013.

Kina, Laura, and Margo Machida. “Miscegenating Racial Representations: Critical Mixed Race Strategies and the Visual Arts.” Panel at the College Art Association Annual Conference, Chicago, Illinois, February 12–15, 2014.

Krauss, Rosalind. “Cy Was Here: Cy’s Up.” *Artforum International* 33, no. 1 (1994): 70+.

Lam, Mariam B.. “Cartographies.” *Asian American Literary Review* 6, no. 2 (2015): 1–58.

———. *Not Coming to Terms: Việt Nam, Archival Trauma and Strategic Affect*. Durham, NC: Duke University Press, 2016.

Lam, Mariam B., Isabelle Thuy Pelaud, Lan Duong, and Kathy L. Nguyen. “Introduction.” In *Troubling Borders: An Anthology of Art and Literature by Southeast Asian Women in the Diaspora*, edited by Isabelle Thuy Pelaud, Lan Duong, and Kathy L. Nguyen. Seattle: University of Washington Press, 2014.

Lê, Việt. *lovebang!*. First film of *Love Bang!* Trilogy. DVD. San Francisco, CA: Independent film, 2014.

———. *eclipse*. Second film of *Love Bang!* Trilogy. DVD. San Francisco, CA: Independent film, 2015.

———. *heARTbreak!*. Third film of *Love Bang!* Trilogy. DVD. San Francisco, CA: Independent

Lee, Anthony. *Picturing Chinatown: Art and Orientalism in San Francisco*. Berkeley: University of California Press, 2001.

Leeman, Richard. "Roland Barthes et Cy Twombly : Le 'champ allusif de l'écriture.'" *Rue Descartes* 34, no. 4 (2001): 61–70.

Lemoine, Mihee-Nathalie. *Who Are You? 2014: 60 Years of Korean Adoption*. Edited by Kimura Byol. Vimeo. Montréal, Québec: Star Kim Project, 2014. https://vimeo.com/117125221.

Lim, Eng-Beng. *Brown Boys and Rice Queens: Spellbinding Performance in the Tropics*. New York: New York University Press, 2013.

Lim, Felicidad "Bliss" Cua. *Translating Time: Cinema, the Fantastic, and Temporal Critique*. Durham, NC: Duke University Press, 2009.

Looking for Langston. Directed by Isaac Julien. DVD. New York: Strand Releasing, 1989.

Louie, Steven G. "When We Wanted It Done, We Did It Ourselves." In *Asian Americans: The Movement and the Moment*, edited by Steve Louie and Glenn Omatsu, xv–xxv. Los Angeles: UCLA Asian American Studies Center Press, 2001.

Love, Heather. *Feeling Backward: Loss and the Politics of Queer History*. Cambridge, MA: Harvard University Press, 2007.

Lowe, Lisa. *Immigrant Acts: On Asian American Cultural Politics*. Durham, NC: Duke University Press, 1996.

Lutz, Catherine. *Unnatural Emotions: Everyday Sentiments on a Micronesian Atoll and Their Challenge to Western Theory*. Chicago: University of Chicago Press. 1988.

Lye, Colleen. *America's Asia: Racial Form and American Literature*, 1893–1945. Princeton, NJ: Princeton University Press, 2004.

Machida, Margo. "Reframing Asian America." In *One Way or Another: Asian American Art Now*, edited by Melissa Chiu, Karin M. Higa, and Susette S. Min, 15–20. New Haven, CT: Yale University Press, 2006.

———. *Unsettled Visions: Contemporary Asian American Artists and the Social Imaginary*. Durham, NC: Duke University Press, 2008.

Mackrandilal, Maya. "Lacuna." Paper presented at the College Art Association Annual Conference, Chicago, Illinois, February 12–15, 2014.

Manalansan, Martin. "Race, Violence, and Neoliberal Spatial Politics in the Global City." *Social Text* 23, nos. 3–4 (Fall–Winter 2005): 141–56.

Mankekar, Purnima, and Louisa Schein, eds. *Media, Erotics, and Transnational Asia*. Durham, NC: Duke University Press, 2012.

Mann, Steve, et al. "Sousveillance: Inventing and Using Wearable Computing Devices for Data Collection in Surveillance Environments." *Surveillance & Society* 1, no. 3 (2003): 331–55.

Melamed, Jodi. *Represent and Destroy: Rationalizing Violence in the New Racial Capitalism*. Minneapolis: University of Minnesota Press, 2011.

Memoirs of a Geisha. DVD. Directed by Rob Marshall. Culver City, CA: Columbia Pictures, 2005.

Mercer, Kobena, ed. *Exiles, Diasporas and Strangers*. Cambridge, MA: MIT Press, 2008.

Min, Susette Min. "The Last Asian American Exhibition in the Whole Entire World." In *One Way or Another: Asian American Art Now,* exhibition curated by Melissa Chiu, Karin Higa, Susette Min, 34–41. New York: Asia Society, 2006.

Mirzhoeff, Nicholas. "The Death of the Death of Photography." In *An Introduction to Visual Culture*. New York: Routledge, 1999.

Moltke, Helmuth von. *Militarische Werke*. In *Moltke on the Art of War: Selected Writings,* edited by Daniel J. Hughes, 45–47. Presidio Press: New York, 1993.

Morrison, Elise. "Performing Citizen Arrest: Surveillance Art and the Passerby." *International Journal of Performance Arts and Digital Media* 7, no. 2 (2011): 239–57.

Muñoz, José Esteban. *Cruising Utopia: The Then and There of Queer Futurity*. New York: New York University Press, 2009.

———. *Disidentifications: Queers of Color and the Performance of Politics*. Minneapolis: University of Minnesota Press, 1999.

Munroe, Alexandra. "Buddhism and the Neo-Avant-Garde: Cage Zen, Beat Zen, and Zen." In *The Third Mind: American Artists Contemplate Asia, 1860–1989*, edited by Alexandra Munroe, 199–216. New York: Guggenheim Museum, 2009.

Munroe, Majella. "Zen as a Transnational Current in Post-War Art: The Case of Mira Schendel." *Tate Papers*, no. 23 (Spring 2005). www.tate.org.uk/research/publications/tate-papers/zen-transnational-current-post-war-art-mira-schendel.

Nakamura, Lisa. *Digitizing Race: Visual Cultures of the* Internet. Minneapolis: University of Minnesota Press, 2008.

Nakano, Mei, and Grace Shibata. *Japanese American Women: Three Generations 1890–1990*. Berkeley, CA: Mina Press, 1990.

Ngai, Sianne. *Ugly Feelings*. Boston, MA: Harvard University Press, 2007.

Nguyen, Mimi Thi. "'In the Arms of Pirates, under the Bodies of Sailors': Diaspora, Desire, and Danger in Nguyen Tan Hoang's *PIRATED!*" In *Charlie Don't Surf: Four Vietnamese American Artists*, edited by Việt Lê, 66–75. Vancouver: Centre A., 2005.

Nishime, Leilani. *Undercover Asian: Multiracial Asian Americans in Visual Culture*. Chicago: University of Illinois Press, 2014.

Noszlopy, Laura, and Matthew Isaac Cohen. *Contemporary Southeast Asian Performance: Transnational Perspectives*. Edited by Laura Noszlopy. New Castle: Cambridge Scholars, 2010.

O'Brien, Genevieve Erin, dir. *For the Love of Unicorns*. Los Angeles, CA: independent film, 2014.

Okubo, Mine. *Citizen 13660.* New York: Columbia University Press, 1946.

Omni, Michael, and Howard Winant. *Racial Formation in the United States.* New York: Routledge, 1994.

Pate, Soon. "Genealogies of Korean Adoption: American Empire, Militarization, and Yellow Desire." PhD diss., University of Minnesota, 2010.

Pearlman, Ellen. *Nothing and Everything: The Influence of Buddhism on the American Avant Garde 1942–1962.* Berkeley, CA: Evolver Editions, 2014.

Pelaud, Isabelle Thuy, Lan Duong, Mariam B. Lam, and Kathy L. Nguyen, eds. *Troubling Borders: An Anthology of Art and Literature by Southeast Asian Women in the Diaspora.* Seattle: University of Washington Press, 2013.

Pentecost, Claire. "Fields of Zombies: Biotech Agriculture and the Privatization of Knowledge." In *agriART: Companion Planting for Social and Biological Systems,* exhibition catalog curated by Ryan Griffis and Mark Cooley, Fine Arts Gallery, George Mason University, 2009, www.yougenics.net/agriart/pentecost.html.

Puar, Jasbir. *Terrorist Assemblages: Homonationalism in Queer Times.* Durham, NC: Duke University Press, 2007.

———. "Transnational Sexualities: South Asian (Trans)national(alism)s and Queer Diasporas." In *Q & A: Queer in Asian America,* edited by David L. Eng and Alice Y. Hom, 405–22. Philadelphia, PA: Temple University Press, 1998.

Puwar, Nirmal Puwar. *Space Invaders: Race, Gender and Bodies out of Place.* Oxford: Berg, 2004.

Rancière, Jacques. *The Emancipated Spectator.* Translated by Gregory Elliott. New York: Verso, 2009.

Rashomon. DVD. Directed by Akira Kurosawa. 1950. Los Angeles, CA: Embassy Home Entertainment, 1986.

Ratnam, Niru. "Art and Globalization." In *Themes in Contemporary Art,* edited by Gill Perry and Paul Wood, 277–310. New Haven, CT: Yale University Press, 2004.

Robertson, Kirsty. "'Try to Walk with the Sound of My Footsteps': The Surveillant Body in Contemporary Art." In Allen et al., *Sorting Daemons: Art, Surveillance Regimes and Social Control,* edited by Jan Allen, Kirsty Robertson, and Sarah E. K. Smith, 31–47. Kingston: Agnes Etherington Art Centre, Queens University, 2010.

Rofel, Lisa. *Desiring China: Experiments in Neoliberalism, Sexuality and Public Cultures.* Durham, NC: Duke University Press, 2007.

Rogoff, Irit. "Gossip as Testimony: A Postmodern Signature." In *The Feminism and Visual Culture Reader,* edited by Amelia Jones, 268–76. New York: Routledge, 2003.

Root, Maria P. P. *The Multiracial Experience: Racial Borders as the New Frontier.* Thousand Oaks, CA: Sage, 1996.

Roth, Moira. "The Aesthetic of Indifference." *Artforum International,* November 1977.

Roth, Moira, and Jonathan Katz. *Difference/Indifference: Musings on Postmodernism, Marcel Duchamp and John Cage*. Amsterdam: GB Arts International, 1998.

Saito, Yoshiko. "The Aesthetics of Unscenic Nature." In *Nature, Aesthetics, and Environmentalism: From Beauty to Duty*, edited by Allen Carlson and Sheila Lintott, 238–53. New York: Columbia University Press, 2008.

Schjeldahl, Peter. "Breaking Away: A Flowering of Young African-American Artists." *New Yorker*, June 11, 2001. www.newyorker.com/archive/2001/06/11/010611craw_artworld.

See, Sarita Echavez. *The Decolonized Eye: Filipino American Art and Performance*. Minneapolis: University of Minnesota Press, 2009.

Sekula, Alan. "The Body and the Archive." *October* 39 (Winter 1986): 3–64.

Serota, Nicholas. "History behind the Thought (Interview with Twombly)." In *Cy Twombly: Cycles and Seasons*, edited by Nicholas Serota, 42–53. London: Tate Publishing, 2008.

Shah, Svati P. "Knowing 'The Unknowns': The Artwork of Chitra Ganesh." *Feminist Studies* (2011): 111–26.

Shimakawa, Karen. *National Abjection: The Asian American Body Onstage*. Durham, NC: Duke University Press, 2002.

Silva, Denise Ferreira da. *Toward a Global Idea of Race*. Minneapolis: University of Minnesota Press, 2007.

Smith, Sarah E. K. "Captured and Controlled: Critiquing Surveillance through the Camera." In *Sorting Daemons: Art, Surveillance Regimes and Social Control*, edited by Jan Allen, Kirsty Robertson, and Sarah E. K. Smith, 49–61. Kingston: Agnes Etherington Art Centre, Queens University, 2010.

Smith, Shawn Michelle. *Photography on the Color Line: W. E. B. Du Bois, Race, and Visual Culture*. Durham, NC: Duke University Press, 2004.

Smith, Sidonie, and Julia Watson. *Interfaces: Women, Autobiography, Image, Performance*. Ann Arbor: University of Michigan Press, 2005.

Soe, Valerie. "Open-Source Identities: Identity and Resistance in the Work of Three Asian American Artists." *Amerasia Journal* 40, no. 2 (2014): 2–24.

Stoler, Ann Laura. *Imperial Debris: On Ruins and Ruination*. Durham, NC: Duke University Press, 2013.

Stray Dog. Directed by Akira Kurosawa. 1949. DVD. Irvington, NY: Criterion Collection, 2004.

Sturken, Marita. *Tangled Memories: The Vietnam War, the AIDS Epidemic, and the Politics of Remembering*. Berkeley: University of California Press, 1997.

Susik, Abigail. "Cy Twombly: Writing after Writing." *Rebus: A Journal of Art History and Theory* 3 (Autumn/Winter 2009): 1–28.

Sylvester, David. "Cy Twombly (2000)." In *Interviews with American Artists*, 171–81. New Haven, CT: Yale University Press, 2001.

Tadiar, Neferti. *Fantasy-Production: Sexual Economies and Other Philippine Consequences for the New World Order*. Seattle: University of Washington Press, 2004.

Takahashi, Jee. *Nisei/Sansei: Shifting Japanese American Identities and Politics*. Philadelphia, PA: Temple University Press, 1997.

Takemoto, Tina. *Looking for Jiro*. DVD. San Francisco, CA: Independent film, 2009.

———. "Looking for Jiro Onuma: A Queer Meditation on the Incarceration of Japanese Americans during World War II." *GLQ: A Journal of Lesbian and Gay Studies* 20, no. 3 (2014): 241–75.

———. "Notes on Internment Camp." *Art Journal* 72, no. 2 (Summer 2013): 55–57.

———. *Warning Shot*. DVD. San Francisco, CA: Independent film, 2016.

Taylor, Nora A., and Boreth Ly, eds. *Modern and Contemporary Southeast Asian Art: An Anthology*. Ithaca, NY: Cornell University Press, 2012.

Theiler, KimSu. *Place-Names: New York City*. Vimeo. New York: NY: Independent film, 2011. https://vimeo.com/28885882.

Thin Blue Line, The. Directed by Errol Morris. 1988. VHS. New York: HBO Video, 1988.

Tongson, Karen. *Relocations: Queer Suburban Imaginaries*. New York: New York University Press, 2011.

Trapp, Elizabeth J. "Cy Twombly's Ferragosto Series." MA thesis, Ohio University, 2010. www.ohiolink.edu/etd/view.cgi?ohiou1276609006.

Tsuchitani, Scott. "Making Art, Making Change: The Tactical Use of Guerrilla Intervention." *Social Policy* 41 no. 3 (2012): 27–33.

Varnedoe, Kirk. "Your Kid Could Not Do This, and Other Reflections on Cy Twombly." *MoMA* 18 (Autumn–Winter 1994): 18–23.

Vendler, Helen. "The Medley Is the Message." *New York Review of Books*, May 8, 1986. www.nybooks.com/articles/archives/1986/may/08/the-medley-is-the-message/.

Villiers, Nicholas de. *Opacity and the Closet: Queer Tactics in Foucault, Barthes, and Warhol*. Minneapolis: University of Minnesota Press, 2012.

Virilio, Paul. "The Visual Crash." In *CTRL [SPACE]: Rhetorics of Surveillance from Bentham to Big Brother*, edited by Thomas Y. Levin, Ursula Frohne, and Peter Weibel, 108–13. Cambridge, MA: MIT Press, 2002.

Warner, Michael. "Queer and Then?" *Chronicle of Higher Education*, January 1, 2012, http://chronicle.com/article/QueerThen-/130161/.

Wechsler, Jeffrey. *Asian Traditions/Modern Expressions: Asian American Artists and Abstraction, 1945–1970*. New York: Abrams, 1997.

Wiegman, Robyn, and Elizabeth A. Wilson. "Introduction: Antinormativity's Queer Conventions." *Differences: A Journal of Feminist Cultural Studies* (2015): 1–25.

Wilson, Judith. "Optical Illusions Mages of Miscegenation in Nineteenth- and Twentieth-Century American Art." *American Art* 5, no. 3 (1991): 88–107.

Wu, Ellen. *The Color of Success: Asian Americans and the Origins of the Model Minority*. Princeton, NJ: Princeton University Press, 2013.

ABOUT THE CONTRIBUTORS

Artist, scholar and global agitator **ANIDA YOEU ALI** serves as the artist-in-residence at the University of Washington Bothell. She is a first-generation Khmer Muslim woman born in Cambodia and raised in Chicago. Ali is the winner of the 2015 Sovereign Asian Art Prize and co-founder of Studio Revolt, an award-winning media lab working between the United States and the Asia-Pacific region. She holds an MFA from School of the Art Institute Chicago.

Born in Los Angeles, **KIM ANNO** is a painter, photographer, and film/video artist whose work has been exhibited, collected, and screened by museums, galleries, and festivals, nationally and internationally. Venues: Goethe Institute, Johannesburg, San Francisco Museum of Modern Art, Honolulu Academy of Fine Art, Berkeley Art Museum, Crocker Art Museum, Brooklyn Art Museum, 14th Annual New Media Festival in Seoul, Pulse, Miami, Dusseldorf, and so on. She is a recipient of awards: Zellerbach, Fleishhacker, Open Circle, James L Knight, Westaf, Berkeley Film, Foundations.

ELIZA O. BARRIOS, based in San Francisco, California, is an interdisciplinary artist and founding member of Mail Order Brides/M.O.B. Barrios's work is primarily new media and site-specific installation, while her collaborative work includes social practice and public interventions. Her work has been exhibited and screened in galleries, museums, and film festivals domestically and internationally. Barrios holds a bachelor of arts from San Francisco State University and a masters of fine arts from Mills College.

JAN CHRISTIAN BERNABE is the operations, new media, and curatorial director for the Center for Art and Thought (www.centerforartandthought.org), a nonprofit cultural hub that starts from the perspectives of the Filipino diaspora and harnesses the potential of digital media and technologies to foster dialogues among artists, scholars, and the broader public. He is a Filipino American gender-queer interdisciplinary scholar of Asian American art history and visual culture, comparative race and ethnic studies, and queer cultural studies. He has a PhD from the University of Michigan, Ann Arbor, in the program in American culture and is at work on a manuscript on contemporary Filipino American photography and video art practices as cultural and historical critiques of United States–Philippines post/colonial relations and US imperial visual regimes and knowledge production. Based in Chicago, he is also the director of news and social content for ChicagoPride.com.

SITA KURATOMI BHAUMIK is an artist and writer who uses food as a strategy to connect personal and public histories. Raised in Los Angeles and based in Oakland, she is an Indian and Japanese Colombian American. Sita holds a BA in studio art from Scripps College, an MFA in interdisciplinary art and an MA in visual and critical studies from California College of the Arts. You can find her work at sitabhaumik.com.

WAFAA BILAL is an Iraqi-born artist renowned for provoking dialogue about international politics and internal dynamics through high-profile, technologically driven projects that employ the use of robotics, the Internet, and photographic mobile mapping. Using his own body as a medium, Bilal challenges our comfort zones with projects like *3rdi, and Counting . . . ,* and *Domestic Tension*. He lives and works in New York City and is an associate arts professor at New York University's Tisch School of the Arts.

HASAN ELAHI is associate professor of art at University of Maryland and is an interdisciplinary artist working with issues in surveillance, privacy, migration, citizenship, technology, and the challenges of borders. His work has been presented at venues such as Centre Georges Pompidou, SITE Santa Fe, the Sundance Film Festival, and the Venice Biennale. His work is frequently in the media and has appeared on *Al-Jazeera*, *Fox News*, and *The Colbert Report*.

Born in Chicago, **GREYSON C. HONG** is an artist and educator based in New Haven, Connecticut. He graduated with an MFA from Bard College in 2014 after receiving her BFA from the School of the Art Institute of Chicago in 2007.

KIAM MARCELO JUNIO (preferred gender pronouns: *they/their/them*) is a Chicago-based interdisciplinary artist creating work through photography, video, installation, performance, and hybrid forms. Their research and art practice centers around queer identities, Philippine history and the Filipino diaspora, American imperialism, the politics of visibility, and social justice through collaborative processes and healing modalities. Kiam served seven years in the US Navy as a hospital corpsman. They were born in the Philippines, and have lived in the United States, Japan, and Spain.

LAURA KINA is Vincent de Paul Professor of Art, Media & Design and director of Critical Ethnic Studies at DePaul University, coeditor of *War Baby / Love Child: Mixed Race Asian American Art* (University of Washington Press,

2013), cofounder of the Critical Mixed Studies conference and association, and a reviews editor for the *Asian Diasporic Visual Culture in the Americas*. Kina is an LGBTQ ally and "hapa, yonsei, Uchinanchu." Her paintings address Asian American and mixed-race identities and histories with a focus on Okinawa and Hawai'i diaspora. Her solo exhibitions include *Uchinanchu*, *Blue Hawai'i*, *Sugar*, *A Many-Splendored Thing*, *Aloha Dreams*, and *Hapa Soap Operas*. She has exhibited nationally and internationally, including the Chicago Cultural Center, India Habitat Centre, India International Centre, Japanese American National Museum, Nehuru Art Centre, Okinawa Prefectural Art Museum, Rose Art Museum, Spertus Museum, and the Wing Luke Museum of the Asian Pacific American Experience.

H. LAN THAO LAM'S practice is at the intersection of research, object-making, installation, film, video, writing, and intervention. As part of the artist duo Lin + Lam, along with Lana Lin, she has been involved with projects about immigration, sites of residual trauma, national identity, and historical memory. Lam is the recipient of the Canada Council for the Arts, Vera List Center for Art and Politics Fellowship, among others. She is assistant professor of fine arts at Parsons.

MARIAM B. LAM is a faculty member in comparative literature, media and cultural studies, director of Southeast Asian studies, and associate vice chancellor for diversity and inclusion at University of California Riverside. She coedited *Troubling Borders: An Anthology of Art and Literature by Southeast Asian Women in the Diaspora* (University of Washington Press, 2014) and a Southeast Asian American studies special issue of *positions: asia critiques* (2013), and authored *Not Coming to Terms: Viet Nam, Archival Trauma and Strategic Affect* (forthcoming, Duke).

VIỆT LÊ is an assistant professor (visual studies) at California College of the Arts. He has been published in *positions: asia critique, Crab Orchard Review, American Quarterly,* and *Amerasia Journal,* among others. Lê has presented his work at the Banff Centre, Alberta, Canada; UCLA Hammer Museum, Los Angeles; 1a Space, Hong Kong; Bangkok Art & Cultural Center (BACC), Thailand; Civitella Ranieri, Italy; Shanghai Biennale, China; Rio Gay Film Festival, Rio de Janeiro; among other venues. His website can be found at vietle.net.

KYOO LEE, a critical theorist and a creative writer, currently an Associate Professor of Philosophy at City University of New York, is the author of *Writing Entanglish: Come in Englysshing with Gertrude Stein, Zhuangzi . . .* (Belladonna Chapbook, 2015) and *Reading Descartes Otherwise: Blind, Mad, Dreamy, and Bad* (2012). She also co-edited the *Women's Studies Quarterly* issue "Safe" (2011) and the *Critical Philosophy of Race* issue "Xenophobia &

Racism" (2014). Her current projects include a monograph that casts a queer perspective on philosophy.

LANA LIN is an artist/writer whose recent research concerns embodied vulnerabilities that emerge at the confluence of race, gender, technology, and malignant cell growth. She has been awarded fellowships from the Javits Foundation, Fulbright Foundation, and Vera List Center for Art and Politics. Her work has been shown at the Museum of Modern Art and the Whitney Museum in New York City; Gasworks gallery, London; and Stedelijk Museum, Amsterdam. She is Associate Professor in Media Studies at the New School.

MAYA MACKRANDILAL is a transdisciplinary artist and writer whose current work imagines radical futures for women of color solidarity and liberation. She holds an MFA from the School of the Art Institute of Chicago, where she was a recipient of a Jacob K. Javits Fellowship. After spending eight years in Chicago, she relocated to Los Angeles in 2016. Her essays have appeared in *New Inquiry, 60 Inches from Center, contemptorary, and MICE Magazine.*

ZAVÉ GAYATRI MARTOHARDJONO makes intercultural, geopolitical, boundary-defying, high-glam performance, video, and installations from a queer and transgender, Indonesian-American-Canadian perspective. He has shown at Aljira Center for Contemporary Art, BAAD!, Bronx River Art Center Gallery, Boston Center for the Arts, Center for Performance Research, Center for Contemporary Arts in Glasgow, Dixon Place, Issue Project Room, Leonard and Bina Ellen Art Gallery, Movement Research at Judson Church, Recess, SOMArts, and Winslow Garage. His website can be found at zavemartohardjono.com.

SUSETTE MIN is Associate Professor of Asian American Studies at the University of California, Davis. Formerly a curator at the Drawing Center in New York City, she has curated exhibitions at the Berkeley Art Museum, Whitney Museum of American Art, Asia Society, Los Angeles Photography Center, and Apexart. She is the author of *Unnamable Encounters: The Ends of Asian American Art,* forthcoming from New York University Press, and currently the arts editor of *Social Text.*

EUN JUNG PARK is an assistant professor of art history at Southwestern College in California. She is an independent scholar and curator focusing on contemporary Korean American art. She received her PhD in art history, theory, and criticism from the University of California, San Diego.

ALPESH KANTILAL PATEL is assistant professor in contemporary art and theory at Florida International University in Miami. His art historical scholarship, art criticism, and curating reflect his queer, antiracist, and transnational approach to contemporary art. His monograph *Productive Failure: Writing Queer Transnational South Asian Art Histories* is forthcoming from Manchester University Press. A grant from the Fulbright Foundation underwrote research for the follow-up to this book, tentatively titled *Transnational Approaches to LGBTQ Artistic Practices*.

VALERIE SOE is associate professor of Asian American studies at San Francisco State University. Her experimental videos, documentaries, and installations, which examine gender and cultural identity and antiracism struggles, have won prizes and been exhibited worldwide. She has published extensively on Asian and Asian American art, film, culture, and activism, and she is the author of the blog *beyondasiaphilia.com* (2012 Art Writers' Grant from the Creative Capital/Andy Warhol Foundation). Her latest film is *Love Boat: Taiwan*.

JEFFREY AUGUSTINE SONGCO is a multimedia artist. He holds a BFA from Carnegie Mellon University and an MFA from San Francisco Art Institute. He has exhibited throughout the United States, including Steven Wolf Fine Arts and the Asian Art Museum in San Francisco. His writings have appeared in *Art21 Blog*, *Bad at Sports*, *Huffington Post*, and *Hyperallergic*. He would like to be the US representative to the 2023 Venice Biennale.

HARROD J SUAREZ is assistant professor of English and comparative American studies at Oberlin College, where he teaches courses in Asian American literature, globalization and diaspora, and transnational American studies. He is currently at work on *The Diasporic Maternal: Nationalism and Globalization in Filipina/o Literature*, a book that examines overseas maternal figures from the Philippines in literature and history in an effort to access what he calls the archipelagic underside of global empire.

TINA TAKEMOTO is associate professor of visual studies at California College of the Arts. She has received grants from Art Matters, the James Irvine Foundation, and the San Francisco Arts Commission and has exhibited nationally and internationally in Milan, Rio de Janeiro, Berlin, Seoul, and Hanoi. Her articles appear in *Afterimage, Art Journal, GLQ, Performance Research, Theatre Survey,* and *Women and Performance*. Takemoto is board president of the Queer Cultural Center and cofounder of Queer Conversation on Culture and the Arts.

KENNETH TAM is a multimedia artist working primarily in sculpture and video; his work is interested in exploring the fraught spaces of the body and interpersonal relations. He received his BFA from the Cooper Union and his MFA from the University of Southern California. He is a recipient of an Art Matters grant, a California Community Foundation Fellow, and a

Core Program Residency Fellow. He has shown extensively around Southern California and participated in *Made in LA 2016* at the Hammer Museum.

SAYA WOOLFALK uses science fiction and anthropology to reimagine the world in multiple dimensions. She has exhibited at MoMA PS1; Contemporary Art Museum Houston; Montclair Art Museum; Chrysler Museum, Seattle Art Museum, Brooklyn Museum; Asian Art Museum, San Francisco; MCA Chicago; the Studio Museum in Harlem; Frist Center for the Visual Arts; Yerba Buena Center, San Francisco; Newark Museum; MCA San Diego; MoCA Taipei; and Performa 09. She has been written about in the *New Yorker*, *Sculpture Magazine*, *Artforum*, *ARTNews*, the *New York Times*, and *Huffington Post*.

INDEX

Note: Page numbers followed by "f" and "n" indicate figures and endnotes, respectively.